Old Man of Storr, Isle of Skye, Scotland
Cover photograph by Karolina Szczerkowska, https://outdoorswithkarolina.com/

BY THE SAME AUTHOR

A Walk by the Sea: A Journey into the New Millennium.
Troubador Publishing, 2016

Treasured Islands

Journeys around the inhabited islands of The United Kingdom, its Crown Dependencies and the Republic of Ireland

John Brant Chatterton

Copyright © 2024 John Brant Chatterton

The moral right of the author has been asserted.

Apart from any fair dealing for the purposes of research or private study, or criticism or review, as permitted under the Copyright, Designs and Patents Act 1988, this publication may only be reproduced, stored or transmitted, in any form or by any means, with the prior permission in writing of the publishers, or in the case of reprographic reproduction in accordance with the terms of licences issued by the Copyright Licensing Agency. Enquiries concerning reproduction outside those terms should be sent to the publishers.

Troubador Publishing Ltd
Unit E2 Airfield Business Park
Harrison Road, Market Harborough
Leicestershire LE16 7UL
Tel: 0116 279 2299
Email: books@troubador.co.uk
Web: www.troubador.co.uk

ISBN 978 1 80514 350 5

British Library Cataloguing in Publication Data.
A catalogue record for this book is available from the British Library.

Printed by TJ Books Limited, Padstow, UK
Typeset in 11pt Aldine401 BT by Troubador Publishing Ltd, Leicester, UK

Matador is an imprint of Troubador Publishing

To my wife Lily and my son Maxim

CONTENTS

	Prologue	ix
1	The Mission	1
2	Great Britain and The Scilly Isles	13
3	St Michael's Mount and Burgh Island, England	27
4	Firth of Clyde, Scotland	31
5	Cumbrian Island Outposts – The Furness Islands, England	43
6	The Mull of Kintyre to the Firth of Lorn, Scotland	47
7	The Island of Ireland and Rathlin Island, Northern Ireland	63
8	(Not quite) the Aran Islands, Ireland	71
9	Isle of Sheppey, England	73
10	Mull and the surrounding islands, Scotland	77
11	Island Successes and Failures in Essex, England	91
12	Random islands in County Cork and Southwest Ireland	95
13	The Isle of Skye and surrounding islands, Scotland	107
14	The Isle (and Calf) of Man, a UK Crown Dependency	119
15	A few convenient Orkney Islands, Scotland	125
16	The Shetland Islands and Fair Isle, Scotland	133
17	Inner Holm and Holm of Grimbister, Orkney Islands, Scotland	161
18	Assorted islands on the Northwest coast of Scotland, and two "Small Isles"	165
19	Canvey Island, England	175
20	Islands off the South Coast, England	179
21	Tiree and Coll, Scotland	186
22	The Gorumna Islands, County Galway, Ireland	193
23	The Outer Hebrides, Scotland	198
24	The islands of Ynys Mons, Wales	220
25	The rest of the Small Isles (Rum, Canna and Sanday), Scotland	232

26	Many more Orkney Islands, Scotland	239
27	Ten more islands in Galway and Mayo, Republic of Ireland	271
28	Lindisfarne (Holy Island) and Piel Island, England	289
29	More Essex islands and The Broomway, England	298
30	Lundy Island, England	308
31	Remaining islands in the Highlands, Scotland	313
32	The remaining Welsh islands	323
33	The remaining islands of County Mayo, Sligo and Donegal, Republic of Ireland	345
34	The Channel Islands: UK Crown Dependencies	377
35	South West Ireland – again	391
36	The GB stragglers: Whale Island, Portsmouth harbour and Osea Island, Essex and three small islands of the Outer Hebrides	419
37	The Ultimate Stragglers	427
38	Epilogue	435
	Acknowledgements	440
	Appendix: Island Statistics	443
	Index	458

PROLOGUE
Inchaghaun Island, County Galway
30th June 2022

The weight of his hand was on my shoulder as we balanced each other through the boulder field and around rockpools. We were both having to use sticks and at any given moment my knee could buckle in a spasm of pain, and we would both have been face-down in a heap on the sharp rock, or eye to eye with a startled crab and I was furious with him. His obsessive obstinate recklessness had now put me six hundred foolhardy feet from the shoreline and the safety of the car and to make matters worse this was now the second assault course tidal crossing of the day.

"You're a bloody nutter!" I had spat out whilst crossing to Illaunmore earlier as we tried to follow a barely recognisable path across the seabed, but here there was nothing as we became a parody of some First War scene of the maimed leading the blind.

Halfway back he stopped to rest and reflect as we got back our breath in what was a tidal seabed in the most serene and wild place imaginable, for poets or painters, and I looked over to my older friend now contemplating his entire life, on a rock in the Gaeltacht.

"I feel alive again" he said, yet knowing that this would be his last adventure; the last seemingly senseless, injudicious act in a life of insane mountain ascents, caving descents and a near suicidal descent into the oven of the Grand Canyon, Arizona.

Now as I regarded him my anger evaporated into the desolate majesty of rock and wind that only a consummate artist could describe. He was lost in his reveries and contemplating the final chapter of his existence, but what better place to do just that? Here in a timeless moment of rock, sky and sea he surveyed his life and purpose ebbing away from him; almost as swiftly as the tide could return and subsume these two aging men with bad legs sitting on a rock surrounded by drama.

We had probably "hopped" better islands but none perhaps more meaningful in a moment. A staggering amount of Guinness, Tayto's crisps and whiskey and nearly every mile of the Wild Atlantic Way had been consumed and argued over.

I only did 71 of the 72 Irish islands with John and he did the other 152 of the archipelago in every kind of weather and conveyance that could be flown, driven or put to float.

I invite you to join him in this odyssey, this final treasure hunt around our Treasured Islands.

John Lawlor

1. The Mission

It had been almost eight years since the 5,003-mile odyssey around the coast of Great Britain. I'd walked for a total of 328 days at an average 15.3 miles a day and the book *A Walk by the Sea* had been published in August 2016 with a celebratory party and book signing at my favourite pub *The Dark Horse*. Well actually next door at its then pretentious wine bar satellite, *Le Cheval Blanc*, in my adopted hometown, the leafy fighting-above-its-weight suburb of Moseley in Birmingham. The event was a great success with a modest sum of money raised for charity, Macmillan's I believe. It was a culmination of 15 years work, planning, walking and writing and I needed a new challenge in my dotage. I'd toyed with the idea of attempting the newly completed 625-mile Ulster Way and thus complete the circumnavigation of the United Kingdom, but my walking was faltering now, to say the least, and the challenge had to be more sedentary.

Then I had an idea: the last journey was accomplished by avoiding ferries. Why not make this journey about only travelling by ferry, boats or other forms of transport. A plan was hatched to visit ALL permanently inhabited islands in the British Isles. I wrongly assumed that those not connected by bridge or tidal causeway would be connected by some sort of commercial ferry, passenger or vehicle. I was, of course, wrong! Oh! And before the Irish jump down my throat the perhaps contentious *geographical* definition of the British Isles is all islands in the North Atlantic's European continental shelf northwest of the French mainland.

I took the galley proofs of *A Walk by the Sea* with me on a business trip/conference to Concepcion, Chile in March 2016 and, whilst reflecting on my epic journey, I tentatively put a modicum of flesh on the planning of my next adventure. I have always liked islands and after the circumnavigation of Great Britain (England, Wales and Scotland) I completed walks around the **Isle of Wight**[1] and **Anglesey**, two of our larger offshore islands. Friends suggested I should tackle walking around all the offshore islands, but this was too ambitious at my age and with legs not as agile as 10 years ago. They had not considered the gravity of this task or indeed the definition of an island.

I had no idea just how many inhabited islands were in the British Isles (including **Ireland** and the UK's Crown Dependencies of the **Isle of Man** and the **Channel Islands**). Are there 50, 60, 70 or more? Again, as with the coastal walking route, definitions are important:

- What is a permanently inhabited island?
- Is an island connected to the mainland by a bridge still an island?
- Is an island accessible at low tide only still an island?
- Is an island in a freshwater lake an island to include?
- What modes of transport would be allowed to access these islands?

The rules were embryonic then and on a lone trip to Tierra del Fuego's (Land of Fire), Chilean sector, largely devoid of people, I was able, in the vast barren but hauntingly beautiful wilderness, to ask myself what motivated people to settle here and more immediately important why am I here? The latter question was easy: to fire my own imagination after a lifetime of wondering what this place is about; a lifetime of reading about Darwin and Magellan; a lifetime of scrutinising maps of places like Patagonia. The former question was more difficult to answer as migrations and settlement were complex conundrums.

My island adventures will be more than ticking off a list of places; they too will be a voyage of discovery, of peoples, their challenges, culture, and aspirations with who knows what adventures unfolding before me. The Chilean sector of Tierra del Fuego has few hotels for an island almost the size of Wales, but one night in the stark but comfortable *Barlovento*

---

1 All islands in **bold type face** are those visited (see index)

hotel in Porvenir I sat after dinner enjoying a bottle of excellent Chilean Sauvignon Blanc. I was rather bored with the 2018 World Cup qualifying football game on the communal TV in which Chile were playing Argentina. I turned my attention to my potential island adventure and reckoned I would manage to visit about 150 islands from the Shetland Islands, deep in the North Atlantic to the Scilly Isles off the southwest coast of Cornwall. This guestimate was bolstered by an unknown number yet to be discovered islands in the Irish Republic. Ireland was included to extend the Celtic journey to the full.

My serious accounting of all inhabited islands north and west of mainland France is currently 223, though this tally changes with time as populations are dynamic. Of these 28 are off the coast of England, six of which include the Scilly Isles, and 14 off the coast of Wales. The rest, of which some 72 are off the coast of the island of Ireland (including one in Northern Ireland) and 97 off the coast of Scotland, owe their heritage and culture to a mix of Scandinavia (Viking and Norse) and Celtic (Gaelic and Irish) history. The Viking raids and later the journeys of the Celtic Saints did not distinguish between our modern conventional political boundaries. To avoid Irish islands would be to deny their existence in an ever-changing diaspora of cultures across the geographical entity that is now The British Isles – my *Treasured Islands*. Finally, the journey includes 10 islands in the Crown Dependencies of Guernsey, Jersey and the Isle of Man. Mainland Eire and Mainland Great Britain complete the totals.

Sceptical friends suggested this was a pointless exercise serving no purpose other than self-indulgence, like ticking off the Scottish Munros (the 282 mountains over 3,000 feet). I disagreed vehemently. Life is full of challenges and with advancing years, challenges are synonymous with romanticism. This will be my Grand Tour of the islands I call home.

Walking the coast was easy, as apart from planning my start and finish points each trip and booking (sometimes) accommodation ahead, it was just about getting fit and placing one foot in front of the other. My island tours needed a modicum of planning. After all, by definition, these were dispersed across numerous bodies of water from The English Channel to the North Atlantic. The rules were formulated thus:

- Any permanently inhabited island in **Great Britain**, **Ireland** and the Crown Dependencies of the **Isle of Man** and **Channel Islands**, based on the most recent and available census information.
- Size, access, ownership, or inaccessibility would be no obstacle.
- Islands connected to the mainland or another island by bridge (vehicular or foot) or causeway would be included.
- Tidal islands connected only at low water to their adjacent mainland, or another island would be included.
- Passenger or car ferries would be the preferred mode of access, though foot access, car access, and private boat hire were alternatives.
- Where services allowed, travel by plane would be considered.
- Islands with temporary annual occupancy by tourists or holiday makers would be largely ignored.
- Only islands in open sea, harbours or tidal estuaries would be included. Inhabited islands in non-tidal rivers or freshwater lakes would be excluded.
- Islands called 'islands' but not completely separated by water, like London's Isle of Dogs or Kent's Isle of Thanet, were to be excluded.
- Islands not thought to be islands by public consensus but accord with my rules, for example **Portsea** (the island on which the city of Portsmouth stands) would be included.

Island populations are dynamic, slowly diminishing in the remote west of Ireland or slowly increasing, after years of decline, in the Northern Isles of Scotland. An estimate of the roll call of islands is as follows with a total but volatile complement of 223, distributed as follows:

- Scotland 97
- Republic of Ireland 72

- England   28
- Wales   14
- Channel Isles   8
- Isle of Man   2
- Northern Ireland   1
- Great Britain   1

Above my fireplace is a striking poster designed by The Ordnance Survey, working with Sheffield University. It illustrates all islands belonging to Great Britain greater than five square kilometres in size. These are all included on my target list except for Scarba, Taransay, Scarp, Mingulay and Hirta which are all uninhabited:

- Scarba is north of **Jura** in the Inner Hebrides and uninhabited since the 1960's.
- Taransay is off the west coast of **Harris** in the Outer Hebrides and uninhabited since 1974. It is the largest island in Scotland with no permanent population. The island was the setting for the BBC so-called reality series *Castaway* where hapless volunteers led by Ben Fogle pitted their collective wits surviving the rigours of isolation in the name of entertainment. Bob Geldof co owned Planet 24 who made the show which saved his faltering fortunes post *Live Aid*.
- Scarp is also off the west coast of **Harris.**
- Mingalay is 12 miles to the south of **Barra** in the Outer Hebrides and abandoned in 1912.
- Finally, Hirta near the remote Atlantic island of St Kilda which was evacuated in 1930.
- St Kilda itself lies 64km west northwest of North Uist in the Outer Hebrides in Scotland and was also evacuated of its permanent residents in 1930 and is now a temporary military base only.

Many islands less than 5 square kilometres in size are inhabited. These are counted in my odyssey.

The largest islands by size (excluding Great Britain and the island of Ireland) are:

- Lewis and Harris (counted as one island)
- Isle of Skye
- Mainland Shetland
- Isle of Mull
- Anglesey
- Islay
- Isle of Man
- Mainland Orkney
- Arran (Scotland)
- Isle of Wight

Generally, in pub quizzes when asked which of our islands (excluding Great Britain and Ireland) is largest, the **Isle of Wight** gets the popular vote as we are deceived by familiarity and assumed population size. The **Isle of Wight** is not even the largest of our islands by population. The pub quizzers are now even more confused! **Portsea** with 207,100 (2010 estimate) is first by population followed by the **Isle of Wight** with 141,538 (2021 census). Perception is embedded in our collective psyche with **Jura** 'a tiny' island of 196 souls in the Inner Hebrides only 14 square kilometres less than the area of the **Isle of Wight**.

For the record, **Arran** in the Firth of Clyde is actually larger than the **Isle of Wight**. The pub quizzers in the *Fox and Ferret* in Godalming will dispute this as, in the narrow perspective of Little England, it simply cannot be true. Next in population size in Great Britain comes **Anglesey** in north Wales, **Sheppey** and **Canvey Island** off the Thames estuary, **Lewis and Harris** in the Outer Hebrides, **Mainland Shetland**, **Mainland Orkney**, **Hayling Island** east of Portsmouth and **Walney Island** off the Cumbrian coast.

A summary of islands by their local authority affiliation and mode of access follows:

THE MISSION

Mode of Transport	Ireland
Car Ferry	2
Private Boat	13
Aerial Tramway	1
Air	1
Road Bridge/causeways	36
Low Tide Access	4
Passenger Ferry	14
TOTAL	**71**

County	Ireland
Clare	1
Cork	15
Donegal	9
Dublin	2
Galway	19
Kerry	6
Limerick	2
Mayo	16
Sligo	1
TOTAL	**71**

Mode of Transport	England
Hovercraft	1
Private Boat Taxi	1
Causeway	7
Foot Bridge	1
Road Bridge	6
Low Tide Access	6
Passenger Ferry	5
Road access	1
TOTAL	**28**

County	England
Cornwall	1
Cumbria	5
Devon	2
Essex	7
Hampshire	3
Isle of Wight	1
Isles of Scilly	6
Kent	1
West Sussex	1
Northumberland	1
TOTAL	**28**

Mode of Transport	Scotland
Car Ferry	35
Road Bridge/Causeway	28
Private Boat	11
Air	2
Foot Bridge	2
Low tide crossing	6
Passenger boat/ferry	11
Dinghy	1
Floating Bridge	1
TOTAL	**97**

County	Scotland
Argyll and Bute	22
Eilean Siar	18
Highland	16
North Ayrshire	3
Orkney	22
Shetland	16
TOTAL	**97**

Mode of Transport	Wales		County	Wales
Passenger Ferry	5		Cardiff	1
Private Boat	3		Gwynedd	2
Causeway/Road bridge	2		Pembrokeshire	4
Foot bridge	1		Ynys Mons	7
Causeway Foot	3			
TOTAL	**14**		**TOTAL**	**14**
Mode of Transport	Northern Ireland		County	Northern Ireland
Commercial Ferry	1		Antrim	1
TOTAL	**1**		**TOTAL**	**1**
Mode of Transport	Channel Islands		Administration	Channel Islands
Car ferry	1		Balliwick of Jersey	1
Air	1		Balliwick of Guernsey	7
Passenger ferry	3			
Private boat	2			
Low tide access	1			
TOTAL	**8**		**TOTAL**	**8**
Mode of Transport	Isle of Man		Administration	Isle of Man
Air	1		Tynwald	2
Private boat	1			
TOTAL	**2**		**TOTAL**	**2**
GRAND TOTAL	221		**GRAND TOTAL**	221
(including Great Britain and Ireland (Eire)	223		(including Great Britain and Ireland (Eire)	223

It is clear that the geographical spread is daunting as are the logistics of modes of transport, especially the sourcing of private boats at often unpalatable costs. A half day boat hire with skipper to the remote island of **Rona** north of the Isle of **Skye** was an eye watering £350. A fast RIB (reinforced inflatable boat) the next day was £125 per hour to **Scalpay**, just a nerve tingling 20 minutes ride from the Skye bridge. This was all part of the experience, though I am always nervous at approaching a complete stranger asking for a trip to a remote island without the obvious cover of ornithology, fishing or wildlife watching. Time is money and the potential boatman rightly wanted to know how long he would have to wait on the island. "No, I don't want to stay long just walk a while, take in the ambience and we will return".

I am foolish to worry as the service industry is there to serve, at a reasonably brokered price, without unnecessary questioning; besides an easy jaunt in a boat at inflated prices is probably more lucrative than a day's fishing these days. We sometimes forget we live clinging to a rock, a rather large rock, in the North Atlantic and the vagaries of the weather can upset even the firmest plan. I tried repeatedly to reach **Soay**, an island about a mile from the village of Elgol on **Skye**. I have even paid my £55 fee on a scheduled tourist trip. This was postponed no less than 4 times because of stormy weather, before a successful mission using a private boat hire in September 2020.

Scotland and Ireland would present the biggest logistical challenges, with many of the inhabited islands, especially in Ireland, only accessible by private boat hire. These were amongst the most treasured challenges, with probably the most serendipitous moments of sheer pleasure. Like pitching up on **Vaila**, a private island to the west of **Mainland Shetland** and being treated to Polish vodka, lunch and fine wines, or **Auskery** 15 miles out in the North Sea from **Mainland Orkney** in fine company if not the best of weathers. Other islands were frustrating in their inaccessibility, like **Foulness** on the bleak Essex coast or **Thorney** on England's south coast, not that these islands were difficult to get onto, but the Ministry of Defence had other ideas.

I decided on a 'clean slate' approach. That is to re-visit the many islands I had visited before in my travels around the UK. The **Isle of Wight**, for example, was a frequent holiday venue as a teenager with my parents.

Many of the Hebridean islands had captured my imagination over the years, like the time in the early 1970's when a group of university friends headed for **Mull** to celebrate Hogmanay. Stuart, a fully-fledged adopted Scot, was keen when we met to show off his newly acquired talents; bagpipe playing and his mastery of the Gaelic language. So much so that we arrived at the ferry terminal as the hydraulic platforms on the Roll-on-Roll-off ferry were securing the vessel for its last journey of the year. We had to plead with the shore staff for the ferry to return to collect us.

I pride myself with the accolade that I have visited more places in Great Britain than anyone else, alive or dead. After all I'd travelled through all coastal cities, towns and villages on my epic walk. Furthermore, as part of my job over 20 years I have trained Environment Agency river inspectors to monitor the degradation or otherwise of river and coastal assets to protect the Nation against flooding. I have been to many remote coastlines that protect and both obscure rural and inner-city streams and rivers. I have yet to be challenged on this claim. Visiting remote islands in the North Atlantic and its sheltered and not so sheltered bays and estuaries would enhance not only my travel experiences but the intrinsic quality of travel.

Another major challenge was grappling with Irish, Gaelic, Old Norse and Welsh place names. These islands of ours have gone through many political and social upheavals through history and place names are a legacy of languages spoken by our ancestors. Old Norse proliferates in Shetland and Orkney and even within the Hebrides. Scotland's islands are rich in the Gaelic heritage of their clan system and even outside the *Gaeltacht*, the Irish speaking west coast of Ireland, Irish names have been retained.

Where the island name is not in English, I have used English equivalent translations where possible along with vernacular names where appropriate (see Appendix). Thus:

> Inis Bó Finne (Irish) is **Inishbofin** (English equivalent) meaning island of the white cow.

Finally, it has become obvious during planning and execution that privately owned islands, almost exclusively in Ireland, may have to be missed where the owner's privacy is of paramount importance and securing transport to these a further block on ambition. There are, for example, 23 Irish islands where, according to the 2016 Irish census, only two or even one permanent inhabitant is recorded and with time these sparse populations may reduce to zero or become temporary holiday lets. It is the intention to get to all, but success will depend on access, price of access, weather at the time of visit and the kindness of boatmen and owners. Those not visited after all avenues have been exhausted will fall under the category of 'The ones that got away'.

In Ireland particularly there are curiously a number of islands with single or maybe two residents on the 2016 census. I learned that this was a clever trick to ensure the jetty or piers for landing on the islands were maintained by the coastal authorities. Permanency depended on safe embarkation and disembarkation. The owners or residents of the islands would go out with the *Garda* (police) on census night. They would register their permanent residency and post the official census form in the ballot box and return with the *Garda* to the mainland. Their income from short lets in the summer season could continue with the knowledge that jetties and piers would be maintained. Without registration of permanency the expensive maintenance would fall onto these 'faux' residents.

The book is not necessarily an 'end to end' read and is structured in the order of visit, first to last, so some information and anecdotes may be repeated where relevant to one or a number of islands. The reader may make choices from the index and maps that support each section or take the whole roller coaster ride around the coast of the British Isles.

TREASURED ISLANDS

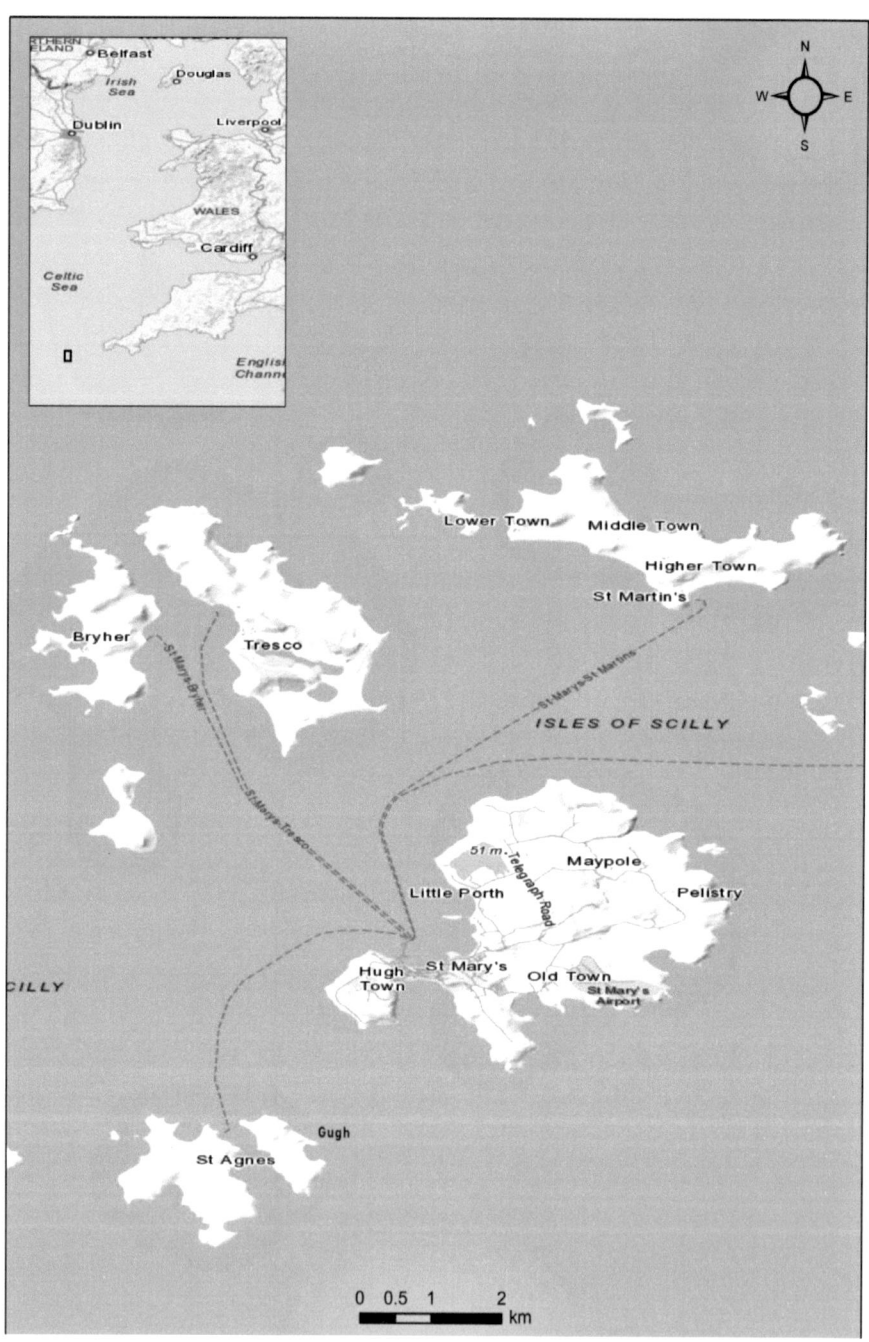

Isles of Scilly (St Mary's, Tresco, St Martins, St Agnes, Bryher and Gugh)

2. Great Britain and The Scilly Isles

The odyssey began in April 2016 almost 8 years since finishing my 328 day *Walk by the Sea*. After a long journey by car from my home in Moseley, Birmingham, it was appropriate that I elected to stay in *The Queen's Hotel*, Penzance the night before boarding the *Scillonian* ferry to **St Mary's** on the Scilly Isles. I had stayed in this modest sea front hotel the night before I made my tentative first steps from Land's End to circumnavigate Great Britain. Memories of that day in August 2001 came flooding back; the hotel was much as I remembered, designed with coach tours for elderly pensioners in mind. The irony was that I had become an elderly pensioner myself.

I was to travel to and set foot on all inhabited islands in the British Isles in no particular order but assemble a chaotic timetable whenever time and resources allowed. Geographers include the island of Ireland in the entity the "British Isles", much to the chagrin of the Irish. Its citizens have been held in check by the English imperial jackboot for centuries, leading to insurrection and bloodshed from the battle of the Boyne in 1690 and the defeat of James II by King Billy, the 1916 Easter uprising and the 30 years of 'troubles' in Northern Ireland. It's no wonder our cousins across the Irish Sea get annoyed with this apparently invasive geographical term!

The term *Great* Britain has jarred with me all my geographically aware life. The adjective 'Great' has nothing to do with political superiority (try telling that to Boris Johnson's band of post Brexit 'cult' followers) but has been hi-jacked by gnarled popularists and latterly Brexiteers to invoke and revive memories of Britain's Victorian 19th Century dominance throughout the world. These people want to return to the halcyon idyll they perceive of the arrogance of Empire and the rose-tinted faded memories of hot summers without end, warm beer, cricket on village greens and the days before 'Johnny foreigner' came to pollute the culture they call English. We are living in the dark shadow of the politics of self-entitlement and exceptionalism.

I am writing this on 8th May 2020, Victory in Europe's 75th anniversary. The celebrations have been muted because of the COVID 19 pandemic sweeping the world, with the unnecessary delayed UK Government response that has cost the lives of many tens of thousands, many of which are the generation who remember the defeat of fascism. Just like Trump's response and the desire to 'Make America Great Again' (MAGA hats are everywhere in USA's 'flyover' States) Little Englander's worry more about the faltering economy than human life. Hitler was beaten but we now have fascism creeping in through the back door. So just why is Britain prefixed by the adjective 'Great'?

As with all definitions there is dispute as to how my island nation got its name. Is it because after the unification with Scotland in 1707 Britain was re-invented as Great Britain? Or, more politically and worryingly sinister does it stem from the 16th to 19th century when this country really was 'Great' in the eyes of the world? The tobacco barons, rubber plantation owners, cotton traders, slave owners and their traffickers, industrial inventors, industrial revolutionaries and so on really were lauded, especially by the Victorians, as really 'Great' people.

I'd like to think some were not 'Great Britons' as there is nothing 'Great' about subjugating African tribes as slaves and creating vast wealth from human trafficking or the exploitation of workers in the factories and mines throughout Britain and the Empire from India to Canada. All too late, but we are waking up to the atrocities of the slave traders and shadowy opportunists, who for personal greed manacled hundreds of thousands of Africans, men, women and children and transported those that survived across the Atlantic. Edward Colston was one of the worst tyrants and his statue was toppled in Bristol in June 2020 and unceremoniously dumped in the River Avon. This was a fitting end to a man who would order cowering African slaves to be thrown into the Atlantic if they became sick so he could claim off his dubious insurance.

This is certainly not the 'Great' Britain of the liberal minded. However much history sanitised the evils of our colonial past some luminaries like Isambard Kingdom Brunel, James Watt, David Hume, the Scottish enlightenment philosopher, Adam Smith, the father of economics and James Hutton, the geologist and many others did contribute to Britain's Greatness in the eyes of the World.

More prosaic there could, it seems, be a French connection. When the Romans left northern Europe, Britons from southwest England settled in the Armorican peninsular, now Brittany and known then as Bretagne, with their own country adopting the moniker Grande Bretagne, or Great Britain, probably simply because it was larger. However, I prefer the theory that the Roman Claudius Ptolemy in the year 148 used "Great" to distinguish from "Little" Britain, or Ireland. Simply put and useful for my island journey, Great Britain (the World's ninth largest island) is the largest of an archipelago of islands off northwest Europe, now comprising a diminishing total of about 223 inhabited islands and an untold number of isolated uninhabited islands as far northwest as the remote volcanic islet of Rockall, some 423km northwest of **Tory Island** in Donegal.

The island outpost of St Kilda, 64km west-northwest of **North Uist** in the Outer Hebrides, was inhabited until 29th August 1930 when the last 36 islanders were evacuated. The most remote inhabited island in the British Isles, apart from the Scilly Islands, which are hardly remote because of great communication links and a population of in excess of 2,000, is now **Foula**. This spectacular island lies approximately 20 miles west of the village of Walls on **Mainland Shetland** with a fluctuating population of around 30 with even a school. Getting there and to other remote islands not connected by road bridges or scheduled ferries would be a real adventure.

I needed a stretch after the trip south and I walked to the *Turk's Head*, a pub reputed to be the oldest in Penzance and beloved of my university friends Geoff and George who were regulars there in the late 1960's. Curiosity had gotten the better of me and I wasn't disappointed with the pub preserved much as it would have been all those years ago. Religious houses ran the earliest true inns to cater for pilgrims and knights on their way to the Crusades in the Holy Land. *Ye Olde Trip to Jerusalem*, whose cellars are carved from the rocks beneath Nottingham Castle, is just such an example. Established in 1189, it claims the title of the oldest pub in England and was a stopover point for forces on their way to meet with Richard the Lionheart. The *Turk's Head* also inherits this historical legacy.

The walk through ramshackle back streets was about a mile there and back and I decided to 'tick off' officially my first island, **Great Britain**. My island anecdotes would not be I decided proportionate either to the size or population of the island. This reminded me of Douglas Adams' seminal book *A Hitch Hiker's Guide to the Galaxy* whose sole entry for planet Earth was "Mostly Harmless", though, with the way mankind is currently self-destructing, I would challenge that terse definition! However, under the Gaia principle expounded by James Lovelock, humans will die out but the earth itself will re-generate. Look at the demise of the dinosaurs if prove be needed. After just six weeks of lockdown during the COVID 19 pandemic, the cleaning of air and water and wildlife taking back control were palpable.

It was bitterly cold for April and the motley collection of sea front B&B's and apartments were showing little sign of occupancy. I was anxious about the three-hour sea crossing to **St Mary's** the next day and researched the weather. It was going to be choppy once away from the safety of the south Cornish coast. I am not a sailor. High altitude did not worry me even when I climbed Cotopaxi in Ecuador in 1991, which at 5,897 metres is one of the highest volcanoes in the world. But put me on a boat and nausea swells immediately. I recall an English Channel crossing with my dear Cousin Dick where the gallant ferry master missed the safety of the harbour entrance to Dover twice with the whole posse of passengers sliding in a quagmire of their own puke. Catholics nervously played with their rosary beads and Muslims mouthed the Koran, hoping for salvation from their God.

I had been to the Scilly Islands before at the end of the last Century on a weekend 'seminar' organised by The Met Office following a project I had been involved with. That time we flew to Hugh Town by helicopter and avoided the treacherous sea passage. The seminar was really a 'thank you' for the hard work put in by the consultants involved and we had a jolly time in *The Mermaid* pub with technical content at a bare minimum. During the downtime from merry making a colleague and myself decided to make the 13-mile coastal circumnavigation of **St Mary's**, the largest of the Scilly Isles. It was that walk that sparked off the urgency to walk around the whole of Great Britain. I remember thinking "If I can walk around **St Mary's** I can walk around Great Britain".

Breakfast at *The Queen's* was taken in the clipped silence associated with all British hotels and a rate was negotiated to park my car in the hotel car park whilst I was away. I had toyed with the idea of simply parking on the promenade free of charge. Luckily all places had been taken as, during the night of my return, the promenade and hotel were relentlessly battered by 20-foot waves lashing my second-floor bedroom window and shaking the whole building reminiscent of the 4.3 Richter scale earthquake I had experienced in Folkestone in 2007 on my perambulation around the British coast. My sturdy Land Rover Freelander could have been lost to the deep and my first island venture thwarted.

Once on board the *Scillonian* the captain, in a matter-of-fact way, announced, as I had feared, that weather conditions were not going to be good. I snuggled down into my aircraft style seat and tried to sleep and not look out of the starboard port hole where sea became land which in turn became sky, which became land which became sea again in a constant loop of hell. Small children and their guardians seemed to delight in the motion, exhibiting little if any ill effect. Matters were made worse when the tannoy announced the journey would take longer because of the extremely low tides on **St Mary's** which inhibited safe landing at the scheduled time. These same low tides were later in that trip to work in my favour in my hectic scramble to visit all six inhabited islands in an impossible logistical nightmare.

After what seemed an eternity we disembarked on the new quay, paid for by European Regional Development money, Cornwall receiving special status for its apparent deprivation. I had not planned accommodation or my trips to any of the islands in the archipelago as the St Mary's Boatmen's Association website was hopelessly vague about which of their boats went where and when. Why couldn't they just publish timetables? Then the penny dropped. It was that old tidal cycle thing where access on and off islands was at the mercy of the seasons and the moon. To make matters worse I had landed on the Scillies when the spring high tides were at their highest and their lowest. I trudged into Hugh Town in despair knowing I could never visit all six islands under these tidal conditions. I had just started my island odyssey and I would almost certainly have to return at some future date to complete.

The Tourist Information Centre confirmed my worst fears regarding the tides and potential boat cancellations but gave me *Shearwater* guest house, owned by Tina (originally from Canada) and her partner Bob (an Islander for many years but originally from Manchester). They were delightful as was their small, inexpensive but more than adequate accommodation. I was to eschew the four-star luxury I usually enjoyed.

Dumping my ruck sack, I set off for the quay again hoping to catch the 14:00 to **St Martin's**. I missed it, so there was to be no more island hopping (or even island hoping!) that day. Instead, I thought I'd better get to know what the protocol was to get to the other islands. Now if you are based on **St Mary's** you are at the mercy of the St Mary's Boatmen's Association who do not appear to communicate with the 'off island' Boatmen's associations (**Tresco**, **St Agnes** and **St Martin's**). The **St Mary's** trips are posted on boards at various vantage points at 09:00 each morning; they sometimes indicate when the day tripper can return, either early or late afternoon; with it so far?

From what I could gather they leave, say, at 10:15 from **St Mary's** quay to, say **Tresco**, and come straight back to **St Mary's** empty as the **Tresco** Boatmen seem to have a monopoly on taking **Tresco** day trippers to the other islands. They each have a Mafia style grip on who they take where and when. When I innocently asked "Could I go out on a St Mary's boat and return on a **Tresco** boat" the question was met with incredulity and derision.

Once I got the idea, I began to plan the next few days, only to be told that the third day of my visit, a Sunday, would be a write off for trips to any island as a gigantic low was to envelope not only the Scillies but the whole of Cornwall. What would further complicate logistics was the fact that neither planes nor the *Scillonian* ever travel on a Sunday. I was exasperated as I had to get to **Tresco**, **Bryher**, **St Martin's**, **St Agnes** and **Gugh** (pronounced 'Goo') in two days. This was wholly out of the question on St Mary's Boatmen's Association boats. Worse logistics were to come on my travels but at this stage I was an island virgin, literally an innocent abroad.

After a pleasant walk around Hugh Town to achieve as I originally planned my 'mile walk on each island' I retired to the *Atlantic hotel* for a pint to re-group. The mile on each island plan was abandoned quite soon on my travels as timetable restrictions almost everywhere on scheduled ferries prohibited this idea without overnight stays. I decided to opt for **Tresco** the next day and it was rumoured that because of the extremely low tides it would be possible to make the half mile crossing to **Bryher** on foot. At last things were starting to go a bit my way.

I felt I could leave **St Agnes** and **Gugh** for the following day. **Gugh** is actually joined to **St Agnes** by a tombola, or narrow neck of beach or isthmus joining two more prominent land masses which for some inexplicable reason is derived from the Italian 'mound'. Moving on from this geography lesson however my plans would leave out **St Martin's**. I did further research and found another layer of transport – the water taxi. For the princely sum of £50 one could avoid the Mafia-style Boatmen's Association altogether and use the network of water taxis, the residents preferred mode of subsidised travel but available to anyone else at inflated prices. In this microcosm of capitalism, it certainly was a sellers' market.

St Mary's was by far the largest island in the group with a 2021 population of 1,818, with Hugh Town its quaint 'capital', set out in two distinct parts joined together by another tombola. The worry is that with increasing storm surges from the Atlantic the isthmus could be breached putting the largely sheltered harbour and quay to the north in peril. I had worked in my capacity as a coastal asset inspector in **St Mary's** to see exactly the scale of damage inflicted on these islands in the unabating trajectory of storms since 2013.

Hugh Town was a favoured holiday destination for sixties Prime Minister Harold Wilson, in the days when we had principled politicians in high office, as opposed to the self-entitled fraudsters we have today. Faux austerity runs through their veins to shore up vulture capitalism and minimise taxation for the corporate chairmen and executives, with secure Cayman Island investments and mansions and yachts in the tax-free safe havens like Monaco and the Channel Islands. Barbara Castle, Harold, Richard Crossman, Dennis Healy and the indefatigable Tony Benn were without peers in their principles of social and economic equality.

These heady days saw me at the University of London, a golden era of social experimentation, dedicated protests against the injustice of Apartheid and the solidarity and resistance against the Vietnam War. Wilson, one of only six Labour Prime Ministers to hold that high office of State, is buried in the cemetery in Old Town church.

The only other British Prime Minister to be buried on a British island was John Stuart, 3rd Earl of Bute, a favourite of George III. He was interred on Rothsey on the **Isle of Bute** in 1792. He was the first Prime Minister (1762-1763) from Scotland following the Acts of Union in 1707 and the first Tory to have held the post. Of the 58 Prime Ministers since Sir Robert Walpole, some 29 or half have been Tory's (or regurgitated as Conservatives by Sir Robert Peel), including such luminaries as Lord North, The Pitts (younger and elder), the Duke of Wellington, Disraeli, and Churchill).

Of coincidental interest to my island adventures the origin of 'Tory' comes from **Tory Island** off the coast of Donegal, Ireland. The word 'Tory' derives from the Middle Irish word *tóraidhe* or in translation outlaw, robber or brigand, from the Irish word tóir, meaning "pursuit", since outlaws were "pursued men". The term was initially applied in Ireland to the isolated bands of guerrillas resisting Oliver Cromwell's nine-month campaign in Ireland from 1649 to 1650, who were allied with Royalists. It was then applied as a derogatory term by political opponents, the Whigs who morphed into the Liberal party. In 2019 the UK voted in the latest 'Brigand' as Prime Minister, Alexander Boris de Pfeffel Johnson. If the cap fits…

The Atlantic Inn and the *Bishop and Wolf* public houses caught my evening's fancy with convivial locals and fine food. Some say **St Mary's** is '2,000 alcoholics clinging to a rock', but on my travels I've heard the same expression used to befit other tiny islands with boisterous licensed premises. Last orders were on time as with five police and community support officers, **St Mary's** has the lowest per capita police presence anywhere in the United Kingdom.

The weather the next day was bleak and damp to say the least so after a delicious breakfast (breakfasts in private guest houses are so much better than those in pubs or modest corporate hotels), I trudged to one of the ticket selling outlets and booked a passage to **Tresco**. A phone call to the **Tresco** Boatmen's Association secured me a water taxi at 13:30 to **St Martin's**. All would be well, or would it? Tides ensured that the tourist boat couldn't dock at New Grimsby as was usual and it was diverted to Carn Near Quay on **Tresco's** southern tip, a full 30 minutes' walk to *The New Inn*. On arrival, a chain of tourists snaked up the concrete roadway past Tresco Abbey Gardens housing a spectacular collection of 20,000 plants, some of which that couldn't even survive in Cornwall, under 30 miles away. I could see the island of **Bryher** in the distance beyond the receding tide. As expected, the onward tourist boat could not dock there because of the extraordinary low tides.

I waited till 11:45 in the *New Inn* when I was told it would be safe to cross to **Bryher** and without getting more than damp feet crossed the muddy strait emptied of its diurnal water and headed for the *Vine café* as part of my then obligatory mile walk. **Bryher**, the smallest of the inhabited islands, was ecstatically beautiful even on that dreary day with white, sandy beaches and crystal-clear coves on its sheltered side, contrasting with the deeply rugged Atlantic coast, notably at the aptly named Hell Bay pummelled mercilessly by relentless storm surges.

After a leisurely cup of tea, I had an hour to return to Carn Near Quay and rendezvous with my water taxi to take me to **St Martin's**. I made it by a whisker and the 20-minute journey was extended to ensure suitable draft to disembark at Lowertown quay. Whilst waiting I chatted amiably to the boatman who was to meet the social worker doing her rounds. I learnt that most of the services, hospitals, schools etc., that we take for granted are in short or non-existent supply on the islands. Anything more than a minor illness or graze necessitates flying off the islands. Although there are primary schools on each island, from 11 to 16 'off island' children must go to **Tresco** and board for the week there. Beyond age 16 students must leave for the mainland, Truro or Penzance. Each island has however its own post van with the Royal Mail clearly subsidising delivery. This will undoubtedly change as the greed of profit tightens its ugly grip at the expense of this vital public service.

Eventually the boat had enough draft to access the quay at Lowertown without any unnecessary contortions of my arthritic limbs. I strolled to the 'town' which was deserted and headed for the *Sevenstones Inn* for a late lunch. The pub was also deserted save for a couple headed for the early ferry back to **St Mary's**. The view from the basic bar was true to the tourist blurb and offered stupendous views to the myriad of tiny islands beyond. I recalled that the late return journey was scheduled from Highertown quay some 40 minutes' walk away so, discretion being the better part of valour, I sauntered the length of the island through quiet lanes bordering compact bulb fields with not a soul in sight.

The mild and temperate climate, created by the Atlantic Gulf Stream, assures early delivery of daffodils and tulips for British supermarkets. There is even a vineyard on the island. I have always been a glass half empty sort of guy and I got an uneasy feeling that the late afternoon ferry was not going to be at the quay. It had been wet all day and the few tourists venturing out would have elected for the early boat. I, of course, had not been on the **St Mary's** boat to **St Martin's** and a headcount on the early boat would indicate that all travellers had been accounted for.

My suspicions were confirmed at the quay; the *Marie Celeste* would have looked busier when it was discovered deserted and adrift near the Azores in 1872. A child's abandoned pink school bag was the only evidence of human activity in the bleak, dank and draughty waiting room, with only public service notices to read and re-read to keep my boredom at bay. Surely the ferry would come. I was resigned to traipsing back to Lowertown in search of accommodation when I noticed a car on the slipway. I approached and tapped on the blacked-out window. The driver's window was slowly lowered and inside were four elderly gentlemen of the cloth, including the ex-Bishop of Plymouth and the Chaplain of the Isles. They took pity on this waif and stray and assured me that a passage to **St Mary's** would be secured. They had been committing the ashes of a parishioner at a service on the island.

As there are no car ferries on the islands, I was expecting my ecumenical companions to perform a 21st Century miracle, driving on water. My imagination was playing tricks with me and to my relief a private water taxi emerged and whisked the Reverends and their assorted entourage back to Hugh Town. I offered the skipper a measly £5 towards the fare, which he gracefully accepted. I slept well that night having walked 12 miles on or between four of the six inhabited islands.

St Agnes and its little sister, **Gugh**, were all that was left to visit the following day – a Saturday. What could now go wrong? Everything. There was no early return on the public ferry to catch the last *Scillonian* to Penzance before Monday. Tides again were thwarting my ambition. The scheduled return at 16:00 would miss the connection out of the islands and all flights to Land's End were booked solid. I had no choice but to throw more money, a further £50, at the problem and book the *Falcon* for my return trip. This luxury transport was reputed, at £300,000, to be the best boat on the Scillies. On the scheduled ferry I offered a discounted rate for an early return to anyone who so desired to part with a fiver. Capitalism is catching I mused.

St Agnes joins the smaller island of **Gugh** by a tombolo (two such geomorphological features in two days) with exposure at low tide. I walked across the uneven strand to **Gugh** first and climbed high up on the 34-metre summit of Kitten hill, as I was told of the existence there of remnants of an Iron age settlement. The tenacity of settlers in premodern history is truly remarkable and whichever islands I chose to visit, especially in the Celtic fringes, evidence of ritual monuments and burial chambers abound. I am not adept at recognising such decaying evidence and stumbled around in wind-pruned, dry, waved maritime heath or dense gorse and bracken. Although notified as a Site of Special Scientific Interest (SSSI) in 1976 its continuing status is in doubt as poor management has choked the abundance of flora with a dense ground cover of bramble. My scratched legs bore witness to this.

Returning to **St Agnes**, and as it was too early for a drink, even by my standards of decorum, I wandered along sleepy lanes with cottages reminiscent of chocolate box covers bedecked with early spring flowers. The still remoteness was beguiling and with little overnight accommodation its timelessness would, it seems, last forever. A jolt out of its perennial slumbers occurs on Friday evenings in the summer with the highly competitive domestic Cornish Pilot Gig races.

After my brief sojourn on the Scillies, I was punch drunk with their tranquillity and indescribable beauty. Time had surely stopped. **St Agnes** and **Gugh** were no exceptions and circumnavigation of each was comfortably achievable before lunch at another *Turk's Head,* a former customs house, owned by the garrulous Nicki. The pub has the accolade of being the most south westerly in the United Kingdom. We talked about the rigours of island life and the necessary insurance, when travelling to far away destinations, of leaving two days at either end of scheduled flight bookings to allow for weather conditions which locked down transportation on and off the islands. *Falcon's* skipper often made the 42-mile trip to Penzance to return fog bound Skybus passengers to mainland Cornwall at a cost of £100 per passenger. I was after all out in the Atlantic Ocean with the next landfall America. I had four paying passengers on the return and money back in my wallet.

The return journey to Penzance on the *Scillonian* was unremarkable and I got some sleep, lulled by the gentle waves and not at all what I had been told to expect. The forecast was not good with a deep low-pressure system due the next day, but there was no boat on a Sunday, a tradition I expect since when the islanders were a tad more religious than today. On arrival I walked the very short distance to the *Queens Hotel* and dumped my bag in the Freelander which I had parked in the rear car park and thankfully not on the promenade. *The Turk's Head* was packed with cold early season holiday makers, and I skipped the modest fare in favour of the *Pirates Rest* Fish and Chip shop nearby that had been so good a few days earlier. I could taste the freshly cooked batter already, not quite on a par with the artery clogging beef dripping batter of my Yorkshire childhood but delicious, nevertheless. I arrived at eight to find Saturday of all days was early closing and my desperate pleas to serve me fell on very deaf ears. I was relegated to the *Lugger Inn* roadhouse, deserted, but serving almost passable roast dinners.

A postscript to the Scilly Isles adventure is, (as will often unfold during the travels and travails through my *Treasured Islands)*, a unique fact unbeknown before but unearthed by my research. The Netherlands and the Scilly Isles hold the record for the longest conflict in World history. The Dutch-Scilly war technically lasted 335 years, from 30th March 1651, until a peace treaty was signed in 1986. The weird thing isn't just that the Netherlands and the archipelago off the west coast of Cornwall were at 'war' in the first place, but also that not a single shot was fired, nor an ounce of blood spilled. The war began when the Dutch took the side of the Parliamentarians in the English Civil war. In the process the Dutch incensed Charles the First's Royalists with whom they had historically been allies. When the skirmishes were over, and the Dutch left the islands nobody thought to sign a peace treaty. In 1986 Roy Duncan, an island historian invited the Dutch ambassador to Great Britain to visit **St Mary's** and formally negotiate an armistice.

3. St Michael's Mount and Burgh Island, England

I retired early as I wanted the next day to visit **St Michael's Mount**, a few miles east of Penzance at Marazion and then onto **Burgh Island**, off the Devon coast, before spending the night with my old friends Richard and Andrea in their palatial home in Teignmouth. They'd moved from the Midlands, forced out of their beautiful barn conversion at the diktat of HS2 high speed rail planners.

I rarely sleep well and woke abruptly at six. In my early morning confusion, I thought "Wow, it's raining cats and dogs out there". I got up to look out of the window; my room on the 2nd floor overlooked the sea, and to my amazement the sounds at the window were not rain but 20-foot waves crashing across the bows of the hotel. The predicted low had come with a vengeance. Cars parked on the promenade were swamped and I remembered that, but for the fact that there had been no space on the promenade prior to my departure on the *Scillonian*, I might have been parked there too with the Freelander meeting a premature, soggy end and scuppering my further island ambitions that weekend.

I checked the tide tables and discovered that low tide at **St Michael's Mount** was around midday and the four or five-mile journey meant I could enjoy a leisurely breakfast looking out at the angry cauldron of a sea. I left the hotel and sauntered to Marazion car park only to be told that the 'Mount' was closed for the day due to inclemency in the weather. Setbacks were to be a common theme on my island ventures. Forlorn, I walked to the deserted café for a think and a cup of tea to be told that the causeway was open and only the attractions had been suspended for the day.

I squinted out to sea to find the stone causeway and all I saw in the

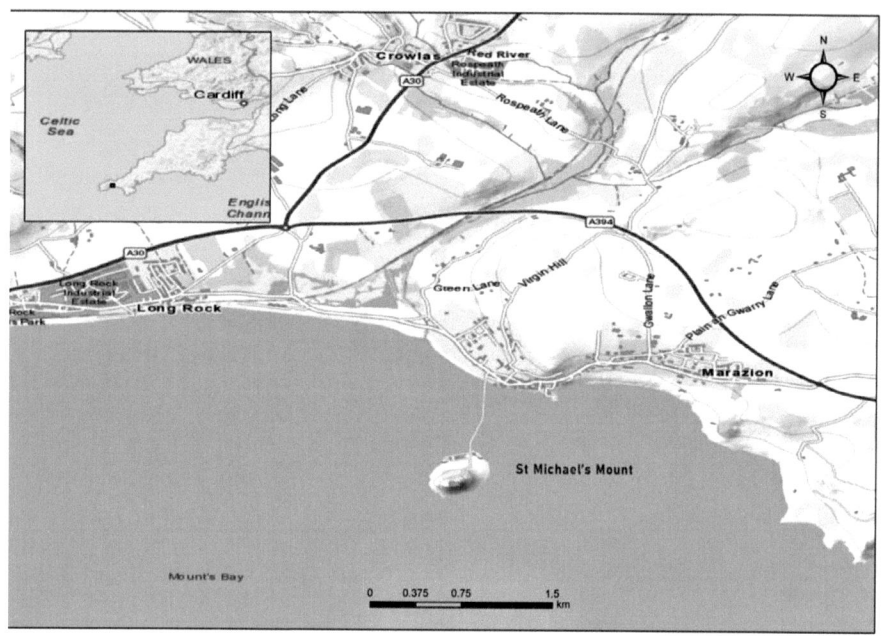

St Michael's Mount, Cornwall, England

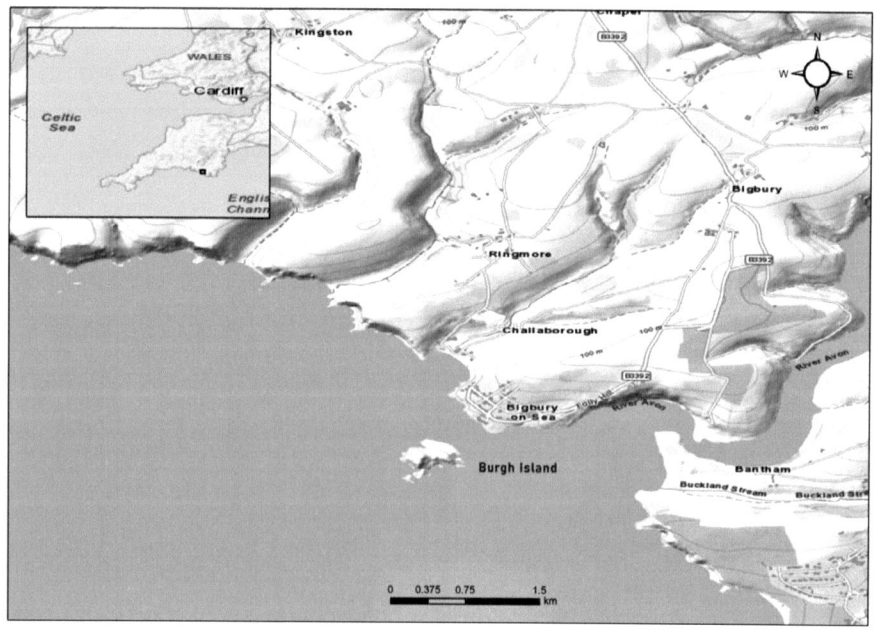

Burgh Island, Devon, England

murky distance was the crashing of waves across what appeared to be the causeway. It is a long way from Birmingham, and I wasn't of a mind to come back at another time when I was so tantalisingly close. I struggled against the wind to research access but only a fool would have attempted such a perilous crossing. I was that fool. I got wet, very wet but was encouraged by a cluster of walkers ahead of me and with each step the tide was in retreat and the causeway more exposed. It was like the parting of the Red Sea for Moses on his flight from Egypt with a straggling band of Israelites; after all **St Michael's Mount** has long been a pilgrim's route.

Historically, **St Michael's Mount** was the Cornish counterpart of Mont-Saint-Michel in Normandy, France, with which it shares the same tidal island characteristics and the same conical shape, though it is much smaller. Edward the Confessor gifted the site to the Benedictine order of Mont Saint-Michel before the Norman Conquest and by 1811 there were 53 houses and four streets, with a population peaking at 221. It is now the property of the National Trust having been gifted by Francis Cecil St Aubyn, 3rd Baron St Levan in 1954. **St Michael's Mount** is one of 43 unbridged tidal islands that one can walk to from mainland Britain, though most are uninhabited. I circled the tiny island before heading for the warmth of my Freelander and the couple of hours drive to **Burgh Island**.

I arrived at the nondescript settlement of Bigbury-on-sea and set off across the half mile sandy isthmus that connects **Burgh Island** to Great Britain at low tide. The April wind was punishingly cold, and I armed myself against its bite with two outer coats over my thick *Weird Fish* gansey. I remembered walking the Pass of the Cattle in northwest Scotland on the way to Applecross in June 2004 and this short walk was every bit as cripplingly numbing. I avoided the *Three Pilchards* pub and set out for the island summit via well marked paths, bypassing the intensely private hotel grounds with its helipad to whisk the pampered guests to and from this exclusive resort. I'd visited the island on several occasions, but this was truly a labour of love, a box ticking exercise, which in my frozen state seemed as pointless as the whole challenge I'd set myself, but intensely satisfying none the less.

The blurb for the outlandish and pricey *Burgh Island Hotel* suggests it is widely regarded as one of the foremost places to see and experience Art Deco in Europe. It salves its conscience and justifies its exorbitant prices by highlighting its eco-friendly credentials, but don't all hotels these days? Water saving, organic produce, energy saving lighting and solar electricity generation are boasted in its brochure.

The hotel was a hideaway for high society in the 1930's with Noel Coward and Agatha Christie being prominent guests. Once the tide was in and access restricted no prying eyes could disturb any untoward shenanigans. It still has an air of pomposity about it today with curious non-resident visitors turned away in a trice. Even the *Pilchard inn*, dating back to 1336, off site but part of the hotel, is largely out of bounds for tourists, who on a hot summer's day have the indignity of queuing at a hatch to order beverages.

4. Firth of Clyde, Scotland

I'd been studying Hamish Haswell-Smith's *The Scottish Islands*, my Bible for exploring the Scottish islands and I'd decided to tackle them sector by sector just as Haswell-Smith had written about them in his remarkable book, with copious maps and illustrations, all hand drawn. These are as artistic and compelling as Alfred Wainwright's *Lakeland Fells* series of books, so precious to me in my youth. Fell walking was a passion I had inherited from my father. The book, or rather authoritative compendium, includes all islands, inhabited or otherwise so long as they are greater than 40 hectares in size. It was compiled essentially for yachtsmen listing safe havens to anchor and other tips for the hardy amateur sailor.

God forbid that I was travelling to them all. Nobody in their right mind would surely attempt islands like Soay, some 40 miles off the coast of **North Uist** in the Outer Hebrides. In the annals of human endeavour there is always someone up for any challenge. Whilst walking across **Fair Isle** (isolated between the Shetland and Orkney Islands) I came across such a man. He was attempting ALL Great British islands and climbing to the highest point of each! He and other island 'enthusiasts' had clubbed together an eye wateringly large amount of money to hire a RIB (Reinforced Inflatable Boat) to take them to Soay.

Being a systematic sort of guy, I started in Scotland with the first sector of Haswell-Smith's book. *The Solway Firth to the Firth of Clyde* sector has 4 inhabited islands: **Arran** and the small island of **Holy Island** in Lamlash Bay close to **Arran**, **Bute** and **Great Cumbrae**. A fifth, Sanda, off the tip of the Mull of Kintyre is not permanently occupied according to local knowledge. I had intended to visit via private charter but, as usual, the weather was against me. After further research I made an executive decision – it didn't count. The island had been bought by a Swiss businessman in 2009 for £2.5 million 'for his personal use', but the

TREASURED ISLANDS

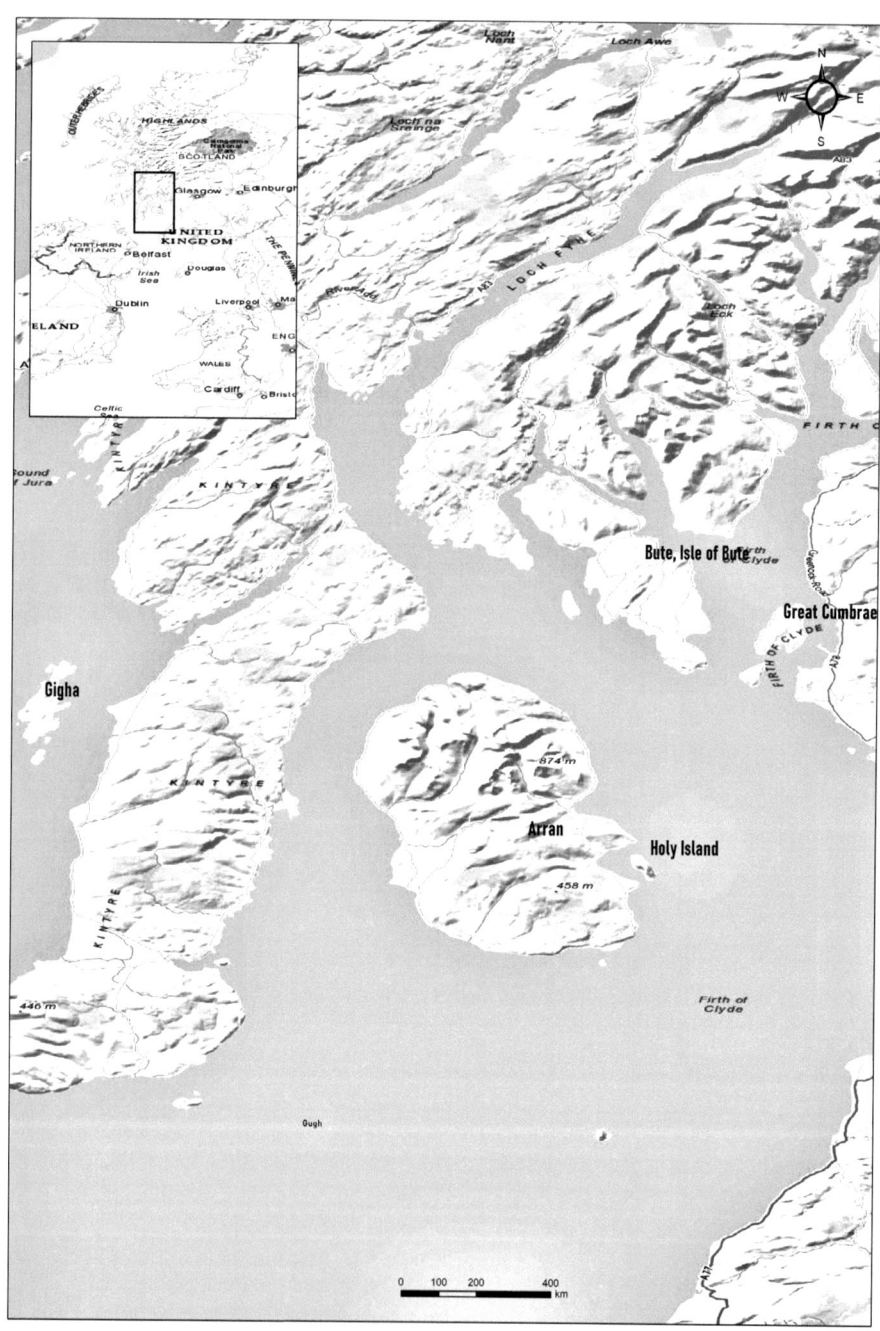

Firth of Clyde, Scotland

2011 census recorded no permanent residents. Maybe following the 2021 census its permanent residential status will change; back to the drawing board? However, and to my delight the 2021 Scottish census was delayed because of the COVID-19 pandemic.

I drove from Birmingham aiming to get the last RoRo (roll-on-roll-off) ferry from Wemys Bay to Rothsey on the **Isle of Bute**. I had been used to these long drives to the starting points on my walk around the coast and I arrived at the ferry terminal after a seven-hour drive, stopping only at the peerless Tebay services in Westmorland which boasts quite rightly the finest farm shop on the whole UK motorway network. On arrival the waiting room was deserted, and I had time to charge my phone and get a summer Caledonian MacBrayne timetable which would be a necessary companion all summer and beyond. The wait gave me time to unpick the complexities of the ferry timetable and help me mentally prepare for the enormity of the task ahead.

The last car ferry I had taken was across the Magellan Straits in Chile on the way to Tierra del Fuego. This latest adventure after the southwest England appetizer was now well under way. I'd been listening to the naturalist Chris Packham on the radio on the way north and his views of earth's fragility mirror my own. His vision for the World's future was not good with man's selfishness and self-seeking strangling the beauty bequeathed to us millions of years since the big bang which created us. It was only a few months before the Referendum on continued membership of the European Union which was to further divide our Nation and much of the World again through the whim of loathsome self-serving politicians.

Bute is largely owned by the 7th Marquess of Bute who prefers to be known as Johnny Dumfries or Johnny Bute, the former Formula 1 racing driver and past winner of the Le Mans 24-hour race. These modern aristocrats seem to prefer catchy ordinary names to align themselves with us 'commoners'. Continuously populated for 6,000 years its prosperity, like many Scottish islands, blossomed with the advent of herring fisheries this time in the 19th Century before tourism emerged as the island's prime economic driver. Rothsey is the main settlement on the **Isle of Bute**.

His then Royal Highness Prince Charles Philip Arthur George, Prince of Wales, KG, KT, GCB, OM, AK, QSO, CC, PC, ADC, holds, amongst his many other 'grace and favour' titles so beloved by the aristocracy, the Dukedom of Rothesay. A little schizophrenic I thought as besides being Prince of Wales, like all heirs to the British throne, he was also the Earl of Chester, Duke of Cornwall, Earl of Carrick, Baron of Renfrew, Lord of the Isles and Prince and Great Steward of Scotland. This political expediency seems to cover all constituent parts of the current United Kingdom. I'm sure these age-old titles, since the Prince's elevation to King Charles III, are now in the possession of the Duke of Cambridge. Overseas visitors must be perplexed with such disconnection between the titles' privileged owners and their sporadic geography. The Duke of Devonshire lives primarily in Derbyshire and the Duke of Norfolk in Sussex.

The town is dominated by the 13th century castle of the same name. Glaswegian Victorians loved the place, "doon the watter" that is the river Clyde, travelling in years gone by, by steamer and away from the fetid, claustrophobic tenements and closes of the city. As with many of our coastal resorts cheap package holidays abroad were the death knell to these enervating days out. Those of us of a certain age remember Lena Zavaroni, who was born on Rothesay, and star of shows of intense mediocrity in the seventies. Her fame was probably contributory to her untimely death in 1999.

The short journey to Rothsey as the sun was setting amplified the beauty of the Highlands in the distance acting as an antidote to the worthless human follies that stricture common sense. The ferries are heavily subsidised by the Scottish Government who champion the principles of enlightenment at every stage in their proud history. This was to be highlighted later that year in their overwhelming desire not to break with Europe unlike the xenophobic 'Little Englanders'. Though a modest fare I declined to take my Land Rover Freelander as I was to stay close to the harbour and return the next day. Rothsey is at the same latitude north as Punta Arenas in Chile is south. Map projections of the World certainly play tricks.

It was good to get away as politically the World was entering "The Weird Zone" with Donald Trump seemingly unassailable as Republican presidential nominee. English local elections showed labour had a better share of the vote than even the triumphant Blair in his early years before being sullied by Iraq's Desert Storm campaign. The likes of Ken Livingstone and especially Jeremy Corbyn were now the whipping boys of both the Labour and Tory establishment. Sadiq Khan became elected mayor of London with a greater number of votes secured by a single political candidate in British history and the first Muslim mayor in Europe. Trump had vowed to ban Muslims from entering USA until "we know what the hell is going on" in the wake of some terrorist atrocities and I wondered if this madness would apply to Mr Khan! This is fuelling the fires of immigration rhetoric which was to peak after the UK "democratically" voted to break anchor from our European brothers and sisters. Leicester City had just won the football Premiership title with 100 to 1 betting odds at the start of the season, so the weird zone was extending to sport as well.

I avoided *The Golfer* pub where the gathering was watching Liverpool in the closing stages of the Europa league final and went next door to a quiet little place where my companion was a truck driver from my childhood hometown of Keighley in West Yorkshire. The economics of trucking defy logic with the short crossing from Wemys Bay costing for an HGV some £220 return. As convivial as our brief exchanges had been I had a mile to walk to reach my B&B, the *Ardyne Guest House* on the beautiful promenade of majestic double fronted stone houses, the summer houses of wealthy Glaswegian industrialists at the height of Empire.

I was up early to catch the ferry to the mainland and head off to Ardrossan to board the ferry to Brodick on **Arran** which I had read is 'Scotland in miniature", on one-pint sized island; though this "pint sized" island is actually larger than the **Isle of Wight**. What appear to be short journeys are often logistically challenging as I slowly headed down the coast to Largs and beyond, tracing my coastal walk in reverse. The ferry to **Arran** was full. I had not booked ahead and a patient hour or so was required to get me and the Freelander onto the next ferry. The idea was to drive to Lamlash and seek out a ferry to **Holy Island**.

It was well after two in the afternoon when I got to the jetty only to be told by a surly young girl manning the ferry owner's shack that the low tides would make a journey to **Holy Island** impossible. My plans, and not for the first or last time, were in tatters. I regrouped with a cream tea at a nearby café and waited for Jim, the boatman, to return on what I was told would be the last boat of the day bringing Buddhists back from the island before hatches were battened down for the pending storm expected the next day from the southwest.

Jim arrived in his boat *Sally Forth*. He was an affable and atypically generous Yorkshireman who had been operating this service for decades and when I tentatively asked about a quick journey, he rejected my offer of £50 to accept the normal £5 fee. I was in luck. A woman too approached him explaining she wanted to visit the island almost as briefly as I did to pay respects to a friend's mother who had had her ashes scattered on this sacred island. The low tide did not faze old Jim and after an hour or so of idling we set off to pick up the last bunch of pilgrims who were deserting the island early to avoid the pending storm.

The evacuation involved more than a boatload, so the good lady and I had ample time to explore whilst Jim made a repeat journey. The weather was excellent, and the island seemed to ooze with spirituality dotted as it was with Buddhist symbolism. A devout Catholic, Kay Morris, who owned the island, apparently had in 1992 a dream from the Virgin Mary instructing her to give ownership over to a Tibetan order of monks, *Samyé Ling Buddhist Community*. They paid £350,000 for the island which affords one of the largest non-denominational Buddhist centres in Europe with up to 200 adherents searching for inner peace.

A condition of sale was the retention of its natural environment. The new owners have taken harmonisation with nature to an admirable level with wholly sustainable living and introduction of thousands of native plant and animal species. Visitors are welcome so long as they abide by the five golden precepts of Buddhism: refrain from killing, refrain from stealing, refrain from lying, refrain from sexual misconduct, and refrain from consuming intoxicants. My thirty-minute visit fell wholly into line with this simple philosophy of life. All precepts were obeyed to the letter!

On my return to **Arran**, I gave three of the pilgrims a lift to the ferry at Brodick and made for Lochranza, the home of the island's only distillery, via Corrie to take the RoRo to Claonaig on the Mull of Kintyre. I'd virtually circumnavigated **Arran** on my coast walk and the island was as beautiful and tranquil as I remembered. Goat Fell, though not a Munro with a height less than 3,000 feet, stands proud like a beacon in the Firth of Clyde. **Arran** is a mecca for aspiring geologists as it lies on the Highland boundary fault with, for such a small island, an unparalleled array of sedimentary, igneous and metamorphic rocks from the Pre Cambrian to the Mesozoic period. Sir Archibald Geikie, the Victorian geologist, described **Arran** as a complete synopsis of Scottish geology. Many a university student has found the trips to the island both liberating in both the academic and social sense, often seen through newly acquired beer goggles in some of **Arran's** excellent inns.

An ancient 13th Century Irish poem, *Agalllamh na Senorach* sums up the charm and mellowness of **Arran**:

> *"Arran of the many stags*
> *The sea strikes against her shoulders,*
> *Companies of men can feed there,*
> *Blue spears are reddened among her boulders.*
>
> *Merry hinds are on her hills,*
> *Juicy berries are there for food,*
> *Refreshing water in her streams,*
> *Nuts in plenty in the wood".*

In summer, the length and breadth of the Highlands and Islands is bedecked with rhododendrons, not a native species to Scotland but introduced in the 18th Century from southern Europe. These, in my opinion, glorious blooms flourish in the mild climate abetted by the Atlantic Gulf Stream.

Brodick castle has one of Europe's finest historical collections. The round tower of the castle dates back to the 13th century. In 1652 Oliver Cromwell's troops, though usually renowned for destruction rather than construction, built the battery and extended the castle before being massacred by the islanders, again an unusual reversal of fortunes for the zealous Roundheads.

The 10th Duke of Hamilton was in ownership of Brodick castle at the beginning of the 19th Century. He married into the infamous Beckford family who were among the first to obtain plantations in Jamaica. They owned hundreds of slaves and, over three generations, grew extremely rich. In fact, one third of all Jamaican plantations were owned by Scots; a blight on their traditional image as innovators and liberal guardians of culture and freedom created during the 'enlightenment'. William Beckford spent much of his ill-gotten fortune on art treasures and a grand house. His daughter and heir, Susan, brought part of the priceless 'Beckford collection' to Brodick which is still on display at the castle. Many of Scotland's baronial mansions and their opulent contents were built on the profits made from the slave trade, conveniently air brushed from school curriculum history lessons.

I headed for the *Argyll hotel*, a tired time warp of a hotel, in Campbelltown as I was still keen to get to Sanda the next day. The owner was married to a Russian and they had owned the hotel for 20 years or so. His opinion was that Sanda was not inhabited permanently though there was some talk of a hotel and holiday lets being opened. Sanda has had a varied bunch of owners including Jack Bruce, bassist in the seminal sixties blues combo *Cream*. Jack should not be confused with the Scottish King Robert the Bruce who was also reputed to have landed there in 1306. Jack Bruce bought Sanda in the seventies but sold it when he heard Hunstanton nuclear power station on the North Ayrshire coast would be built to 'spoil his view'.

I reported to the authority of *Appendix 2 of the Scottish Census of inhabited islands* for 2011 (my yardstick for permanent population) and the recorded inhabitants was zero. No boats were available in any case as the weather from the southwest as predicted was atrocious. My job here was done and after noting the memorial garden to Linda McCartney, who had been well known in the town, set off back for Claonaig.

I noticed on my road map that Largs was the ferry terminal for **Great Cumbrae** and hopping across **Arran** was by far the best way back to Largs and so avoiding maybe half of the 136 miles via Inveray and Arrochar. I set off with **Great Cumbrae** on my mind when I noticed I could pinch an island from Haswell-Smith's Sector 2 (*Mull of Kintyre to Firth of Lorn*), namely **Gigha**, before catching the **Arran** ferry. A short 20-minute journey by RoRo from Tayinloan was too good to miss out on. My paranoia was however kicking in as a Londoner was reputedly renovating a house on nearby Cara with a view to living there. Trusty Appendix 2 suggested otherwise; Cara was not permanently inhabited.

I left the Freelander at Tayinloan and caught the very frequent ferry and ambled across **Gigha** for a couple of hours enjoying cake at the multi award winning *Boathouse* tea rooms, opened especially for me, which was worth the £5 ferry fare alone. My sights were set on Achamore House, once owned by Sir James Horlicks (of night-time beverage fame) beyond the scattered and peaceful village of Ardminish and the tempting but closed *Gigha hotel*. **Gigha** is run as a very successful community collective, and the island trust has built about 18 new houses aimed specifically at people with special needs.

Gigha lies some 3 miles off the west coast of Kintyre with the population on this small island peaking in the 18th century at a reputed 614. The community buy out in March 2002, for around £4 million and largely paid for by the National Lottery fund, has allowed the present population of about 163 (50 percent more than at the time of the buyout) to flourish and businesses are thriving. The 15th of March each year is celebrated as 'Independence Day'. Although the exotic Gigha cheeses don't appear to be made on the island, *The Wee Isle Dairy*, one of the emerging businesses on the island, makes delicious artisan ice creams from the milk from local cows grazing on the lush pastures of Tarbert farm.

It is 5 minutes by car ferry to **Great Cumbrae** slip from Largs and I circumnavigated the island anti clockwise before arriving at Millport, the only settlement on this strange island which was a go-to holiday destination for Glaswegians before Rothsey became popular. The town would have been especially busy during the annual summer shipyard and factory shut down in Glasgow, known as 'Fairs week'. This took me back to my childhood in the West Riding when all the knitting wool and worsted cloth factories in Yorkshire and the cotton mills in Lancashire would stagger their holidays to avoid overcrowding of the popular holiday resorts in the North of England, especially Blackpool, Morecambe and Scarborough.

I recall the expansive beaches between Blackpool's three iconic piers, crammed to an uncomfortable cheek by jowl capacity with not an inch of spare sand in between us and our neighbours. We changed into our trunks in full view with only the awkward positioning of our towels protecting our dignity. The exhilarated holiday makers made the best of the lottery that is the English summer with collective memories that occupied their thoughts as they tended their noisy looms throughout the drab winters of the north of England.

The paddle steamer *Waverley* still plies its trade from Glasgow to **Great Cumbrae** in the summer months. In 1906 steamer companies boycotted the island because of excessive harbour dues and but for an intervention by politician David Lloyd George this could have been the death knell for the island's modest prosperity throughout the 20th Century.

After the last ferry back to Largs in mid evening Milltown is a ghost town except for its five packed pubs. I had by coincidence rolled into town the same weekend as Paul, my caving pal from London University speleological society (*CaveSoc*) back in the early seventies. He had checked into the *National Water Sports Training Centre* to get his qualifications to drive a small offshore motorized boat. I picked up Paul and did another tour of the island before we made a determined assault on all five pubs with the usual cacophony of drunks to be expected on a small island with little else to fill the evenings. Thirty minutes in each pub was sufficient, escaping Karaoke in the *Kilburn Bar* and the frenetic dancing in my hotel the *Royal George*. We escaped the carnage of the night and walked the promenade on a fine early spring evening with the uninhabited Little Cumbrae glowering menacingly in the distance.

TREASURED ISLANDS

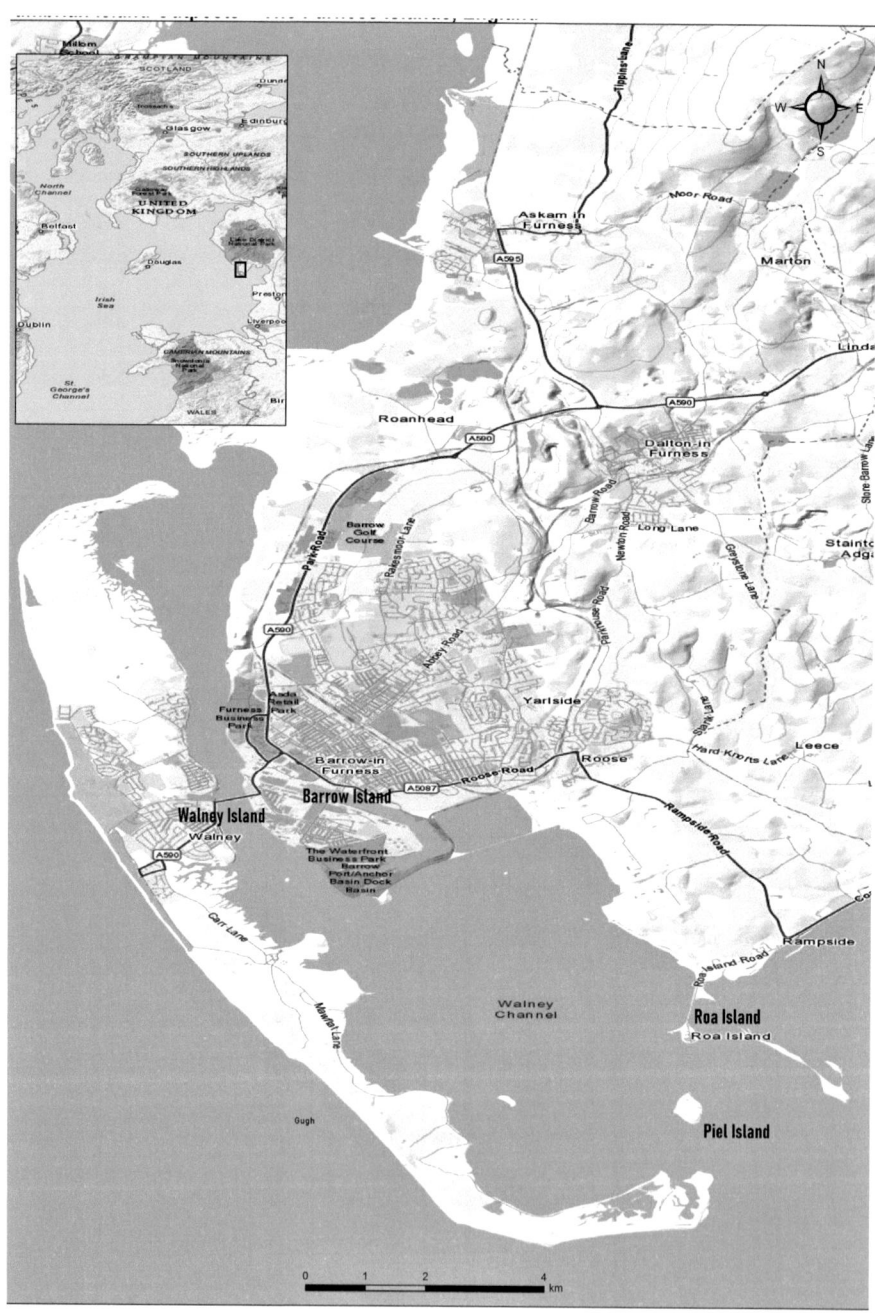

Cumbrian island outposts – The Furness Islands, England

5. Cumbrian Island Outposts – The Furness Islands, England

After dipping my toes into the first round of Scottish islands I headed south and made an on-the-spot decision to visit four of the English islands off the coast of west Cumbria; **Barrow Island, Walney Island, Roa Island** and **Piel Island**, known as the Furness islands. Three other uninhabited islands, Sheep, Foulney and Chapel make up the largest island group between **Anglesey** and the Firth of Clyde.

Heading south I left the M6 to meet the coastal road through Workington and Whitehaven, once proud industrial towns of some prowess, but now relics of a bygone age. Terraced housing reminiscent of south Wales in linear settlements were incongruously juxtaposed adjacent to the stunningly beautiful west Lakeland fells. I was heading for Barrow-in-Furness, as remote from the rest of England as it was possible to be. Barrow too was falling on hard times in this post-industrial age, with huge unemployment.

During the Tory eighty seat landslide in the General Election of 2019 this depressed forgotten part of the UK voted in a Conservative Member of Parliament in the guise of Simon Fell. His constituents are the working-class Northern 'Red' Tories who secured an unassailable Boris Johnson his tenure as Prime Minister, believing the Brexit lies espoused by the ideological Tory tabloid newspapers. The debacle of the Tory response to COVID 19 the following year and the despicable contempt shown by Johnson's special adviser Dominic Cummings to the lockdown rules, actually created by him, is surely now an embarrassment to these erstwhile Labour voters. Their relatives were literally dying. At the height of the first wave of the pandemic Barrow led the cluster of Northern towns with highest rates of coronavirus infections in England and Wales, with 882 cases per 100,000.

I'd spent a little time there when my mother was hospitalised after falling down her neighbour's stairs breaking her leg. The once proud shipyards are now home to select warship re-fits. In the past the vast hangers still dominating the town were where the first British Polaris ballistic missile submarine, *HMS Resolution*, was laid down by Vickers-Armstrong on 26th February 1964. The suburban landscape had been transformed as anywhere else in the western world with ugly, garish retail parks à la mode American. The one in Barrow is even called Hollywood Park. They keep the capitalist dream alive even after the adversity of unemployment ballooning since the demise of Vickers.

I reached **Barrow 'Island'**, characterised by bleak run-down tenement buildings with few people venturing out. It is hardly an island now, like Barry Island in south Wales. It nestles between the now derelict docks and the town centre. In the 1860's the two docks *Buccleuch Dock* and the *Devonshire Dock* were opened by Prime Minister William Gladstone, and these suffocated the channel which had maintained its island status. For some peculiar reason it is still referred to as one of the Furness islands and known as '*Baz I*' by the locals.

I had seen enough of the dereliction and headed for the A590 trunk road which runs across the northern edge of **Barrow Island** before crossing the Jubilee Bridge to **Walney Island**. Vickerstown is the main settlement and as the name suggests was built as a dormitory settlement to house Vickers' workers. Its west coast is reputed to be the windiest lowland site in England, and I can vouch for this during my coastal asset inspections with engineers from Barrow council. Between the crumbling and largely ineffective flood defences are salt-marsh, shingle, sand dunes and brackish ponds with the expected plethora of bird hides. On the horizon in the Irish sea are six offshore wind farms, taking full advantage of the windy location, with a grand total of 378 turbines (and counting) and a capacity of 1,657 Megawatts. The continued development of sources of sustainable energy provides a much-needed employment opportunity.

It was getting late, and I had booked into the surprisingly amenable *Clarke's Hotel* in Rampside at the landward end of the causeway leading to **Roa Island**. **Roa Island** is a tight knit community of about a hundred people, which until the mid-19th century was only accessible at low tide or by boat. Today it has a passing interest for tourists in an 'end-of-the-road' sort of way with a good selection of modest cafes. It is the staging point for pleasure trips to **Piel Island**, now owned by Barrow borough council and lived on by the King of Piel, with the pub as his kingdom.

I walked around the perimeter of **Roa Island** and its many boat yards and opted to wait on the quay wall to enquire as to the timings of the boat to **Piel Island**. I waited and with no one to ask I sat patiently in the warm spring sunshine looking towards the small island. It had been a long drive from Largs. I was joined by a pleasant enough guy who, obviously a local, indicated that the last sailing had been at 16:00. He could see my disappointment and gave me the telephone number of the boatman. I phoned and he cheerily indicated that a trip tomorrow could be possible.

Relieved I continued chatting to my new friend who invited me across the road to his modest terraced house for a cup of tea. I agreed as I had had no time to stop for refreshment in my rush to achieve my Furness islands ambition. Once inside, a 'Tardis' opened up before me with a huge kitchen the like of which is reserved for those James Martin TV cookery programmes. It transpired that this was the house of Dave Myers of *Hairy Bikers'* fame, the loveable rogue who along with Simon King had injected a bit of spark into the growing number of otherwise tedious celebratory chef extravaganzas. The kitchen accessories had been paid for by some TV production company costing around £40,000.

After more than a comfortable night in *Clark's* I set off for the quay on **Roa Island** and my 'booked' trip to **Piel Island**. There was no sign of activity on a rather colder Monday morning. Annoyed, I phoned the proprietor to be told he would no longer be making the trip that day. I mumbled expletives under my breath and headed back to the M6, leaving an audience with the king for another time.

6. The Mull of Kintyre to the Firth of Lorn, Scotland

I arrived at *The Argyll Inn* in Lochgilphead after another seven-and-a-half-hour drive from Birmingham. It was a nostalgic journey from the Erskine bridge, crossing the river Clyde, as much of the journey followed the route I'd last covered on foot in April 2004 during *'A walk by the Sea'*. The trip was like turning over pages in my mind reliving the once in a lifetime experience all over again. I'd travelled the route several times since to holiday in Crinan with friends, but this journey was special as it was the start of a new leg of the newest adventure, a random selection of islands which would ultimately turn into a collection of the 223 inhabited islands off the shores of the British Isles.

The hotel was deconstructed in every way, one of a small chain, basic and passably comfortable with a public bar which slumbered until the post eleven o'clock revellers descended on the only licensed premise remaining open in this sleepy town. Lochgilphead was a staging post to Campbeltown some 50 miles away and I assume to the nearby Caledonian MacBrayne ferry port at Kennacraig, the gateway to **Islay**, my first island of this trip.

It was less than an hour to the ferry port and I arrived exuding optimism. What could go wrong? The port was thronged which surprised me as this was May and the holiday season had not yet started or so I thought. I offered up my debit card to purchase a return ticket for me and the Freelander. "Sorry sir, next available sailing is Monday". That was in four days' time. "Why is this?", I spluttered incredulously. The salesclerk became agitated. "It is the annual whisky festival".

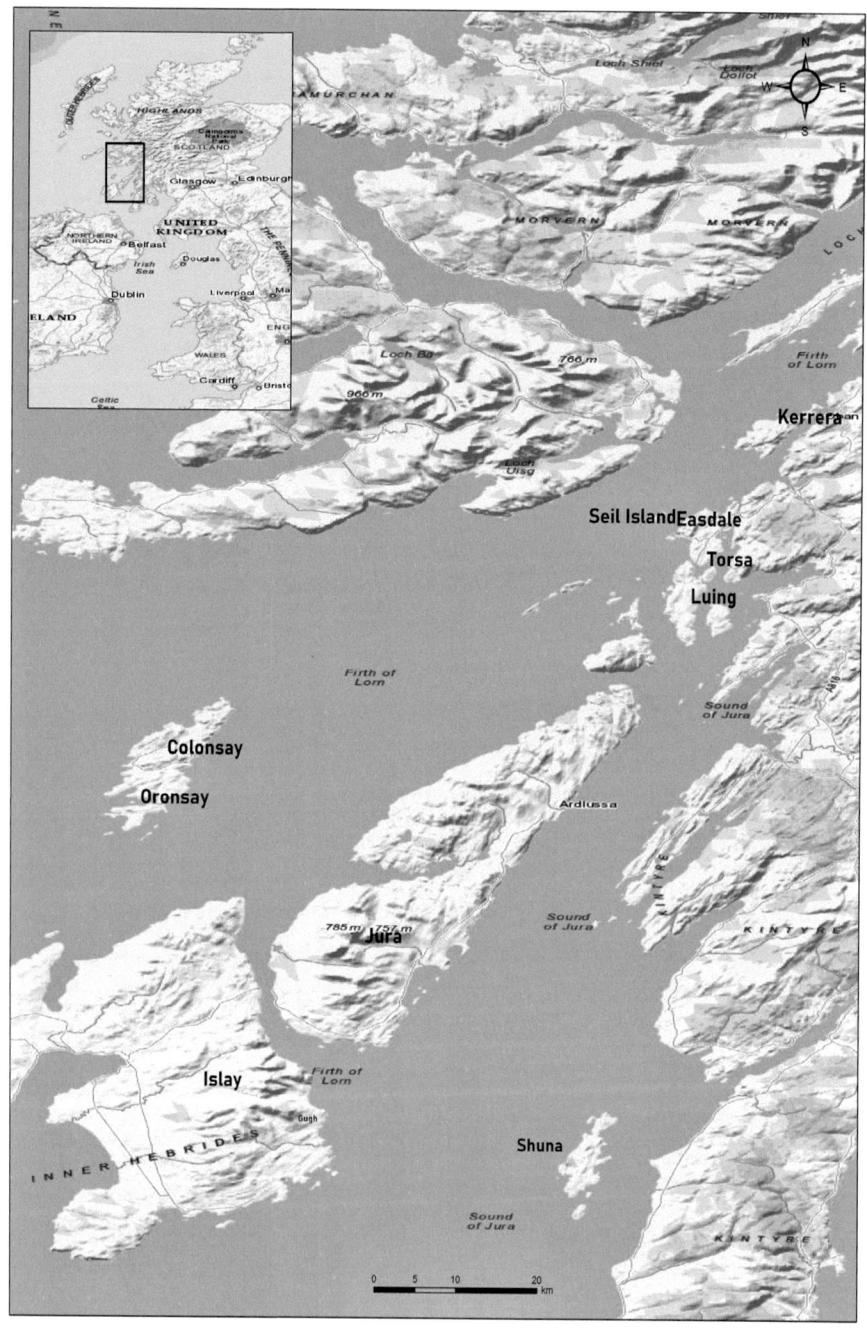

The Mull of Kintyre to the Firth of Lorn, Scotland

Feis Ile as this festival is affectionately known draws crowds from all parts of the world. **Islay** is a veritable cornucopia of whisky distilleries, nine currently operating and the famous Glen Ellen, now closed down but still offering aged malt at sky high prices. Of course, planning my trip, I simply as usual did not do sufficient research. OK I thought I will repack my bag and go as a foot passenger. The agitated clerk became even more impatient. "Have you booked accommodation" she enquired. "Don't worry I will get some when I get there". She laughed hysterically. "Look, everywhere has been booked for months; there are no beds left on the island". Now I've always been stubborn and of the 'bird in the hand is better than two in a bush' philosophy, so I booked my return, parked my Freelander, and embarked on the first ferry to Port Ellen, a two-hour twenty-minute journey to the south of the island as against a slightly shorter journey to Port Askaig in the island's northeast.

The ferry was packed with whisky revellers. On arrival I headed for the *Islay hotel* on an unseasonably warm afternoon. A light lunch and a local ale cheered me up a little until my worst fears were indeed confirmed. There was no room at the inn or anywhere else on the island. Undeterred I enquired about a bus service at the shop next door and was told I had just missed one which departed some 10 minutes before the ferry arrived for Bowmore, the capital, and onto Port Askraig. "A coordinated bus service would not have been too much to ask for, would it, I chuntered?" "Taxi?" I enquired. Again laughter. "The festival has a cartel on taxis to drive the imbibers between distilleries……you'll be lucky".

My patience was depleting rapidly, and I decided to wait for the bus due to arrive in about an hour and head for Port Askaig and board an evening ferry to **Colonsay**; surely there would be accommodation there? With time to spare I researched rooms on **Islay's** neighbouring islands of **Colonsay** and **Jura**. I may as well have been searching for a room in East Timor. Nobody knew where I might book. The bus arrived which I boarded with a couple of young Japanese lovers, and we made the 45-minute journey to Bowmore where I decided to disembark. This was another 'bird in the hand' idea.

I bade farewell to the bus driver and the lovers and headed for the Bowmore Tourist Information Office to be greeted by Judith and Janice who, charming as they were, soon ran out of patience with this elderly guy insisting there must be a room…. somewhere. They tried **Jura** with no luck. They tried **Colonsay** with no luck and I was about to throw my hat in and get the bus to Port Askaig and onto Oban with a view to trying to get to **Colonsay** the next day, when out of nowhere Judith said triumphantly, "we have a single room for you at the *Lochside hotel* for £95". It was two minutes' walk away and, though, by my dishevelled appearance I looked as though I couldn't afford it, I bit their hand off to accept. How fortunes change? Flexibility is indeed a virtue. I quickened my step to the said hotel, checked in and with a couple of hours to kill boarded the bus to Port Askaig with a view to taking the RoRo to **Jura**, thus ticking off another island.

The tiny RoRo with room for about 10 cars was open to the elements and gave a panoramic, no mesmeric, view of the Jura Mountains. It is held that 15 pairs of golden eagles soar freely over these peaks with hen harriers lower down their slopes. The ferry is not part of the CalMac monopoly and operated on behalf of the Argyll and Bute council. It docked at Feolin which has no facilities for the tourist other than a rudimentary bus shelter. The nearest village, Craighouse, the main settlement and home to the famous Jura distillery, is over eight miles away and buses were as rare as hen's teeth coordinating with school hours only.

I walked in absolute solitude for 30 minutes southwards on the coast road and then turned back to Feolin, with an eye on the return timetable. A calm returned on that bright spring evening. **Jura** at 142 square miles is almost as big as the **Isle of Wight** and with only 196 inhabitants it has one of the lowest population densities of any of the Scottish islands: 1.38 people per square mile. This is a sparse population by any reckoning. In comparison Scotland's population density is 174 people per square mile and there is a lot of wilderness in Scotland!

Jura is also famous for the Corryvreckan or speckled cauldron, a ferocious whirlpool, where on certain states of the tide, the sea cascades like a waterfall and is a real danger to shipping. George Orwell, aka Eric Blair, rented a cottage, *Barnhill,* on the island from 1946 till his death. He completed his dystopian novel *1984* there and almost drowned swimming through this quirky torrent. On a previous visit my son Maxim proudly navigated his way through it on his first venture at the helm of a boat. He was lucky as the phenomenon is at its most dramatic and perilous on a spring flood tide running westwards at speeds of 10 knots against a strong west wind.

Orwell's representation of a brainwashed future is mirrored in today's society as right wing popularism takes a grip on countries worldwide. There are seven landlords on **Jura** who now carve up the ownership of the island between them, mostly absentees, so feudalism is alive and well. It is wise not to venture out onto the hills from mid-August as these estates host stag hunting for the rich and privileged. Princess Anne and former Prime Minister David Cameron have been frequent visitors. It is said that 20,000 acres are owned by his wife, Samantha's stepfather Lord Astor. Cannily and suspiciously the registration of ownership is in Nassau, Bahamas with no overt connection to the Cameron family. This is the trick of the over privileged quasi aristocracy who hide their wealth in 'offshore' affiliations to avoid taxation.

The hypocrisy is overwhelming with Cameron and his wealthy successors asking us to tighten our belts whilst they under invest in public services, especially the National Health Service, until the country's population's collective pips squeak. Meanwhile, their investments flourish, supported by hedge funds, in on the trick of pre-empting market failure. With an estimated 16 million of the UK population not able to find £100 in an emergency (if fixing a boiler or replacing a fridge is such) the Government strategy is no worse than the lairds orchestrating the 'Highland Clearances' in previous centuries. Although relatively few forced clearances on **Jura** were recorded, the emigrations, which decimated the population to today's levels, were far from voluntary, being the result of factors such as hunger and spiralling rents. *Plus ca change.* To quote Orwell from his classic, *The Road to Wigan Pier:*

"England is the most class ridden country under the sun. It is a land of snobbery and privilege, ruled largely by the old and the silly."

Whilst on the subject of 'silly' and at the opposite end of the poverty spectrum 'K Foundation Burn a Million Quid' was a performance art action on 23rd August 1994 in which the K Foundation (an art duo consisting of Bill Drummond and Jimmy Cauty) allegedly burned cash to the amount of one million pounds in a disused boathouse on the Ardfin Estate on **Jura**. The money represented the bulk of the K Foundation's funds, earned by Drummond and Cauty as KLF, one of the United Kingdom's most successful pop groups of the early 1990s. It's a funny old world from Orwell to Drummond via Cameron.

Returning to the ferry I nonchalantly asked the ferrymen about a connecting bus to Bowmore. "You've missed the school bus, but why not ask for a lift from one of the cars on board". It was a captive audience, so I tapped on the window of the first car, feeling like a Romany car window washer at the Bristol Road A38 traffic lights back home in Birmingham. A face appeared, a not too friendly face. Three Americans had been visiting the Jura distillery and they, though with some immediate reluctance, agreed to drop me off at Bowmore, a little out of their way.

There was no time to rest, and a whisky party had begun in the bar of the *Lochside hotel*. A genial guy sat next to me on his bar stool and soon enlightened me to the traditions of *Feis Ils*. We were joined by Irvine Wilson Tchaikovsky, the unlikely whisky ambassador for Diageo, the world's largest producer of spirits and famous for selling *Johnny Walker* blended whisky in 180 countries. Now *Johnny Walker* would not be on the menu that evening. I spied the dregs of a bottle of *Glen Ellen* single malt on the bar and asked the barman if I might taste it. He grimaced and explained that the *Lochside* were selling this at £200 a dram or 1/8 of a fluid ounce or 3.55 millilitres! I recoiled and was allowed a quick sniff of the cork. The "dregs" had been left by a group of obviously rich Swedes who had purchased the full bottle for an unbelievable £7,000.

The barman asked me what I wanted to drink and conscious of the impending expense I asked for the whisky menu where prices started at £60 a dram. I opted for a pint of Guinness another Diageo product. Irvine was by now well-oiled and well into his stride with a detailed account of Lagavulin's 200-year history which has been distilling whisky, he quipped "under 32 British Prime Ministers and 7 terrible Coldplay albums". He liked a joke did our Irvine!

Islay is also known as 'Queen of the Hebrides'. Many regard it as the malt whisky capital of the world with famous names like *Bruichladdich, Bowmore, Laphroaig, Lagavulin, Caol Ila, Bunnahabhain* and *Ardbeg* the established brands and well known all over the whisky loving world. The annual *Feis* pays tribute to all of these and many more with connoisseurs and billionaires the likes of the Russian oligarch Roman Abramovitch regular visitors. **Islay's** whiskies are mostly known for their "pungent peaty, smoky and oily flavours, with just a hint of salty sea air and seaweed". In recent years with the popularity of gin taking off in an unprecedented way, gin distilling, a much simpler process, is flourishing as a complementary industry. The Islay gin company was set up just north of Bowmore at Bridgend with an infusion of wild Islay heather giving its *Nerabus* brand a unique taste.

Islay produces around four million proof gallons of whisky every year, most of which is exported. Nevertheless, the duty collected by HM Government from sales in the British market alone is the equivalent of a generous income for every man, woman and child on the island. Its per capita Gross Domestic Product (GDP) is probably equal to that of Qatar or other oil rich Gulf States!

With a mild climate courtesy of the Gulf Stream (no relation!), a plethora of bird and mammal species and a long historical legacy, some summer days see nearly 6,000 tourists on the island and over 15,000 during the *Feis Ile* whisky festival. No wonder bed space was at a real premium. Winter-visiting barnacle goose numbers have reached 35,000 in recent years with as many as 10,000 arriving in a single day. Minke, pilot and killer whales and bottle-nosed dolphins are regular visitors.

Islay is the closest British landfall to the Republic of Ireland and its size and strategic geography led the Norse settlers from the 9th Century to establish the 'Kingdom of the Isles', which became part of the crown of Norway following Norwegian unification. The Lord of the Isles council, holding court over much of the Hebrides, was held on an island in Loch Finlaggan near Port Askaig where its ruins are still to be seen. To Norway, the islands became known as *Suðreyjar* meaning southern isles. For over four centuries this Kingdom was under the control of rulers of mostly Norse origin. By 1336 Gaelic clan dominance was re-established and its rulers were known as 'Lord of the Isles', this accolade now being hi-jacked by Charles Windsor the then Prince of Wales, so it seems. Written records go back further in time here than any other Hebridean isle.

I awoke drunk and disorientated having fallen in with the Diageo entourage till very late in the *Lochside* bar but had a bus to catch yet again to Port Askaig to meet the CalMac ferry to **Colonsay** a pleasant hour or so away. **Colonsay** is a jewel in the Hebrides accessible from both Oban and **Islay** and home to a thriving population of 124 permanent inhabitants. Arriving at what might laughingly be called the capital, Scalasaig, the *Pantry* was the first stop to re-fuel my hungover body before heading the five or so miles to **Oronsay** which can be accessed across the strand at **Colonsay's** southern tip if the tide is right which it was, just. I had a suitcase with me and didn't want to drag it all the way to **Oronsay** so I enquired at the CalMac booking office where I could leave it for the day. "Just leave it in the corner, it will be quite OK" was the reply. And so it was. Theft is way down the list of anti-social behaviours on this island. Apart from a solitary burglary in 2006 the last recorded crime was treachery against the King in 1623!

The roads were deathly quiet and the terrain gently undulating though a little exacting for an unfit ex-walker. I'd heard that a popular pursuit is something known as "MacPhee-bagging" – you've heard of Munro-bagging, well none of the hills on the island rise above 469 feet (in the case of Carn an Eoin), but those more than 300 feet are known as "MacPhees". There happens to be 21 of them on **Colonsay** and a solitary one on **Oronsay**. It is possible to do the lot in a single day – a 20-mile trip. Sadly, these challenges are for me a thing of the past. The name MacPhee derives from the erstwhile owners of the two islands during the 15th century.

I made the short trip to **Oronsay** across blinding wet mirror-like shell sands known as the Strand. The tiny island is now privately owned but farmed on the American owner's behalf by the RSPB. The carefully defined route brought me to the halfway mark denoted by the sanctuary cross. In the past any **Colonsay** fugitive who reached this point was immune from punishment if they stayed on the smaller island for a year and a day. This would be the height of social isolation as **Oronsay** has hardly ever been home to more than 10 souls. Aptly the etymology is probably Old Norse meaning island of the ebb tide. As ever there is evidence of monastic traditions with two substantial Celtic crosses adjacent to the ruins of the medieval Augustinian priory. I rested to catch my breath but not for too long as getting cut off by the tide was certainly not an option. The clouds were scudding across the horizon with the perfect picture post card of the Pap of Jura in the distance.

On a muggy but midge free day with the sound only of the cuckoo, I trudged back across the Strand but wasn't relishing the undulating five-mile return leg. A car, yes, a car approached and a kind lady from the island's oyster farm took pity on me and invited me for a lift. At first, I declined but then I remembered that walking was not the purpose of my island hopping. She dropped me at the *Colonsay Hotel* which was deserted in late afternoon and a couple of fine Colonsay craft beers slaked my thirst.

The TV in the bar was showing footage of the almost far right take over in Austria. This was the calm before the turmoil of Brexit a few short weeks away. Already there were dark mutterings over immigration and enhanced xenophobia was setting fire to reasoned discourse with hatred rising from the smouldering ashes of liberal democracy. The horrors of Donald Trump, Nigel Farage and now Boris Johnson were still to come, with rational Britain still upbeat about remaining part of the European family.

Islands like **Colonsay** which benefit from EU regional development grants would soon be set adrift to fend for themselves.

I was hungry and retired back to the café to await the ferry past the 'well of the south wind', so called because fishermen stopped a while to pray for a fair south wind before their travails at sea. The residents today depend on the burgeoning tourist trade and their advertising blurb reflects this with **Colonsay** being promoted as 'The Jewel of the Hebrides'. I wondered if they had checked with other islands' web sites to see whether they too had used this superlative accolade to promote themselves. The usual buzz words are used; "tranquil, unspoilt natural beauty, rich heritage" with a gushing request to lovingly share it with you.

Archaeologists had discovered that Mesolithic man was growing and harvesting hazelnuts on **Colonsay**. Now this is a real insight into the past climate in the Hebrides as, although hazelnuts can withstand temperatures down to about 16 degrees Centigrade, their trees are best grown in warmer climates where the summer season is at least six months long. Despite the proximity to the Gulf stream, this is a far cry from the current temperature regime. Even long-term average temperatures on the island only just nudge 17 Centigrade even in July and August. With days of hazelnut production long gone the island has more recently turned to distilling and brewing with **Colonsay**, the smallest island in the world to host a brewery. More recently the micro-brewery has branched out to create Wild Island Botanic Gin, distilled with hand gathered wild botanicals from the island.

The ferry back to **Islay** was on time; they always are. At Port Askaig I changed ferry to meet the return boat to Kennacraig from Oban. These are big boats and look majestic plying between the narrow sound that separates **Islay** from **Jura**. I shuddered at the thought of 'jumping' a similar sized ferry in my student days sailing from Dubrovnik to Rijeka in Tito's Yugoslavia in the late sixties. I had had an altercation with the police; they had beaten me up for calling them fascists; heady days of student politics indeed. I was dragged before a judge and summarily fined all the money I had leaving me penniless, or rather 'dinar' less. What is more on release the cunning police had planted marijuana in my ruck sack. Luckily, their ruse was pre-empted by a kindly onlooker who had recognised me, and he realised the score. Without warning he hurled my rucksack, and my only possessions into the harbour. With no money and no spare clothes, I booked a ticket to Korcula, (the birthplace of Marco Polo), on money given to me by my kind benefactor. "Stay on the ship till Rijeka" he firmly advised. Hence my dramatic escape. On my hitch hike to Maribor, close to the Austrian border, where I had a safe haven I, for the only time in my life, knew what hunger pangs really were. I waited patiently with my hosts for two weeks until my father managed to send me a one-way train ticket back to Bradford.

It was dark by the time the ferry reached Kennacraig and I drove to Lochgilphead and the cold comfort yet again of the *Argyll hotel*. I still had some small islands in the locality to tick off in Sector 2 of Hamish Haswell-Smith's island compendium: **Seil**, **Easdale**, **Luing**, **Torsa** and **Shona**, collectively known as the slate islands. **Seil** on the east side of the Firth of Lorn is attached to the mainland by what is quaintly known as 'The Bridge over the Atlantic' as, until the Skye bridge was completed in 1995, it was the only bridge that linked mainland Scotland to the islands beyond in what might loosely be called the Atlantic.

In effect the narrow sound at all of 10 to 15 metres wide is spanned by a stone humped bridge, the Clachan bridge built in 1792 by Thomas Telford. Fast flowing water cascades through the narrow aperture as tides ebb and flow. Gavin Maxwell's famous book about otters *The Ring of Bright Water* was filmed on **Seil**, home to the mother of Princess Diana, Frances Shand Kydd, until her death in 2004. Its sleepy lanes lead past long forgotten slate mining quarries and just when it appeared that nothing else significant appears to have enhanced or beset the island you can always rely on St Columba to take central stage in its early history.

Scotland is full of legends, the most famous of course being the Loch Ness monster but curiously a little known but nonetheless fascinating a legend is that the Clachan bridge can almost claim to link another country. After the Jacobite 1745 Rebellion, it was pronounced illegal to wear the kilt in Scotland and those loyal to the Stuart cause could only wear it "overseas". The island of **Seil** was recognised as such and returning supporters of the Jacobite cause would enter the nearby inn, the *Tigh an Truish* (house of the trousers), to change back into the forbidden garment. Richard Crace and I had slaked our thirst there one sultry June day during the 'A walk by the Sea' adventures.

At the southern end of **Seil** is **Easdale Island** reached by pressing a button to call a private ferry. I want to be the ferryman with clear instructions not to be disturbed between 10:50 to 11:20 (elevenses); 12:30 to 14:00 (lunch) and 15:50 to 16:30 (tea). This compact but densely populated island has a perimeter walk and a pleasant community spirit. Although only 10 hectares in size, and therefore does not qualify as a 'Haswell-Smith island', it has 59 inhabitants.

Easdale was one of Britain's great centres of slate quarrying from the 17th Century and, at its peak in Victorian times, had a population in excess of 500, with most working in the vast slate workings beneath the sea. A storm in November 1881 flooded the quarries sounding the death knell for the industry. By 1960 just 4 residents remained until its recent revival as a tourist 'day out' culminating with lunch and a couple of pints at *The Puffer*. These marginal islands struggle to survive and need popular gimmicks to attract the curious. Whilst some rural communities have 'welly wanging' in Somerset or cheese rolling in Gloucestershire, **Easdale** hosts the World Stone Skimming Championship which has taken place annually in September since 1997 with the disused flooded quarries the popular venue. Necessity is and will always be the mother of invention.

Waiting for the small RoRo to **Luing** (pronounced Lung) I fell afoul of the Scottish lunch break. I decided to take the car over as the fares, being subsidised, are ridiculously cheap and I needed to access, again at low tide, the seemingly inhabited island of **Torsa** situated just off **Luing's** eastern shore. I missed the call to board the pre-lunch ferry and had an hour's wait whilst the crew disappeared for their Irn Bru and deep-fried mars bars or whatever was on offer at the local café that day.

Luing 'nestles' (note the romance) a short 200 metre ferry ride off the Oban coast across the Cuan sound. Like **Easdale** it was a centre for slate mining, its slate being used in the construction of Glasgow University and **Iona** cathedral. At its zenith 150 miners produced 700,000 slates every year. The island now slumbers with a modicum of beef farming, lobster fishing and tourism. The lobster pond between Eilean Loisgte and Fraoch Eilean is one of the largest in Scotland.

Having absorbed all that was of particular interest I drove slowly around the island trying to locate a suitable access to **Torsa**. The challenge unfolded with **Torsa** dubbed by me as the 'inaccessible pinnacle' of the island hopper, though more inaccessible islands were to come. After lots of false leads down ancient drovers tracks not used for years, I miraculously found a convenient beach which painfully (my legs are fragile with arthritis, did I ever mention this?) and painstakingly took me to the narrowest of channels between the two islands just as the tide had ebbed to its lowest. The rocks were slippery, and I worried about my safety in this hostile environment with little sign of habitation, save distant sea fishermen, and certainly no mobile phone signal.

Breathless I crossed the 10-metre channel to **Torsa** and headed for the only house on the island which I later discovered was not permanently inhabited and therefore outside the rules of combat. It was a holiday let and my journey had been wasted. The 2011 census suggested one permanent inhabitant, but on reaching the well-preserved cottage I witnessed no sign of life. I re-crossed the channel and met a much better-defined drovers' track, a low tide access in former days when the island had surely been permanently inhabited.

I spent the time before boarding the return ferry exploring the hidden beauty of **Luing** with inspiring views over the sound of **Luing** to Lunga. Rows of neat, whitewashed ex slate miners' cottages in Toberonochy were marred by the multiple 'wheelie' bins which local councils have now imposed on most of us to separate the various types of re-cyclable waste. A laudable aim but why colour them purple?

The grave of Alex Campbell lies in the well-tended ruins of Kilchatton chapel in the village. Now this guy was a Covenanter, a religious group of huge significance in Scotland in the 17th Century which denounced the Pope and the doctrines of the Roman Catholic Church in favour of the austerity of Presbyterianism. His mawkish invocations adorned his grave "digged my grave before I died" with warnings against 'women that wear Balylonish garment, men that have whiskers, Quakers, Anabaptists, and Independents'. He was clearly a man of eccentric and dangerous views. I was reminded of the Martyr's stake just outside Wigtown in Dumfries and Galloway. Margaret McLachlan and the teenager, Margaret Wilson were martyred for refusing to rescind their Presbyterian faith and accept King Charles II as head of the Scottish church. In an act of barbarism rarely equalled since the burning at the stake of Joan of Arc, they too were tied to stakes, but this time slowly drowned as the tide in the Cree estuary rose.

The last inhabited island in this sector was **Shuna** farmed by Catherine and her husband escaping to the 'Good Life' from Yorkshire. The only access was by private boat, and I tentatively phoned Duncan who kept a boat at Craobh Haven. I always feel nervous requesting the hire of a boat. This is illogical as they are there for that very purpose. It is just like going to Curry's and being reticent about buying a laptop or tablet. "Excuse me, is this laser printer for sale?" the nervous buyer would tentatively ask. "No" would come an aggressive reply; "What do you think this is, a shop".

I recall in Lerwick, after a vast cruise ship had swallowed up its Korean visitors at the end of a hectic day, spying a lady packing away her very expensive home knit **Fair Isle** scarves. The streets were deserted after the fray of southeast Asians had been tendered back to their floating palace and I enquired as to the cost. She looked at me with disdain (I was rather unkempt with my shirt tails hanging out in the style of Boris Johnson) and muttered, hopefully joking, "You can't afford one". I bought one to spite her.

Maybe that is my problem as boat hire to obscure islands not specifically for fishing or wildlife spotting may seem cranky and as projected fees are rather expensive the prospective boatman would eye me up with some suspicion. Or, if the tentative booking is by phone, the recipient may think he is subject to a crank call made as a result of a drunken bet. In short, I am just too sensitive.

For the modest sum of £50 Duncan took me on the 20-minute journey to **Shuna** and waited on the jetty whilst I explored the island. Catherine the present tenant was there to greet us as were a handful of holiday-let inhabitants looking for seclusion and contemplation and hopefully sightings of the healthy populations of Red, Roe and Fallow deer; along with otters, common and grey seals, porpoises and dolphins reputed to be out on the water. We talked about island life on that calmest of days with tales of being marooned for weeks at a time during bad weather. **Shuna** was another slate island but apparently with very little slate. For half an hour I explored the dangerously unstable Shuna castle, though more a castellated mansion, built in 1911 before being abandoned in the 1980's. Its architect perished as a passenger on the *Titanic* the very next year.

The island had been bequeathed to the City of Glasgow in 1829 with the stipulation that any income from the island, mainly agriculture I suspect, should be 'devoted to benevolent purposes.' The Corporation preferred the capital and promptly sold it; so much for the largesse and philanthropy of the City fathers.

Time for once was on my side and I skipped over to complete **Kerrera** my first island in Haswell-Smith's next sector *Mull and the Surrounding islands*. The ferry service from a mile or two south of Oban is passenger only and islanders have an old car for getting about their island and another newer vehicle for use on the mainland. This explained the packed car park clustered around the jetty. The first mate on an otherwise empty ferry was a likeable young chap like me fascinated by islands and he too was studying Hamish's Book *The Scottish Islands* between crossings. His boat *MV Carvoria* is the smallest vessel in CalMac's fleet. **Kerrera** is said to have almost doubled in size since the 2011 census with a remarkable 18 children living in three small settlements across the island. The school closed in 1997 but the daily commute to Oban is no problem thanks to the all-weather ferry service.

It appears that the island is somewhat matriarchal as at least three of its farms are run by young women who had been born on the island and returned to take up sheep farming and to some degree managing this closely knit community whose population is clearly booming. On my short walk I felt a real sense of remoteness amongst these hardy pioneers, though the reality is that Tesco's in Oban is barely three miles away as the crow flies! **Kerrera** provides a natural breakwater for Oban Bay and its busy ferry terminal to the Hebrides.

The MacDougall's are the prominent clan here with a foothold on **Kerrera** since the 12th Century. During the Covenanting wars of the mid-17th Century the Protestant minister John Neave persuaded the invading Protestant troops to slaughter every Catholic MacDonald on the island. None survived. General Leslie's men sacked Gylen castle and amongst the glowering proud ruins an inscription 'Trust in God and sin no more' can just about be made out. The mysteries of religions built on the central theme of 'loving your neighbour' are beyond civilised imaginations. History is littered with events of unspeakable cruelty 'inspired' by distorted religious beliefs.

7. The Island of Ireland and Rathlin Island, Northern Ireland

Work in Belfast allowed me to 'tick off' the second largest island of my journey after Great Britain – Ireland. I'd been going there since about 1990 for work and pleasure and I love both Northern Ireland and the Republic for all social, geographical and cultural aspects; from the buzz of Temple Bar in Dublin and the 'Wild Atlantic' west coast to the geological freak of nature that is the Giant's Causeway on the exposed shores of County Antrim. The people are positive and good humoured despite the political turmoil that has wreaked havoc on both sides of the divide for much of the 20th Century.

I first made the flight to Belfast around 1990 to see Bob Dylan in concert at the Dundonald Bowl. There was a 'moodiness' then either real or self-inflicted by years of watching news clips of the euphemistically described *Troubles*. I arrived at Belfast City airport and my taxi driver, for £20, drove me up and down the Catholic Falls and the Protestant Shankhill Roads and onto the Peace Line and all the sites this inquisitive Englishman wanted to experience. There was a frisson of danger as we stretched our legs in both loyalist and republican areas both coloured by their flags of honour with ornate murals marking out their territory. The city centre was caged in those days with army check points everywhere.

This was about eight years before *the Good Friday Agreement* and death and destruction were the reality. This 1998 peace agreement has transformed the island of Ireland with renewed prosperity and peace between the religious factions. Sadly, the wretched intransigence of politicians through a stubborn desire to carry out 'the will of the people' following the Brexit referendum result in 2016 to leave the European Union, may wreck the

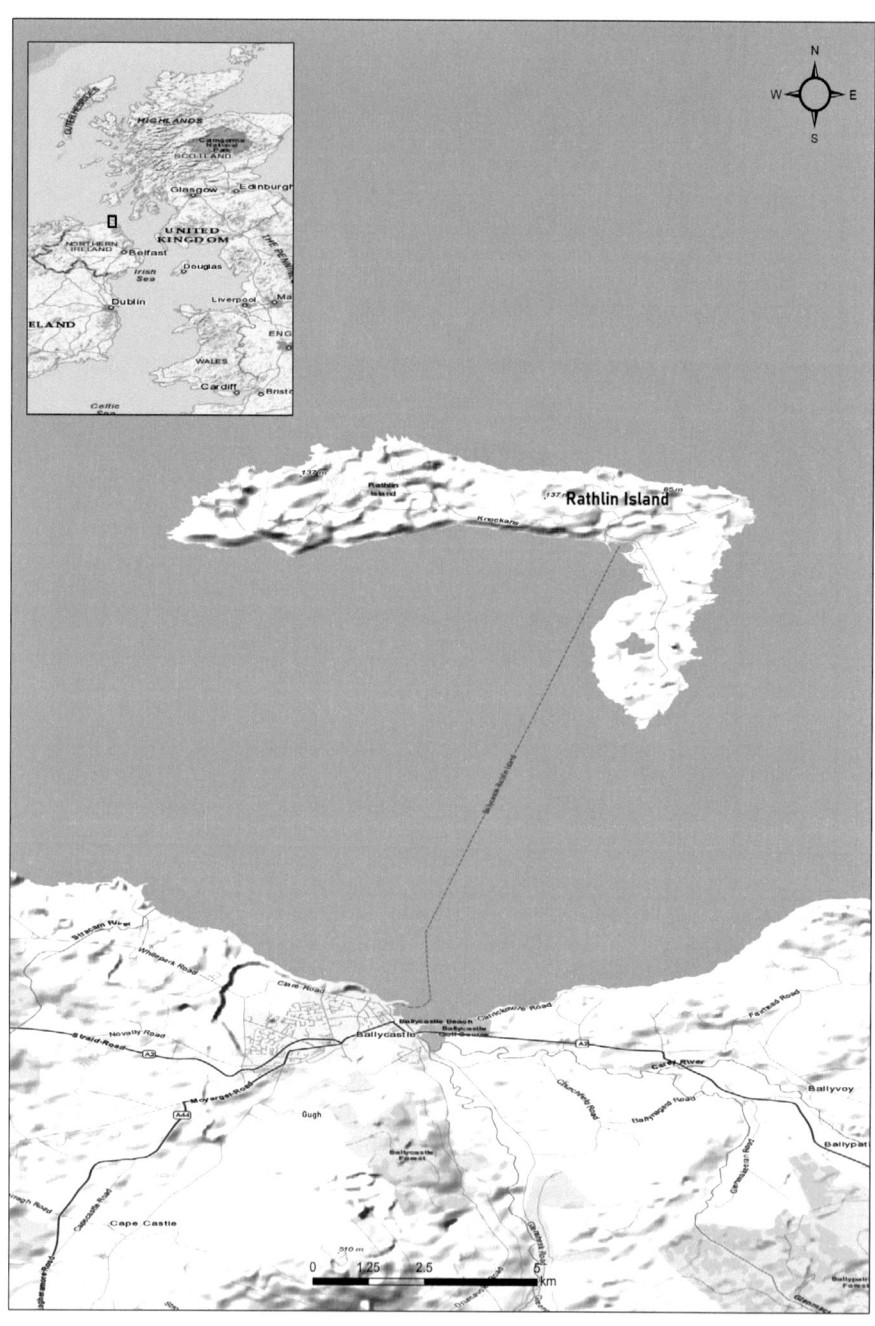

The island of Ireland and Rathlin Island, Northern Ireland

process. This could well return Northern Ireland to the days of sectarian gloom. For goodness's sake, when did any Conservative Government ever care before about what *the people* want? Re-establishing a border between north and south to retain customs integrity within the European Union is unthinkable. The bribes by Theresa May's Westminster Government to those die-hard reactionary fringe of 18th Century Protestants, the Democratic Unionist Party, created by Reverend Ian "No Surrender" Paisley, then led by the intractable Arlene Foster, could have scuppered the integrity of the hard-won Peace.

In the new Millennium I made several trips each year to Belfast and experienced the metamorphosis of a city in transition. I tried to stay at the *Europa Hotel* on Great Victoria Street, which has the dubious accolade of being the most bombed hotel in Europe. I liked it as though it was a stone's throw from Sandy Row, a Protestant bastion with appropriate menacing murals, the cosmopolitan comfort of *The Crown* pub, with its Victorian private wooden snugs, was immediately opposite the hotel and thus avoided any potential confrontation with local malcontents. I rarely strayed any further, my mind steeped with TV imagery of UDA or IRA gang cultures.

I've had many a flight to either George Best City airport or the more distant international airport at Aldergrove. Our passports indicate we are citizens of "The United Kingdom of Great Britain and Northern Ireland". That is 'The UK'. Tell that to the now defunct BMi Baby airline who advertised "Cheap flights to the UK" without an appreciation of our political footprint. This incensed some of my colleagues; "Where did they think we are now" one muttered on dropping me off one trip. It seemed the 'Troubles' had disassociated Great Britain from the rest of our United Kingdom. Even in the Olympics it is 'Team GB' athletes who win medals, not 'Team UK'. This political distinction is not lost on Northern Irish competitors.

However, since 1998 when anybody born in Northern Ireland can apply for a Republic of Ireland passport or play sport for either side of the divide it confuses the National psyche. With many UK citizens having immediate Irish ancestry the application for Irish passports is brisk in the wake of Brexit. We English, Welsh and Scots are being denied our European identities, and the benefits of freedom to travel, work or live in any of the 27 member states of the European Union, whilst those of Irish ancestry are offered a lifeline for their future as Europeans.

My dislike of BMi Baby extends beyond their lack of political astuteness. On one of my trips back to Birmingham I was denied boarding one of their flights for coming to the rescue at the boarding gate of two elderly passengers who were 'forced' to pay £40 each for having the wrong size carry-on baggage. I saw red. My spontaneous temper is a fault I cannot correct. I intervened at this injustice and was ejected from the boarding queue. The police were called, and I was refused boarding despite the mild protestation of even the armed officers.

A kindly policeman escorted me out of the airport and gave me a lift to the docks to get a car ferry to Liverpool. He was a Liverpool football supporter, and this was a great and inexpensive way to get to Anfield. Luck was not on my side as the ferry was delayed and I opted for an uncomfortable night in the city centre *Travel Lodge*, booking an early FlyBe flight before turning in. Queuing up to check in early the next morning an officious employee of said airline asked me for £40 to check in my bag. Exasperated I blurted "I think I am having a nervous breakdown". "Sir, you can't travel if you are ill", she briskly retorted. I paid my money. Some days later I received a letter from BMi Baby explaining I was banned on all future flights for life. I wrote back and asked did they mean my life or theirs! They did not reply. Some years later they ceased to operate. A Pyrrhic victory, I mused.

I have two titanium resurfaced hips and airport security checks are an inconvenience. On a further trip to Belfast after a thorough search the clearly gay security officer asked me to accompany him to a private room to see the scars. He took his friend. They demeaned me by asking me to drop my pants and looked at my operation scars long and hard with one of the guys saying to the other "ooh isn't it big!" Annoyed I left for the bar.

The bar was closed. How ironic as this was George Best airport. Northern Ireland of course was home to two flawed sporting geniuses: George Best and Alex "Hurricane" Higgins. Both died ravaged by alcohol. Alex ended his life playing snooker in seedy Belfast clubs for £10 a game. Another amusing irony at the George Best airport is a sign in security advising one to drink responsibly!

I've by coincidence met a number of celebrities on my travels from the irrepressible jazz legend George Melly to Ronnie Wood of the Rolling Stones. One of my personal but tragic stories relates to Alex. Whilst travelling by train to Portsmouth on a Sunday afternoon in 1993, a stumbling, cadaverous figure, clearly worse for drink, lurched up to me asking for a light for his Benson and Hedges cigarette. I obliged and we engaged in conversation. It was Alex Higgins on his way to play in the Grand Prix tournament at the Hexagon, Reading. He was past his glory days and a sad, pathetic figure, with a ready insult for all players I enquired about. It was gut wrenching to see and hear 'The Hurricane', who I had long admired, at this stage in his career. We talked the whole journey and at Reading he staggered, utterly drunk, off the train leaving his cue, bound in tatty cardboard, behind. I quickly called out his name, but a hefty minder snatched the cue from my grasp with menacing insults. This was a truly sad memory of a snooker legend. He was knocked out in the first round of the completion and never played at the highest level of the game again.

I arranged to meet John, who is like a much-loved younger brother to me at my hotel, a cheap sister of the Radisson chain. The Europa had been fully booked. He had recently returned to live in his family home in Abbeyleix, County Laois, in the Irish Republic and we set out for a catch up, eschewing the *Crown* for something more adventurous. John is fascinated with, and was a 'supporting artist' for, *the Game of Thrones*, phenomena much of which is filmed in Belfast's Titanic Quarter and sets along the Antrim Coast. He had agreed to be my guide the next day as the locations were close to Ballycastle, the ferry boarding point for **Rathlin Island,** Northern Island's only inhabited island.

His compatriot extras would meet up for 'Thrones reunions' at a number of city centre pubs and we crawled around them all: *Muriel's café bar* with an eclectic collection of brassieres hung from the ceiling; from there to *Whites Tavern* and thence to *Kelly's Cellars*, eating at the delectable *Mourne fish bar* before ending the tour at *Spaniard rum house*. I had to work the next morning early so I left John to the delights of *Filthy McNasties*. The city was unrecognisable from the 1990's and renovations were in full swing. Belfast is now a must go-to destination despite the usual appalling weather with tourists from over the globe drawn by George R R Martin's adapted novel 'A song of Ice and Fire' featuring the fictional continents of Westeros and Essos. With the Titanic quarter leading the way Belfast is much, much more than that, a true World city.

My work complete I met John at George Best airport and we drove up the Antrim coast through Carrickfergus staying at the *Londonderry Arms* at Camlough, once owned by Winston Churchill in 1921. The deeds indicating his former ownership were displayed proudly in the hotel. Of more fictitious significance and drawing worldwide tourists to Camlough was its backdrop to scenes from *The Game of Thrones*, bringing unexpected trade to this not too shabby coaching inn. This is Protestant country with British and Ulster flags tattered but still flying proudly in the wind.

We arrived at Ballycastle in time to catch the passenger ferry to **Rathlin**, a 25-minute crossing of some discomfort to me but not to the hyper excited children enjoying their school holidays. The weather was not good, but we decided to walk to the East Lighthouse before lunch at *McCuaig's bar*. When the sun broke through, we could see the Mull of Kintyre in Scotland, after all the Antrim coast is only 12 miles at the narrowest point of the Straits of Moyle (North Channel) from the Scottish mainland.

It was rumoured that the folks of **Rathlin Island** wished a post Brexit secession to Scotland to take advantage of Scotland's inevitable Independence. Scotland by some 60% were in favour of staying in the European Union. After all Northern Ireland was settled by Scottish and English Plantationers from the reign of James VI of Scotland who became James I of England too. Before political boundaries restricted and contained travel, inhabitants of Kintyre, and the islands of **Jura** and **Islay** would make the journey to the larger island (Ireland) to the south for commerce.

It is close to the East Lighthouse that a plaque heralded the site of the cave where Robert the Bruce in 1306 was hiding from the English after one battle or another. The legend goes that he watched a spider trying unsuccessfully to spin its web from one corner of the cave to another. Its tenacity paid off eventually and inspired Robert to return from his exile and inflict a number of victories against the sworn enemy. If you try and don't succeed, then try and try again. Wherever I go there is always some interesting anecdote or connection which I now call the Robert the Bruce or even the Marconi moment.

I had travelled to Cape Breton Island in Canada that summer with my lifelong friend Trevor and Len, an Irish American from Scottsdale, Arizona and I had booked four nights in the town of Sydney. We had been told the previous year in a bar in Truro, Nova Scotia that Cape Breton was unmissable. It was. Sydney, a town struggling after the closure of its mines and steel works finally in 2001, wasn't. At its height, the steel works were the largest in the World.

On our first day we decided to give Sydney a fair crack of the whip and visited the only two tourist attractions: the mining museum and the Marconi Museum close by. The first was fascinating and our guide with a curious Scots Irish Brogue (the accent of Nova Scotia) portrayed graphically the horror of the life of miners working as indentured labourers of the *Dominion Coal and Steel Corporation* in the early 20th Century. The British not only subjugated India and sub-Saharan Africa but also its Canadian citizens, grinding them into abject poverty with 15-hour days coupled with swingeing wage cuts. Modern neoliberalism is mild compared with the unconscionable profits made in the name of the British Empire. Len was particularly humbled and suffered back breaking stumbling for a quarter of a mile underground to reflect on memories of his father who had worked as a student in the 1920's coal mines in Kentucky under similar brutal conditions. In the words of Merle Travis in his song *Sixteen Tons*, these poor downtrodden miners quite literally "owed their soul to the company store".

Chastened by the experience we headed for the other attraction, the Marconi Museum. It was here on 17th December 1902, a transmission from the Marconi station in Glace Bay, Nova Scotia, became the world's first radio message to cross the Atlantic from North America; the destination being Poldhu, Cornwall. Walking to East Lighthouse on **Rathlin Island** I invented the "Marconi moment". On my travels to seemingly random places like this lighthouse there is always something that connects or interests. This time it was Marconi's telegraphy transmission test for Lloyds of London, who needed rapid information on the ships they were insuring. The tests on 6th July 1898 took place between Ballycastle on the mainland and East Lighthouse on **Rathlin Island**. This was one of the world's first successful telegraphy transmissions leading to the transatlantic transmission from Nova Scotia four years later. By coincidence **Rathlin Island** saw another transatlantic first when Richard Branson's hot-air helium balloon crashed into the sea nearby in 1987 after its record-breaking transatlantic flight from the USA.

Returning to the mainland we explored John's battle sites filmed under extreme weather conditions and privation not dissimilar to that suffered by the Sydney miners albeit pay was better and voluntary exit to avoid further hardships was swift.

8. (Not quite) the Aran Islands, Ireland

My work often takes me to the coast and fortuitously I was to work in County Clare during September 2016 and my island gazetteer indicated that the Aran Islands, **Inishmaan** the largest; **Inishmaan** the middle and **Inisheer**, the smallest, could be accessed from nearby Doolin. Though I had originally intended my island quest to be restricted to the UK, I fancied extending the project to embrace the whole Celtic theme. This would include the many inhabited islands of the Republic either reached by ferry, bridge or causeway, or in one memorable case by cable car.

This was a serendipitous moment to begin the extended mission as I had a late flight from Shannon airport and time to kill. I drove along the Wild Atlantic Way, a tourist road stretching 2,500km from Donegal to County Cork, listening to the Niall Boylan show on the radio. Now this station is a gem interspersing soft rock with our talk show host and the dulcet tones of his listeners richly interspersed with expletives the Irish use without offence being taken. Radio 2 in UK would have been closed down long ago if this rich colourful language had been allowed. The listeners of Tunbridge Wells would not have been amused.

The subject matter that afternoon was the condemnation of an inebriated guy crossing the busy motorway ring road in the vicinity of Dublin, who was jailed for his troubles. Listeners were in animated debate taking sides over his plight with the minutia of his offence being picked over for the best part of an hour. Each call had a mischievous nuance, well-chosen expletive, and a fascinating take on an otherwise innocuous story. This was pure radio gold unique to Irish humour.

I arrived at Doolin in a fierce gale and the Doolin ferry terminal was well and truly shut. My plans were in tatters, and I was resigned to go to these islands at a more leisurely pace in the future. I missed the annual inter-island football competition which was taking place that weekend and consoled myself with lunch at *Gus O'Connors* in the most charming of villages. I climbed back into my hire car, rocked by the wind, and headed back to Shannon airport.

The Aran Islands, part of the *Gaeltacht* Irish speaking Ireland, owe their continued existence to tourism. Storms, increasing in frequency, can make the difference between profitability and desperation and even ruin. The 2020 COVID-19 pandemic decimated the economy of the Aran Islands, along with many others on my journey. Islands by definition are usually remote. As the lure of urban living attracts islanders more and more, the fragility of existence is amplified by the ever-increasing ferocity of storms. My work on the west coast on that visit was to assist the authorities in mitigation strategies to alleviate the negative effects of storm damage to both communities and their lucrative Links golf courses. This is merely a temporary sticking plaster. Furthermore, the threat and reality of global lockdowns can only result in future unsustainability. Globalisation, climate change and pandemic almost certainly will condemn the fate of the Aran Islands and their depleting inhabitants to that experienced by the plethora of now deserted islands around Ireland's shores.

9. Isle of Sheppey, England

I find myself in all parts of the country, randomly it seems, accrediting river inspectors for the Environment Agency. I like this work as it feels real, not report writing or strategising for some distant project never to be completed. I spend the day with the fledgling or experienced inspectors, and we travel to inspect their flood mitigation assets; sluices, outfalls, walls, embankments and the like which try to keep the country flood free. I don't care to conduct my 'tests' like a driving instructor, furtively glancing at his clip board and barking unfriendly instructions at the terrified candidate. I chat and get to know the inspector as we drive, often many miles, from site to site. Over years of meeting the same people (their accreditation ticket lasts 5 years) I develop a bond and we reflect on times gone by and crises or otherwise that have beset them or me in the intervening time. We try and solve both professional and personal problems together and I go home feeling a sense of achievement in lending a hand to their careers.

I was in Kent on a fine autumn day meandering along the flood defence assets at Faversham, home to the fine Shepherd Neame brewery. We finished the inspections early and after a long walk along the flood embankments of Faversham Creek remembered from my epic walk, I headed for the **Isle of Sheppey**. This is an island of over 40,000 people and the 3rd largest populated island in England. Now cataloguing the islands of England is tricky as unlike Scotland there is no Appendix 2 of the census. Essex, for example, has a number of small islands like **Osea** or **Northey** in the Blackwater estuary joined to the mainland by tidal causeways, but their populations are associated with the 'mainland' civil parish. Some detective work would be required to establish habitation or otherwise.

Sheppey however, accessed across the Sheppey Crossing, opened in 2006 at a cost of £30 million, is separately designated as an island with, unusual

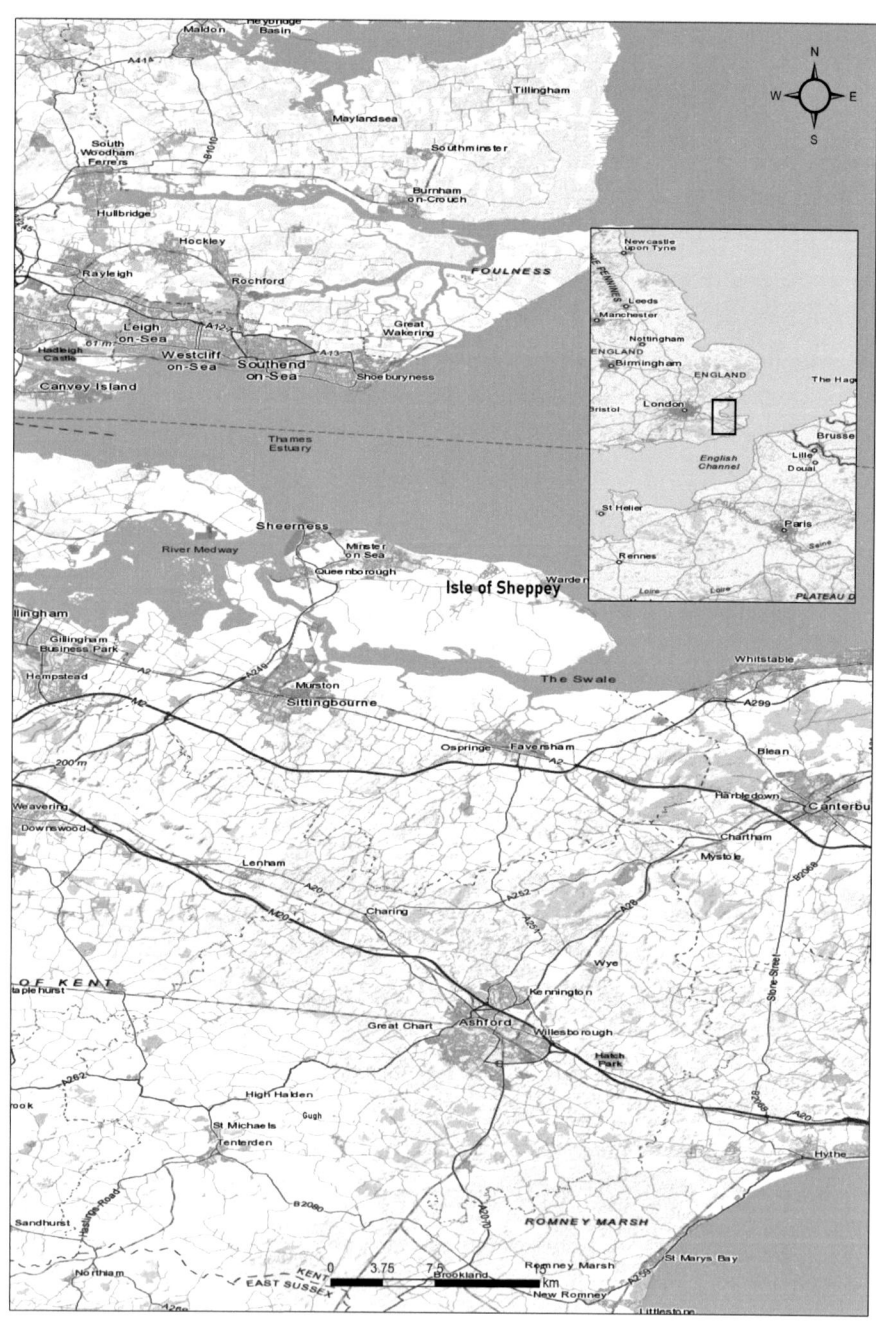

Isle of Sheppey, England

for an English island, an accurate 2011 census population. The bridge rises steeply in a sweeping arc over The Swale, a channel which separates the island from mainland Kent. The flat expanse of marshland gives way to the largest settlement on the island, Sheerness. This is a humdrum sort of town nestling five to six metres below the colossal prison wall-like flood defence concrete bastions which protect the exposed populace from the rigours of storms from the North Sea and up the wide Thames estuary. I found a stairway up the giant defences and onto the exposed berm looking across the estuary. Flood gates had been closed permanently for the winter denying ease of access. Not only does the town seem imprisoned by the estuary but three actual prisons are located on the island, remote and easy to protect.

It is a frightening place with citizens probably oblivious to the defences and their vital role in maintaining the integrity of the community which simply could not exist without them. It was post-Brexit, and this part of estuary England has the reputation of being UKIP (the once popular xenophobic United Kingdom Independence Party, founded by arch Brexiteer-in-chief, Nigel Farage) with almost two thirds of Swale (62.5%) voting to leave the European Union. I eyed people up with suspicion trying to work out the Brexiteers. Instead of using postcodes to determine how Eurosceptic a community is it would be more appropriate to use social characteristics, smokers, those with tattoos, the dispossessed pensioners yearning for the days of empire etc., but maybe this is a tad prejudicial.

I lost interest in the place quickly and headed back to the mainland via Minster. My friend Clive, a Jamaican Brummie, found himself working in Minster and did not contradict the bleak narrative I portrayed when describing this island community, insular in geography and insular in attitude.

In some quirk of historical fate, after the Dutch occupied **Sheppey** during the 1666 second Anglo-Dutch war, the town of Queenborough was never handed back to England and on 17th June 1967 a ceremony was held for the official handover.

On a far more sinister note, the town of Queenborough is about a kilometre across the Swale from the notorious Deadman's Island. My task is to visit all *inhabited* islands in the British Isles. Deadman's island has inhabitants but true to its name they are all dead! In 2016 as a result of coastal erosion some 200 bodies were discovered. It is believed that these were the poor souls who had died on floating prisons moored in the Thames estuary at the beginning of the 19th century. Men and boys had succumbed to diseases of one kind or another and had been unceremoniously buried on the island, now out of bounds to all visitors.

10. Mull and the surrounding islands, Scotland

I felt I could squeeze a few more islands into my schedule before winter truly set in. I elected for the islands accessed from the island of **Mull** and was accompanied by my stalwart university friends, Stuart (whose father was born in **Kerrera**) and Paul. I had struck up a friendship with them again after 35 or so years. People don't change in spirit; they just get older. Stuart and Paul were no exceptions. Both are now retired and enjoying the fruits of the baby boomer final salary pensions; Stuart an ex-Glasgow headmaster at a highly regarded school and Paul was a consultant anaesthetist, both now firmly established in Scotland. I was looking forward to many trips with both of them in my future island hopping; our *'Last of the Summer Wine'* experiences.

We picked up Paul in Clackmannanshire, Scotland's smallest local authority, a part of the world I know little if anything of, but the autumn colours on wide avenues of trees underlined my deep love for Scotland and its natural beauty. My two companions are both optimists par excellence with adventure etched into their veins. These trips were going to be fun. The idea was we would tick off **Lismore** at noon and make the 16:00 ferry from Oban to Craignure in **Mull**. These trips are always fraught and there is "never any time to lose", a motto in constant use on all our joint trips together. Stuart is a good driver but too fast for my stomach.

The noon ferry was an optimistic goal and we missed it by six or seven minutes and retired to the nearby restaurant for coffee and oysters and a wee nip of malt. Port Appin was quiet and cold, and missing our ferry was fortuitous as instead of having to wait on **Lismore** with no shelter for the

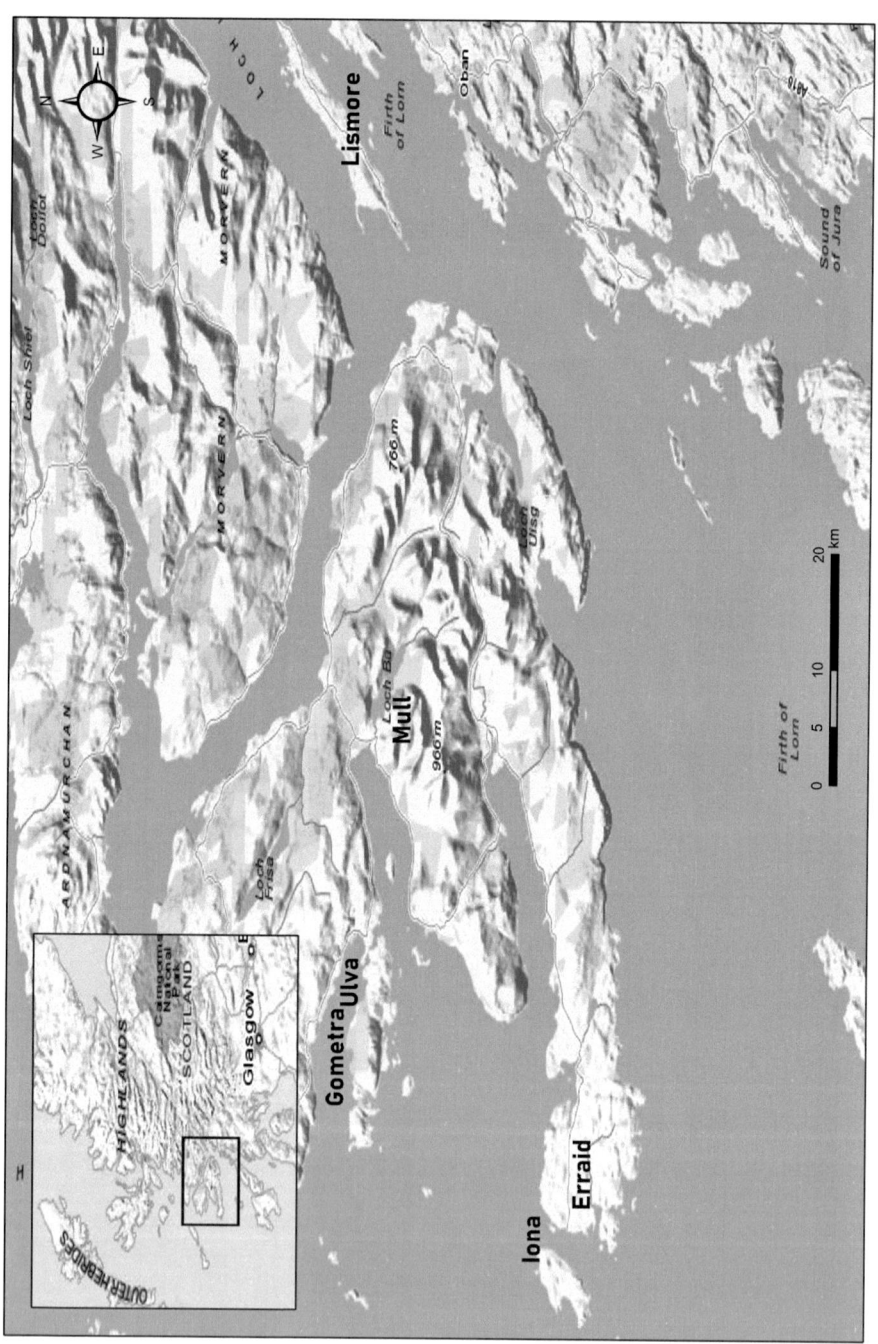

Mull and the surrounding islands, Scotland

best part of two hours before we could return, we warmed ourselves in the *Pierhouse Hotel*.

The time went quickly with reminiscences of our last trip collectively to **Mull** in New Year 1975/6. Stuart, a Derbyshire lad by birth but Scottish at heart, had decided to emigrate to Scotland after university in London and take on board the full Scottish experience (Bagpipes, Gaelic speaking, the lot). Keen to show off his newfound talents whilst Paul carved out a gasket for Stuart's clapped out Mini out of a fruit pie box, he played a tune on his bagpipes unaware that the last ferry before New Year was about to depart. We missed it but frantically waved the CalMac vessel back to avoid a ruined holiday in a rented cottage in Tobermory. Missing ferries was getting to be a habit.

The passenger ferry to Port Ramsay on **Lismore** eventually arrived to take us there with an assorted group of islanders. We claimed concessionary fares on an already heavily discounted trip. Now concessions are only for islanders, not tourists, and our collective senior citizen bus passes were given short shrift by the grumpy young first mate, who didn't know what to make of us. He was rigged in full life jacket, which made us nervous in this rickety old tub. We docked, photographed the footfall on yet another island and returned almost immediately to the mainland.

Lismore lies in Loch Linnhe at the heart of the Lynn of Lorn National Scenic Area, one of forty such areas in Scotland, which have been defined so as to identify areas of exceptional scenery and to ensure its protection from inappropriate development. In his 1997 book *Mountaineering in Scotland* WH Murray describes **Lismore** thus:

> "the skyscape is vast and made so not by its emptiness, but by the throng of high and pointed hills lifting out of the glittering seas and islands. Nowhere else on the Highland coast can you enjoy a view of the mountainous mainland to equal this one."

As with all Scottish islands, decimated by Highland Clearances, the population is now recovering with a 30% increase between the 2001 and 2011 censuses. Like **Kerrera** its proximity to the mainland is surely a contributory factor; that and the fact that mains water was installed by Scottish Water only as recently as 2007. Even the Gaelic language is still in a healthy minority on the island. Maintaining this heritage is one of the aims of the Comann Eachdraidh Lios Mòr, the **Lismore** Gaelic Heritage Centre.

Now the ferry to **Mull** was a different matter, one of CalMac's finest and more reminiscent of a cruise liner in contrast with the ones we remembered 40 years ago. I recalled CalMac do a malt of the month deal which we relished on the 50-minute journey to Craignure. We had opted for the overheated *Isle of Mull spa hotel* about a minute's drive from the ferry terminal, taking advantage of off-peak break deals. The £32.50 taster dinner menu was excellent, and the price lulled us into thinking we had a good deal. Over yet more malts we planned the next two days with the weather apparently set reasonably fair. We had four inhabited islands to negotiate from our base. There are two main roads on **Mull**, one heading northwest from Craignure and the other southwest. We elected to take the first road to **Ulva** and its sister island **Gometra**, leaving **Iona** and nearby **Erraid** for the following day.

Mull, after **Skye**, is the second largest island of the Inner Hebrides and ranks fourth largest of all Great Britain's islands, with Tobermory its bustling main settlement. Finlaggan on **Islay** was the historic seat of the *Lords of the Isles* under Clan Donald. Throughout Scottish history this was a powerful position and a title of Scottish nobility with historical roots going back beyond the Kingdom of Scotland. It emerged from a series of hybrid Viking/Gaelic rulers of the west coast and islands of Scotland in the early Middle Ages centred on **Mull**. Why the present incumbent at the time of our visit was Charles, Prince of Wales seems a travesty, besetting a proud tradition going back centuries.

The **Ulva** ferry takes at most five minutes from Lagganulva, with the smaller island **Gometra** a good five miles across the island accessed by a small pedestrian bridge. We discussed over lunch at the *Pier house* the day of our arrival, that cycling would be a better option than walking and tried to secure bikes from a wee shop in Salen. We even found a local electric bike hire emporium on the website. It was the fag end of the season and bike hire was all but impossible with a kindly proprietor indicating that the **Ulva** ferry had closed for the winter on October 31st. It was November 1st. This was another serious planning error. The nice lady failed to tell us that the terrain on **Ulva** was unsuitable for cycling so we had been lulled into a euphoric state that the paths would be well maintained and the terrain uncomplicated. How wrong could we be?

The day dawned glorious, and our spirits were up. We declined the malt whisky with our porridge and basked in the low early morning sunlight watching from the breakfast room the stately ferry dock and set sail again. For reasons unknown, this was my first experience of a British cooked breakfast where baked beans were not on the menu! Whilst finishing our repast Paul tentatively asked, "Should we book the ferry to **Ulva**?", refusing to heed the words of the cycle shop proprietor. Now, as the readers of my stories know I am no planner. I frowned at the idea, but Paul insisted. I called and just as well as the ferry was not on any sort of established timetable and indeed, as the lady of the previous day had firmly indicated, had stopped its daily sailings for the winter. Reluctantly the boatman agreed to do a special trip for us, and we arranged to meet at 10:30. Our passage was secured for the princely sum of £18 in total (return). "When do you want to come back?" the boatman asked. 15:30 was agreed. We asked if we could use the now closed *Boathouse* restaurant for shelter should we return early. His knowing and rather patronising smile was lost on us! We soon found out why.

We were unbriefed as to the arduous nature of the track and he scowled rather sarcastically, thrusting a leaflet into our hands with routes to guide our way. We ignored the small print as I knew I was in the capable hands of a geographer (Stuart) and a sea farer (Paul). Navigation would be no problem. It was not but the terrain and what passed for tracks were severe on my elderly legs. The scenery to Ben More, **Mul**l's only Munro, and across the island was spectacular, but the path to **Gometra** never ending.

We reached **Gometra** (an island, off an island, off an island, off an island: **Ulva**, **Mull**, Great Britain) exhausted. This was, we mused over a spartan lunch, livened only by Stuart's home-grown apples, a 4th order island as unless you sailed direct it was accessible only by 2 ferries and a footbridge. Conscious of the early darkness and the need to meet our ferryman we could not rest long. This was becoming another "Inaccessible pinnacle" of island hoppers. For those who do the Munros (the 282 peaks in Scotland in excess of 3,000 feet) only one, on the Cuillin ridge on **Skye**, must be done as a rock climb – the Inaccessible Pinnacle (perched 150 feet atop of Sgùrr Dearg) as it is known. **Gometra** had the same feel of remoteness and inaccessibility.

Ulva and to a lesser degree **Gometra** have suffered sad plights through history as witnessed by the dozens of abandoned cottages (referred to as Desolation Row) lining our inadequate track. Its tourist blurb bills it as "a hidden gem, nestled in the crook of neighbouring **Mull's** embrace; **Ulva** is an island paradise for wildlife, scenery and escape". That maybe so today but belies its past as a once vibrant community before the horrors of Highland Clearances. The 1841 census records 15 communities farming on **Ulva** with a total population of well over 400, maybe at its zenith as many as 637 on this 48 square kilometre island. It has been recorded that in these halcyon days every family owned at least one boat and there was a surplus of potatoes to sell.

Then came first the failure of the kelp industry, a vital fertiliser, then potato blight but most significant of all the notorious Highland Clearances. William Clark, a lawyer from Stirling, was the island's 19th Century owner. He ordered the burning of crofts with two-thirds the population fleeing for their lives. Just like the Duke of Sutherland in northwest Scotland, sheep were deemed by Clark to be more economical than crofters. The heinous Duke's wife on seeing the starving tenants on her husband's estate, remarked in a letter to a friend in England, "Scotch people are of happier constitution, and do not fatten like the larger breed of animals." It is no wonder that self-entitlement is alive and well amongst 21st Century oligarchs and aristocracy. Donald MacKenzie's book *As It Was/Sin Mar a*

Bha: An Ulva Boyhood wrote about those who stayed, exiled to Starvation Point on the north coast:

> "...Where the old and feeble folk cleared from their crofts were placed by Clark, to exist as best they could on shellfish & seaweed till they died".

The Clark family continued to own **Ulva** and **Gometra** till 1945.

Hoping for better times a community buy-out at £4.65 million was completed in 2018. **Ulva** has been the focus of attention not only for its famous visitors, from Walter Scott to Boswell and Johnson to Beatrix Potter, but for the luminaries born there and excelling in life away from this small island. David Livingstone's grandparents lived there. Lachlan Macquarie, the Governor of New South Wales from 1809 to 1821, often referred to as the father of Australia, also hailed from **Ulva**. His family had a 900-year association with the island, though Lachlan had to sell the island to settle his debts. His fate clearly sealed the fate of his fellow islanders as ownership passed to uncaring absentee landlords.

Gometra was used as a granary by the monks of nearby **Iona** but today supports a reputed four families living 'off grid'. Gometra house was reoccupied in 1993. We felt we needed at least two and a half hours for the return leg. We checked the map given to us by the suspicious ferryman when we said **Gometra** was our destination. He had every reason to doubt my agility as I found it difficult to get out of the boat. The short leaflet indicated a 6-hour outward and return journey, which fortunately we hadn't read as we set off. Paul and I were nowhere as fit as keen cyclist Stuart and we stumbled and tripped our way slowly across the excuse for a path pitted by what must have been a procession of quad bikes used by the isolates of **Gometra**. The blind were indeed leading the blind. We made the whole journey in a remarkable five and a half hours greeted by a bemused but irritated ferryman ready to ship us back to **Mull** as a chill wind descended on the narrow sound.

We headed for refreshment at the *Mishnish Hotel* on the Tobermory waterfront and attempted, with various degrees of success, to use the dictating facilities on my Samsung android to catch up with any anecdotes and musings from the day. We reflected on our journey across **Ulva** to **Gometra**. There appears to be something in the psyche of remote islanders to become global adventurers, but for most travel was not a choice but a dire necessity.

The *Mishnish* is billed as "one of the few iconic bars left in Scotland", a ridiculously grand claim but which cannot be acknowledged or refuted. It was only five o'clock in the afternoon and drink was already making us incapable of pronouncing its strange name, whose derivation remains a mystery. We drunk our Bellhaven's St Andrew's real ale and Speyburn malt chasers muttering shy and retrospective memories into my phone with the *Buzzcocks "Ever Fallen in Love (With Someone You Shouldn't've?)"* playing loudly in the background. The poignant lyrics reminded me of my unhappy first marriage to Shan who accompanied us to the same pub all those years ago.

After a night of more catch up and reminiscing with copious malts, we were 'fit' to tackle **Erraid** in the southwest of **Mull** and onto **Iona**. Stuart is still an enthusiastic traveller and his oft repeated apt catch phrase "Not a moment to lose" is a testament to his determinism of spirit. **Erraid** can be reached at low tide across the strand, and we searched out the best route over wide shimmering sands. Panicking about tide levels (I don't think we had checked the tide tables!) we split up, each thinking we knew the quickest route, only to be corrected by a chance encounter with 'an angel of mercy' heading back to her island home.

The island is home to the Findhorn Foundation, a spiritual retreat where members "work in co-creation with the intelligence of nature and take inspired action towards our vision of a better world". The island is also known as one of the locations in Robert Louis Stephenson's *"Kidnapped"* where the eponymous hero David Balfour was marooned for a while on the island having been shipwrecked on the Torran rocks nearby. He was unaware that the island was joined to the mainland at low tide twice a day. The young Robert Louis visited the island many times whilst his father was designing and building nearby lighthouses.

Erraid has the accolade of being statistically not only the driest but the sunniest location on northwest Scotland's coast. Stevenson's description of the island suggests:

> "It was still the roughest kind of walking; indeed, the whole, not only of Earraid (sic), but of the neighbouring part of **Mull** (which they call the Ross) is nothing but a jumble of granite rocks with heather in among".

We relaxed in the weak sunshine close to the Foundation premises and exchanged pleasantries with its occupants before heading to join our car on **Mull** for the short journey to Fionnphort and the ferry to **Iona**.

Iona is world renown as a spiritual retreat and the monastery was founded in the year 563 by the monk Columba who brought Christianity to the Picts of Scotland. The Celtic stone crosses found there have inspired much of Celtic art and religion to this day. In front of the abbey stands the 9th century St Martin's Cross, one of the best-preserved Celtic crosses in the British Isles.

The long arm of Henry VIII's draconian measures to rid the nation of Catholicism extended even to **Iona** with all but three of the 360 stone crosses destroyed in the Reformation. **Iona** seemed to be on all its invaders 'to do' lists of destruction. The monastery was repeatedly sacked by Viking and Norse raiders and its religious significance was almost lost in the 18th century. Remarkably this holy place always seemed to rise from the ashes. Columba's relics were removed and divided two ways between Scotland and Ireland in 849 as the monastery was abandoned.

When Samuel Johnson visited in 1773, he painted a bleak picture:

> "The inhabitants are remarkably gross, and remarkably neglected: I know not if they are visited by any minister. The island, which was once the metropolis of learning and piety, now has no school for education, nor temple for worship, only two inhabitants that can speak English, and not one that can write or read".

Today the abbey is the most elaborate and best-preserved ecclesiastical building surviving from the Middle Ages in the Western Isles. The monastery contains the graves of 48 Scottish kings at the sacred burial ground of Reilig Odhrái. The graves include 'Macbeth', eight Norwegian kings and four Irish kings though few are identifiable today. John Smith, the former Labour party leader before Tony Blair is buried in the graveyard. His epitaph reads (from Alexander Pope's *'An Essay of Man') "An honest man's the noblest work of God".* Honesty is in short supply amongst many of today's politicians. Arguably Smith was the best Prime Minister Britain never had.

The island is now home to the **Iona** community founded in 1938 by George MacLeod as an ecumenical Christian community of men and women from different walks of life and different traditions in the Christian church. Its Christian roots have thus been revived. We stayed some time on the island in quiet contemplation – **Iona** has that effect – and even gave up the chance of an earlier ferry. The peace and tranquillity were truly infectious. Stuart pointed out an inscription on one of the many tablets in the monastery which when roughly translated read:

> 'As long as there is the sweet sound of Gaelic singing the world will be at peace'.

Though having religion battered, quite literally, into me at my austere Methodist boarding school in Harrogate in the early sixties I have always had a spiritual edge, nurtured by my mother's respect, no deep love, for nature. She was at her happiest in autumn gathering the beech leaves turning to a majestic gold, and making bouquets for church charities, the leaves held fast by glycerine. As I sat on ancient pews, deep in thought, I remembered the barbarity of boarding school. I was sent as an 11-year-old to Ashville College on the outskirts of Harrogate. On the first night I missed my mother and tried conversation with my neighbouring bed mate. "Who is talking?" came a brusque voice. My mother told me always to tell the truth and I owned up, to be extricated from my bed and beaten senseless by this sadistic brute, the housemaster Mr Ken Groves. I shall never forget his name or the bunch of other sadists, Braithwaite (sentenced later for child abuse) and Lockwood who were amongst our torturers.

Paul became 'my wife' for a couple of hours as we took advantage of my pair of English Heritage membership cards which have a certain discount currency even in Scotland. There were no cafes, pubs or restaurants open on this late early November afternoon so after our contemplative tour of the monastery buildings we waited patiently for the ferry and the hour's journey back to the mundanity of the *Isle of Mull hotel*.

I had booked to have a massage courtesy of Morag before dinner, and we were running very late. Stuart decided to 'go for it' on the darkening, winding country lanes with Paul rally-style navigating using the road atlas to warn of impending bends! Our recklessness was reminiscent of our caving days. I was slightly older than the others and the only university approved minibus driver in the grandly named London University Speleological club. Heading back to our caving cottage in Eyam, Derbyshire, after far too much to drink at the remote *Three Stags Head* in Wardlow Mires Paul, Stuart and the other young Turks would climb through the minibus windows of the speeding van, across the roof rack and back in the other side. I shudder to think of what carnage could have ensued.

Our cottage in Eyam, rented for the princely sum of £25 per year, was our less than adequate base. Eyam is well known as the village heroically self-isolating during the 1665 plague. The virus was brought in from London in a package containing a rather damp suit of clothes. In the fourteen months the danger lasted, plague claimed 260 lives out of a population of around 800. Graves are scattered around the village and at the village boundaries hollows were carved into the millstone grit wall stones and filled with vinegar to sterilise the money left by the villagers in exchange for food. The current UK poet laureate, Simon Armitage, pays tribute, in his poem *Lockdown* to the brave souls of Eyam written during the 2020 COVID 19 pandemic:

> "And I couldn't escape the waking dream
> of infected fleas
> in the warp and weft of soggy cloth
> by the tailor's hearth
> in ye olde Eyam.
> Then couldn't un-see
> the Boundary Stone,
> that cock-eyed dice with its six dark holes,
> thimbles brimming with vinegar wine
> purging the plagued coins.
> Which brought to mind the sorry story
> of Emmott Syddall and Rowland Torre,
> star-crossed lovers on either side
> of the quarantine line
> whose wordless courtship spanned the river
> till she came no longer."

My life, too, was almost lost in Derbyshire, not by plague but sheer folly. I joined the caving club in 1970 as a driver but was soon coerced by Stuart and Paul to join them in their subterranean exploits. I enjoyed the frisson of danger. On one trip to explore the uncharted Critchlow cave in the Lathkill Dale valley, near Monyash I came close to meeting my maker. I was bigger than my snake hipped colleagues (well not Paul) and usually was forced through tight passages first using the logical argument that if I fitted then so would they.

On turning to leave the dreadful bedding plane crawl that was Critchlow and some 200 metres from daylight, I became immovably trapped with my body jammed against limestone floor and ceiling and my mouth trying with little success to avoid ingesting the muddy filth. No amount of pushing would shift me. I was doomed but at 22 years old one's own mortality is not the most pressing issue. I knew I was going to die as did the others as this was, or so we thought, a one-way exit. Suddenly a voice ahead of me was heard. Our insufferable colleague Steve Newton had discovered an alternative passage, actually the one we'd crawled in on. I had inadvertently found the bifurcation. After much pushing and pulling I was eventually released from my Jurassic tomb and, new neoprene wet suit ripped to shreds, emerged blinking into the new dawn of a Derbyshire day. The experience haunts me five decades later.

Winter is not a good time for island hopping in these often bleak and windy conditions. After all we live on the edge of Europe way into the Atlantic ocean. Islanders choose isolation and solitude, and it appears post Brexit that the mother island – Great Britain- is also choosing isolation from its European neighbours. Nevertheless, we had immensely enjoyed the camaraderie of the last few days and as we boarded the ferry back to the mainland Stuart with his inimical loquaciousness exclaimed:

> "The earth to the Lord belongs and all that it contains, excepting the Western Isles for they belong to McBraynes!"

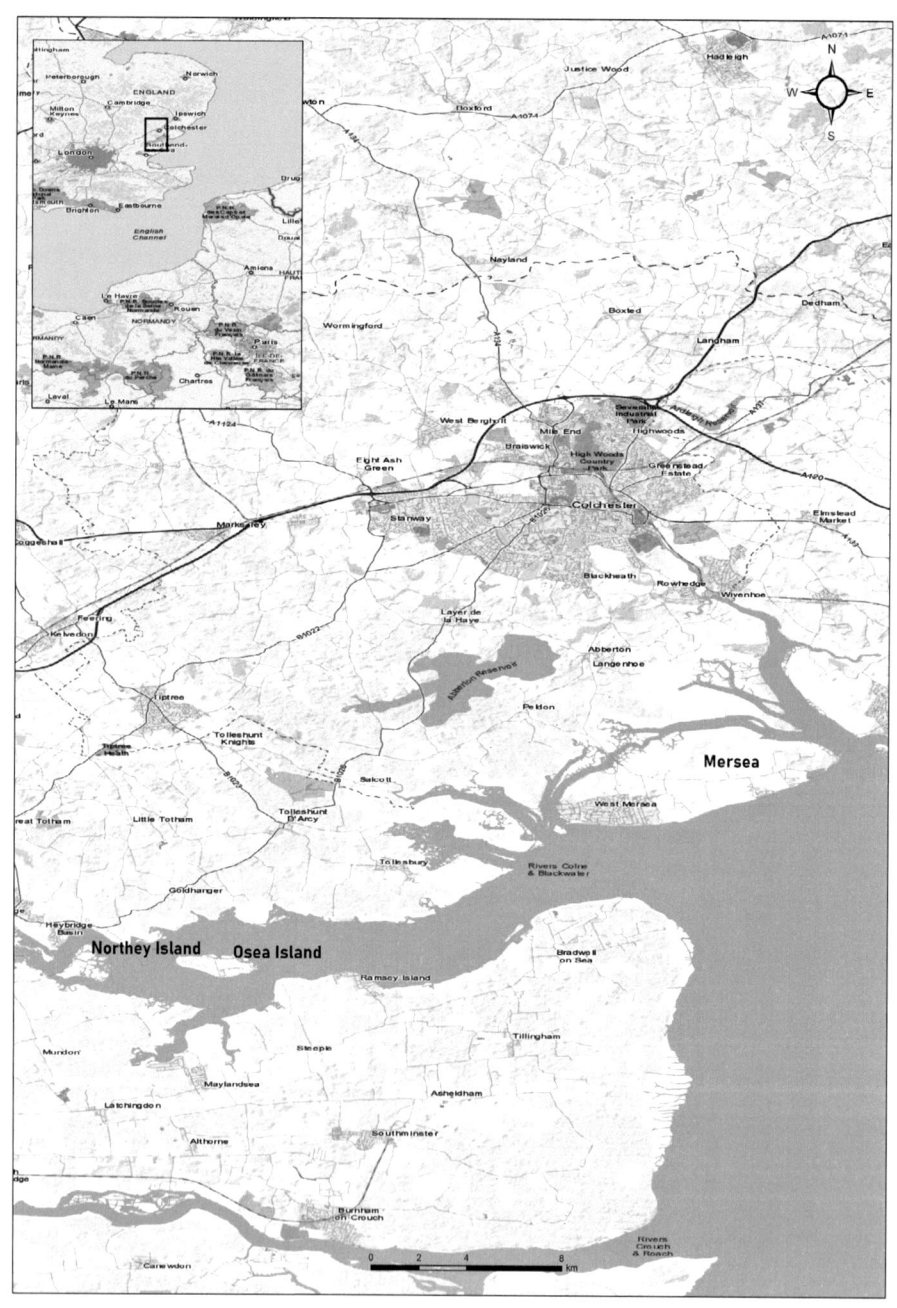

Island successes and failures in Essex, England

11. Island Successes and Failures in Essex, England

The Scottish islands are grouped in convenient batches of half a dozen or a dozen or maybe more, each group 'do-able' in a single trip, but in England the inhabited islands are eccentrically placed with a special effort often required to gain legal access. My work in flood risk management takes me to seemingly random places and if an island is nearby, I try to "tick it off". I was fond of the *I-Spy* series of pocketbooks in the 1950's and 1960's – find an oak tree and tick it off; find an island and tick it off is just an extension of this. Having completed my 5,003-mile journey around Great Britain's coast and visiting for 20 years random towns and villages with their rivers and coast to inspect I pride myself with the fact that few people past or present have visited more of Great Britain than I have. I have yet to be disproved!

I found myself in Essex and took the opportunity to track down **Foulness**, near Southend, the fourth largest island off the English coast and **Mersea Island** near Colchester. **Osea** and **Northey Islands** could easily be 'ticked off' on this venture too, or so I thought. I got to **Foulness** after a four-hour drive from Birmingham. I had as usual not done any in-depth research. The whole island is a Ministry of Defence artillery training ground and is not accessible to the public other than for four hours on the first Sunday of each month between April and October from 12:00 to 16:00, when the **Foulness** Heritage centre opens its doors. I was fooling myself I could outwit these access rules.

The island sits on the north bank of the mighty Thames estuary a short distance east of Southend and a haven for migrating birds. It was the proliferation of these birds that eventually scuppered plans to build London's proposed third airport on the adjacent Maplin Sands. As I drove south, I thought "How hard could it be to sneak past the security and scamper onto the island for a few moments?".

The approach to the check point (still on the mainland) was menacing and well-guarded, clearly a terrorist target in these troubled times. I said a cheery hello and explained the purpose of my mission. The guard was unmoved and informed me that written consent was required to gain access, unless you were visiting one of the *bona fide* islanders who rent their houses and land from the MoD. My pleas fell on stony ground and deaf ears, and I was ordered off site; a special return journey would be required during the Summer. A cheeky scamper would have been useless anyway as the uninhabited Havengore island separates the mainland from **Foulness** itself.

Northey Island near Maldon was nearby, as was **Osea Island**, both reached by tidal causeways situated in the river Blackwater. **Northey** is a National Trust nature reserve and occupied by the warden only. The two islands are amongst the 43 (unbridged) tidal islands which can be walked to from the British mainland and two of six such tidal islands in Essex. **Northey's** size varies anywhere between 80 and 300 acres depending on the tides and provides a barrier against tidal surges, protecting settlements at the head of the Blackwater estuary. The salt marsh and mud flats are home to geese, shelducks, and golden and grey plovers.

The poorly maintained tidal causeway, about 250 metres long, leads to a quiet tranquillity. It was not always so and hosts the site of the battle of Maldon in 991, where Ethelred the Unready's Anglo Saxon forces under the command of Earl Byrhtnoth lost to a Viking invasion. **Northey Island** is the oldest recorded battlefield in Britain. My retreat from the island was almost as ignominious as Ethelred's as the tide was fast incoming and I had to circumnavigate the estuary to gain further causeway access to **Osea**.

It was November and gloomy and the access to this secretive island was elusive. After several attempts I found the access, but this was gated and locked, and the tide was quickly advancing onto the snaking sliver of a causeway some several hundred metres long. CCTV cameras guarded the route, and I was too nervous to use the intercom to explain my mission. I retreated for another time and headed for **Mersea Island. Osea Island** looked menacing and sinister in the gathering gloom. It used to house a treatment centre for wealthy alcoholics, set up rather ironically by the Charrington brewing family. It was revived as the *Causeway Retreat* between 2005 and 2010 and amongst its patients was the flawed musical diva Amy Winehouse, but its worthy ambition did little to save her. Its license was revoked when the district judge in charge of these matters suggested that 'its standards would shame a third world country'.

On reaching **Mersea**, apparently according to tourist blurb, Great Britain's most easterly inhabited island, I took a whistle stop drive around the island – East and West **Mersea** – before darkness took a permanent hold for the night. The access road, flooded on extreme high tides, via the Strood causeway was originally constructed by the Saxons in the late 7th Century. Island populations are subject usually to plummeting declines, but **Mersea** appears to have bucked the trend with population more than doubling rising from 3,140 in 1961 to 6,925 in 2001. It is proud of its isolation and attracts a growing number of visitors, despite the decline of tourism in nearby Clacton, trading on peace, tranquillity and independence. As the daylight failed, I saw little of its apparent attractions and headed for Colchester. **Mersea** may not be amongst my favourite islands, unlike the Romans who visited it as a holiday location from their garrison in Camulodunum or Colchester, the first capital of their distant province of Briton.

TREASURED ISLANDS

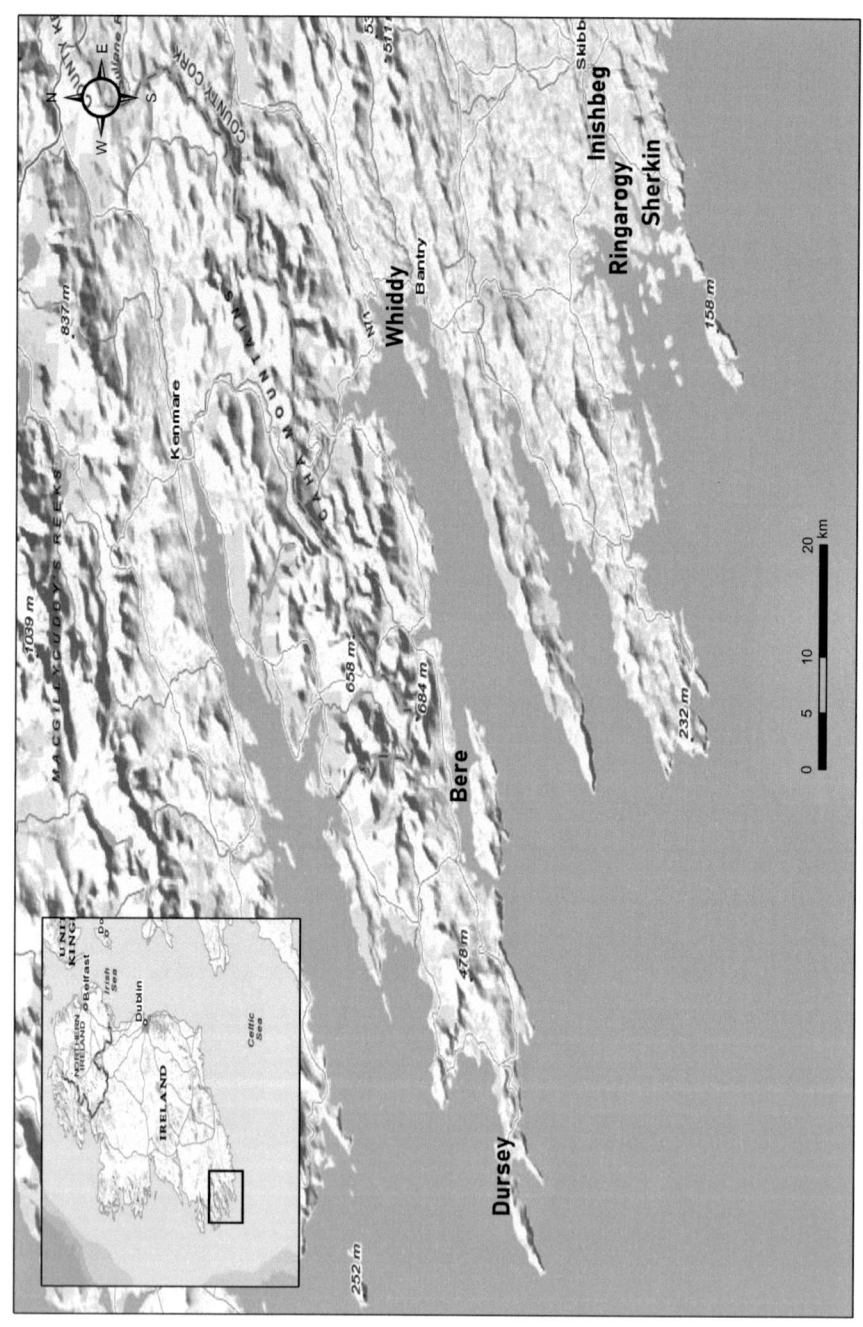

Random islands in County Cork and southwest Ireland

12. Random islands in County Cork and Southwest Ireland

With spring 2017 approaching I was eager to escape the geopolitics of Trump and Brexit and the evil mendacities that global politics had become. Angela Merkel and Trump had just met, and his stubborn intransigence was as ugly as ever. In a few months the mantle of the leader of the free liberal world seemed to be passing from USA to Germany. How is that for upending socio-political reality in 75 years.

Since attempting to visit the bleak Essex marsh islands, I had visited two far distant islands in southeast Asia; Bali (twice) and nearby Timor Leste. Though geographically close each was of a quite different character and temperament. Passport irregularities meant I was marooned in Bali on my December trip, holed up in inexpensive luxury in Kuta, the Magaluf of southeast Asia. The Alaya hotel was simply the best hotel I have ever stayed in but costing a mere fifty US Dollars per night.

My extended stay saw an endless pampering by attentive staff with afternoon tea or tiffin on the airy mezzanine and a rose petal filled bath drawn for me at the end of the working day before exquisite massages. This oasis of calm contrasted with the endless tacky bars and cheap massage parlours which were the order of the day in the bustling streets beyond, choked with traffic, mostly taxis trying and mostly failing to make a living. The romantic notion of a tropical paradise has long since gone, with commercialism the watchword. There is even a Trump hotel there now. On my second trip the island was "graced" by the Saudi King, holidaying with a 1,500 strong entourage with over 500 tonnes of luggage.

In stark contrast is the new country of Timor Leste (East Timor), gaining independence from Indonesia in 2002 following a bloody war. A detailed statistical report prepared for the Commission for Reception, Truth and Reconciliation in East Timor cited a minimum of 102,800 conflict-related deaths in the period 1974–1999, namely, approximately 18,600 killings and 84,200 "excess" deaths from hunger and illness. This tropical island of little more than one million in population is connected to Indonesian Timor to the west though with a closed border. Its population, largely Christian in contrast to its Muslim Indonesian neighbour, is fiercely independent and in recovery mode with assistance from UNDP (United Nations Development Programme) and other non-Government organisations. Our aim was to help rural communities to become resilient to the rigours of a worsening climate. This will not be easy and compounded in difficulty by a then Trump administration, including astonishingly the head of the Environmental Protection Agency, who denies the very existence of climate change. With almost a quarter of UN funding coming from the USA, supporting projects like this around the world via the Green Climate Fund initiative looked fragile.

On my return a long-awaited trip to Ireland beckoned and a start of the islands inhabited off the coast of the Republic. Many of these islands are connected by road bridges or causeways so I foolishly expected the task to be simple, but as most are in the southwest of the country where the coastline is heavily crenulated travel times on rural roads would be lengthy and arduous.

I was impetuous, I always have been as explained by my four marriages! I booked a flight to Dublin, where apart from a couple of islands including **North Bull Island** in the Dublin area, the nearest islands are in west Cork 362km distant, or a four-hour drive! Unperturbed I drove to Abbeyleix where my good friend John Lawlor lives in isolation out of almost a duty to his beloved late father who was born there and had occupied the bungalow for over 30 years prior to his death. John had been stuck in a rut in England. His employer seemed to have one mission and that was to strangle his aspirations and keep him at the very bottom of their socio-economic scale.

Small town Ireland was stultifying, and he like me was eager for a road trip. After several pints of Guinness and a Paddy's whiskey or two in *Morrisseys*, a well-known, traditional roadhouse pub then past its best on the old Dublin to Cork road, I stayed overnight as I often do at the *Abbeyleix Manor Hotel*. It is a good economical establishment even after the Brexit announcement had sent the pound into freefall.

John is not a natural map reader but a writer of thoughtful, often beautiful prose and a dreamer, who sees himself, with a sense of irony, as a character out of one of JP Donleavy's seminal sixties novels, perhaps not the rogue Sebastian Dangerfield in *The Ginger Man*, but more Balthazar B in his *Beastly Beatitudes*. The latter novel described in the august words of *The New York Times* as "one of the most perfect love affairs in modern literature". I think John ever the elegiac roué aspires to this accolade.

Though our route initially took us on one of the many motorways built during Ireland's 'Celtic Tiger' period at the turn of the century, progress was slower than I would have liked, punctuated by stops to argue over map reading. We took a short detour off the Dublin to Limerick motorway and took coffee at the Obama Plaza in Moneyball, County Offaly, a tribute to one of the US president's Irish ancestors. Falmouth Kearney, Obama's great- great- great- grandfather left an Ireland ravaged by famine to carve out a better life, as did many of his country men and women. An estimated 37 million Americans claim Irish ancestry.

We reached Baltimore in the far southwest of County Cork at around one in the afternoon and discovered a ferry to **Sherkin**, one of the several inhabited Carbery Hundred Islands, was due to depart within the hour. This was a ferry for the locals at this time of year and friends greeted each other, laden down with their shopping from excursions to Skibbereen, the market town a few miles up the coast. The return journey gave us about an hour and a half on the island and we were told there were two pubs to enjoy.

We quickened our step up the steep hill from the harbour past the medieval Franciscan priory to find refreshment. Of course, the season had not begun, and *Murphy's* pub and restaurant and *The Jolly Roger* were firmly closed. This was a pity as a sign along the road instructed us that the latter pub had been voted the second-best coastal pub in Ireland. We wondered by who and by what criteria (and wondered which pub was voted #1). Apart from the views the pub itself looked unkempt and run down but maybe renovations were ongoing.

Like all Irish islands the Great Famine in the 19th Century had decimated the population. In the 10 years from 1841 to 1851 the population fell from 1,131 to 696 and declined to a low of 70 in 1981, recovering to its present (2016) level of 111. **Sherkin** has its own special character. A west Cork anecdote has it that **Sherkin's** residents live off their art: island craft, paintings and book writing all inspired by the island's tranquil lifestyle. We sat in the weak spring sun before ambling quietly back to the ferry.

The landscape was dominated by a white obelisk (The Baltimore Beacon) pointing to the sky. The beacon is locally known as "Lot's Wife", after the Biblical woman turned into a pillar of salt. The Book of Genesis describes how she became a pillar of salt after she looked back at Sodom. A salutary tale etched in the minds of devout Irish Catholics. This is the very southern tip of Ireland with Fastnet Rock visible in the distance. Due to its location, Fastnet is known as "Ireland's Teardrop", because it was the last part of Ireland that 19th century Irish emigrants saw as they sailed to north America to an uncertain future. Folklore abounds, with the particularly quirky story that in 1631 Barbary pirates attacked the village taking about one hundred unsuspecting inhabitants to the slave markets of north Africa. There are clearly descendants of these hapless sons and daughters of Cork dreaming of their ancestral homeland in Mulligan's Bar, Marrakech (yes, there is a bar of that name!).

Planning a logistical route in a logical fashion was way beyond me as preparation is not my strong point having been impatient and irascible most of my life. I will never learn. I discovered that there were other inhabited islands accessible from Baltimore, for example **Clear Island** but they would have to be for another time as we needed to get to the village of Allihies for our random overnight accommodation some 98km distant. It never seemed to bother me that a return visit to this remote corner of west Cork would take more time and more money. It was simply extending the adventure.

The R595 route north and west follows the newly designated Wild Atlantic Way past the myriad of other Carbery Hundred Islands, two of which, **Inishbeg** and **Ringarogy**, were easily accessible from the mainland by road causeways. There are reputed to be 100 Carbery Hundred Islands but who's counting; poetic licence is much more preferable to pedantry. These two were 'ticked off' without ceremony driving around their narrow, uncared for roads without doing them the courtesy of a full inspection. They comprise rugged outcrops dotted with small crofts and the convoluted coastline of each merges imperceptibly with the mainland. Perhaps they weren't worth a lengthy visit after all, I mused. Purest island hoppers, if there are such people, might not class these as islands at all.

My great grandfather went by the name of Jabez, a depressing biblical name if ever there was one (from 1 Chronicles, chapter 4) meaning pain or sorrow. **Ringarogy's** meaning is equally depressing, coming from the Irish Rinn Ghearróige, meaning the 'point of the defeat' after some unsuccessful skirmish in 1537 with a gang of Waterford mariners when the island's villages were burnt in the attack.

Ringarogy's largest neighbour is the similarly causewayed **Inishbeg**. The owners of the Inishbeg estate today have "undertaken a uniquely sympathetic renovation and rejuvenation of this island paradise" and it is open all the year round to the public. Of historical interest the island was once home to American president and Second World War hero Dwight D Eisenhower's chauffeur and some say his lover, Kay Summersby. She accompanied him during his period as Supreme Commander of Allied Expeditionary Forces in northwest Europe. Summersby says the 'affair' went no further than "stolen kisses" during walks or on aeroplanes, holding hands, and horseback riding or golfing together. Nevertheless, the potential scandal was an embarrassment to both Field Marshall Montgomery and President Truman. Those in high office today who are known multiple philanderers with the most reprehensible of moral compasses are on the contrary adulated by their adoring sycophants.

We chose Allihies as an overnight resting point as it was close to **Dursey Island**, unique in that its only regular access is by a rickety aerial tramway built in the 1960's to allow all year 'safe' access. The strait between the mainland peninsular and the island was and still is notorious for its treacherous tidal race with the submerged Flag Rock close to the centre of the navigable channel. With suitable knowledge and care it is still navigable on calmer days to transport sheep.

As with all my Irish trips what seemed to be a relaxed amble turned into a mad chase. We passed by some pleasant looking sea food restaurants at Castletownbere but felt we needed to reach our booked accommodation before nightfall. This option proved a wise move, with swirling mists and weak sunshine creating an almost surreal setting across the Kenmare River. Our destination was attained as the last light of the day edged below the growling ocean, the wild Atlantic. It was a serendipitous spectre of beauty, as we looked down at the retreating sea mist. Coming back to earthly reality food was our main goal before relaxing with a couple of pints of Guinness. It had been a long drive from Abbeyleix.

Our affable landlady, Marie, soon dampened our spirits. It was out of season, a very short season in these parts, and the three pubs in the tiny village, which would have been closed permanently if in England through a distinct lack of profitability, would not be serving food of any kind that evening. She owned the shop next door to her B&B and offered us pizza (warmed on the premises) to ensure our bellies had some lining before the Guinness drinking ensued in *O'Neil's* and the *Lighthouse* pubs side by side on the town's main street. The drinking fraternity would have insisted that the elixir of St James Gate was food enough and, if taken with baked beans, is some topers say the only daily sustenance any man needs!

Dursey beckoned, and for once advanced logistics were necessary as the cable car, no more than a converted farm trailer (holding six passengers), sets off each day at 09:30 and runs back and forth for an hour before retiring until later in the day. If you are on the island after the 10:30 car has left, then isolation would ensue. Not wanting to be outwitted by the quirky timetable we made the first crossing along with a couple of shepherds heading out to do what shepherds do. My Biblical upbringing in the West Riding of Yorkshire during Sunday school at the Glusburn Baptist chapel led me to believe that shepherds "watched their flocks by night" not at ten o'clock in the morning. The young guys were good natured and fit for their job which was more than could be said for the cable car which lurched from side to side in the stiff breeze, some hundred feet above the rocks below.

In summer this is quite a tourist attraction for those foreign visitors wending their way up and down the Wild Atlantic Way. Patience is their virtue as a single journey takes about 20 minutes and the return trip costs 10 Euros. Being at the front of the queue is no guarantee of a place in the contraption as locals get priority. The Germans in particular, who are used to reserving their places early (towels on their package holiday sun loungers) apparently get more than a little agitated by the delays. Looking through the slats on the floor of this rickety old Heath Robinson of a device, which has 'eased' the journey to **Dursey** since 1969, was the menacing and restless sea. The trip was indeed hope triumphing over adversity. We held on tight as the car lurched forwards. My eye caught a copy of Psalm 91 pasted on the wall, an apt Biblical reference for such a journey:

> "Whoever dwells in the shelter of the Most High will rest in the shadow of the Almighty. I will say of the LORD, He is my refuge and my fortress, my God, in whom I trust".

We were indeed at the Lord's mercy.

Progress is often not to be respected. Cork County Council and the Irish tourist board, *Failte Eire* proposed in 2020 a 10 million Euro development replacing the existing cable car with a state-of-the-art two-way system capable of carrying 300 people an hour. The project included all the tourist trappings of a visitor centre, gift shop and a glazed elevator on the mainland and dismissed the negative impact on the chough feeding and nesting habitats. An island of remote beauty would have become a scar on the landscape like the Cliffs of Moher further north in County Clare now attracting over a million visitors a year using the Wild Atlantic Way. The balance between maintaining natural sites of beauty and exposing them for tourism, education and profit is a very fine balance. The cable car was closed during 2022 for major maintenance but the grander ideas seem to have been shelved.

This small island bears witness to a little-known but bloody travesty by Ireland's Imperial rulers (those self-entitled pompous English again). During the nine years war (or Tyrone's rebellion) from 1593 to 1603, in an attempt to end English rule, Dursey castle was sacked and 300 islanders were killed. A further thousand attempted the long journey to Leitrim in what is now the Border region between Connacht and Ulster, but only 35 survived. The selective teaching and sanitising of history avoids many such stories. Little now remains of Dursey castle.

On safely alighting, we walked in the drizzle with poor views for what seemed an appropriate length of time and returned to the aerial pod and back to the Beara peninsular and onto Castletownbere, the modest oasis which we had foolishly avoided the night before. I discovered that a car ferry served **Bere Island** from Castletownbere and, if we made the 11:30 crossing returning at 13:00, we could make the last return ferry of the day to **Whiddy Island**, which also lies in Bantry Bay a couple of miles off the town of Bantry. If our plans worked, we would have 45 minutes to cover the 51km to the ferry. A tall order; but hope springs eternal!

The ancient ferry had seen better days. With only one other traveller yet again the economics of island ferries perplexed us. We later learned that one of the **Bere** islanders won a Euro millions jackpot. Perhaps they could donate some of the money to a ferry re-fit. Given Ireland's reputation for pubs it was odd that in the space of two days we had already encountered four closed ones. Hope again triumphing over experience we noted that there was a pub for lunch on **Bere Island**, but as with the two on **Sherkin Island** the previous day this too was closed.

The island has a tranquil, sedate feel about it, strategically set at the entrance to Bantry Bay. We whiled away the time ambling the narrow lanes criss-crossing the island without meeting a soul.

As with all ferries the return journey was on time and we put caution to the wind driving at speed to Bantry with moments to spare to make the ferry, *Ocean Star III*. John was ravenous and I promised him that if the *Bankhouse* on **Whiddy island** was closed as we fully expected it to be we would forego the delights of this small island for another time. The ferryman, Tim, assured us that the pub would be open as did the motley assemblage of passengers, locals not tourists, who were returning from the town laden down with shopping. Our fellow travellers comprised the ferryman's mother and an over garrulous young guy with a zest for life rarely seen in youths of his age. He was not a native of the island and the islanders viewed him with suspicion, maybe because of his uncertain sexual orientation.

Irish social life was, until 20 or so years ago, dominated by the Catholic church with an estimated 80% of the population being regular attendees at Mass. The more recent exposure of a plethora of paedophile priests created an opportunity to eschew the authority of the church and create a more liberal minded national psyche. Gay marriage was made legal in the Republic before any other country in the World and though the pro-life campaign still had a tight grip, forbidding abortion, a popular vote in early 2018 resulted in a victory, by quite some margin for the pro-choice in an ever-increasing section of society.

The then incumbent Prime Minister or Taoiseach in Gaelic, Leo Varadkar, is not only of mixed parentage with an Indian father but was at the time of my visit only around the age of 40 and gay. The country has come a long way from the Ireland of John Lawlor's youth with respect to inclusiveness and liberal attitudes. My dear late friend Tony would shudder when detailing the cruelty that he suffered at the hands of his Christian Brother Jesuit teachers. How a religion, based on love, can turn into an institution that cows its followers into trembling submission is a mystery.

We docked and made the short walk to the *Bankside*, followed by the mischievous skipper, Tim who, unbeknown to us, doubled up as barman whilst the women folk busied themselves getting the place spic and span for the upcoming season. Food comprised of a limited selection of confectionary, Tayto's crisps and cups of tea for me, the driver, and the ubiquitous Guinness for John. The ferry business had been in the same hands for 20 or more years and with summer visitors attracted to this unique island sheltered in the lee of the Beara Mountains, Tim was not going to let the business go easily.

In 1979 the oil tanker *Betelgeuse* exploded at the **Whiddy Island** terminal killing 50 crew with only 29 bodies recovered. Laden with 114,000 tonnes of Saudi oil the aging tanker was ill equipped and the jetty infrastructure inadequate to offload its cargo safely. The greed of nations, oil companies and their lust for oil has cost countless thousands of lives in exploration and especially in wars. The fate of the *Betelgeuse* is just a tragic footnote in the rape of and disregard to the exploitation of the World's natural resources. The Iraq war between 2003 and 2011 cost in excess of US$1 trillion that is, wait for it, 1,000,000,000,000 US dollars.

I was travelling to Madras (now Chennai), India in the early 1990's at the time of the first Gulf war. A colleague and I travelled British Airways via Kuwait. On one trip our bookings were changed, and we travelled on an earlier flight. Our original flight was intercepted by Iraqi soldiers and hostages taken including a small child, used by Saddam Hussein as a propaganda tool. An acquaintance on the intercepted flight was taken to Baghdad and used as a human shield. On his release his oil company employer had sacked him in his absence. Profit before humans has always been and always will be the clarion call of the vulture capitalist 'elite'.

We returned to Bantry with Tim's sister one of the *Bankside* spring-cleaning ladies and at four in the afternoon were Dublin bound some four hours and 392km away. After another hectic day, driving in the smallest hire car known to man, Dublin was too ambitious a target, so we opted instead to retreat back to Abbeyleix for the 'comfort' of *Morrisey's* pub and the convenience of the *Abbeyleix Manor*. Dublin would be for another time, and I promised John that I would at least try a modicum of planning for future jaunts and secure a more comfortable vehicle.

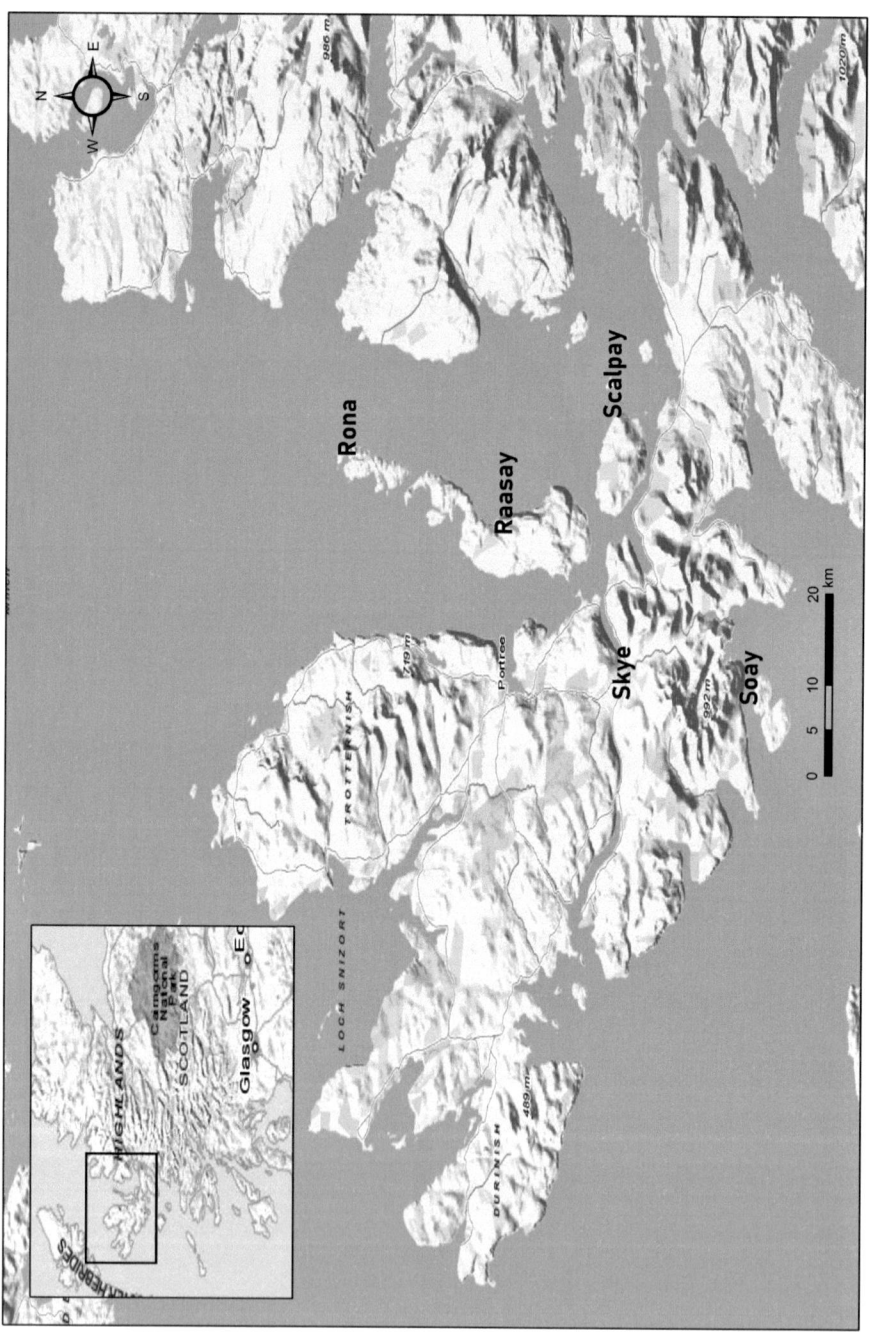

The Isle of Skye and surrounding islands, Scotland

13. The Isle of Skye and surrounding Islands, Scotland

April 2017 saw the first anniversary of my island hopping and a trip to **Skye** and its surrounding islands was neatly planned with Liverpool Sue as my companion. Now planning was a novelty but only **Raasay** had a scheduled CalMac ferry, an up-to-date fuel hybrid of which the company was justly proud. The islands of **Soay**, in the shadow of the Cuillin Mountains off Elgol fishing village, **Rona** tucked way to the north of **Raasay** and **Scalpay** were only accessible using eye-wateringly expensive private hire boats. Of course, **Skye** itself is accessed conveniently via the Skye bridge at the Kyle of Lochalsh. Haswell-Smith's original edition of *The Scottish Islands* didn't even class **Skye** as an island now, but this is just purism gone mad.

Skye, after **Harris and Lewis**, is Great Britain's second biggest offshore island. **Skye** will always be remembered for the legend of Bonny Prince Charlie (aka Charles Edward Stuart) who embarked from **Skye** for France on 20th September 1746 never to set foot in Britain again following the Jacobite's final defeat at the Battle of Culloden by the Hanoverians. This finally put an end to the Stuart dynasty, started in 1603 by James I (VI of Scotland). Flora MacDonald, aged 24, travelled with Prince Charlie, whom she disguised as her maid, Betty Burke, across the sea from **Benbecula** in the Outer Hebrides to the Isle of **Skye**. He was a wanted man with a £30,000 price on his head, or over £7 million at today's prices. The *Skye Boat* song, whose lyrics have been slurred endlessly by a generation of Rab C Nesbit lookalikes recorded the emigration for posterity:

> "Speed, bonnie boat, like a bird on the wing,
> Onward! the sailors cry;

Carry the lad that's born to be King
Over the sea to Skye".

As with many romantic myths, this journey to **Skye** was factually incorrect.

Skye is dominated by the magnificent Cuillin Mountains and its famous ridge the basalt and gabbro Black Cuillin containing twelve of Scotland's Munros, acknowledged as the hardest of all to attain. Linking them is even tougher, with many narrow ridges to scramble and concentration is required with every step. The inaccessible pinnacle affectionately known by the climbing fraternity as 'Inpin' rises from the summit of Sgurr Dearg and is the only Munro requiring serious rock-climbing skills.

Skye's very shape is beguiling with it being described as "sticking out of the west coast of northern Scotland like a lobster's claw ready to snap at the fish bone of **Harris and Lewis**". Its irregularity in shape is so extreme that the mountaineer WH Murray wrote:

> "**Skye** is sixty miles long, but what might be its breadth is beyond the ingenuity of man to state".

I like that description.

Skye's population peaked in 1841 until, like many other islands, the Highland Clearances raised their ugly spectre. Now, at 10,008 (2011 census) it is not much lower than that of 1755. The once inspirational Liberal leader, Charles Kennedy, was its Member of the Westminster Parliament for 32 years, the youngest MP at 23 when first elected. He lost his seat in 2015 and died soon after, following a long battle with alcoholism. The Highlands and Islands were always a stronghold of Liberal politics with luminaries like Jo Grimond and David Steel at the helm. Today with the upsurge of Scottish nationalism they barely cling on to political power.

Scottish nationalism is proudly left leaning and socially democratic with policies and principles harking back to the enlightenment movement of the 18th Century. This renaissance was characterised by an outpouring of intellectual and scientific accomplishments from the likes of Adam Smith's *Wealth of Nations*; the philosopher David Hume; and that pivotal figure of the Industrial revolution, James Watt. Their legacy has given Scotland, amongst other things, freedom of movement with no trespass laws, free university education, free medical prescriptions and health care for the elderly. In contrast English nationalism conjures up xenophobic Brexiteers and illiberal, misogynistic racists with little enlightenment of any kind. Their followers and political leaders hark back to the pink world map where the sun never set on the British Empire and slavery was just a business opportunity with no thought for humanity.

Apart from the Talisker distillery the population are mainly public sector workers or engaged in the burgeoning holiday market which since the opening of the Skye Bridge, completed in 1995, has spiralled to unprecedented levels. At the height of summer accommodation of any sort is nigh on impossible unless pre-booked. Our trip was during Easter, and I had, unusual for me, the foresight to have booked my accommodation and trips ahead. In mid-April the season was not yet under way. The weather was in the high teens in England, but a very blustery and dreary 9 centigrade on **Skye**. Was my planning to be thwarted? I had secured a four-hour trip on the *Brigadoon*, which cost the equivalent of a family of four flying to Majorca and back with a week's accommodation thrown in. George its skipper would be sailing out of Portree, the capital of the island, and I waited with bated breath for the phone call calling the trip off because of the poor weather.

I had also contacted David, proprietor of the *Bella Jane* sailing out of Elgol in the south of **Skye** to hitch a ride to **Soay** on her twice daily trips to the nearby Small Islands, **Canna** and **Rum**. Finally, after no luck in eliciting a trip to **Scalpay**, a private island noted for its self-catering to satisfy the demands of deer hunters, I hired a RIB courtesy of the owners of Seaprobe Atlantis who also operate a glass bottomed boat out of Kyleakin close to the Skye Bridge. I kept asking myself "was it worth it". Was it too expensive and too much of a hassle? Then I thought life is a hassle unless you kick away the obstacles.

Crossing the Skye bridge, we soon reached Sconser for the 13:00 ferry to **Rasaay**, sheltering in the very modern waiting room with two fellow passengers; a resident who was keen to drive us around the island on our arrival and a young Polish woman, escaping a troubled marriage for the Highlands. The kindly lady gave the Pole a lift to her accommodation at Rasaay House, now a hotel catering for all pockets. Sue and I then embarked on a magical mystery tour of the lady's island, cursing (well actually not cursing as she, as the rest of the islanders were, was a strict "wee free" Presbyterian) tourists in their shiny four by fours. We embarked on a modern-day tour of the Hebrides, or so it seemed, mimicking Boswell and Johnson's visit there in 1773. No track was left untouched and an hour and a half later we were despatched back to Rasaay House desperate for refreshment and the ferry back to **Skye**.

Raasay was the unlikely setting for iron mining in the early 20th Century and a sombre row of miners' cottages in the main village of Inverarish was all that was left as a legacy to this industry. Our guide owned one of the cottages and was bursting with pride for her island and its heritage. The island's current slumbers were soon to be desecrated by the opening of a whisky distillery, bringing in welcome jobs but despised and loathed by the closed community of apparent religious zealots with strict adherence to the Sabbath. They were proud of their heritage and especially Sorley MacLean, one of Scotland's poets of national and international stature, and one of the most distinguished of all Gaelic poets who was born on **Raasay**. His most famous poem, translated by Nobel laureate Seamus Heaney, captures the mood of this remote Hebridean isle:

> "I will wait for the birches to move,
> The wood to come up past the cairn
> Until it has veiled the mountain
> Down from Beinn na Lice in shade.
> If it doesn't, I'll go to Hallaig,

> To the sabbath of the dead,
> Down to where each departed
> Generation has gathered".

A fateful lot the wee frees, I thought as we rushed to meet the ferry back to a semblance of civilisation.

On a lighter literary note Roger Hutchinson wrote the acclaimed *Calum's Road* in 2006, about **Raasay** crofter Calum MacLeod who hand-built a road to his croft. The book was shortlisted for the Royal Society of Literature's Ondaatje Prize. There was no road from Brochel to Arnish two and a half kilometres north and the eight families living there were threatening to leave. Calum the local postman in 1966 bought a four-shilling book (20 pence) on road building and constructed the road himself.

The MacLeods of **Raasay** were Protestant but for some contrary reason they supported Bonnie Prince Charlie, the Young Pretender, and even sent 120 men to fight for him at Culloden. This was a bad mistake as in revenge Government troops destroyed homes and led a vicious campaign of murder, rape and looting. It was reported that in the aftermath "there was not left in the whole island a four-footed beast, a hen or a chicken."

Sue cooks for a band of Buddhists in a retreat near Callander in the Scottish Trossachs and she knew a couple of them who live as remote crofters near Stein in the north of **Skye**. She would stay with them and meditate; I would book into the nearby *Stein Inn* and not meditate. From a magazine I idly flicked through in my cosy room (there were no TVs) I discovered the inn was amongst Scotland's top 100 bars, a bedfellow with *Gleneagles* and the chic gin establishments emerging in Glasgow's Merchant City and Edinburgh's Georgian new town.

Accommodation booked, check; boats chartered, check. What could go wrong? Firstly, it is a three-hour round trip to both Kyleakin and Elgol from the Stein inn; secondly the weather was closing in. I settled into my new accommodation, popular with continental Europeans. [After Brexit

I continue to refer to myself as a British European]. Donald, the barman was dour in the good old Scottish tradition of dourness. He didn't lose his **Skye** accent for anyone, let alone our mainland European friends, rightly proud of their command of English. They would nervously ask for a table to be told to wait in a queue as booking was not part of the busy pub's ethos. Donald would serve drinks – alone- at his own pace, oblivious to the confused hordes of thirsty foreigners who were either too scared to challenge the man or didn't understand what he was saying. The result was organised chaos until 9pm (tired tourists eat early) when the bar would gradually empty to be replaced by the local fishermen and English tourists who, unlike their continental counterparts, don't just drink before dinner, but before, during and especially after.

Whilst observing this nightly ritual from the comfort of the only bar stool, my phone trilled and it was *Brigadoon's* skipper saying that the trip to **Rona** was on, but it would be a bit lumpy on the way back, whatever lumpy meant to a non-sailor. I relaxed with a glass or two of Tallisker with my newfound friends; a photographer called Steve who loved the *Stein* and **Skye,** a chef from Durham and his ex-England cricketer partner, Rachel.

The rooms in the *Stein* date back to 1790, making it the oldest pub in **Skye**, conjuring up images of smugglers and contraband. I slept as sound as I do these days anticipating a great trip to **Rona**. I'd invited Sue and her two crofter friends along and the next morning we left for Portree harbour to greet George and his *Brigadoon*. A covey of fishermen spied me and mockingly asked if I had my sea sickness pills. Answering to the negative I quickly retreated to Boots the chemist for a ready supply. The next few hours would be, for me, a nightmare and the boat certainly did not live up to its name. It was not idyllic and in no way remote from reality. We were to be pummelled fiercely by crashing waves for what seemed an eternity.

Brigadoon was unkempt and untidy, and shelter was confined to four shipmates. Most of the maximum complement of 12 as advertised would have got very wet. Once he had let his guard down George was easy to talk to and casually enquired if I had spoken to Bill Cowie. Bill had lived on the island for a good number of years, managing the estate for a Danish lady, Dorte Mette Jensen, who restored Rona Lodge at An Acarsaid Mhór, and built a new landing jetty. I replied to the negative and he slowed the engine. Contacting Mr Cowie would be a requirement as well as a £5 per head (more expense!) mooring fee, as the construction of a new jetty in this hostile environment clearly doesn't come cheap.

I phoned Bill who seemed pleasant enough. He had gone to **Rona** to recover from a broken marriage and now lived there with his new wife after many years alone. Now marriage is tough. I should know; I have married four times. But to live on a remote island cut off from civilisation for many months a year would really test marital resolve and patience, of which I have none. The COVID 19 2020 lockdown has tested many a happy family to its frayed limits. I spent that terrible time alone, so my only worry was my own mental resilience. I quickly developed Stockholm syndrome enjoying my captivity. Much of the research and writing of this book was done during this time of deep reflection.

Though Bill and his wife are the only permanent residents the population peaked in 1891 at 181. The common theme throughout the Islands and Highlands was greedy largely absentee landlords contemptuous of the residents eking out a miserable existence a step away from poverty. You can only poke a hornet's nest for so long and throughout the Western Isles what was left of the depleting population rose up in 1882 in retaliation in what became known as the battle of the Braes across in **Skye** opposite **Raasay**. The subsequent Crofter's Act of 1886 protected the few remaining holdings but failed to return dispossessed lands. Rona's fate was already sealed not helped by a contemporary description of the island as:

> "the most unequal rocky piece of ground to be seen anywhere……. To an ordinary observer its aspect is quite repulsive; presenting no picturesque features and but little verdure to chequer its grey and sterile surface".

A tad harsh I thought.

The journey of just over an hour was uneventful and cold with views limited on a grey, blustery day. We planned to walk across the island and were too timid to knock on Bill's door where Rona whisky and Rona postage stamps were on offer, along with showers and provisions for yachtsmen using the moorings. We walked towards Church Cave as far as the coll, the highest point on our rugged and slippery path, giving us spectacular views both to the north and the south. Discretion being the better part of valour we sensibly returned before the weather really set in. Bill was waiting and regaled us with his island stories before the return journey.

Now I know what lumpy means. We were heading into the wind and George admitted that any worse weather would have forced us back. His reluctance to do so was also anxiety as to where we would spend the night if marooned. I sat in the fore cabin biting my lip with every wave crashing across and over the bows. Some hour and three quarters later we made it to the calm of Portree harbour and bade farewell to a very relieved George. The sea sickness tablets were an essential buy.

My queasiness had subsided by the time I was dropped off at the *Stein Inn*, but I wanted fresh, clean air to banish my residual nausea. I took myself up to the ruins of Trumpan church above Ardmure Bay, scene in 1578 of one of the bloodiest episodes in Scottish history. The MacDonalds and the MacLeods were constantly at odds with each other and on this occasion the MacDonalds of Uist in the Outer Hebrides headed for the church to burn it down with all the MacLeods inside at worship. Their plan was thwarted and the MacLeods stormed the newly arrived boats in Ardmore Bay and slaughtered every last one of their sworn enemies. On my way back to the comfort of the inn I felt despair at the constant horrors of history with man the only mammal to habitually kill its own kind.

The skipper of the RIB seemed non-plussed about braving the elements to whisk me to **Scalpay** the next morning after an hour and a half's drive from the *Stein Inn*. A group of far eastern tourists were huddled together to experience the glass bottomed boat trip whilst I was directed to a 12-seater RIB with the young skipper who although in his mid-twenties had only left Scotland once and didn't like it, but then he did choose the Canaries. I ventured to Tenerife to visit an old university friend once, just to prove it wasn't for me. Ensconced amongst the karaoke bars of Playa de las Americas, selling San Miguel at a Euro a pint I was proved right. My companion to **Scalpay** had left his job salmon farming in Torridon to settle back in his beloved Broadford vowing never to leave, and who could blame him.

We set off in the RIB riding effortlessly over the heavy waves. "Aye, these don't worry about the weather", muttered my agile companion. Not so agile, I was thrown against a modest steel rail and decided for my safety that despite the cold and lack of gloved protection I would grab this rail till my knuckles were white and freezing. We scudded under the Skye Bridge heading past Pabay with the Crowlin Islands and Applecross (on the mainland) in the distance. The skipper's boss was born on Pabay, but this small flat island is now not permanently occupied. I'd hired the RIB for 1 and a half hours at £120 per hour so time was at a premium. Squally showers were mixed with warm sunshine, and we reached **Scalpay** in 40 minutes.

I walked to Scalpay house and back up a muddy track with the sort of views across Loch na Cairidh that entices tourists to **Skye**. After 30 minutes of reflection, we were back on the sea speeding with the wind back to port. My young friend racked up the speed under the Skye bridge to 42 knots, an exhilarating few minutes of adrenaline pumping pure joy. The high cost of rental was dissipated with the elation of this short trip. Money like time (if you have both) is a relative construct.

Dean Munro, a clergyman often known as Dean of the Isles described **Scalpay** in 1549 as:

> "..a fair hunting forest, full of deer, with certain little woods and small towns, well inhabited and manured, with many strong coves, good for fishing".

The island is now owned by a merchant banker and farmed by his son. The rich still hunt deer on **Scalpay** but rather for sport than sustenance.

I spied after leaving the RIB that The *Bella Jayne* was docked at Kylekin, and this explained the phone call I received from the captain back at the *Stein Inn* postponing my trip. I now, for once, had time on my hands and thought I would drive to Elgol to get my money reimbursed. The office was closed but the road to Elgol gave inspiring views of the Cuillin Ridge in the glory of ever-changing moods brought on by minute-by-minute changes in the weather. It had been a good day, but **Soay** was for another time, if ever.

My last evening in Stein was enhanced by a well-to-do group enjoying the Easter holiday break. The garrulous head of the party regaled us with stories of her grandfather, the *Daily Mirror* columnist, William Connor, who used the by-line, Cassandra. Diaries found after his death had not been published at the express wish of his wife. We discussed their content with accounts of the scandals of celebrities of the 1950's and 1960's; a social history treasure trove probably lost for ever. In 1959 one of the most extraordinary libel trials of all time took place in Britain. The flamboyant American entertainer Liberace had sued Cassandra for implying that he was homosexual (not legal in those days). Connor, who didn't hold back his disgust for the pianist, wrote that Liberace was:

> "...the summit of sex - the pinnacle of masculine, feminine, and neuter. Everything that he, she, and it can ever want... a deadly, winking, sniggering, snuggling, chromium-plated, scent-impregnated, luminous, quivering, giggling, fruit-flavoured, mincing, ice-covered heap of mother love."

Liberace won the case and was awarded a then-record £8,000 in damages (about £500,000 in today's money). At the height of our fake news culture, we expect such outrage from the right-wing tabloids these days, but not the *Mirror*.

The party left and I retired to the bar and was rewarded with a giant

Talisker bought by two well-heeled honeymooners (in advertising in London) who had escaped the clipped luxury of the £350 per night *Two Chimneys* boutique hotel and Michelin star restaurant in Dunvegan to taxi to a real pub. They were "mini mooning" after a lavish wedding at the hotel in which the opening wedding (Angus to Laura) in *"Four weddings and a Funeral"* had been set.

Donald called last orders and Donald didn't mess around. "But our taxi is not coming till midnight" the unhappy couple implored. "Then you'll have to wait outside" was his gruff retort, and promptly closed the bar. It was raining hard and not like the England of eternal summer, a land which consists almost entirely of green and pleasant countryside, as portrayed by Richard Curtis' films. I was summarily despatched to bed with a long drive home the next day.

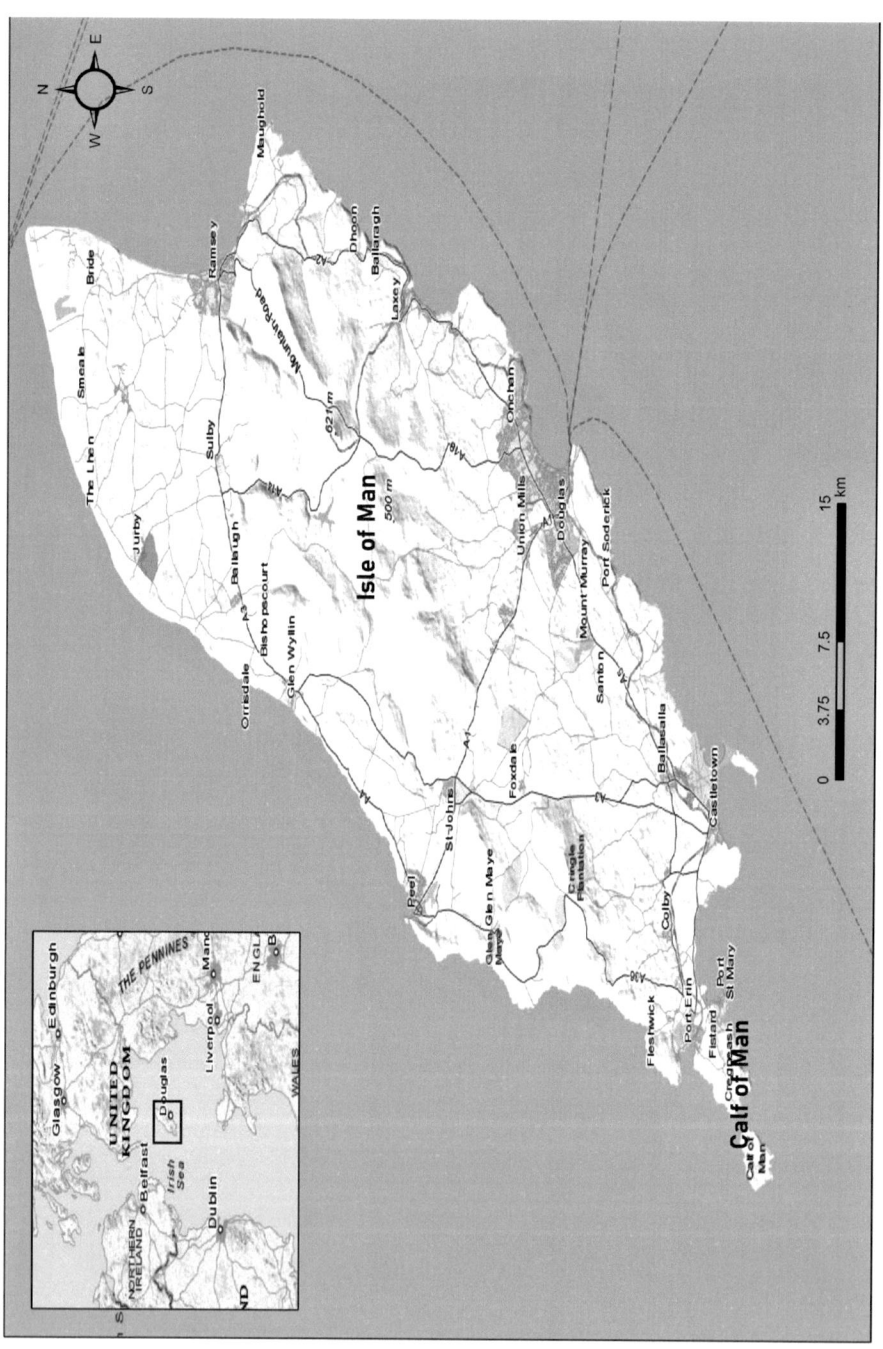

The Isle (and calf) of Man, a UK Crown Dependency

14. The Isle (and Calf) of Man, a UK Crown Dependency

I'd been to the **Isle of Man** three times before. The first time was a lifetime ago when I visited Peel where my second wife had a friend. I seemed to remember we spent all our time in the *Creek Inn* and recall little else. The second time was a quick trip from Liverpool to Douglas. My teenage daughter, Lauren, had never flown so I surprised her and Liverpool Sue's daughter, Mary, with a couple of days away. I seemed to remember we spent much of the trip in A&E courtesy of my bad bout of gout, lightened (for the girls) only when, much to the amusement of Lauren and Mary a triage nurse accidentally stood on the offending big toe. The third time my work took me there to train staff on asset inspections at Manx Utilities.

This time I again was serendipitously asked to go back to provide further training. This was to be too good an opportunity to miss out on especially getting a trip to the **Calf of Man** which is inhabited six months on and six months off by a conservation warden. Research suggested it might not be permanently inhabited but I adopted an insurance policy in case its residency status changed.

Detailed planning was required as was the case with most islands where populations are tiny and commercial ferries non-existent. I rang a boat operative in Port Erin, the nearest harbour to the Calf and was directed to Bob at Port St Mary who owned *Gemini*. A genial sounding guy answered the telephone and was happy to oblige but concerned about whether I could afford the trip by myself on his 12-seater charter boat. I explained the project and a date plus a fee was set. The forecast didn't look good for the elected day with near gale force winds predicted. It was May but that means very little weatherise in the unpredictable Irish Sea. I was woken on the Sunday morning before the trip and the worst was confirmed. The trip was off for at least 2 days, but a window was expected on the evening of 17th May. I held my breath.

The **Isle of Man** is an hour's flight from Birmingham on a Stobart air Flybe propeller aircraft. The modern airport at what used to be called Ronaldsway was quiet and reminded me of the sort of airport being revamped now in small towns and cities across the former Soviet bloc. It was a couple of weeks before the annual TT race where maniacal motorcycle riders attempt the 37 and three-quarter mile circuit at speeds in excess of 200 mph. The Dunlop family are legendary competitors, with Joey notching up 26 wins in several categories between 1977 and 2000. Guy Martin, whose easy northern twang has made him quite a TV celebrity, is also famed, largely because as of 2016 he has never won despite his natural prowess as a racer.

Michael Dunlop recorded the fastest lap in 2016 of 16 minutes 53.929 seconds or an average speed of 133.962 mph. It sounds like, and is, breath takingly stupid on what are after all normal country roads wending through otherwise tranquil scenery. Houses and spectators are only protected by flimsy cushioning. Some 251 fatalities have been recorded since its inception in 1907 including 110 spectators and other non-competitors. The *Tourist Trophy*, for that is what TT stands for, is one of the oldest motor sports races in the world.

The **Isle of Man** is also known to the rest of the world as a tax haven, just like its sister 'Crown Dependency' the Channel Islands where the likes of the Barclay brothers, who owned the Daily Telegraph, hide their ill-gotten loot from the HMRC, a tax evasion of mind-numbing arrogance. It has, from Victorian times, been a favourite holiday destination for the UK, especially from the north of England before the advent of cheap package tours to the continent. Ferries ply across the Irish sea from Heysham in Lancashire and Liverpool. My uncle Jack was a regular visitor in the 1930's where he and his pals would stay in male only camps for a fortnight. He used to brag that for five pounds you could get a fortnight's holiday and still have change for fish and chips in Settle on the coach journey back to his native Skipton.

Ask a British citizen what is meant by a Crown Dependency and he or she will stare blankly. However, farcically one of the favourite questions in *Life in the UK* tests for those seeking UK citizenship is to name a Crown Dependency (well now you know) and a Crown Protectorate. The latter, better known as British Overseas Territories, are the motley assortment of countries that are the rump of Britain's Imperial rule, like Gibraltar, the Falkland Islands and Pitcairn Islands or the Cayman Islands – the daddy of all offshore tax evasion territories. I have a barrister friend, Andrew, who each year is summoned to one of these BOT's, St Helena, to represent miscreants as there is no judiciary on the island.

Maybe my next venture should be a visit to each of the current list of 14, mostly remote islands and with a combined population of little more than 200,000. Now that would be a challenge. The strangest of these is Pitcairn home, in the middle of the Pacific, to 67 inbred souls mostly descendants from the mutiny on the *Bounty*. On 28th April 1789, led by Acting Lieutenant Fletcher Christian, disaffected crewmen seized control of the ship from their captain, Lieutenant William Bligh, and set him and 18 loyalists adrift in the ship's open launch.

Talking of the Empire I stayed for three nights at *The Empress hotel* on Loch Promenade, Douglas overlooking the Irish Sea. It was full of the northern elderly on coach tours. Even though I too am elderly I never mix with my age cohort, and it was quite disconcerting watching those of my age with the afflictions associated with longevity; they too like myself would have frequented 1960's pop venues in Liverpool's Cavern or London's Oxford Club or the legendary Marquee club on Wardour Street. Now these baby boomers are cannon fodder for the real rulers of our nation, the press Barons. It was four weeks before the 2017 General Election, called by the unelected Prime Minister, Theresa May, to bolster her support for a hard Brexit.

These *Daily Mail* and *Sun* readers are being fed distortions at best and lies at worst and, despite the erosion of their NHS, their pensions and their heating allowances not to mention their grandchildren's education, will blindly vote Tory, or Team May as the Conservatives seemed then to be called. It's like turkeys voting for Christmas. At breakfast I heard one lady blurt "Them on benefits, they've all got dogs you know". Another said with scathing menace "Do you know I've got a friend who gets £2,000 a month as a nurse for working two days a week; and those Corbyn commies say they need to rely on food banks". I cringed into my Manx kippers, yet another symbol, like the tail-less cat, of the **Isle of Man**.

I had a successful day's training and found the *Queens* public house for a couple of pints of Okell's excellent local beer, where topers were talking about nothing but the upcoming TT, all torque and fuel tank slap. To escape this tedium, I retired rain soaked to the *Empress* piano bar. The pianist in residence was strangling old favourites like *Lara's Theme* from *Dr Zhivago,* a film most of the residents would be only too familiar with from the 1967 David Lean epic starring the impossibly beautiful Julie Christie and the inimitable Omar Shariff. I met my first real girlfriend, Anne, whilst watching the film in the *Empire* Leicester Square. The nostalgia of Empire seemed to be a feature of this trip.

The weather was still poor, and I strolled down the promenade in between squalls. There is a memorial to the RNLI, the Royal National Lifeboat Institute, formed originally as the *National Institution for the Preservation of Life from Shipwreck* in 1824 by Sir William Hilary, a Manx resident. The Tower of Refuge was a memorial to the shipwreck of the *St George* on Conister Rock at the entrance to Douglas harbour. Sir William skippered the lifeboat to rescue all on board. The work of the RNLI is legendary; there were 8,462 lifeboat launches in 2014, rescuing 8,727 people, including saving 460 lives.

My phone trilled. It was Bob. "Meet me at the outer harbour in Port St Mary at five thirty this evening". He sounded enthusiastic. "Are you fit", he asked? "Not really", I replied. I pressed the phone off and mused as to why he asked this question. After all I was only going to climb a few steps from the mooring to *terra firma*. The day was quite superb with not a cloud in the sky and the sea as flat calm as it ever gets in these parts. I couldn't wait till the evening. I arrived at the appointed meeting point to be greeted by Bob, Dave from Manx radio's morning show, his wife, and another Dave and a guy called Mark. Quite a reception committee I didn't expect. We set off heading past the stacks and sea cliffs to the southeast of Man with bird life in profusion and a fleeting glimpse of marine life. After 30 minutes the **Calf of Man** was in sight and soon we were within feet of the rocky, treacherous looking shore, with a colony of seals a hundred or more strong within touching distance. Landing was going to be impossible without serious damage to *Gemini*.

I expected Bob to shrug his shoulders and head for port. Not a bit of it and now I saw his cunning plan. I had paid to land on the island and land we would. This is where the two Dave's and Mark came in. Ropes and boat hooks were deployed with the ropes threaded through iron rings, one on a rocky outcrop and the other on the **Calf**. *Gemini* was wedged in position with slack and taut ordered by Bob with military precision. I was worried but managed with some discomfort to tip toe on the outcrop with bemused seals looking on. "Don't suppose that'll do?" Bob asked. The younger Dave was now despatched to "the mainland" with the agility of some of the Loaghtan sheep which we had seen grazing at impossibly precarious angles on the cliffs above us.

I was coaxed from the boat in a makeshift bosun's chair to stand on the **Calf** whilst the crew were responding to Bob's pleas for slack and taut. "That's enough", I spluttered and attempted to re-join my ship mates, but stability took some ten minutes with some heart in the mouth moments. I can hardly bend these days, but a shot of adrenalin dissipated both fear and infirmity. Back on board we traced two of Bob's lobster pots, both containing trapped crustaceans but both too small or too pregnant to keep. Bob nonchalantly returned them to the deep, re-bated the pots and set off back to harbour.

It had been a memorable journey with a wonderful support crew. I paid my modest excursion fee, got a lift to the bus stop at Port Erin and set off happily back to the flesh pots of Douglas for the princely sum of £3.10. What a delightful bus ride with hardly half a dozen passengers getting on during the 80-minute trip, including a stop at the by now deserted airport. Bus stops were all named, including the delightfully prosaic *Brown cow cattery* and the *Isle of Man rest home for old horses*.

15. A FEW CONVENIENT ORKNEY ISLANDS, SCOTLAND

The summer of 2017 saw a snap general election called by Prime Minister May in order to secure the overwhelming mandate she felt was sure and give her a carte blanche for the hardest of hard Brexits. A Remain campaigner, she like all converts, became a zealot to her new cause with her Cabinet with equal zeal campaigning for the impossible, self-flagellation at the expense of Britain's standing in the World. The vote on June 8th should have been the death rattle of ill-conceived and half-baked policies in the wake of a stolid block by Juncker, the President of the European Commission, and his disconsolate 27 member states. She won with a much-reduced majority and mandate but lumbered on in self-delusion likely to suffer her "*Et Tu Brute*" moment at any time.

The reality of Brexit, with a 'No deal' seeming very probable, was unlikely to herald in a future making 'Britain Great Again' in the same retrogressive vein as mid America's MAGA generation. It foreshadowed a poorer Britain with obstacles to trade, human rights, environmental justice, free movement and working conditions. The Brexiteers were promised £350 million a week in additional NHS funding, 'taking back control' from so-called despotic faceless 'unelected' mandarins in Europe and the cessation of uncontrolled immigration. The reality is that a paralysis of travel and free movement of goods was likely. Restrictions on European's living, working and travelling to the UK has backfired in the faces of those who voted "leave" as after withdrawal their movements to live, work and travel to EU member states would also be restricted.

Meanwhile Jeremy Corbyn suffered hateful smear campaigning of his and Labour's unfounded endemic racism and anti-Semitism orchestrated by the wealthy press barons. Their tax privileges would at last have been

TREASURED ISLANDS

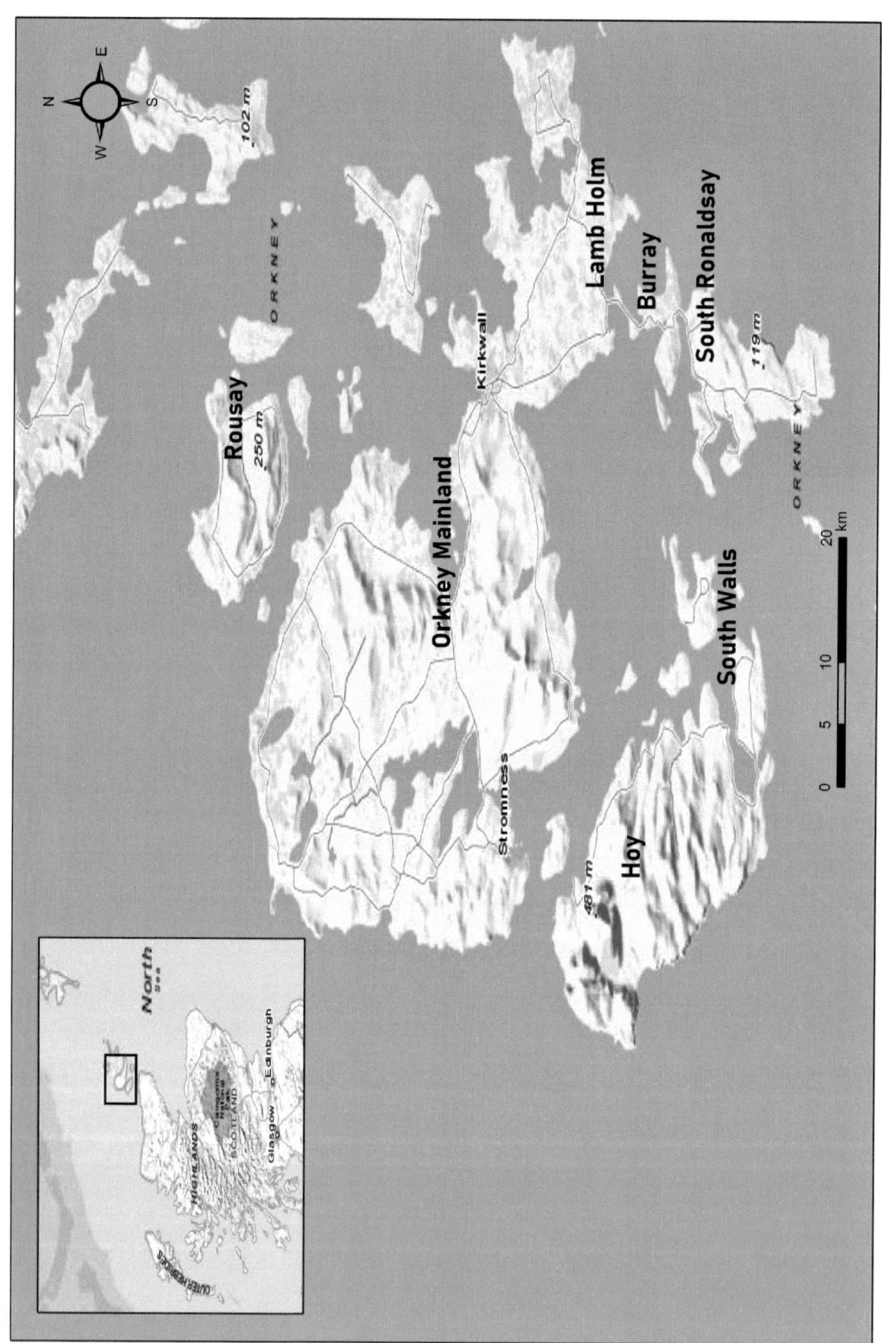

A few convenient Orkney islands, Scotland

denied by a so-called Socialist Government. The rallying cry of red top reading working class Tories is "we don't want to be taken back to the Britain of the 1970's". I was amused by one tweet I read: "I for one welcome the lack of medicine and doctors after Brexit, the Victorians got on OK taking heroin, blaming demons for bad moods and fixing headaches with hammers and that was when BRITAIN WAS REALLY GREAT".

The following week found me in Edinburgh known as the 'Athens of the North' or more disparagingly, 'Auld Reekie'. It is a city surpassing magnificence in my opinion. What is now the picturesque Princes Street Gardens, was once the drainage site, outside the city, for the citizenry's waste and effluence, as well as a popular site for dumping dead bodies. The foul smell that would thus rise from its stagnant waters was overwhelming; hence the name Auld Reekie.

I have spent many years in August at the Edinburgh Fringe following Bob in his various comedic enterprises and memories are rekindled on each visit. The *Café Royal* in West Register Street never fails to satisfy with its cosy dining area and Enlightenment wall ceramics of the luminaries who made the city what it is. As though I had come home to roost my venue for the week for my SEPA (Scottish Environmental Protection Agency) lectures was next door to the *Café Royal* in the grandeur of the National Statistics Office. The week was spoilt by the news of the Grenfell Tower disaster in west London for which the Tories were already deflecting blame onto the residents, the brave fire fighters and anyone else but them that they could muster as culpable.

I had driven to Edinburgh and after the business end was over continued onto Gills Bay on the Scottish north coast to take a ferry to the Orkney Islands and hence to conquer the 15 or so inhabited islands of the Shetland islands. I was joined on this venture by Ian, a larger-than-life solicitor, who as a keen photographer would record the adventures ahead.

We made a stop at John O' Groats so I could bring back treasured memories of the halfway point of my walk around Great Britain. I spotted a trio of cyclists who had just completed the journey from Land's End. I contributed to their charity and mentioned my walk. They seemed embarrassed that a grey-haired old man with a lazy gait would brag about such an implausible feat.

We stayed overnight at the *Castletown hotel* in Castletown a dozen or so miles from the ferry port. Although mid-June the temperature was autumnal and the sparsely furnished rooms cold and unwelcoming. The weather was a portend of things to come in the far northern islands of Britain.

The crossing to St Margaret's Hope on **South Ronaldsay** using the Pentland Ferries, was a pleasant hour's journey. Our Northlink ferry to Lerwick on **Mainland Shetland** didn't leave till almost midnight the following day so we checked into the *Murray Arms* at St Margaret's Hope with a view to visiting a number of easy island pickings on the Orkneys. Causeways known as the Churchill Barriers, link **South Ronaldsay** to **Burray** and **Burray** to **Mainland** (as the most populated islands on both Orkney and Shetland are called).

In October 1939, just as the Second World War was getting started, a German U boat sank the Royal Navy battleship *HMS Royal Oak* and to prevent further attacks Winston Churchill, first Lord of the Admiralty at the time, ordered the barriers to be built. The construction was really a red herring as the construction was not officially opened until four days after VE day in May 1945. Such was its complexity that 1,200 Italian prisoners of war were commandeered to build it, in contravention of the Geneva convention which forbade prisoners of war from engaging in projects to support the war effort. At whatever cost the Barriers now allow unfettered road travel from **South Ronaldsay** to Kirkwall, Orkney's capital.

The drive skirted the infamous Scapa Flow where on 21st June 1919 whilst awaiting their fate after the end of the First World War the German commander, Admiral Ludwig von Reuter, decided to scuttle the fleet rather than hand the ships over to the Allies. Some 52 of the 74 vessels were sunk and though salvage operations continued for decades the carcasses of some, now popular with divers, are evident almost 100 years later.

Orkney with about 70 main islands of which around 20 are inhabited, is pastoral and, unlike its neighbouring Shetland Islands, at a low enough latitude for trees to flourish. The islands have been part of Scotland since 1472 when they were annexed from Norway for failure of payment of a dowry by King Christian of Norway and Denmark for James III's bride Margaret, maid of Norway.

It was on **South Ronaldsay** that first commercial attempts were made to harness wind power, but use of early turbines was thwarted by high maintenance costs making electricity costs prohibitively expensive. These were the pioneering days when sustainable energy sources were regarded as quirky experiments. How times have changed. May 2020 saw the first week that not a single watt of electricity was generated by coal fired power stations in the UK.

To pass the time, we travelled rather aimlessly around **Mainland** and picked a random ferry from Tingwall to **Rousay** after visiting the village of Twatt, which has a sister settlement on **Mainland** Shetland. We giggled like naughty schoolboys and Ian rather predictably photographed the road sign. This linguistic double entendre is matched by such other rude British place names as Cocks, Cornwall, Minge Lane, Upton-upon-Severn, Worcestershire, and Bell End also in Worcestershire. It had to be done though we wondered why the road sign was still in place. Indeed, on returning two years later the sign had been removed, either as a trophy or by embarrassed locals. The only evidence of the village name is now etched on the church sign board.

Rousay has been nicknamed 'the Egypt of the north', due to its archaeological diversity and importance with over 160 archaeological sites identified, and we had a couple of hours to explore before the twenty-minute ferry ride back to Tingwall. We chose Taversöe Tuick with two burial chambers, one above the other, an arrangement seen at only one other Orkney tomb. It was a short walk up hill from the ferry and exposed my total lack of fitness. The discovery of the rich vein of cairns, brochs and burial chambers in both **Rousay** and neighbouring islands was made possible through funding in the 1930's by the whisky magnate Walter Grant who lived in Trumland House near the ferry terminal.

Our smugness at securing this bonus island was short lived when we discovered that I would have to return in the future as the ferry to the nearby islands of **Egilsay** and **Wyre** call first at **Rousay**. We would have been better selecting an island with sole access from **Mainland** but like many of my island visits they are poorly planned and spontaneous rather than well organised.

We discussed which island to visit prior to our midnight sailing the following night and chose **Hoy**, sailing from Houton on **Mainland** to Lyness with a conveniently timed Sunday sailing only to discover that again I needed to go there at a later date to secure **Flotta**. The booking clerk was concerned at my disappointment that the Sunday ferry didn't dock at **Flotta** as she was adamant that "there was little of interest to make the journey worthwhile". This flat island, hence the Norse name, was a tranquil farming community until in 1974, Occidental Petroleum started construction of the island's oil terminal. This became the second largest oil terminal serving the UK North Sea, especially the Piper fields, the largest being Sullom Voe in Shetland.

I have always wanted to visit **Hoy**, especially the Old Man of Hoy, ever since being captivated by the exploits of Chris Bonington, my boyhood mountaineering hero. This 137 metre old red sandstone sea stack, the tallest sea stack in the British Isles, will certainly succumb to the elements someday but its status remains iconic. The stack was first climbed by Bonington, Rusty Baillie and Tom Patey in 1966 and about 50 climbers negotiate the climb each year with the 1966 route classed as extremely severe. In 2014, at the age of 80 Chris re-climbed the Old Man to raise awareness and funds for motor neurone disease charities in memory of his wife Wendy. When I think of the meagre pains that I constantly moan about I think of this amazing feat.

We took the car over to **Hoy** to drive to Rackwick where a three-mile walk would disgorge us on the high cliffs overlooking the Old Man. We ate our improvised lunch on a fine afternoon transfixed by this geological spectacle that I had admired for so long. It reared up above the cliffs just metres away from our picnic spot, so close we could almost touch it.

Hoy is the highest, wildest and wettest island in the Orkney archipelago and contrasts in its geography from all the other islands with Ward Hill its highest, roughest peak defying the bucolic low-lying landscapes of virtually all other islands. A chill was setting in as we retraced our steps, noting that temperatures in England had soared to 33 degrees.

On reaching our car we passed the Dwarfie stone a short distance from the almost deserted Rackwick. This is reputed to be the only example in northern Europe of a rock cut tomb similar to those in the Mediterranean region. It has been the subject of many necromantic legends with Sir Walter Scott no less beguiled by sightings of a giant and his wife who made this tomb their retreat.

We drove south to **South Walls** which in my opinion is an island in its own right separated from **Hoy** by a causeway though its population is counted with that of **Hoy** in the Scottish census. I didn't want some know all pointing out sometime in the future that I'd missed the island and its small settlement of Longhope, so we made a deliberate decision to make footfall. Although the Scottish islands *Appendix of the 2011 Scottish census of inhabited islands* makes no reference to **South Walls**, it has as much right to be considered separate as **Burray** and **South Ronaldsay** or **East** and **West Burra** on Shetland, all connected by similar causeways.

We were early for the return ferry so, observing a Russian flag, we stumbled across the Russian memorial to the Word War Two north Atlantic convoys near the *Hoy Hotel*. The four-year struggle to provide material to support the Soviet war effort cost the lives of around 3,000 sailors and merchant seamen. Over 100 civilian and military ships were lost, with the nadir coming in the summer of 1942 when convoy PQ17 was mauled by the Luftwaffe and nine U-boats. The memorial was poignant but around the compound was an array of dilapidating military armaments and other paraphernalia, a sad postscript to a brave campaign.

Saddened we took refuge in the *Hoy Hotel*, an establishment as cold as charity with three lone drinkers that Sunday afternoon. A request for a cup of tea was greeted with some incredulity. This was like Peter Kay's *Phoenix Nights*. The juke box was playing Willie Nelson's version of "You were always on my mind" a melancholic refrain of missed opportunities. The sparse audience were in deep reflection with few words spoken.

On arriving back on **Mainland**, we still had several hours to while away before the ferry to Lerwick so, tide willing I was to 'tick off' two more islands listed in the Scottish census but not part of Hamish Haswell-Smith's islands as they were smaller than his cut off limit of 40 hectares.

We arrived in Stromness and found a bleak hotel to gather sustenance and await the falling tide. We found a route to **Inner Holm**, home to a handful of folks but a foot crossing was impossible. The tides were not willing though the daylight was as we were now at mid-Summer in what the Russians call "White nights". Time was also not on our side, so we abandoned hope of securing **Inner Holm** in Stromness harbour and set our sights on the causeway leading to the **Holm of Grimbister** just east of Finstown and on our way to the Shetland ferry. The causeway was not quite clear of the tide and in the impending gloom reluctantly we left the crossing for another time catching a pre-ferry pint in a busy Kirkwall bar.

16. The Shetland Islands and Fair Isle, Scotland

I was first in the ferry queue which meant, at 07:30 the next morning, I would be first off or so I thought. The ferry marshals waved me forward and then, to my absolute horror, asked me to back onto the ferry. My reversing is renowned for being abysmal and I have broken many taillights to verify this. "Just reverse at an angle between that HGV trailer and that coach" the marshal cheerily instructed. I had only had a single pint all day, but my attempts were atrocious, and I was summarily asked to vacate the driver's seat for the manoeuvre to be made for me. I held my head in shame and headed for the passenger deck to watch re-runs of some football game or other. Bedtime beckoned as we had a busy day island hopping in the morning and I went off to find my pre-booked 'pod'. Ian opted for the empty ship's cinema, a tip given to us by the bar staff as the performance had ended for the night and lights were dim.

I found my allotted pre-booked pod in a room crammed with maybe a hundred passengers cooped like chickens in a battery farm, in various stages of undress and with various levels of nocturnal utterings. Claustrophobia kicked in and I fled to the cinema for some fitful sleep before morning. The ferry landed on time, and we declined breakfast on the boat and headed for our second, third, and fourth islands (**Mainland Shetland** being the first). **Trondra, West Burra and East Burra** were reached from Scalloway via road bridges and all three were secured within the hour and we headed back to Lerwick for breakfast and our first encounter with the island's capital, our home for the next ten days.

First impressions were a disappointing slew of mediocrity, made worse by the constant summer chill to be expected at these latitudes. **West Burra** was to be my first fifth order island (**Great Britain** to **Mainland**

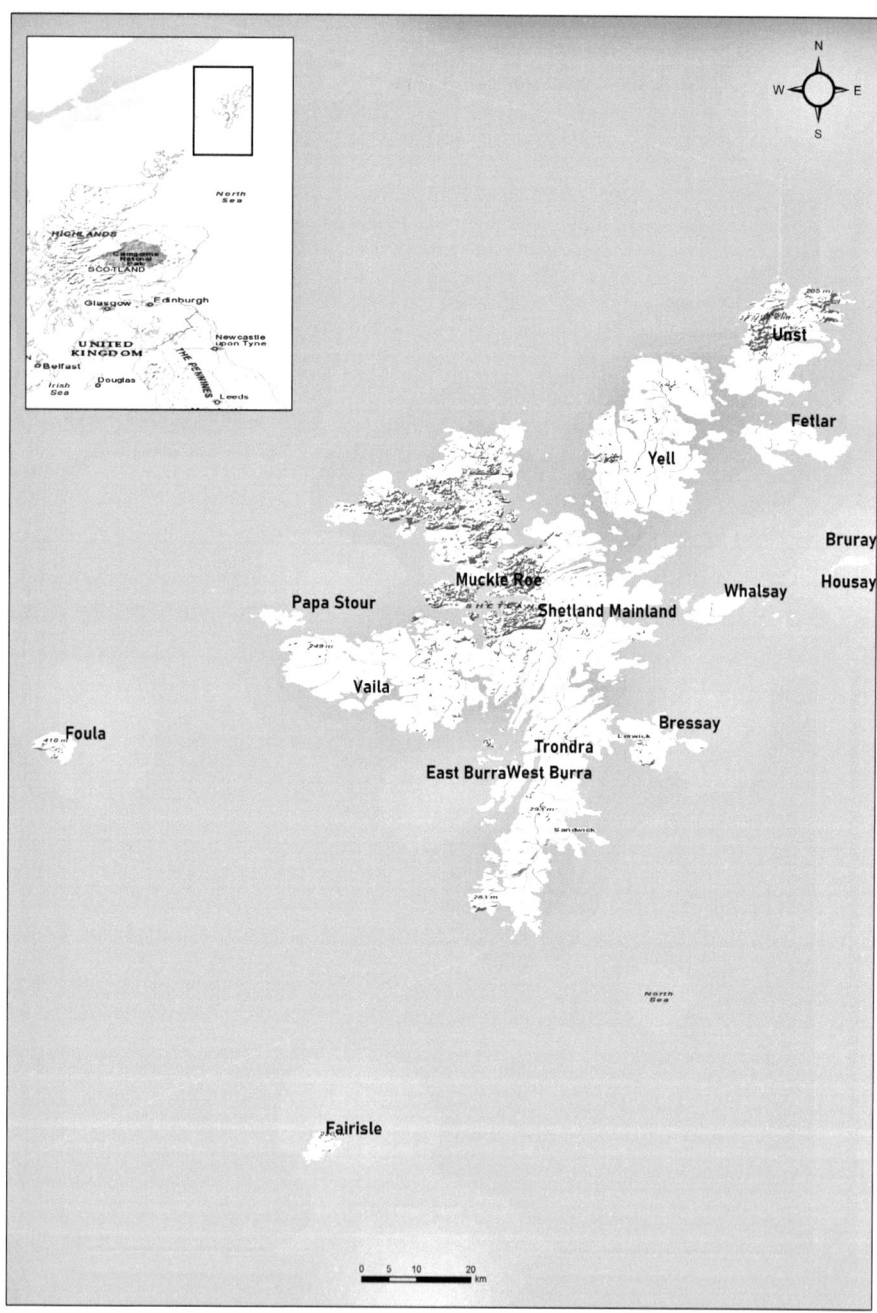

The Shetland Islands and Fair Isle, Scotland

Shetland to **Trondra** to **East Burra** and finally, **West Burra**). Sated and satisfied at this most auspicious start we discovered the frequent RoRo to **Bressay** sailed from Lerwick harbour. Five islands by ten o'clock in the morning, now that was an achievement! These Scalloway islands were becoming alarmingly and rapidly depopulated before being connected to the **Mainland** by the road bridges. **West Burra** and its main settlement of Hamnavoe are now within easy commuting distance to Lerwick.

The previous March I had gone to Tierra del Fuego, or the Land of Fire at the bottom of the World. The southern latitude of Ushuaia, dubbed the southernmost city in the World, is at 54 degrees actually only as far south as Newcastle upon Tyne is north. Lerwick is really north. The remoteness of the Shetlands from even mainland Scotland is never really fully appreciated as British map makers always put the islands into an inset. In October 2018 a Scottish law was passed to place Shetland in its rightful place on maps of Scotland. The reality is that Lerwick is closer to Bergen, Norway than Aberdeen. Even more staggering is that the remote northern-most landfall in Shetland at Muckle Flugga off the island of **Unst** is further from the Scottish/English border than the border is to Land's End.

The Norsemen held sway here for centuries as a staging post for their territorial raids elsewhere in the North Atlantic from Ireland to Greenland and beyond. They could read the Atlantic swell and were simply the finest of navigators. Their name for Shetland was *Hetland* or *Hjaltland* meaning high land and a number of alternative suggestions have had scholarly support before Shetland became the established name for this group of 30 islands of substantial size of which 16 are currently inhabited. A 17th was permanently inhabited during the first months of the COVID 19 crisis in 2020 when Chris Lewis an ex-soldier and his dog, Jet self-isolated on the 108-acre island of Hildasay after a walk of over 12,000 miles from his home in Swansea. At the time of writing, he was still walking the British islands and tackling the thankless task of cleaning up the flotsam and jetsam on beaches on the way.

The terrain of **Mainland** is mostly smooth and low and covered with rough grass and heather and upland peat. Its highest point, Ronas Hill rises only to 450m. The contrast with **Orkney Mainland** came as a shock as we drove to the Scalloway islands of **Trondra** and both the **Burra** islands which have a distinct Scandinavian feel in architecture and civic amenity. Trees are largely absent at this latitude 60 degrees north and on a par with the southern tip of Greenland.

Lerwick harbour is in the lee of the Isle of **Bressay**. Its sheltered position might explain why it became the Shetland Island's capital. Neither Lerwick nor **Bressay** could exist without the other. It was said that in the 15th century one could step from boat to boat to get from Lerwick to **Bressay**, the Dutch being predominant in the burgeoning herring industry.

We took the car on the short ferry ride to explore the island as on the west side is the National Nature Reserve of Noss separated from **Bressay** by the Noss Sound. We drove to a vantage point above the sound and contemplated a ferry crossing, but the ferry was not running on Mondays, so we satisfied ourselves in the knowledge that no permanent residents live there. We discussed whether we were looking at the Atlantic or the North Sea, a tricky question for geographers.

The sandstone cliffs of Noss have weathered into a series of horizontal ledges making ideal breeding grounds for gannets, puffins, guillemots, shags, black-legged kittiwakes, razorbills, fulmars and great skuas. The excitement mounted as we attempted some primitive ornithology. We had heard that Orca whales had been spotted in the sound, but we were not fortunate to see them. They leave the deep ocean to prey on seals marooned on rocky outcrops that become inundated at high tide, easy pickings for some of the world's most cunning and dangerous but possibly misunderstood predators.

We had no binoculars to try to identify the myriad of sea birds (even if we knew what we were looking at) so retired to the bleak interior of the *Maryfield Hotel* for mid-morning coffee. We'd after all accomplished a lot already that day and had yet to find a base for our stay. I panicked at this point as we poured through *booking.com* and Shetland tourist literature small ads for suitable premises. It was high season and accommodation would be at a premium or so we thought. Rather than calmly reviewing options I, in my "bull in a china shop" fashion, opted for the expensive *Harbour View* self-catering with four bedrooms (two of which would be redundant to our needs). This was not cheap and for some reason I have never quite fathomed, I discovered I was subsidising Ian, for the pleasure of his company I assumed. My motto has always been to "throw money at the problem". At least we now had a base convenient for the 'flesh pots' of Lerwick.

It was from Bressay Sound that Harald Hardrada's ships sailed south in 1066 to be defeated by the last crowned Anglo-Saxon king, Harold Godwinson at Stamford Bridge in Yorkshire. Known to all as King Harold his success was short lived being pummelled on all sides first by the Vikings in the north and finally at the Battle of Hastings by William the Conqueror. England would, except from a couple of quirky infringements, never be defeated in battle again, thus fermenting the exceptionalism of the landed classes which has lasted for just short of a thousand years.

On our return we paid a king's ransom to a Lerwick solicitor, based on the main thoroughfare, Commercial Street, who owned a number of residential lets, and settled down to our "holiday", exploring the town. Cruise ships love the place and dock for about four hours a day when the town is awash with thousands of Koreans or Germans, but at other times the town centre, apart from locals going about their business, is largely deserted.

Our visit coincided with the increasingly popular Bergen to Lerwick yacht race which was first held in 1986 attracting only three entries, two of whom failed to finish, leaving Bjarne Moster, the original organiser, to complete it on his own! These days over 40 yachtsmen and women compete, and the town was crowded with very fit, very tall, very blond, very sea weathered Scandinavians.

Our task that first night was to source eating and drinking establishments. These were quirky in the extreme. *Da Wheel* on Commercial Street with menacing clientele was rated two stars on Trip Advisor, and that is very generous; *The Hoy Hotel* had much less edge but could have been any dreary commercial hotel in any part of the United Kingdom. *The Thule bar*, even more menacing, was not even rated but *Captain Flint's* with three and a half stars was a passable upstairs pub with bright attentive staff and, if you were lucky, local cask ale.

The Lerwick rugby club use it for three-day benders and get off their faces on Gilk – a mixture of Gin and Milk – and tasting as revolting as it sounds. Now the rugby club is affiliated to the Scottish Rugby Union who subsidise their away games. Think about it: Kirkwall in Orkney is their local derby, a seven-hour ferry ride away with Aberdeen 15 hours away for connecting with mainland Scotland fixtures. Their favourite fixture is Stornaway in the Outer Hebrides and how they get there, probably flying, is subject to very complex logistics. An eighty-minute game can involve a three-day absence and some serious drinking!

The Queens Hotel and *The Grand* (owned by one and the same company) are throwbacks from a bygone age, the former with passable bar food. Other than that, there was *Monterey Jacks*, a pizza joint worth one flying visit, a Thai restaurant with extortionate prices and *Da Steakhoose*, which though appealing, was about as easy to get a reservation for as getting into Fort Knox. We systematically failed on every night of trying resorting to the excellent *Harbour* fish bar. We were even allowed to consume their products in the comfort of *Captain Flint's*, which became our evening hostelry of choice.

So that was our evening territory marked out for ten or so days. The self-catering accommodation, not that we would be doing much of that, was between five- and ten-minutes' walk from all these salubrious 'flesh pots'. The digs themselves were adequate if not bland and soulless and once the central heating was fixed (it was June after all!) our HQ was established.

We had eleven further islands to visit using RoRo ferries, conventional ferries, road bridges or flights with one island, **Vaila**, near the village of Walls, off **Mainland**, privately owned with no public access. I had studied timetables of flights and ferries over many weeks and thought I had a semblance of a plan, a fragile plan, but a plan, nevertheless. Some of the more provincial new universities must have a degree course in reading ferry timetables and if not, they should as most I downloaded were impregnable. You can imagine Jeremy Paxman's *University Challenge*, "I'm Ferry Mcferryface of the University of Walsall reading "Ferry Timetables of the Scottish Isles".

I'd booked a couple of rather expensive flights operated on behalf of Shetland Islands Council by Airtask Group operating out of Tingwall a few miles south of Lerwick. **Papa Stour** was a 10-minute flight, (but we eventually opted for the ferry), and **Foula** and **Fair Isle** about 25 minutes each way. **Foula** and **Fair Isle** were accessible by private boat hire or passenger ferry, but leisurely sea travel was not on our tight schedule. Timetables probably necessitated overnight stays which would have been an altogether different challenge on these remote islands with precious little if any accommodation. Avoiding sea sickness was also uppermost in my land lubber's mind.

The charming Airtask booking agent some weeks before had not wanted any security against my bookings and on reaching the air terminal, or rather a small room with 8 chairs, I discovered why. These flights are regularly cancelled because of inclement weather either on the outward leg or projected for the return so a refunding policy would be an administrative nightmare. It proved better and made more sense to take the money when flights were guaranteed, which seemed to be rare.

The day after our arrival we reached the airport at the appointed flight time only to be told the flight to **Foula** had been cancelled, so it was back to the drawing board with my logistics spreadsheet in tatters. Yes, I did have one as I didn't want to return at great expense to conquer an island I had inadvertently forgotten (which was to happen in the Outer

Hebrides). Our alternative that day was to get to **Muckle Roe** a charming little island accessible across St Magnus Bay by road bridge some twenty or so miles north. The 1905 bridge (replaced by the current bridge in 1999) cost £1,020 and was met by public subscription thus reversing the declining population. The small island was charmingly encircled by red granite cliffs but with no other significant memories.

That afternoon there was little to do except explore **Shetland Mainland's** North Roe and the legendary Sullom Voe oil terminal now operated by British Petroleum, which on completion in 1982 became the largest in Europe and secured jobs not only for the Shetlands but in the years of the North Sea oil boom, all across Europe. Those were the days when carbon was king, and the oil companies not seen as Beelzebub but the future of UK prosperity. Unlike Norway which poured massive oil and gas profits into publicly owned Sovereign funds, Her Majesty's UK Government squandered its oil wealth instead of re-investing it in and on behalf of the British taxpayer. What a difference 35 years has made with hydrogen or electricity powered car filling stations increasing stealthily across the nation. Diesel cars are to be rapidly phased out in Scotland by 2032.

Back in Lerwick I suggested we called into the Vaila Fine Arts shop which on passing earlier showed little sign of life let alone trading. It turned out that visits were by appointment and the establishment was only open on days with a 'T' in them. I had done my research and found that **Vaila**, the most elusive of our Shetland Islands, was lived on and owned by a London solicitor, Richard Rowlands and his Polish wife. To stand any chance of securing a visit we had to make contact with this mystery lady who we discovered owned this quirky shop.

I parked in the harbour car park and sent Ian, my emissary, to break the ice. I gave him a copy of my "*A Walk by the Sea*" as a gift to indicate my travel writing credentials. I am hopelessly shy in these matters, but Ian has panache (bullshit) like all solicitors. He was gone for some time which was a good sign, I felt. On his return he sternly indicated that there was no chance of a visit, but this is the usual mischievous prank he plays when a successful mission has been accomplished. Apparently, we had to head to the **Vaila** shore station near the village of Walls on Thursday (two days hence) at 11:00 prompt. Dorata was to give her husband my book and if he approved, she would confirm our visit. The hard work was done and a pint or two at *Captain Flint's* was next on the agenda.

The northern isles of **Yell, Fetlar and Unst** would fill the time the next day with smart timetable planning and unnecessary angst at missing the ferries. I'd taken the precaution of booking a number of ferries from **Mainland** (Toft) to the island of **Yell** (Ulsta), driving across **Yell** to Gutcher with a return car ferry to the island of **Fetlar** (Hamers Ness) and from Gutcher a further car ferry (Bluemill Sound ferry) to the island of **Unst** (Belmont) and onwards to find the fabled Muckle Flugga lighthouse the most northerly outpost of the British Isles. Are you keeping up? We took six ferries in all for the princely sum of a little less than £20 for my 4 by 4 Freelander and two passengers. Subsidies are outlandishly generous with the Shetland Island ferry company and apply to both locals and tourists.

Though ferries were booked, and times precisely gauged there was no real requirement for booking even in June with ample space on all ferries taking 31 or more vehicles and up to 95 passengers. Ferry discipline was strict with clearly demarked lanes between booked and speculative vehicles. Ferries, with no requirement to vacate the vehicle during their voyage, were perfect for a nap with the ship's engine whirring and gentle movement the perfect rhythm for sleep.

Once on **Yell**, the closest of these northern isles to **Mainland Shetland**, no showing of tickets was necessary for other journeys as this was the end of Britain and vehicles would have had to start at Ulsta to go further north in the first place. I became more relaxed and at Gutcher we spied a café. In my eagerness not to screw up the complex logistics, no real breakfast had been consumed. *The Gutcher Goose* was more than a café but the only shop for many miles and I was even able to get my favourite Nivea shaving foam that I'd been forgetting to buy for a week or so. We idly asked the owner if **Fetlar** had a café and, not wanting to lose precious trade, he answered to the negative. What a businessman.

Replete, we boarded the **Fetlar** ferry. Though the next eastward landfall from **Fetlar** is Norway, and it is a remote island to say the least, there are, contrary to the advice previously given, two cafes and a shop serving the isolated sporadic communities totalling some 61 souls. Trade wars in the north Atlantic indeed. The café we visited in **Fetlar** was as inhospitable as the owners were hospitable, but with little stock of any sort to entice the weary traveller. They were an English couple who had recently bought the shop, off licence and B&B as a project and it was real work in progress. We wished them well as for sure they would need every encouragement to survive in those hostile climes.

It was June 21st, the longest day in the calendar and we joked we must come back in summer! Despite the cool weather, **Yell** proved to be a glowering but beautiful canvas of ever-changing scenery with bleak majestic moorland covered with peat blanket bog and idyllic, hidden coves. The sea was never far away from the two or three main roads that traverse the islands and link communities together. **Yell** or Proto-Norse Jala or Jela may have meant 'White Island' referring to the beaches. Is this where English Yellow comes from, as we often refer to sand as yellow, but it hardly ever is the yellow exhibited in Dulux paint samplers. A 16th Century contemporary writer wrote that **Yell** "is such an uncouth place that no creature can live therein except such as are born there". So isolated is **Yell**, actually half the size of the isle of **Arran**, that German U boats used to boast of sheltering from the British northern convoys in its coves.

With time short on each island, we tried to get some mood of the life and times of people in these remote parts. A few miles from the Bluemill Sound ferry in the far north of the island, the Gloup Memorial commemorates the fifty-eight fishermen who were drowned when disaster struck the 'Haaf' fishing on the night of July 21st, 1881. The Shetland sixreen, open boats would row and sail to the fishing grounds 30 to 40 miles away. Many were lost but this was the biggest tragedy leaving few men and boys in the sparsely populated villages of **Yell**.

Haaf fishing took place in Shetland between 1750 and 1900 and involved spending two to three days at sea in big, open, six-oared wooden boats. Using landmarks for navigation they would set six miles of lines, hauling them in again and then sailing the 40 miles back with a boat full of fish. If there was no wind, the six-man crew rowed the huge distance! This was a tough existence and for the male population often the only way of sustaining a living as many had lost their crofter lands to unscrupulous landlords.

By contrast to **Yell**, **Fetlar** is known as the "Garden of Shetland" due to it being by far the greenest of all the islands. Indeed, the name **Fetlar** is reputed to originate from the Viking term "Fat Land", suitable for cropping despite the hostile climate. Houbie is a thriving community with incongruous social housing more characteristic of Glasgow than a remote island community. The Interpretative Centre in Houbie is worth a visit, representing a treasure trove of **Fetlar's** history. On display is a bottle, found by a local fishing vessel in August 2012 which, according to the *Guinness Book of World Records*, is the oldest message in a bottle ever retrieved, released in June 1914.

One of the strange features of **Fetlar** is a huge wall that snakes across the island known as the Funzie Girt or Finnigirt Dyke. It is thought to date from the Mesolithic period when to avoid continual arguments as to which community owned which lush pasture the wall was built to settle any future dispute. So sharp was the division between the two halves of the island, that when the Norse arrived around the 7th Century they talked of East and West Isle separately. They didn't necessarily regard an island as surrounded by water but any land where access was thwarted. As I write this Trump, whose quotes were becoming more outrageous and downright weird, said in the aftermath of Hurricane Maria destroying Puerto Rico; 'This is an island surrounded by water, big water, ocean water'. His idiocy though usually well founded is not so daft in this case if we appreciate the Norse ancient definition of an island, not necessary surrounded by water.

Now I am not in any way defending Trump and never will but yes, an island does not necessarily have to be surrounded by water; what of the Isle of Ely in the Fens or the Isle of Axholme on the River Trent flood plain; even the Isle of Dogs in London, which has become the powerhouse of finance that is now Canary Wharf. Nevertheless, walls are divisive as the walls separating the Palestinians from Israel or the farcical Mexican/USA wall proposed by Trump. With incredulity he once even suggested that the refugee crisis in Europe could be solved by building a wall across the Sahara Desert!

Fetlar maintained its isolation throughout history mainly because of the lack of a safe harbour, with shipwrecks abounding. Stoical crofters eked out a living until its owners the Nicolson's in true landed gentry style threw them out by 1858. **Unst** has the unfortunate accolade of being the first Shetland Isle to suffer from the Highland Clearances which had swept through the Highlands and Islands like a plague. I'd already seen in the Inner Hebrides just how heartless these landowners were. Sir Arthur Nicolson fell short of genocide but cleared some 30 townships and used the stone from their cottages to build himself a three-storey folly to stamp his arrogance on this poor island community.

Unst, as the most northerly island on my excursion of the islands of the British Isles, is most famous for Muckle Flugga lighthouse the most northerly outpost of the UK, with western Norway only 300km away. To put this into context Skaw, UK's most northerly settlement, is 650km from Edinburgh. We just had to get as close as was possible to the lighthouse which had once been accessible at low tide. It was built by brothers David and Thomas Stevenson as are many of the Scottish lighthouses and as a result of a visit by David's young son Robert Louis, **Unst** became his inspiration for the map of *Treasure Island*, though this notoriety is also claimed by Fidlar, a small island in the Firth of Forth, east of Edinburgh. The wind can be fierce in these northern latitudes and in

1962 wind speeds were recorded at Saxa Vord at 177 miles per hour, after which the anemometer was blown away. Beyond Muckle Flugga is only the icy wastes of the Arctic.

The **Unst** website bills this remote island as *"the ultimate destination for those with adventure in their soul"*. I like going to journey's end like Cape Comorin, the southernmost tip of India where the Bay of Bengal meets the Indian Ocean or Tierra del Fuego across the Magellan Straits. So **Unst** was to me very special. We didn't have time on our tight ferry schedule to take the hour or so walk from the Hermaness National Nature Reserve north of Birrafirth to get to the closest vantage point to Muckle Flugga so we headed for the deserted radio masts on the hills above Saxa Vord. This had served as an RAF station until 2006 but is now a tourist resort and home to Valhalla Brewery, the northern most brewery in the United Kingdom, but then it would be, wouldn't it.

The chase against time nearly thwarted our ambition as we frantically drove up dead end tracks before reaching Skaw. Eventually the correct road took us to a distant view of the lighthouse, and I was semi satisfied. In the panic to achieve this goal Ian, whose phone is usually permanently welded to his hand lost, temporarily I might add, the said device. No more pictures of food (his habitual photo opportunity) I sighed with relief - but each to their own. We made the ferry with time to spare and on our way south looked forward to our trip to **Vaila**.

We were more than a little smug to be going to **Vaila** at last, the only inhabited Shetland Island that was not joined to another island by causeway or bridge nor reached by a scheduled car or passenger ferry. The 20 or so miles to the appointed rendezvous at the shore station near Walls increased the excitement to a crescendo. We were told by the redoubtable Dorota Rychlik not to be late, but late we were losing our way several times, thinking that the shore station was in the vicinity of *Burrastow House,* a bleak foreboding hotel looking out across to our island.

We'd tried in vain to ask for directions and in a panic to repeat our request in Walls came across a battered and indistinct sign marking the entrance to our point of embarkation. Dorota was waiting patiently by her small, aluminium boat, practical rather than especially seaworthy. Greetings were dispensed with, and a short wind-swept journey took us to her island abode.

The island is little more than a square mile in area and home to Dorota and her indomitable husband Richard Rowland, a London solicitor. It was a short walk from the pier to the fine imposing manor house extended in 1890 by Herbert Anderson a Yorkshire woollen mill owner who acquired the island in 1837. The oldest part of the house incorporates the original laird's house built in 1696. Herbert was a descendant of Shetlander Arthur Anderson co-founder of the Peninsular and Oriental (P&O) shipping line in 1840. Unlike many of his contemporary landowners, the elder Anderson, MP for Orkney and Shetland, was part of the early liberal tradition within the Northern Isles carried into the 20th century by the likes of Jo Grimond leader of UK's Liberal party from 1956 to 1967. Apart from his well-known philanthropy, founding a home for seamen's widows in Lerwick, Anderson suggested the construction of the Suez Canal long before Ferdinand de Lesseps.

We had in the few short days of knowing of Richard's existence, built a fearful picture of him. We couldn't have been more wrong. He greeted us warmly and laid on Polish vodka to toast our visit. The warmth of the day and the vodka loosened our tongues and Richard began quizzing me on the finer points of my book. It seemed he had speed read the whole 500-page tome the night before, an art well-crafted by the legal profession who are paid by the number of pages in their briefs.

The hall had an intimidating baronial feel to it with drapes, oil paintings and suits of armour decorating its magnificence, clearly inherited with its purchase by our hosts some 30 years ago. No expense had been spared in its construction with skilled labour brought from Yorkshire. A brass cannon cast in Yorkshire adorns the battlements and was ceremoniously fired whenever Anderson and his entourage arrived on Vaila. Dorota tended a flock of organic sheep and Richard writes and draws when not commuting to his offices in London's Gherkin tower. What a contrast between the extreme isolation of long winters and Metropolitan bustle. It was mooted that Herbert liked to party and his dubious sexuality and colourful acquaintances would have been utterly frowned on by the God-fearing non-conformist folk of Yorkshire. **Vaila** was the ideal place for house parties away from prying eyes.

I was brought up in Glusburn a dour, Yorkshire mill village where temperance was the watchword and trips by dissenters to the *Dog and Gun* public house across the parish boundary were frowned upon by the pious and abstemious population. My mother used to brew nettle beer in the summer for the hay makers to slake their thirst after a long day's labour. She followed recipes to the letter and was pleased her beverage was well received, quaffed in volume with much merriment. She had made the brew, so it could not have been alcoholic!

Of course, the villagers turned a blind eye to the lifestyles of their employers; the Horsfall's who ran the knitting wool mill where my father was Chief Engineer and the Taylor's who ran the brewery in nearby Keighley. Mild hedonism was for their ilk and eschewed by the chapel going workers. Dr Renwick our Scottish GP always smoked during surgery with a cigarette in one hand and sometimes a whisky in the other but then he was a doctor, and this was allowed in our structured community's social hierarchy. We had the village institute, 'slipper' baths (as the mill houses did not have bathrooms), a library, a Baptist chapel and even a public indoor swimming baths. This was a sort of faux philanthropy common amongst the Yorkshire mill owners. They had their grand tours through Europe or in Herbert Anderson's case his island of **Vaila**.

Toasts completed we were to have a grand tour of our own in Richard's rusty but functional car. Firstly, we visited the renovated Mucklaberry castle tower with fine views 20 or so miles across to **Foula**, the remotest of any inhabited island in the British Isles. We moved onto the remnants of the farm estate where in a large outhouse was the fully reconstructed skeleton of a sperm whale, washed up nearby some years ago. Arriving back at the hall we were invited for lunch featuring chicken reared on the island and liberally plied with fine wine. Conversation was garrulous with Highland Park malt completing our repast in the comfort of the opulent hall.

The fun did not end there. Dorata whisked us back to the aluminium tub for a whistle stop tour circumnavigating the island at great and inebriated speed, keeping too close to the imposing cliff coastline and through magnificent sea arches. What a day! We bid farewell at the shore station promising to buy souvenirs at her Lerwick shop the next day. Organic woollen blankets and black sheep skins adorn my house, a fitting memory to a serendipitous day. In 2020 the island was put up for sale, 63.75 acres for £250,000 with planning permission. I suspect that the sheep farming was now too much for Dorata but hopefully they would continue to live contentedly in the expansive baronial hall.

Our plan the next day was to visit **Foula** using the Airtask inter-island services Cessna C241C 8-seater aircraft, postponed earlier in the trip because of poor weather. This seemed preferable to taking the ferry, the *New Advance*, which sails from Walls and takes around two hours to reach **Foula**. Seas can be rough out in the North Atlantic, but it was logistics that put us off rather than weather. There was no way we could go and return on the same day so flying (expensive) was our only option. We arrived at the airport at Tingwall on another 'dreich' Shetland day. Flights were cancelled, again. I wanted and needed to set foot on **Foula**. It was a long and expensive trip back to Lerwick at a subsequent date. The timetable left only one feasible option, 28th June, our last day on the Shetlands before the long trip home. However, a return trip meant almost certainly missing the car ferry to Orkney. Out of desperation I booked a ticket.

Whalsay island was a poor but necessary substitute and had to be visited though island fatigue was beginning to set in. We embarked by ferry on a quick, obligatory island run to **Whalsay** with a permanent population of over 1,000, though the correlation between population and houses was as ever baffling. Housing density as we travelled the length of the island seemed far greater than population divided by 2.4 or thereabouts. **Whalsay**, known as the Bonny Isle, was an unlikely place for holiday homes but did boast Great Britain's most northern golf course. A drive across the island from Symbister to Brough and north to (another) Skaw proved uneventful with little to fire the imagination.

Though lush pastures abound the islanders have always been fisher folk. **Whalsay's** fortunes or lack of them very much relied on the vagaries of the herring trade with boom and boost throughout its history. After the Second World War Government subsidies allowed the purchase of superior dual-purpose vessels to allow both herring and in- shore haddock fishing. Local fishing was secured until 1965 when 200 state-of-the-art Norwegian built ships swept the oceans around clean of fish stocks. The future of North Sea fisheries post-Brexit is very much in doubt.

On the plus side, knowledge of the sea and its fisheries remains an inherited skill with, it is said, 20 millionaire industrialists from **Whalsay** investing in super trawlers seeking further fortunes in the world's oceans.

We didn't stay long on the island even though the Heritage centre, like all Heritage centres the world over, promoted its facilities far above their fighting weight. We arrived back at Lerwick just after a cruise ship had left with the cafes on Commercial Street getting back to their normal sleepy trading levels and the proprietors counting their takings. My imagination was caught by a tented **Fair Isle** knitwear stall, mainly intricately designed scarves at sky high prices. We engaged the patron in conversation, and she lamented that her credit card machine had died just at the peak of the tourist rush, thus significantly stifling her takings.

I like the scarves and offered to buy one, not just out of pity but because I genuinely liked them. I looked unkempt and she eyed me slowly up and down. I could read her mind. "Surely this elderly guy is not serious; he can't possibly afford it". My pride was hurt, and I bought one of her finest scarves. Foolish, impetuous, but a beautiful garment to treasure. The value of possessions is more than their worth. We don't need "things"; we need experiences, and this expensive garment encapsulated the 'Shetland experience'. Yes, it will be left one day forlorn on the coat rack of a cheap Chinese restaurant in Birmingham but for now it remains the physical manifestation of treasured memories.

I had too much drink that night having had a tiff with Ian. It is hard not to as sometimes his smugness is overwhelming, and we have a love/hate relationship usually reserved for siblings. Alone, I even tried running the gauntlet of *Da Wheel* public house which was as unsavoury as ever.

The ferry to **Papa Stour** wasn't until late the next afternoon so after a pleasant breakfast in Scalloway I returned to base and occupied myself trying to avoid Ian who seemed to have barricaded himself into his bedroom. I really wanted to 'do' **Papa Stour** alone, but Ian had other ideas. We set off with the mood as black as the late afternoon sky, with rain all the way to West Birrafirth. There was no sign of activity, and I began to question the veracity of the ferry timetable. The 2011 census suggests the population of **Papa Stour** is 15 but rumour has it that now as few as three families and a single occupant live permanently there. Why, indeed, would anyone want to travel there on a Saturday evening? Its 22 miles of indented coastline are rich in history, geology, archaeology and wildlife and it boasts some of the best sea caves in the North Atlantic but with no accommodation or shop chances of tourists rushing for the late ferry were remote.

In common with many small Scottish islands, **Papa Stour's** population peaked in the 19th century and has experienced a significant decline since then. By 1970 the island's school had closed, and the population had declined to sixteen 'fairly elderly' residents, but an advertisement in *Exchange and Mart* reversed the decline. A croft and five sheep were offered free of charge to incomers which brought a flood of applicants. By 1981 the census recorded a population of 33. The island became a refuge from the rat race and earned the nick name 'The hippy isle'. Disheartened with the spartan living in extreme climatic conditions numbers quickly declined. The Sound of Papa, though narrow, can fulminate in bad weather leaving islanders cut off for long periods.

The ferry dutifully did show up and Ian and I were joined by a single crofter who enlightened us as to further reasoning for the decline in population. Anyone living within 32km of the island can qualify as an absentee crofter. The contrast with our experience in **Vaila** couldn't have been greater. We set foot on **Papa Stour** and after a cursory exploration returned to **Mainland Shetland** on the same ferry, delayed by the hitching and unhitching of a crofter's trailer, leaving whoever was still on the island to their lonely devices. In the fading summer daylight we could see that the island's nature is as majestic as its population is becoming depleted. The most impressive and tallest sea stacks of Muckle Fru, clustered around the entrance to Housa Voe as we approached the pier, were barely visible in the impending gloom.

That night we learned about the Festival of *Up Helly Aa*, originally held around Christmas but now moved to every January. What appear to be no more than drunken rituals, festivals and processions have been held since Victorian times with cancellations only as follows:

- 1900: Two weeks due to influenza
- 1901: The death of Queen Victoria
- 1914 to 1919: First World War
- 1936: Two weeks due to the death of George V
- 1940 to 1948: Second World War and aftermath
- 1965: One week due to the death of Winston Churchill

A patriotic lot the Shetlanders seemed to be despite having more in common with Norway than the UK. I suspect COVID 19 added 2020 to the years when *Up Helly Aa* was cancelled.

On Christmas eve in 1824 a visiting Methodist missionary wrote in his diary that:

> "the whole town was in an uproar: from twelve o clock last night until late this night blowing of horns, beating of drums, tinkling of old tin kettles, firing of guns, shouting, bawling, fiddling,

fifeing, drinking, fighting. This was the state of the town all the night – the street was as thronged with people as any fair I ever saw in England."

I see now where the Lerwick rugby club and the fraternity of *Da Wheel* get their ideas of a good time from.

The **Outer Skerries** are a mere 200 miles from the coast of Norway and contain two populated islands **Bruray** and **Housay** connected by a short road bridge. We chose a Sunday to visit and arrived at Vidlin on **Mainland** as usual well in time for the ferry departure. We discussed going as foot passengers as we could walk between the two islands easily on arrival. There is only one mile of road on the two islands. However, it was raining, and we weren't sure about shelter, let alone whether the promised shop would be open for a makeshift lunch. We would need to spend about four hours on the islands after the ferry journey of an hour and a half on the *Filla*. We checked the cost of a car in addition to the passengers and the whole return journey was not much more than £8 return, with a senior concession rate for me and the car as I was the driver. So, we took the car as our shelter!

Ferry prices are eccentric and our **Skerries** journey reminded me of a 12-hour ferry journey from Turku in Finland to Stockholm across the magnificent Gulf of Bothnia with an archipelago of thousands of tiny islands without parallel. Roger and I were worried about what might have been a cripplingly costly ferry ride between two of the most expensive countries in the world. We gingerly walked up to the gruff booking clerk, who looked like the singer out of *Lordi*, who won the Eurovision song contest for Finland in 2006 and asked timidly for a single for two people and a Freelander 2. "86 Euros" he replied tersely. Adding "Inside or outside cabin?". This was included in the overall price. We couldn't believe our luck. Our lunch came to more than the whole fare and flouting strict 'no smoking' rules in public places throughout Scandinavia, Roger was even allowed to smoke in the ferry bar before retiring to a spacious cabin that would put the average *Travel Lodge* to shame.

On the journey to the **Skerries** we were the only vehicle and the only passengers (until the very last minute). There were in total four crew and three passengers and as soon as we set sail the captain, Ivan Reid, invited us onto the bridge for wildlife observation for the whole journey. We were unlucky not to see any whales, porpoises or dolphins as promised by the young captain. The bridge was hi-tech with dials and buttons reminiscent of an airplane. Ivan seemed oblivious to this paraphernalia and sat with his sneaker-clad feet up talking to us animatedly whilst the boat self-steered. Occasionally he would give a modicum of throttle. Ian gently snoozed between reading obscure murder mysteries on his Kindle. It was a blustery day deep in the North Sea, though where the North Sea becomes the North Atlantic is still a mystery. Ivan came to life when some reverse thrusting was required to dock us safely on the jetty on **Bruray** and we were off to park up until our return journey at four.

Sunday on the **Skerries** is quiet to put it mildly. After we parked, we went exploring for the shop. Not a soul stirred. A note on the door indicated it would open for one hour at two pm. Anticipating the cornucopia of delights we pressed our noses to the window and counted down to opening. We feasted on Anderton's stale pork pie and jelly babies listening to a poignant rendition of *Me and Bobby McGee* sung by Kris Kristofferson at Glastonbury a million miles away. Incidentally I noticed that the shop sold L plates for learner drivers when there is hardly any tarred road and no police. Some 20 cars are owned by the population of 74.

We drove across the bridge to **Housay** and back killing all of ten minutes of our wait and I walked to Bruray Wart at 53m the highest point on **Bruray** to pass the time. The views to Grunay, the third main but unpopulated island were stunning in between squally rain showers. With few tourists this is a lonely place though boasts the smallest cinema in Scotland with 20 seats. In 2016 the primary school only had one student. The story went viral, and he received over 10,000 Christmas cards that year from all around the world. Astonishingly the island also had a secondary school till 2014 with the close-knit islanders of exceptional stoicism believing in as much self-sufficiency as their remoteness would allow.

The return ferry was busy with three cars in total! With these ferries costing around five to six million pounds each with annual refits in Fraserburgh, ferry economics are mystifying. The routes only survive by huge subsidies from the Highlands and Islands Council. Having little else to do on the way back we estimated that the day's takings were the princely sum of £32.40. And, of course, islanders get a further discount! **The Outer Skerries**, owned with the exception of one house by the Cussons (Imperial leather soap) family was on sale, without properties included, for a quarter of a million pounds with a total annual revenue from crofters of £106. This seems like the Highland Clearances revenge where the crofters are getting their own back on the Landlords.

The next morning, we drove to Tingwall airport with a certain amount of trepidation. Our delay today was for air ambulance duties rather than the weather, so after a bit of an anxious wait in the booking office/waiting room/security area getting to know our fellow passengers we were ushered to the plane and the short hop to **Fair Isle**. The island is sort of in no man's land between the Shetland and Orkney Islands, known the world over for its Fair Isle jumpers. All Scottish islands seem to be famous for producing some form of knitwear or woollen garments. It must be in the DNA or more likely because there is little else to pass the time in these outposts of civilisation. **Harris** for Tweed, Shetland and **Aran** for jumpers and so forth. The origins of the trademark Fair Isle jumper, hand knitted in traditional bright colours, are way back in the mists of time when islanders exchanged their hosiery for scarce fresh produce from passing ships. The genuine article is still only produced on **Fair Isle** by a small co-operative using hand framed machines.

Civil aviation rules insist on a fire engine to accompany the arrival and departure of passenger planes and as most of the islands served by plane in Scotland have very few inhabitants, the residents of the islands double up as fire fighters and into the bargain baggage handlers-cum-cabin attendants. It is quite unnerving when these guys are dressed head to tail in fire resistant clobber whilst the paying passengers are in their waterproof, but certainly not fireproof, Gortex.

After a perfunctory safety drill, we were off. The trip was expensive for a four-hour stopover, but it had to be done as the boat journey simply didn't fit into our logistics. For some reason I paid for Ian who seems to have a pathological fear of parting with money. Some months later, for no reason ever discussed, I paid for him to fly to the Ashes cricket in Australia and the expensive tickets both at the Melbourne and Sydney cricket grounds. This overt generosity is wholly out of character for a Yorkshireman. They always say a Yorkshireman is a Scotsman bereft of his generosity! The true story below suggests otherwise or maybe it is just my naive stupidity.

Many years ago, I had an acquaintance who had, like me, gone through a messy and traumatic divorce. We bonded because of this one communality. He was the local drug dealer, it turned out. He was always asking me to finance his marijuana deals. I have never 'done drugs' and I steadfastly refused to be his loan 'tadpole'. One weak moment I lent him five thousand pounds with a guarantee of a 24-hour return. The next day he came to the pub saying he had some good news and some bad news. "Give it to me", I sighed. "Well", he retorted. "The bad news is the 'gear' is poor quality". "OK" I spluttered. "Give me the good". "It's all yours", he replied, passing me a large bundle before making excuses and leaving.

I was now a drug dealer. I went home and cried, hastily hiding the 'loot' in my handy concrete floor safe. A hefty prison sentence was certainly on the cards and certain loss of employment. My life would be in ruins. The next day, at work, I had a call from a neighbour. "That's it", I deduced. "The old bill has tracked me down". The agitated neighbour said she had found a 'n'er do well' lurking in my yard. She insisted he spoke to me before turning him into the police. "John. It's Harry", came a well-known voice down the phone. Now Harry was a Loughborough lad, an acquaintance of my dear cousin Richard, with the look of a cross between Charles Manson and Meatloaf. "Do you know anybody who can get me some good Moroccan, there's a drought in Leicester", he implored. These were the days before ultra-strength skunk. "I'm on my way, H, you've come to the right man". Six months later my safe was empty and my drug dealing days were thankfully over.

The journey was delectable, heading down the emerald coast of Mainland to Sumburgh Head, the striking headland to the southeast of Jarlshof, the southernmost tip of the Shetland Islands. Jarlshof has been described as "one of the most remarkable archaeological sites ever excavated in the British Isles" with over 4,000 years of human settlement. We had experienced its impressive excavations some days earlier.

There was no room for trolley service on this cramped flight! The landing strip on **Fair Isle** was halfway up a contoured hillside with steep drops to the sea at either end. The fire engine was there to greet us or save us from any mishandling of the descent. "Where now?", I asked Ian. Of course, instead of turning left to the Bird Observatory we turned right for a couple of miles walk across the island to the southern lighthouse hoping to find refreshment on the way. This was a big mistake as the Observatory, far from being a series of hides frequented by impossibly intense twitchers, was a working bar and restaurant. As usual we had been too busy drinking in *Captain Flint's* to do any useful research.

It is all about birds (and knitwear) in **Fair Isle**. Some 373 different species have been recorded at the Observatory. The island is on the 'flight path' of bird migration from Scandinavia, Iceland and the Faroe Islands. As such, impressive and rare varieties of birds arrive for the bird watchers to enjoy during the breeding season. From April to August its cliffs are alive with the sounds (and smells!) of thousands of fulmars, kittiwakes, razorbills, guillemots, gannets, shags and puffins whilst white skuas fiercely defend their nests on neighbouring moorlands.

The day was unusually fine and the walk south pleasant enough. We were soon in sight of an open shop doubling as a post office as they usually do in these remote parts. We stopped for a breather and encountered a couple coming the other way. The male was eager to engage in conversation which I am usually reticent to do. "What are you doing?" he asked with more than a touch of inquisitiveness. I don't like to explain my business but Ian enlightened John (for that was his name) and his wife of our wider island-hopping ventures.

John Mackay, born on the Isle of **Lewis** but now living in the Kingdom of Fife, was a proper adventurer and soon made us aware of his double ascent of the 282 or so Scottish mountains over 3,000 feet to their summits. These are the Munros as defined by Sir John Munro in 1891. I have a friend who has also climbed them - twice and a feat I have always wanted to do, well once anyway. With arthritis and advancing age this is a pipe dream now. In all John had also tackled 602 Munro tops, that is those officially classed as Munros and those with a secondary 'top' prior to the summit. The Munro club has over 6,000 members with 600 claiming double ascents. Apparently one guy runs them all each year.

It reminded me of when I stopped at a pub in the bleak Medway town of Rochester on my "*Walk by the Sea*" odyssey. A woman worse for wear from her afternoon drinking session suggested I must be bored to want to walk the coast of Great Britain. Some might say the same of our annual Munro bagger. Trig points measuring summit height on top of high points are a thing of the past but the 7,600 built in our islands have no doubt been visited by some passionate devotee to record breaking. My erstwhile walking companion Geoff and his partner, Steph, have visited the 'County tops' or the highest points of all England's pre-1974 ceremonial Counties. I'm reminded of the quote "Two men look out through the same bars; one sees the mud, and one the stars" written by Frederick Langridge in 1896. Each to his or her own. Who are we to judge?

John and I got talking and he put my paltry mission into perspective as he proudly boasted that not only had he visited almost all inhabited Scottish islands but had climbed to the top of the highest point of each! What is more he had climbed the summits of all the Hamish Haswell-Smith islands, inhabited or otherwise. Haswell-Smith's book "*Scottish Islands*" describes in detail, with exquisite hand drawn maps and illustrations, 162 islands of 40 hectares (about 100 acres) or more.

Not content with this feat, which included trips to the North Atlantic outliers of St Kilda and Soay and Rona, the latter some 44 miles to the north of the Butt of Lewis, he is now tackling islands greater than 30 hectares. Dedication indeed! His trip by a reinforced inflatable boat (RIB) to Soay cost him and 12 other enthusiasts some £7,500. His working spreadsheet of statistics and logistics which he proudly sent to me is a work of art. This resolve and tenacity reminded us of the drunken Lerwick rugby club's annual three-day trip to play 'local rivals' in Stornaway. I could never match such derring-do.

We walked on and I admit to more than a tad of jealousy. The south lighthouse (1 degree 39 10 West and 59 degrees 30 83 North) built by David Stevenson in 1892 was the last manned lighthouse in Scotland and finally vacated in 1998. On our way back to the airport shepherding was the only activity in evidence and my image of aging little old women in cramped crofts knitting Fair Isle jumpers was well and truly shattered. We returned to the airport in good time to meet John, his wife and a lone traveller, Ray Goodman, who casually dropped in that he had circumnavigated Great Britain too, but in a yacht! We all have tales to tell.

The 10 days or so we made Shetland our home, apart from cruise liners coming and going and the sailors from the Bergen to Lerwick yacht race, the harbour was overshadowed by an enormous, deconstructed oil rig built in South Korea and headed for the North Sea oil fields. Sullom Voe oil terminal on Shetland was built between 1975 and 1981 with 6,000 people employed during its construction. Whilst capitalist oil companies have a grip on the energy market the industry will continue with little thought of environmental consequences.

Oil activity and extraction of fossil fuels is hopefully to become an anachronism as the IPCC (International Panel on Climate Change) report published in October 2018 warned of apocalyptic predictions should global temperatures rise more than 1.5 degrees in the next 30 years. Of course, neo-liberal America calls this a Chinese hoax and trillions of dollars are required to stem the predicted temperature rise and allow our planet to become carbon neutral; with the construction of solar farms the size of Australia, planting of thousands of square miles of forest and a plea for us to eat less meat and yes, even to return to drying washing on lines in our gardens.

I applaud small initiatives introduced by large numbers of people, but these are generally derided by conservatives who only listen to *Fox News* or read the *Daily Mail* and believe the self-centred oligarchs in whose interest it is to maintain investments in fossil fuels.

I now had one last island, **Foula**, to tackle before heading back on the *Norseman* Ferry to Orkney where I would leave Ian and send him onto Aberdeen, a 15-hour ferry trip in total. This remote rock 20 or so miles out in the Atlantic was home to 30-odd souls, who really knew what isolation was. Since the de-population of St Kilda in the 1950's **Foula** inherited the accolade of the most remotely populated island in The British Isles. Scotland is proud to maintain services on its islands and worries not about cost savings. After all, it would be cheaper to send all islanders to a purpose-built social housing estate in the Glaswegian suburbs, but where is the romance in that. Around the time of my visit, the island had advertised for a teacher with a salary of £45,000 per annum, including a house. There was no sign of austerity politics denying the handful of children their rightful local education. This "extravagance" would be anathema in England, with Tory council's rather voting themselves the latest iphone than being part of this "monstrous abuse of public money".

The weather had to be right. I refused to pay for Ian's trip as it would be an on-off flight to allow us to catch the ferry to Orkney later that evening. This may seem extravagant, but rumour has it that a resident, Professor Smith orders food from the *Burristow Hotel* in Walls and has it flown to **Foula**, to break the monotony of limited supplies available from the one shop on the island. The reality of remoteness is surely a PhD topic for the enthusiastic psychologist.

I was up at 07:00 to gain the early flight and was back in the bosom of Lerwick by 10:30 after calling on this wonderful island all too briefly. The pilot was happy to leave but, weather uncertain, unsure of extricating passengers (including John and his wife and the redoubtable Roy) on the early evening flight. After the exiting passengers had departed with John headed for the island's summit the pilot invited me into the co-pilot seat for the return journey, just me and him, back to Tingwall. He treated me to a rare circumnavigation of **Foula**, an experience I will always cherish, before heading home. We hovered over the breath-taking 376m sheer drop at the back of Da Kame which competes with Conachair on the now abandoned St Kilda as the highest sea cliff in Britain. This was his office and a finer workplace there could never be.

The islanders spoke Norn (a southern Norway tongue) as their only language until the 19th Century. The current owner's ancestors are from Brecon in Wales having bought the island in 1900 and after occupation noted that the only wheeled vehicles on the island were wheelbarrows and these were eyed with some suspicion! Modernity was slowly embraced with wireless telegraphy arriving in 1937 and the telephone in 1954 but piped water supply not until 1982. Although the Julian calendar was disbanded in the rest of Britain in 1753 it is still used in **Foula** with Christmas celebrated on January 6th.

Foula often referred to perhaps a little over dramatically as "The Edge of the World" has had a lasting impression on me; maybe it was the quality of the light, unpolluted by civilisation, its five dramatic peaks, the remoteness, the community way of life or something more intangible and ethereal. Whatever unique or collective characteristics appealed it has to rank amongst the most treasured of my island visits.

17. Inner Holm and Holm of Grimbister, Orkney Islands, Scotland

We spent the evening in a cramped and stuffy lounge on the ferry. After arriving in Kirkwall, I said farewell to Ian, who had a further seven or so hours sailing to Aberdeen, and I ventured into the Orkney night to find my Bed and Breakfast in Finstown, 15 minutes' drive from the Orkney ferry terminal. It was after 11 at night when I arrived at *Hammersmiths* B&B.

I had to be up early to meet the low tide and 'bag' the two wretched tidal islands I had failed to secure on our outward journey. Low tide at both **Inner Holm**, in the Stromness harbour, and **Holm of Grimbister** in the Bay of Firth near my lodgings at Finstown was predicted to be around about 08:00, so an early breakfast was ordered and a speedy goodbye to my erstwhile hosts. All access routes, a raised Heath Robinson causeway to the latter and the ocean floor to the former would be flooded by 10:30. I had bought a pair of green and rather cheap Dunlop wellington boots in Lerwick just in case I became waterlogged. It was pure random luck that the tide was at its lowest prior to my ferry departure from Stromness to Scrabster on the north Scottish coast. As usual planning had not been a priority.

Inner Holm had a single resident according to the Scottish 2011 census and **Holm of Grimbister**, which sounds like a place or character in a Harry Potter novel, had two. Both do not feature in Haswell-Smith's tome based on his size criteria. I'd already sourced the best vantage point to cross to **Inner Holm**, so I donned my fearfully uncomfortable wellingtons and set off across the drained harbour taking care not to fall on the slippery covering of seaweed. Some ten minutes later I made

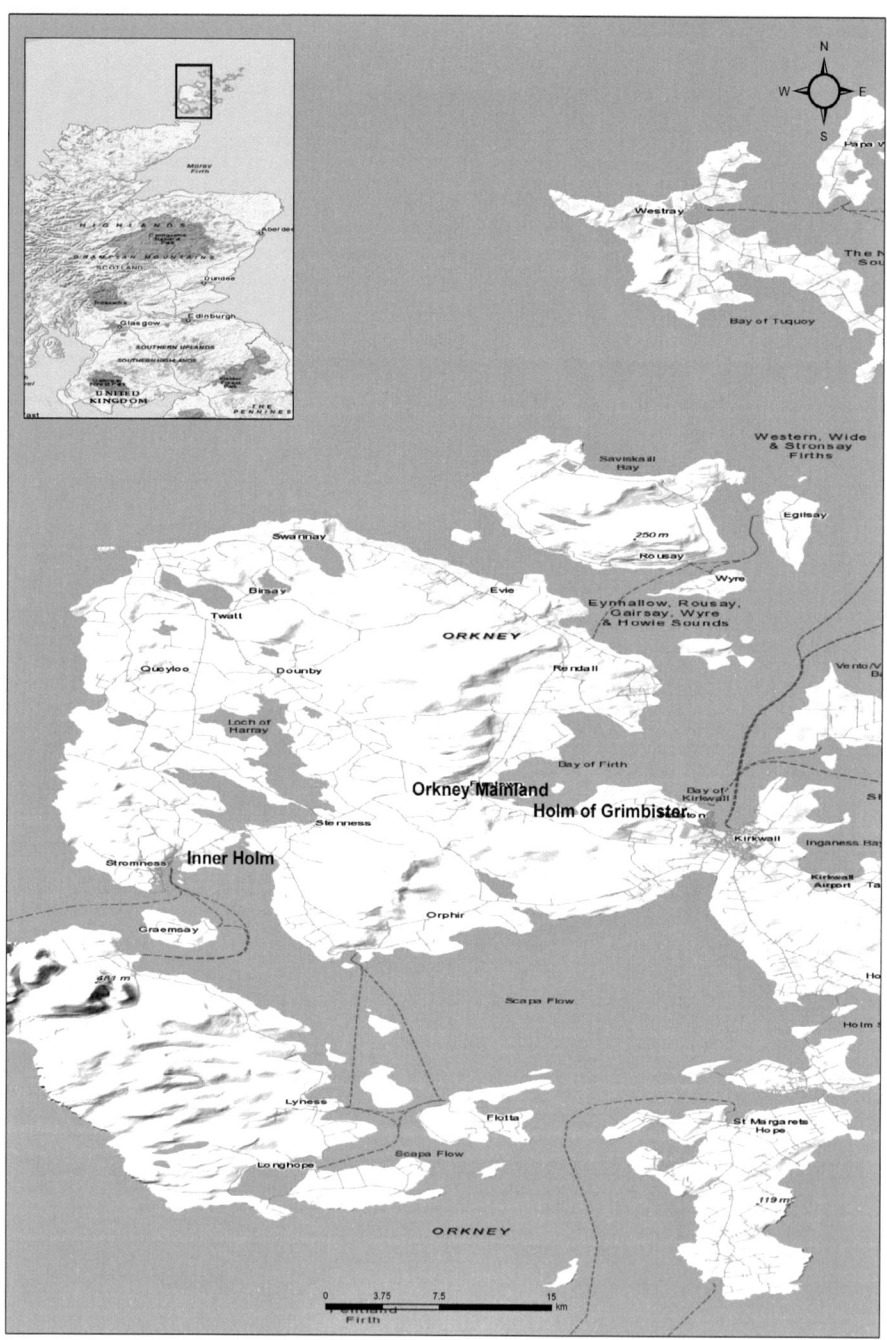

Inner Holm and Holm of Grimbster, Orkney Islands, Scotland

landfall on the island and headed straight back to avoid the single resident taking me for a trespasser, even though enlightened Scotland does not have a law of trespass.

A twenty-minute car ride brought me to the access to the **Holm of Grimbister** causeway which was emerging out of the murky Bay of Firth like a twisting sea monster. Going was rough underfoot on the unworked stone pavement which formed the causeway, and I was glad to be back on **Mainland Orkney** and away to Stromness with a smug satisfaction of success having completed these two irksome island landings by nine in the morning. The latter island went up for sale in 2016 for a paltry £300,000. It had been the home of a candidate for election to the Scottish Parliament.

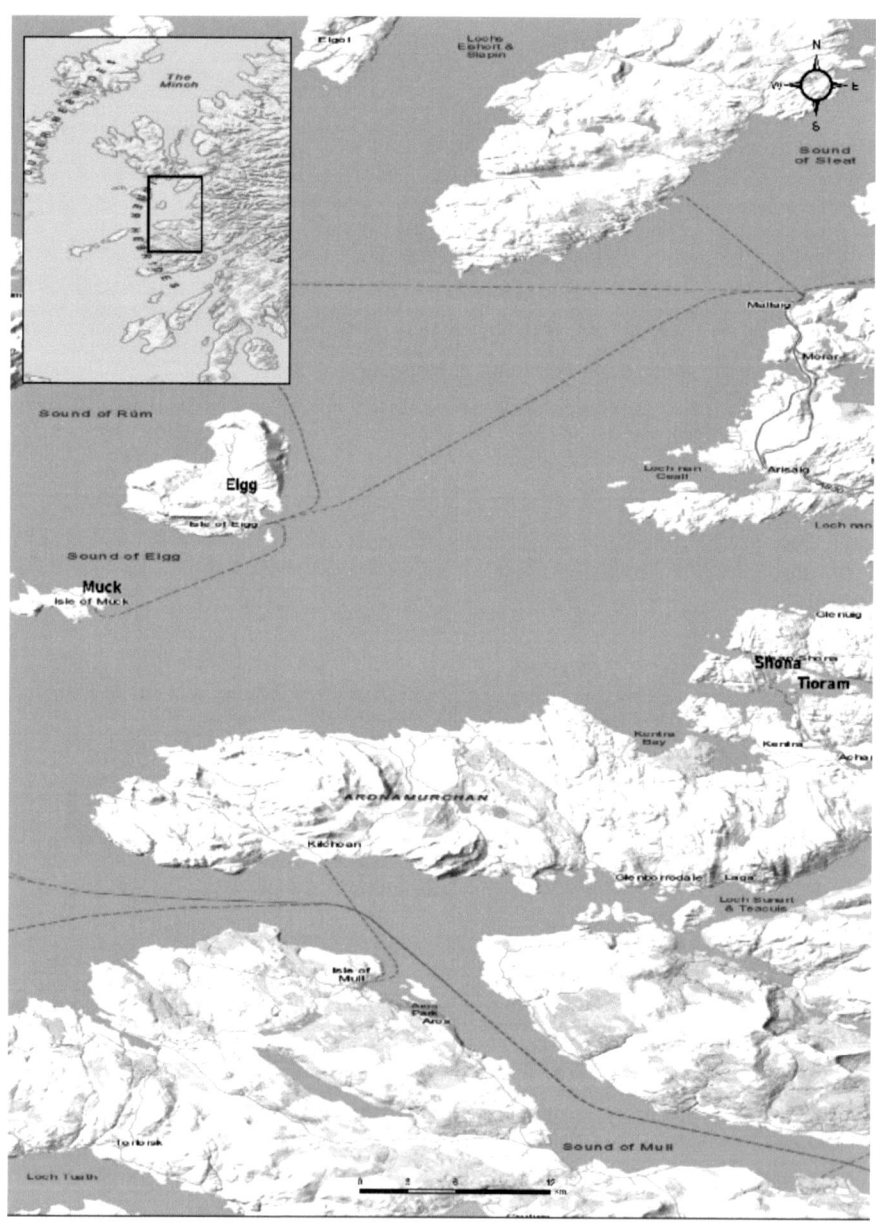

Muck, Eigg, Shona and Tioram, Highland, Scotland

18. Assorted islands on the Northwest coast of Scotland, and two "Small Isles"

After the Shetland adventure, I was heading home and partly out of nostalgia (re-visiting much of my *Walk by the Sea* in the West Highlands, but in reverse) and partly to pick up isolated islands not so far accessed I chose the long way via the remote west coast along the tourist route known as the North Coast 500, a rival in beauty and remoteness to Ireland's Wild Atlantic Way. It was a long drive to my first port of call near Achiltibuie from where I would access the only inhabited Summer Isle, **Tanera Mor**. The other islands in my sight were the **Isle of Ewe** near Gairloch, **Eilean Tioram** (**Dry Island**) and **Eilean Shona**, tidal islands in Loch Moidart, and **Danna** at the southern end of the Tayvallich peninsular with an easy bridged crossing. All except **Tanera Mòr** and the **Isle of Ewe** did not feature in Haswell-Smith's magnum opus.

Logistics would be a nightmare, I thought as I stopped at the *Bettyhill hotel* for mid-morning coffee. I had last stopped there in October 2004 on my epic walk for the princely sum of £20 per night, and at that time it was derelict and wholly run down with no redeeming features. The then new English owners from Hampshire, I believe, were clearly at a loss in this new hostile, remote environment. By 2017 under new corporate ownership, it had become a sophisticated, modern hotel, all gleaming and clean, selling itself as a hotel provider for the North Coast 500 (NC500), which in turn sells itself as:

"Scotland's answer to the legendary Route 66 (in the USA) and the prolific Wild Atlantic Way. Measuring at just over 500 miles, this meandering

TREASURED ISLANDS

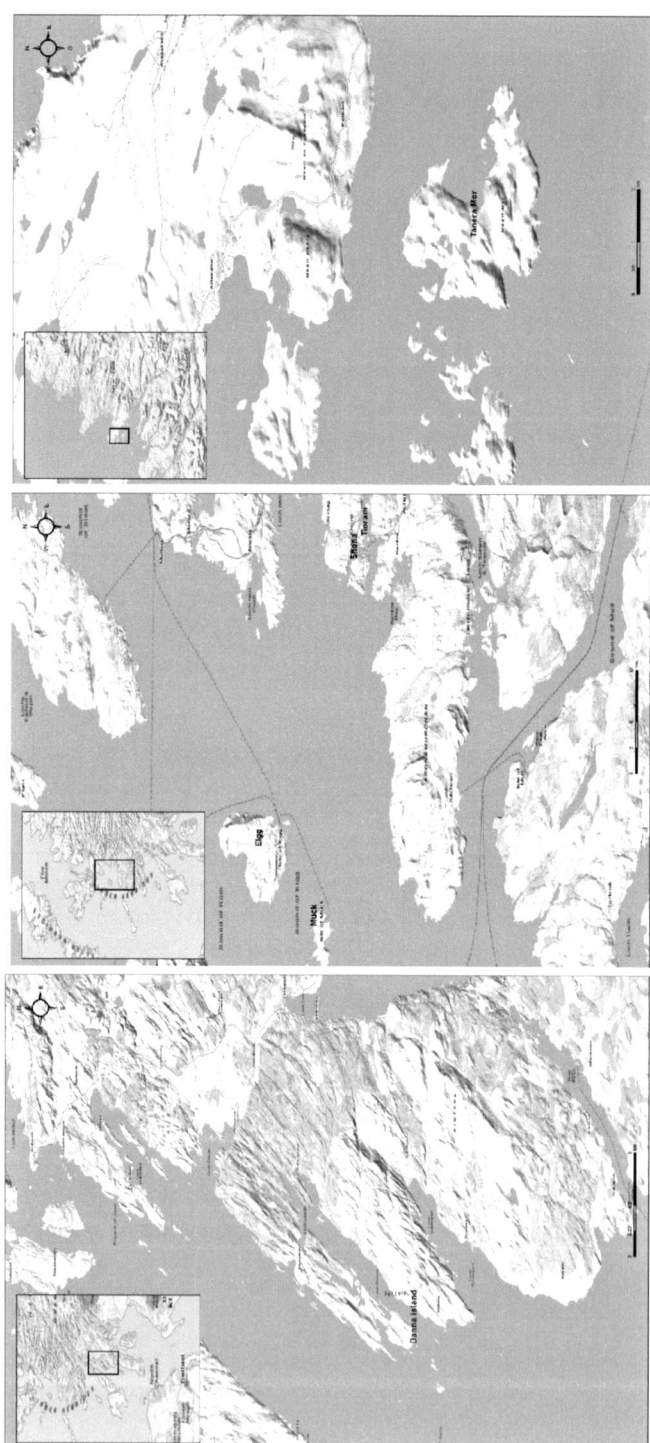

Assorted islands off the northwest coast of Scotland and 2 'Small isles' (l to r) Danna, Muck, Eigg, Shona, Tioram, Tanera Mor

route snakes along the Highland's rugged coastline bringing together ancient castles, serene lochs and glistening beaches".

This is tourism selling itself. The Wild Atlantic Way in Ireland passes by the dramatic cliffs of Mohr, which saw nearly 1.5 million tourists in 2016, up 14% from the previous year. Like its Irish sister the downside to the burgeoning trade now rejuvenated at the likes of the *Bettyhill Hotel* is a saturation of visitors transforming quiet backwaters into whistle-stop must-see destinations. In my 2004 walk along the north coast of Scotland cars were a rarity. Now they, and packs of motor cyclists, reliving their Peter Fonda/Dennis Hopper *'Easy Rider'* fantasies travelling at break-neck speeds, have become an engrained feature of the landscape.

I stopped at the *Summer Isles hotel* briefly to get directions to the **Tanera Mòr** shore station as I'd confirmed with the timetable posted in the Achiltibuie community café that a boat was imminent. I am usually too impatient to take in given directions and I totally missed the narrow road accessing the small jetty, several miles from the village. By the time I arrived, chasing non-existent signage, the boat had disappeared. There was much commercial boating activity with the *Cromarty Queen* arriving which I optimistically mistook for the ferry boat.

I sat in the car hoping the ferry would eventually arrive back and I could 'throw money at the problem' and coax, or rather bribe, the boatman to make an additional trip. It's a long way back to Achiltibuie from Birmingham. Soon a boat arrived disgorging its day trippers and I confronted Ian McLeod, the skipper, offering £50 for a personalised trip. He was a dour Scot hoping for refreshment or a wee dram or two after a hard day at sea, but I managed to persuade him to squeeze me in so long as I kept my time on the island to a bare minimum. That suited both of us.

Until 1931 Tanera Mòr had been the base for a thriving herring fishery and since then has had a large price tag on its sale. In June 2017, Ian Wace, a British financier, purchased the island for £1.7 million, far less than the £2.5 million asking price when it was put on the market in 2013. He was to oversee a four-year development to what he anticipated could become an "idyllic retreat capable of hosting up to 60 paying guests".

After 10 minutes on the island, I re-embarked and chatted idly to the far from dour Mr McLeod and after he moored the boat for the night I bade him farewell and made for Gairloch to plan my next island.

Passing the *Summer Isles hotel* reminded me of a stay there during *A Walk by the Sea*. The hotel overlooked **Tanera Mòr** and was a high-class oasis. I'd wondered why it was so expensive when I booked back in the summer of 2004, but in the remote far north I had little alternative. It appears that these remote hotels have to offer a carrot to attract visitors. The carrot in this case is a Michelin star restaurant with main courses upwards of then £55 and rooms starting at £150. The management guaranteed discretion and privacy. For lovers and those in the public eye conducting secret affairs this is most definitely the place as it can only be accessed, except by fool hardy walkers, via a single-track road past the magnificent Stac Polly mountain. The likes of the late Robin Cook, Tony Blair's foreign secretary and staunch Iraq war opponent, conducted his romantic business there. I did not have the cash, stomach, or evening wear to do justice to the five-course meal.

I reminisced - I entered the foyer at seven thirty in the evening, bedraggled from my ordeal from walking over treacherously steep open moorland, my musty sweat mingling with the pre-diner cocktail set in their pink gowns and DJ's. The incongruity threw me into paroxysms of apologies. 'Mein Host' however had no problem with my dishevelment. The rule in these places is if you can afford the prices then who cares about eccentric dress. There was no chance of unkempt campers looking for beer and gammon and chips turning up here to spoil the intimacy of the idle rich.

My bath was drawn for me and after a welcome soak I made my way to the cocktail lounge in my spare clean but creased walking clothes and insisted on a steak in the overflow restaurant rather than join my fellow guests in their luxurious surroundings. I could have asked for anything. The enjoyment of my beautifully cooked steak was enhanced by eavesdropping on the rich set and the intimacy of their conversations and brief stolen time together; the men uncomfortable, with one thing on their mind; the women exhibiting a soupcon of embarrassment.

After dinner, I made my way to the public bar (yes it did exist, but mainly for the staff) and waived the opportunity for liqueurs and coffee. I was greeted by the haunting eyes of the sous-chef Ellen, a beautiful, sultry Dutch Australian, a free spirit who hibernates for six months in the likes of Achiltibuie to pay for far eastern travel to the beaches of Thailand. "How was your steak?" she enquired. I answered appropriately. I was flattered by her conversation and interest in me, a scruffy, late middle-aged man. We drank far too much Black Bottle whisky, and I was flabbergasted by her insistence in joining me in my room for her last bottles of Oranjeboom Dutch lager. By three in the morning, we were firm friends exchanging e-mails and kisses, but I never got to see the full extent of her ten-foot dragon, tattooed from her shoulder round her body with the tail entwining the base of her left ankle. Of course, we never were in contact again and I can only hope she wasn't caught up in the Boxing Day tsunami of 2004.

After the journey south, I checked into the *Gairloch hotel*, a far cry from that in Achiltibuie, and mingled with the crowds of coach trippers and other assorted guests before and after dinner. The lounge was the venue for a Friday night one-man karaoke, playing the bubble gum hits of the sixties and seventies that were familiar to the ageing clientele, my fellow baby boomers. I was soon bored with his '*Smokie*' and '*The Brotherhood of Man*' repertoire and went outside for a breath of air, to be dazzled by the green, flashing aura of the Northern Lights, or *Aurora Borealis* to give them their scientific name. This unique natural spectacle made up for the mediocrity of this bland hotel. I consumed a final nightcap served by charming Romanian waiters, who were to be summarily kicked out back to the long grass of the EU after Brexit, precipitating a modern form of the Highland Clearances. Back in my dreary room I struggled with the portable Sony TV set, the sort of device which wouldn't be seen dead in any other than this tired production line hotel.

I awoke, knowing the time had come to telephone the family who owned, or at least tenanted, the **Isle of Ewe**. This island has found fame as a honeymooners' island and newlyweds' queue to sail around it. Why, may you ask? Well, say it slowly and what do you get but "I love you". The island's name also came up in 'The Goon Show', during the November 1954 episode "Lurgi Strikes Britain." Neddie Seagoon (Harry Secombe) is informed that the "dreaded lurgi" has appeared on the **Isle of Ewe**, to which he replies, "I love you too. Shall we dance?"

The tricky bit however was to gain instant access to the island, and I eventually found a number for Mrs Grant, the matriarch. The phone rang out and there was no answer and instead of heading for Aultbea and finding a fisherman to make an easy quid or two to take me over, I chickened out. I felt that I would have better luck heading for Elgol on **Skye** and the *Bella Jayne* and use the ticket I had not yet cashed in since April to take me to the elusive **Soay**, a mile or so off the island's coast. I would leave the love island until another time.

I journeyed yet further south following in reverse the dozens of previously trodden roads hugging sea and loch whilst walking northwest Scotland, illustrating just how imperious the *"Walk by the Sea"* had been. The phone trilled and again, the winds that constantly plague this corner of the north Atlantic had kept the *Bella Jayne* on her moorings and me no closer to setting foot on **Soay**. This southern **Soay** is proving as elusive as its northern counterpart near St Kilda. Thankfully, my rules avoid this latter intrepid voyage.

I changed tactics and thought I would keep things simple and 'tick off' the two tidal islands of **Tioram** and **Shona**. Of course, I needed luck with the tides and for once luck was on my side, but only just. I discovered the entrance to a track which led to **Shona** and left the car on the main road and with eager anticipation set off a mile downhill to the causeway.

On arrival, the narrow strait between the mainland and **Shona** was still in spate with no chance of crossing. A lonely four-wheel drive vehicle was on the shore waiting patiently for the tidal stream to abate. Inside was a lone young woman, who assured me that a two-hour window either side of 16:50 would allow me to cross. I asked if I could accompany her but in such a remote, out of the way spot she tactfully declined my request. Who can blame her? She insisted there was nothing to see anyway. Instead of an embarrassed wait making uneasy small talk with this woman who lived on the island with her husband and child, I opted to walk back to the car and find **Tioram**, access the island and return later that evening to conquer **Shona**.

It was a stiff climb to the road, and I wasn't relishing a return journey until I noticed the gate was merely chained shut and not locked so I would be able to drive down to the shore the next time, though the steep, scoured track was not for the faint hearted. I easily found the road to **Tioram,** and the access was dry, though it was apparent that tides here were not diurnal, with a sand bar prominent. In fact, Eilean **Tioram** means **Dry Island**. Eilean **Tioram** is one of 43 tidal islands that can be walked to from the mainland of Great Britain and one of 17 that can be walked to from the Scottish mainland[2].

The island is dominated by a ruined castle, known to the locals as Dorlin castle, dating originally from the 14th Century. It was torched during the 1715 Jacobite rebellion and has been unoccupied since. Proposals to restore the castle by the new owners, Anta Estates, were announced in 1997 and received planning consent from the Highland Council. This included the creation of a clan centre/museum, domestic apartments, and some public access. However, Historic Scotland refused Scheduled Monument Consent; a decision upheld after a local public inquiry. The 2011 Scottish island census suggests a solitary permanent resident but talk at my hotel that night suggested that this was a cynical attempt to prove the castle is deserving of connection to mainland utilities. After all my efforts to access **Eilean Tioram**, I later discovered this was not the island

---

2   Caton, Peter (2011) *No Boat Required - Exploring Tidal Islands*. Matador.

mentioned in the Scottish census, but an island of the same name near Gairloch from where I had just come!

I returned to **Shona** after a hair-raising drive down the treacherous track to the shore and, sure enough, the tide was out and I was able to drive onto the island where I found a boat, the only means of access for the young family when the tide was in. Until the middle of the 18th century, **Eilean Shona** was populated by a number of crofters. In the 1920's J.M. Barrie rented the island for the summer as a holiday home, where he was joined by Michael Llewelyn Davies and some friends. It was Michael, along with his four brothers, who had been the inspiration for Barrie's characters Peter Pan, the Darling brothers, and the Lost Boys. Today, Shona House, Barrie's "Neverland" is an exclusive 11-bedroom retreat with rates rising from £4,500 for a 3-night stay.

I needed to rest for the night and remembered the *Glenuig Inn* south of Arasaig. Whilst chatting to the landlord over a pint he mentioned a charter company, *MV Sheerwater* which operates out of Arisaig marina nearby and visits three of what are known as 'The Small Islands', namely **Rum**, **Muck** and **Eigg**. I studied the timetable and discovered a day trip to **Eigg** and **Muck** operating the next day. This trip could at least make up for the disappointment of missing out on 'Love island' and **Soay**.

I arrived at the marina in good time and booked a trip which calls first at **Eigg** and thirty minutes later goes onto **Muck**, a much smaller island with its café and about two kilometres of single-track road. It was July 2nd and yet there were only three other passengers on the 130-capacity motor vessel for which I paid £20 for a return trip. I had a perfectly acceptable lunch in the well-stocked café at **Muck** and headed off to kill two hours before the return journey to **Eigg** and back to the mainland. I was hoping to get views of An Sgurr on **Eigg**, the anvil shaped volcano, a dramatic stump of pitchstone, sheer on three sides prominent across the Small Isles but the weather was overcast and the views disappointing.

The two islands sustain populations each vying to be the greenest of sustainable islands. 'Eigg Electric' generates a combination of solar, wind and hydro power to provide an electricity network that is self-sufficient and powered 98 percent from renewable sources.

I made the gentle stroll back to the ferry quay and then back to **Eigg**. A thirty-minute pit stop allowed me to enjoy a pint of local beer from the Laig Bay brewing company at the *Galmisdale Bay café*. It was late Sunday afternoon, and the place was packed with the "good old boys" of the island drinking their "whisky and rye". With an island population of only 83 this café was certainly punching above its weight with an extensive seven day a week menu. The community buy-out in 1997 resulted in the population being increased by 24%, some six times greater than other Scottish islands' average. The vibrancy of a once declining island was plain to see.

On leaving the *Shearwater* I headed for another hotel I was familiar with, The *Morar Hotel* and managed to secure the last cramped but available single room The whole hotel was occupied by hard-drinking, elderly German coach trippers. I kept myself to myself chatting with the barman, another Land's End to John O'Groats veteran which seems a prerequisite for hotel staff these days! He was also a *geo-nerd* (now that's a new word I've coined) as he was able to recite capital cities of the world at will. Who'd have known that the capital of Equatorial Guinea was Malabo, a sure-fire winner on BBC's quiz game *'Pointless'*. Exchanging countries and their capitals certainly passed the time in between serving a constant flow of German's, with surprisingly poor English, heading to and from the bar.

All that was left was to secure **Danna** at the southern end of the Tayvallich peninsular, with views to **Jura**. On the way I remembered a tiny island a few metres from shore in Crinan harbour. I'd stayed several times in the extravagantly expensive *Crinan hotel* at the western end of Crinan canal. It was a haunt for David Cameron, the yellow livered Prime Minister who sold us the unnecessary Brexit referendum and then disappeared without trace earning thousands for after dinner speeches, no doubt on the successes of postmodern capitalism. His wife, Samantha, was somehow related to the Astor family who owned much of **Jura** across from Crinan. Princess Anne was also a frequent visitor. With such distinguished guests its price tag was sky high for modest accommodation. My dear friends the family Anderson were also keen visitors which explains my sporadic occupancy of the hotel.

I headed for the harbour; the island, this time definitely listed in the Scottish 2011 census as inhabited, was tantalisingly close, 100 metres at most. A random boatman told me it had been taken over by Richard and Sally Stein, bought for around £500,000. I asked if he could take me the short distance to the island but was given short shrift. The Steins were not in residence and would not appreciate uninvited visitors. I turned tail and headed for **Danna**.

The Tayvallich peninsular is little visited as it leads nowhere with most southern bound visitors heading for the much larger and better known peninsular, the Mull of Kintyre. Though crossing the sturdy stone bridge onto **Danna** was unmemorable the glacial, pitted scenery passed on the way was worth this futile but necessary detour. The town of Tayvallich is a gem and a regular RIB service is on offer to **Jura**. I had an alfresco lunch in bright sunshine at a most acceptable café and made my weary way to the Scottish Lowlands and back home. The 'Shetland' trip had been exhilarating with 29 islands covered. The next adventure awaited.

19. Canvey Island, England

The mundanity of the small band of English islands contrasts starkly with their Scottish cousins. I was to assess the merits (or otherwise) of Essex County Council river inspectors and duly set off for Chelmsford. The end of the longish car journey was thwarted by new-fangled 'pay by card' parking machines and a frustrated hour ensued fathoming out how to pay. I failed but a kindly and thankfully young hotel receptionist assisted, much to my embarrassment. The next day the flood defence inspections were going to plan when I suggested a visit to the massive sea defences which protect **Canvey Island** some miles south. They were unaware of the real reason for my desire to go there.

What an eclectic mix of associations **Canvey** conjures up: Orthodox Jews, a rock icon, Brexit champions, a Catalan style independence movement, not to mention catastrophic flooding in 1953.

In 1972, after getting married for the first time we lived in a cramped one room flat in Old Hill Street, Stamford Hill. In those days it was a poor north London suburb. Today it is the 'go to' choice along with Hoxton and Shoreditch of thrusting young professionals. I worked all day revising my PhD thesis which had been summarily rejected as a first draft, whilst Shan busied herself as a lexicographer at the offices in Holborn of Harrap's German/English dictionary publishers. I was driven not to fail, and the hours passed quickly as I re-drafted my *opus magnum* as it was to become. The thesis was pioneering the concept of tree planting as a sustainable means of flood mitigation, decades before the current trend in natural flood management.

With what little free time (and money) we had we spent in the *British Oak* across the road, a stronghold of IRA supporters. Rebel songs were the order of the day and at closing time all, including us, stood in silence for

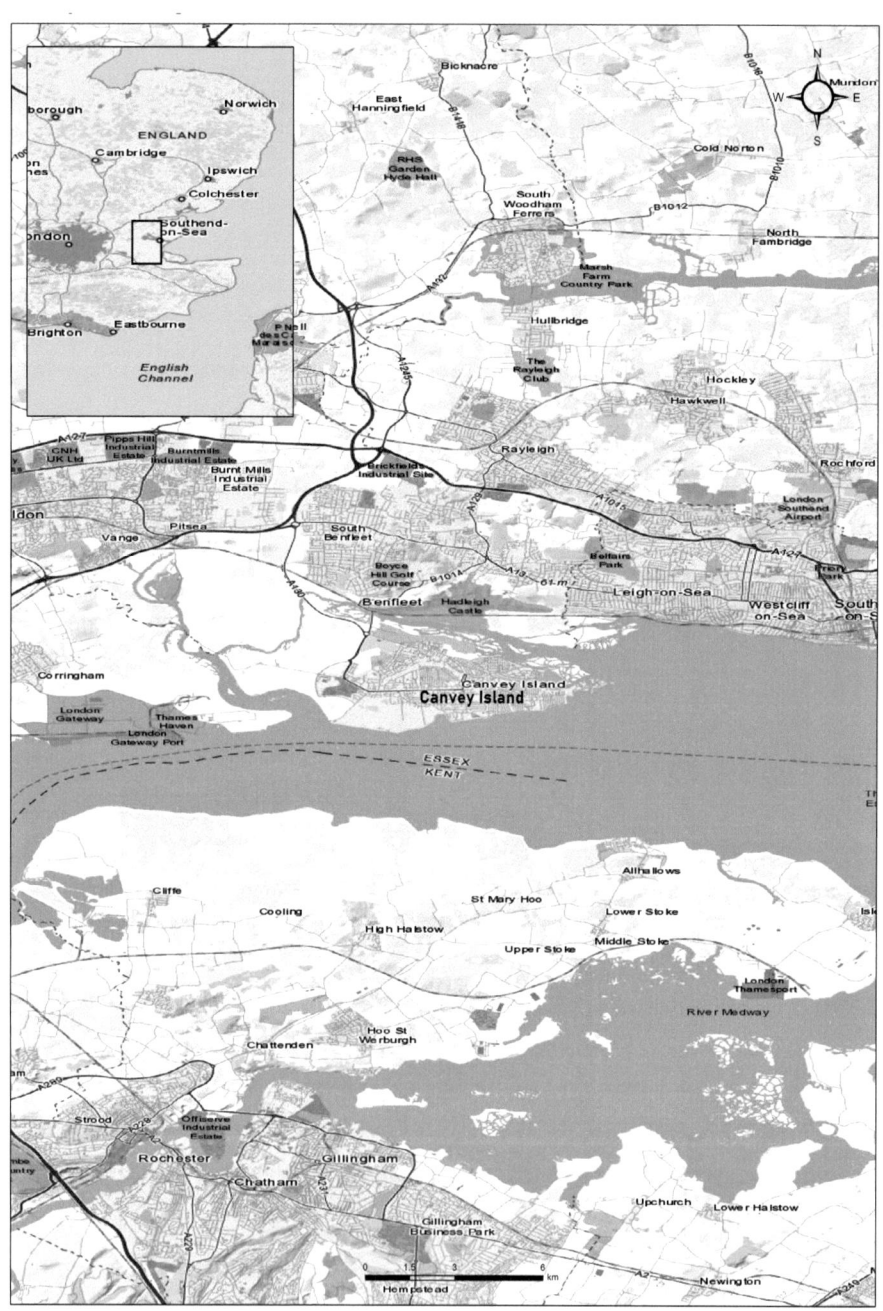

Canvey Island, England

the Irish National anthem. Friends visiting were quickly put in their place should they disrupt this daily ritual by giggling or, worse still, remaining seated.

Many of our other neighbours were orthodox Jews, the men with side curls, beards, long coats and fur hats, the women with wigs and the sort of outer garments with little style or fashion. They had very large families and kept well within their communities. Of course, 45 years on Stamford Hill and its more prosperous neighbour, Stoke Newington, have been transformed into very desirable areas with house prices to match their appeal. In search of a new life and cheaper housing, a number of London's Haredi orthodox Jews are relocating to **Canvey Island** in Essex. Eight children are not uncommon, and they needed a ready supply of large, affordable houses within an hour's commute of London. Scouting parties were sent out to **Canvey**, Milton Keynes, Harlow and Southend. House prices, crime statistics and traffic levels were scrutinised. **Canvey** came out on top and mass emigration ensued. These deeply religious families are an anathema to this island set apart in the Essex marshes often caricatured as a land of boy-racers and "Essex girls", retired gangsters and hard-line Brexiteers. The **Canvey** constituency of Castle Point was among the five most pro-Brexit wards in the UK.

The juxtaposition of two such diverse cultures doesn't yet appear to have presented any racial resentment. A similar mass migration of orthodox Muslims would I am sure be treated with hostility from the islanders' key demographic. The story of **Canvey** becomes even more bizarre when I discovered the Canvey Island Independence Party whose aim is to wrestle back control of this Thames estuary island from the mainland's Castle Point Borough Council. The insularity of island communities and their desire for self-control should not be underestimated even from an island of little more than 40,000 people, separated from mainland Essex by narrow tidal muddy creeks.

From the crests of the massive concrete flood defences the financial towers of Canary Wharf are clearly visible. We walked along these edifices, paying a little deference to the day's objective. It was in January 1953 that **Canvey Island** was inundated by the biggest North Sea surge in recent history. The flood cost 58 people their lives and led to the evacuation of over 13,000 residents. **Canvey** felt the full force of the flood surge, which some say, prevented more serious flooding in London. In the aftermath of the flood, some two miles or more of monolithic linear flood defences (known as sea walls) were built around the island. These stand five and six metres above the properties they are protecting. The severity of this flood paved the way for the design and later construction of the Thames barrier, and its supporting linear defences, by the Greater London Council.

The weather was closing in and the rising tide, washing against the Essex block lower ramparts of the defences, was foreboding, so we retired to the *Lobster Smack*, a clapper board clad pub, which features in Charles Dickens' epic novel *"Great Expectations"* set in the estuary marshes. Conversation turned to music and the eponymous seventies band, Dr Feelgood. The group's original distinctively British R&B sound was centred on Wilko Johnson's choppy guitar style. Johnson was born on **Canvey** Island. His long fight against pancreatic cancer ended in 2022 but the Godfather of pub punk-rock left a rich legacy of music for us to enjoy.

20. Islands off the South Coast, England

I often boast I have visited more places in Great Britain than anybody dead or alive; a formidable claim? Not so. My 5,003 walk around the British coast took in most coastal cities, towns and smaller settlements and my twenty years as an accreditor of river inspectors has taken me not only back to the coast but also settlements situated on the rivers and estuaries throughout the UK. Lorry drivers and travelling salesmen travel more perhaps but have set routes and itineraries whilst thespians and musicians travel to centres of population where their art can attract optimum audiences. Neither group will find itself in Maiden Newton, Dorset or Mundesley, Norfolk. In any case my theory can without doubt never be proven wrong.

River inspections were planned for Hampshire, West Sussex and the South coast, so a whistle stop tour of four islands seemed likely: **Portsea**, **Hayling Island, Thorney Island** and the **Isle of Wight**. The latter will be familiar to the reader, the other three less so. The three largest of the British Islands are **Great Britain, Ireland** (and please before Irish nationalists are sent to kneecap me, please take this in a geographical rather than political sense) and the combined **Lewis and Harris** in the Outer Hebrides. Number three is hotly debated with many barrack-room geographers insisting the **Isle of Wight** is bigger. The two largest islands by area also unsurprisingly have the largest populations. The third largest by population again is hotly disputed with our armchair quizzers opting again for the **Isle of Wight**.

When corrected, with **Portsea** being the undisputed third largest island by population, eyes glaze with bewilderment. Where is it? On explanation that **Portsea Island** includes the City of Portsmouth and Southsea most

TREASURED ISLANDS

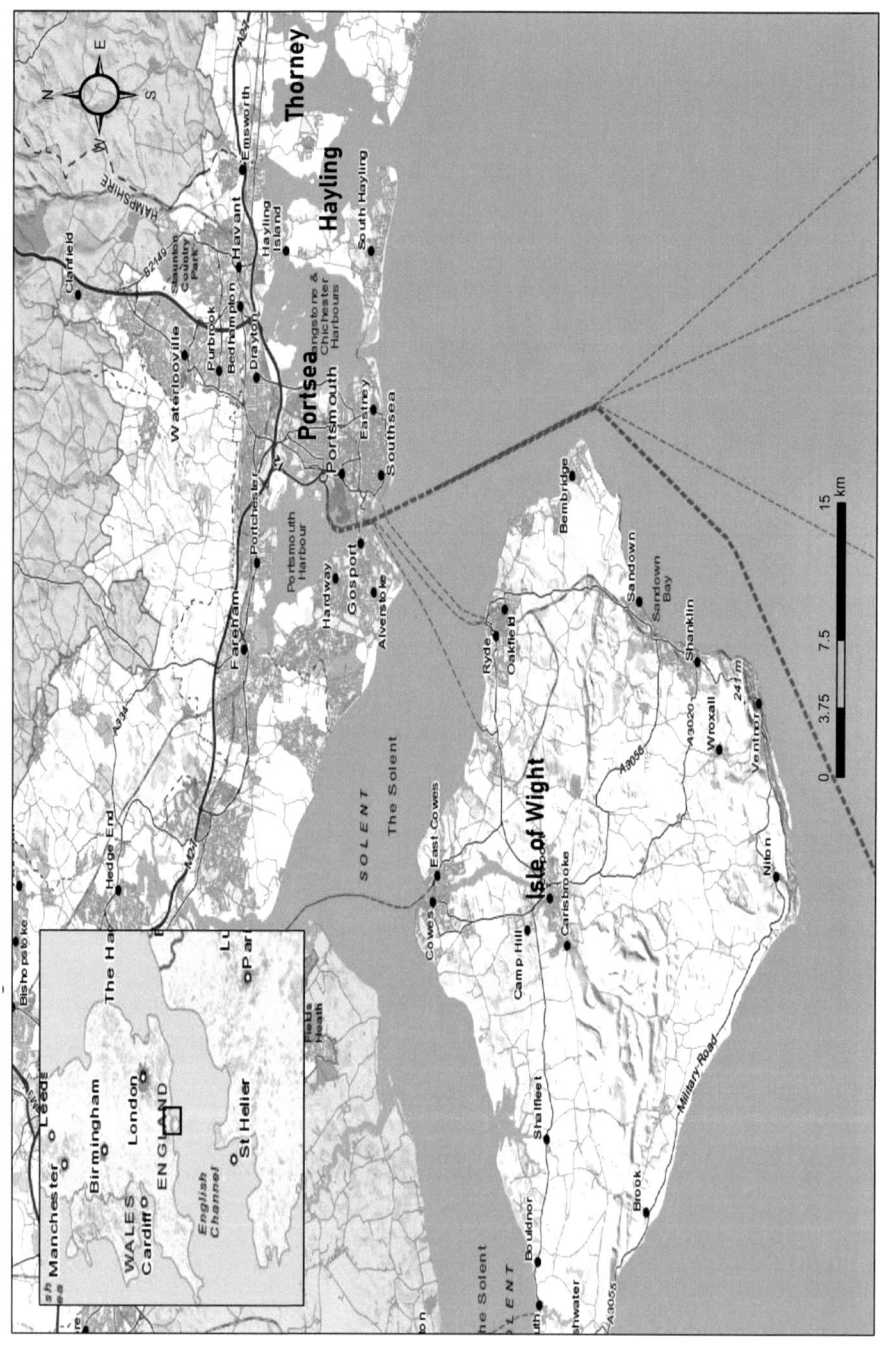

Islands off the South Coast, England

will deny its island status. This is because on close examination of an Ordnance Survey map, the creek to the north separating **Portsea** from southern England is largely hidden beneath the busy east to west M27.

Entering **Portsea** by car is easy with Southsea, a popular resort and an embarkation point for the **Isle of Wight** and Portsmouth, or Pompey as it is affectionately known, rich in maritime history. Portsmouth is the only island city in the United Kingdom and is the only city whose population density exceeds that of London. The city built its wealth on shipbuilding and as late as 1951 some 46% of the workforce was employed thus, rapidly reducing to 14% by the mid-sixties. A naval port of Empire since the days of Henry VIII, Portsmouth regained some sort of naval prowess as the embarkation for ships and their troops to fight Thatcher's Falklands War in 1982.

Now, the historic dockyards are for tourists only with Admiral Horatio Nelson's iconic flagship *HMS Victory* taking pride of place along with *HMS Warrior*, the fastest, largest and most powerful warship in the world when she was launched in 1860. Her construction was a response to not being outdone by the French, who had just built *La Gloire.* Such was *Warrior's* reputation that enemy fleets were intimidated by her obvious supremacy and deterred from attacking Britain at sea - yet she never fired a shot in anger.

October 21st marks the anniversary of the battle of Trafalgar in 1805. Everyone has heard of Nelson's column in Trafalgar Square but in October 1809, the first monument to Lord Nelson to be funded by public subscription in **Great Britain** was erected in Birmingham. If you visit the Bull Ring shopping centre this short rather nondescript monument overlooks St Martin's church. The 44m tall monument seemingly abandoned in a trading estate in Great Yarmouth is my personal favourite Lord Nelson memorial.

The **Hayling Island** ferry from Eastney, on **Portsea's** eastern coast crosses the short neck of Langstone harbour and takes a matter of minutes thus avoiding a long car journey to the road causeway at Langstone. I've worked on **Hayling island** but can't pretend I know it well. It has a quiet feel about it with what appear to be dormitory settlements in Eastoke to the south, with easy access across the causeway and the rest of Hampshire. Normally an island has surprises (look at **Canvey** for, example) that might impress the reader. Try as I might I could not find much of interest in **Hayling**. St Peter's church apparently has one of the oldest bell peals in England, though "one of" indicates that no-one really knows. Just like the church's yew tree with a nine-metre girth which is "believed to be" (by who?) between a thousand and two thousand years old (well that narrows it down, somewhat).

The third and probably the most established (and possibly interesting) fact about this church is it is the resting place in 1959 for Princess Yourievsky (Katia). She was the illegitimate daughter of Czar Alexander II of Russia, assassinated outside St Petersburg's magnificent Church of the Spilled Blood in 1881, where incidentally I met my fourth wife, Liliya in 2002. Bizarrely the good princess chose **Hayling island** to live in an attempt to suppress her asthma but died in relative poverty in a nursing home on the island.

I felt there must be something more sensational that has happened in **Hayling Island** apart from the Real Tennis court (one of a few still used in UK) opened by one of my cricketing heroes Colin Cowdrey. Or the golf club voted in the top 100 in England. Then I found it: on October 20th 2013 at least one hundred properties on the island were damaged when it was hit by a tornado. No injuries were reported. At this point I gave up my quest for interesting facts about **Hayling** Island and headed for nearby **Thorney** Island.

I'd been on **Thorney Island** on *A walk by the Sea*. It hadn't been necessary, but I needed the mileage to make the anticipated 5,000-mile target. It is separated from the mainland by a narrow tidal channel called the 'Great Deep', evocative of some Steven Spielberg block buster. The island is home to 12th Regiment Royal Artillery and the 18 UKSF Signal Squadron, but a coastal path is still accessible provided that walkers declare their name, address and telephone number (and inside leg measurement!) at ominous looking unmanned guard posts at the east and west sides of the island. I remember this walk being tedious but with great views to **Hayling Island** and **Portsea**. I didn't intend to repeat the walk but just step onto the land south of the Deep.

I parked my car and headed for the eastern checkpoint rather nervously. Ahead of me was an ominous looking gate protected by menacing strands of razor wire. On closer inspection it appeared that the intercom was now not working so expectant visitors had to telephone a number to gain access. The number was unavailable. The bridge across the Deep had seen better days but I wasn't going to let either that fact or the lack of means of access deter my mission. On the island side of the Deep was a metre-wide bund in front of the security fencing, so I stepped onto this narrow and unstable strip of land and clung to the fence hoping that the CCTV camera would not pick up this bizarre behaviour. I had made the island and after a few moments reflection made a hasty retreat back to Great Britain. This was not the access I was hoping for but access, nevertheless.

The next day I finished my river inspection duties early and headed for Southsea, the embarkation port for the **Isle of Wight** hovercraft to Ryde using Hovertravel, operating since the mid-sixties. It is the only passenger hovercraft company currently operating in Britain since Hoverspeed stopped using its craft in favour of catamarans. In my teenage years hovercrafts were the vehicles of preference when crossing the English Channel as they were quick and required limited infrastructure other than a concrete landing and take-off apron. Some operators even used just the sand. The idea of the modern hovercraft is most often associated with a British mechanical engineer Sir Christopher Cockerell. His invention was rejected by the military and Cockerell joked "the navy said it was a plane not a boat; the air force said it was a boat not a plane; and the army was plain not interested."

Luckily for me Hovertravel run three trips per hour, so I was able to park, buy my ticket and disembark at Ryde in the space of about 40 minutes. The **Isle of Wight** is evocative of languid family holidays to a grand mansion in the village of Seaview, a few miles east of Ryde This rather magnificent property for its day had been bought by The Baptist Holiday Fellowship. Although a teenager, these holidays were wholly innocent with tennis and croquet between meals and Bible studies. This was 'light touch' religion where hymns and fellowship were as important as prayer; God seemed to be an afterthought. This soft touch version of Christianity is a far cry from what the Baptists have become with evangelism, talking in tongues and loud proclamations of faith the key to salvation.

Our Baptist chapel in Glusburn, Yorkshire was part of the community hubs provided by the owner of the woollen mill, whose beneficence to its workers meant they were provided with all their spiritual and temporal needs. This included an institute, a library and even a swimming baths as part of the suite of 'slipper' baths where once a week the weary workers could enjoy their ablutions as the terraced housing (also belonging to the mill) did not have baths. Alcoholic sales were forbidden, and the nearest public house was *The Dog and Gun*, just across the parish boundary. This model was common in the late 19th and early 20th century with similar villages set up, for example Sir Titus Salt's, Saltaire near Bradford, now a UNESCO World Heritage Site, and Cadbury's Bournville in Birmingham. Paternalistic benefactors ensured the workers needs were, at best, catered for or at worst, controlled.

After I finished my *Walk by the Sea,* I was eager to pursue my continued passion for walking with reasonably stern walks around **Anglesey**, along the Severn Way and the Thames Path and Hadrian's Wall. Circumnavigating the **Isle of Wight** was amongst these mini challenges. On the thirty or so minutes journey across The Solent, I thought back to these days with pride and rued the day I let my fitness wane. Landing at Ryde I found one of its many fish and chip shops and ate a healthy portion before my return journey to the mainland to avoid incurring a parking fine. This two-hour trip had been reflective with reminiscences of childhood, both good and bad.

Before the Norman conquest of England in 1066 the **Isle of Wight** had become a kingdom in its own right, Wihtwara, occupied by the Jutes, making up the third of the triumvirate of powerful German tribes, along with the Angles and Saxons, who had occupied Great Britain. It is intriguing to note that in common with the Crown dependencies of the **Channel Islands** and the **Isle of Man**, the British Crown was represented on the island by the Governor of the **Isle of Wight** until 1995. There are still people who believe that the island is semi-autonomous; well until a little less than 30 years ago it was.

Osbourne House, near Cowes, was the favourite home of Queen Victoria. The bombastic Kaiser Wilhelm II of Germany was Victoria's grandson and was a frequent guest, though often unwelcome, at the annual Cowes regatta before the First World War. He was first cousins with both George V and Czar Nicholas II, who loathed him for his lack of decorum and charm. Fate decreed that George and Nicholas would be rulers of their two countries and arch protagonists of the Kaiser during the Great War. Though George and Nicholas had been close, often holidaying with their respective families in Denmark, George was unable, through political machinations, to offer his cousin asylum in Britain. His bloody fate and that of his entire family was sealed in a blood bath in Yekaterinburg in July 1918.

21. Tiree and Coll, Scotland

I headed north on the Virgin west coast train to Glasgow, walking the half mile to Queens Street station to catch the local Scotrail train onwards to Oban. I had time on my hands and wandered into a bank-turned-pub (as so often they are), *The Counting House* on George Square. It was four in the afternoon and the place was packed to the rafters and I witnessed at first hand just how much Glaswegians drink. Feeling claustrophobic I retreated to *Waxie McFees* and witnessed the same with not a seat to be had. I managed a glass of red before the three-hour train journey to Oban with darkness drawing in and any magnificent panoramas of the Highlands obliterated in gathering gloom. I resorted to working on a project I was involved with in Timor Leste, an independent island nation since 2002 following its bloody war with Indonesia.

I met up again with Stuart and Paul in Oban to relive our youth. The Halloween trip to the Scottish isles was now in its second year and after several decades of separation we were now very comfortable with each other, only our aging appearances defined the passing of the years. We met in the *Royal hotel*, exchanging anecdotes. I led a London University caving expedition to the Julian Alps in 1970 in the then Yugoslavia. I was selected as leader partly out of deference to my age and partly because I was the only one of our group eligible to drive the university union minibus. We found few caves but spent several weeks exploring the deserted mountain karst scenery in between excuses to secure provisions in Ljubljana, the capital of what is now Slovenia. Our 'shopping' trips were little more than an excuse to meet up with the town's speleological club and get wasted on slivovic (plum brandy), the popular national spirit of choice.

The late sixties and seventies were heady years for we university students

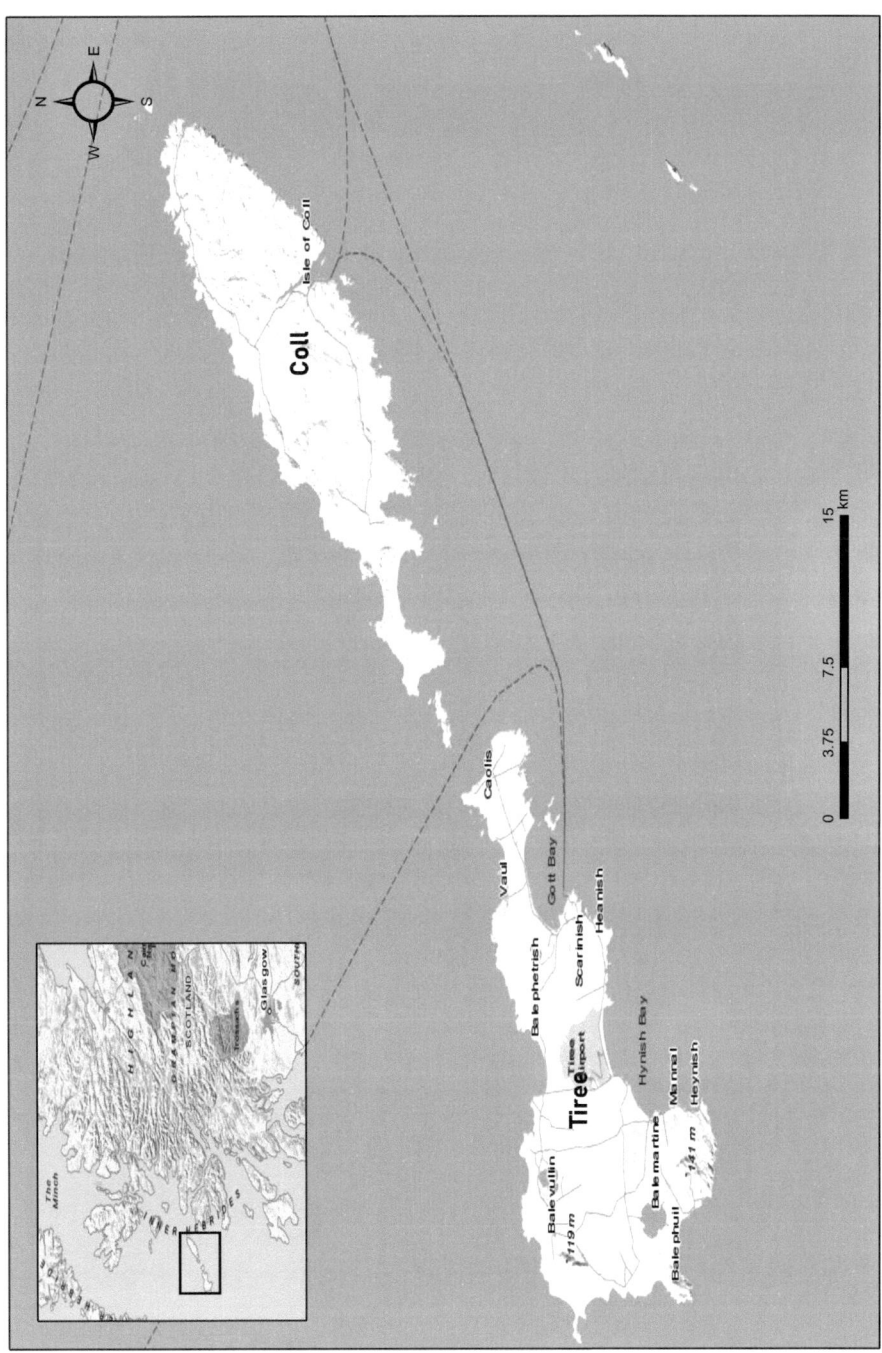

Tiree and Coll, Scotland

and Stuart lived with fellow hippies in a filthy hovel in Grove Road, South Woodford with, if my memory serves, matt black walls. They were the Union elite and spent more time on anti-apartheid or CND rallies than studying. These were the seed bed campaigns which saw the likes of a young Islington activist Jeremy Corbyn getting arrested for his strong beliefs.

Although the privileged 5% were eligible for local authority grants to support them whilst gaining access to free tertiary education, extra money was to be had in the Summer giving guided tours around London to Mormon youths from Salt Lake City. The sixties hippy look seemed to give these tours a greater authenticity and the wide eyed and gullible girls were fair game to Stuart and his flat mates, who fell in and out of love on a weekly basis. Research was minimal to say the least and most of the itinerary was made up. To this day these tourists, now grandparents, are probably returning to London remembering from our misinformation just where the apple fell on Isaac Newton's head! The highlight of every week was a trip to see *Fiddler on the Roof* with the indefatigable Topol in the original lead role. To the young Americans, away from the religious rigours of their Utah upbringing, this came as a major disappointment as they had set their hearts on a visit to the acclaimed seminal sixties musical *Hair* with its hip music and nudity. Stuart used his not insignificant influence to secure tickets from dubious ticket touts with a crazy mark up for the willing and impressionable youths.

Reminiscences over, our mission was to visit **Tiree** and **Coll**, two islands of the Inner Hebrides served by a daily RoRo ferry. Logistics wouldn't allow us more than a perfunctory stop on **Tiree** before the onward journey to **Coll** where we were to spend two nights in the *Coll Hotel*, a bleak sort of pub and the only one on the island.

Tiree is about ten miles long and five miles wide and has the accolade as one of the sunniest places in Britain and has been referred to as "Scotland's chilly St Tropez". For surfing enthusiasts, it is rather rashly known as the "Hawaii of the North". Tourist bombast indeed. The locals like to keep the island a secret but with daily ferries and two flights a day from Glasgow this seems an implausible goal. I remember one of my mothers-in-law, on the opening of the M1 motorway services at Rothersthorpe (now Northampton services), expressing delight in its facilities but reflecting that "it will be spoilt when people find out about it". **Tiree** too was no longer a secret.

We boarded the Caledonian McBride "*Clansman*" ferry operated since 1998, built in Appledore, Devon and the lifeline for those living in **Barra** in the Outer Hebrides and **Tiree** and **Coll**, the latter being our goals this trip. Both islands are low and exposed, which as Haswell-Smith says gives them more than an edge of the world feel about them than any other of the Hebrides. During the Second World War **Tiree** was the most westerly point from which coastal command would fly aircraft in the battle of the Atlantic with something of the order of 40,000 service personnel stationed there. In the event of a German invasion of Great Britain the Royal family were to be taken to **Tiree** prior to evacuation to Canada.

As **Tiree** was elusive, excepting a ten-minute visit whilst the ferry took on passengers, we decided to make the most of **Coll**, which like all other Scottish islands visited had fallen foul of ruthless landowners with famine followed by mass exodus throughout the 19th Century. A quick late afternoon walk told us all we wanted to know about the island which was largely featureless apart from Ben Hogh in the southwest. The island has no streetlights and little other light pollution. On the downside we needed in late Autumn to curtail our walk by four, but on the plus side this meant that the island had been designated 'dark skies' status with unadulterated views of the night sky when the weather allowed.

The hotel on **Coll** was pleasant enough though the central heating was broken for the entirety of our stay, for which a paltry £50 deduction to our room bill was made. We discovered the pub had bicycles for hire and arranged a circumnavigation of the island the next day, about ten miles on roads to the airport, off road across the dunes to the southwest, joining the road at the Gap Year Charity Trust Project and back to our hotel.

After breakfast we set out on our bikes to negotiate our circular route guided by a tourist map that was inadequate for the job. After, for Paul and myself, lung bursting switch back roads on rickety bicycles we went native, that is off road. The day was dry, and I felt in reasonably high spirits despite the fact I hate cycling with a passion unlike Stuart who is the epitome of a fit cyclist. He was in peak fitness after training for the Deloitte *Ride across Britain* mass ride from Land's End to John O'Groats nine days later: that's over 100 miles a day. He had been taking training very seriously with the purchase of a *'squillion'* pound racing bike and figure-hugging lycra to match. This jaunt on **Coll** would be a walk in the park for him even on our ancient bikes.

We made the airport in good time despite the mini switch backs which were irritating me. The tiny airport 'lounge' which had been left open had been renovated thanks to the generosity of the European Regional Development fund, though the next scheduled flight was four months away with the summer timetable ending on 28th October. Brexit would soon put paid to European subsidies to the Highlands and Islands or anywhere else in the UK for that matter. What bemused me is that, in the designated most deprived regions of the European Community, namely Cornwall and west Wales, who gain most from EU grants, the majority voted to leave at the 2016 referendum. Turkeys voting for Christmas! Fortunately, Scotland had more sense as they still have some sort of European affiliations, a residue from the 18th Century enlightenment movement.

The airport lounge had been a blessed sanctuary, with comfortable seats and excellent toilet facilities and significantly more heating than our hotel, but soon it would be dark with time and tide waiting for no man. We ventured into the cold and were bemused by maintenance notices suggesting work by a company from South Staffordshire; surely a local Hebridean firm would have been cheaper?

Cycling the sand dunes was like swimming through treacle and progress was dangerous and slow with tracks frequently covered with blown sand.

After several kilometres of dangerous desert-like terrain, we eventually arrived at the Gap year charity trust project and were inquisitive to discover what this was all about. The building was filled with bright young things either rushing around or huddled over expensive computer machinery – a stark contrast from the wild landscape outside soon to be lost in a deepening gloom. I approached one of the young interns desperate for a drink of water (we had foolishly overlooked to take any provisions). He gladly obliged and began to talk to us about the charity's vision. They annually select around 300 young people from across the UK for 8 to 12-month overseas teaching, social care, and outward-bound projects. Whilst admiring this ethos and their obvious dedication I couldn't help but feel that this was a cover for Missionary work.

Why do Christians have to impose their belief systems on other cultures? I write this in the week that a young American missionary was killed by poisoned arrows whilst attempting to land on the North Sentinel Island, which lies under the theoretical jurisdiction of India near South Andaman Island in the Bay of Bengal. He was alone with the foolhardy task of spreading the Gospel to a tribe reputed to be the most isolated people on earth who have rebuked any contact with so-called civilisation for tens of thousands of years. Leave primitive cultures alone and certainly don't preach Christianity which has lost all or most of its true meaning to many 21st Century believers especially in the evangelical communities of the USA. These neoliberal fanatics who follow a religion based on inclusiveness and equality have lost sight of the original tenets of their faith.

> *'You shall love your neighbour as yourself.'* Mark 12:32

> "When a stranger sojourns with you in your land, you shall not do him wrong. You shall treat the stranger who sojourns with you as the native among you, and you shall love him as yourself, for you were strangers in the land of Egypt: I am the Lord your God." Leviticus 19:33-34

The mid-west Bible belt live their narrow lives with mind numbing hypocrisy apparently upholding the Ten Commandments but, amongst other divisive outrages support Trump's border wall, his imprisoning of child immigrants and spraying the central American immigrant camps at Tijuana with pepper spray.

I was uneasy at the Hebridean Centre, Ballyhaugh; my heart supported their efforts, but my instinct suggested a hidden agenda of proselytising. We had to be back before dark, so our cycling adventure continued without the offer of a cup of tea. The helter- skelter switchbacks were getting the better of Paul and I, not helped by fresh winds on that darkening winter afternoon. We endured what can only be described as a sea of pain. I was feeling poorly so my resident medic, Paul, a retired consultant anaesthetist, took my pulse and sternly asked if I was aware of my irregular heartbeat. I replied to the negative and his tone became sterner. We were on a remote island with no medical facilities, and he was scared for my health. We limped back to base and over dinner discussed my medical options.

The next day we were reunited with the *Clansman* with its 32-crew serving a sparse 40 passengers as against the full complement of 650. The policy of Scottish Government subsidies to island ferries is laudable in these sad days of privatisation for maximum share holder profit. On returning home I checked into the Queen Elizabeth hospital and so began the worst six months of my life.

22. The Gorumna islands, County Galway, Ireland

After our visit to **Coll,** I became part of a trial for Atrial Fibrillation and was a receptacle for all manner of medication. The prescribed betablockers had worsened both my mental and physical health with inexplicable bouts of anxiety and late onset asthma. My retirement ambitions of walking the Scottish Munros were now well and truly scuppered. I pleaded to be taken off the trial medication and return to more tried and tested drugs. Digitalis from the common foxglove for the treatment of heart conditions was first described in the English-speaking medical literature by William Withering, in 1785. He worked at Birmingham General Hospital from 1779. The story is that he noticed a person with dropsy (swelling from congestive heart failure) improve remarkably after taking this traditional herbal remedy. I felt happier with the prescription of a derivative of this traditional drug with over 200 years of evidence-based application.

To clear my mind of ill health I took a trip to Ireland to visit John Lawlor and we decided to head for the Aran Islands in Galway Bay. Access had been attempted a year or so earlier but was thwarted by the weather. After an obligatory but desultory evening in John's Abbeyleix local, *Morrissey's,* where we more than doubled the Tuesday night clientele, we headed for Doolin, the embarkation point for the Aran Islands. This was more in hope than expectation.

We stayed the night in a nondescript hotel close to *Gus O'Connor's* public house. I remembered this, when travelling with my dear late cousin Dick in the late eighties, as a vibrant hostelry with Irish rebel songs sung with gusto by local bands with witty conversations deep into the night. Now it is like many Irish pubs in the country more like a restaurant serving drinks largely to tourists with overpriced meals, on their way to or from

TREASURED ISLANDS

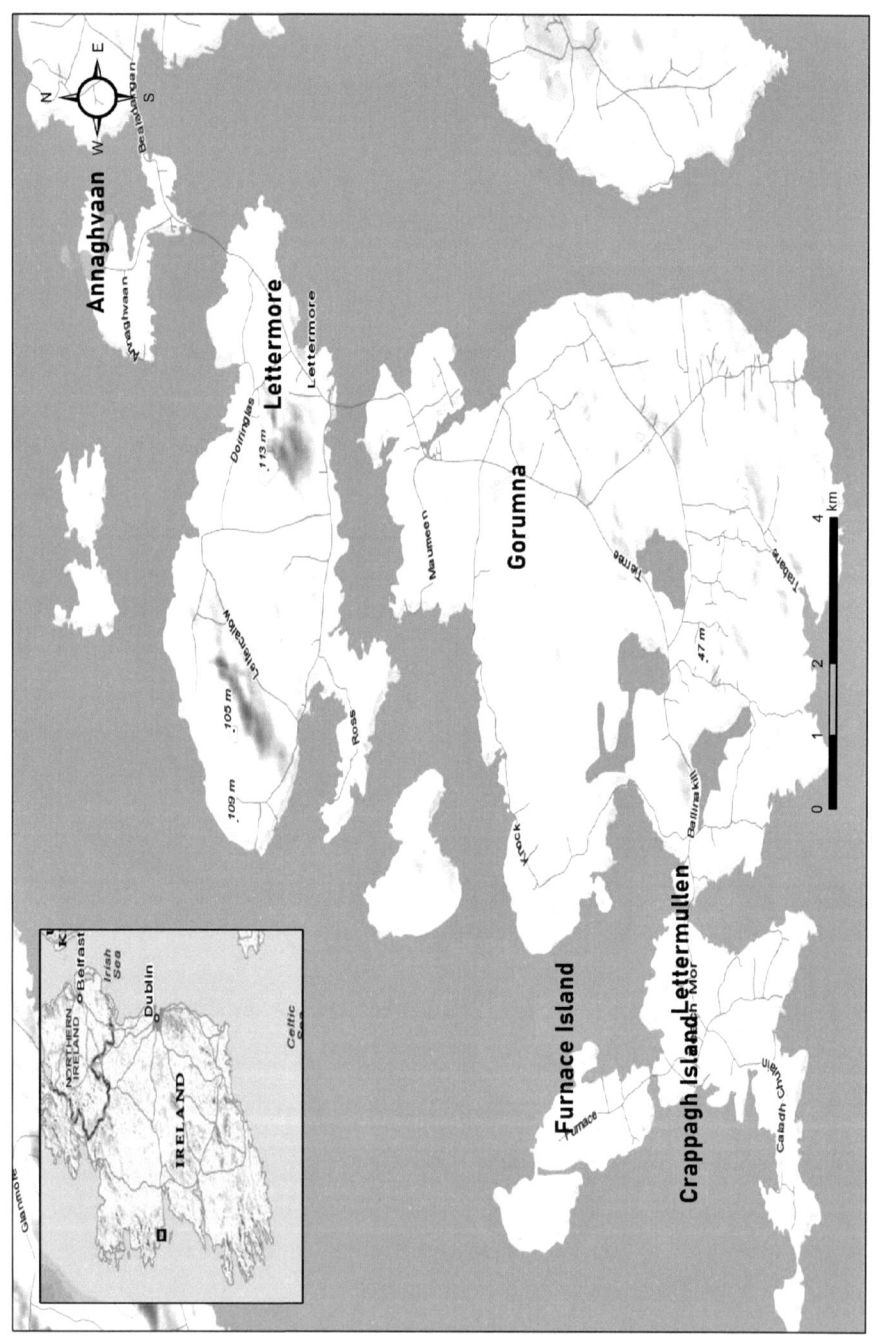

The Gorumna Islands, County Galway, Ireland

the Cliffs of Moher. The Wild Atlantic Way, dreamt up by a genius at Fáilte Ireland (Irish Tourist Board), ensures that largely European tourists find their way to Doolin. Days of heavy drinking with locals are long gone. It was once seriously suggested that to maintain the viability of rural Irish pubs that drink driving laws should be relaxed. Only in Ireland!

Talking of the Irish and their glorious eccentricity radio talk shows are littered with expletives without a thought for censorship. The richness of the English language used in Ireland explains the unique literary status of the likes of James Joyce, William Butler Yeats, George Bernard Shaw, Oscar Wilde, Seamus Heaney, and I could go on. Pre-decimalisation, I once visited Yeats' grave in a church yard under the magical mountain Ben Bulben in County Sligo. Coach parties visited often, largely Americans seeking their heritage. On arrival they were joined by a local who on their departure threw, 'out of respect', a half Crown (12 and a half pence) coin on the grave. The party to a man and woman followed suit and headed back to the coach, leaving the local to pick up his haul.

We made Doolin harbour early the next morning and all three boat trip options for visiting the three islands comprising the Aran group were unavailable. All booking offices were boarded up with apologies for bad weather. The Atlantic is indeed wild. I quickly checked my list of Irish islands and found six inhabited islands in Galway Bay all connected to the mainland by a series of bridges and causeways. The trip would not be a disaster after all. We headed up the 'wild west coast' through the Burren, a bare but beautiful limestone landscape shaped by the last ice age, and onto Galway. The coastal scenery is breath taking with coastal crenulations ensuring ever changing views as the road winds at the mercy of the geomorphology.

We had bought Ordnance Survey 1:50,000 maps in Galway city to ensure efficient navigation as, as ever, time seemed to be at a premium. Driving out of the city I couldn't help but hum *"Galway Bay"* resurrected by The Pogues and Kirsty McCall as a timeless though controversial perennial Christmas record.

'I could have been someone, well so could anyone.... the boys from the NYPD choir were singing Galway Bay and the bells rang out for Christmas day'.

I was suddenly aware that the bi-lingual road signs had been replaced by Irish only signs. Like the Aran Islands over the bay this was Irish speaking Ireland known as the Gaeltacht. About 1.77 million speak some sort of Irish today, mostly learnt at school as a second language. Unlike in Wales there are few schools left teaching in Irish. Only around 82,000 people speak it daily outside of school.

We were entering a Gaeltacht area. Gaeltacht refers individually to any, or collectively to all, of the districts where the government recognises that the Irish language is the predominant vernacular, or language of the home. The 2011 census counted the Galway County and City population of Irish speakers as 48,907 and this represented 47% of the total Gaeltacht population. The number is sadly on the decline, although recognised by the European Union as an official language of the Community. Opening Ireland to all member states, under the enlightened rules of free movement for all member States has meant that Polish speakers in Ireland, 122,515 in 2015, significantly outnumber the vernacular Irish. Whilst in the UK retrogressive Brexit policies will deny further free movement to British citizens, the deluded Tory spin still continues to suggest leaving the EU will "open up Britain to the world".

The six islands comprising the **Gorumna** group are reached from the mainland via the Béal an Daingin Bridge. **Gorumna** is by far the most populated with the other islands in order of population **Lettermore, Lettermullen, Annaghvaan, Furnace** and **Crappagh**. I was impressed to find several 4th order islands in Scotland (accessing the 4th island via three others, unless travelling by sea), but **Furnace** and **Crappagh** were 5th order islands from Great Britain with access via the **Irish mainland, Annaghvaan, Lettermore, Gorumna** and **Lettermullen** first.

We made quick progress onto all these linked islands stopping only to set foot on each. It seems sad we couldn't linger but it is unlikely there was much to linger for and a return to Abbeyleix and my return flight beckoned. The inhabitants are chiefly employed, as for centuries, in the herring and cod fisheries and in the collection of seaweed (kelp) for manure. I was pleased with this raid on five islands, but post visit research suggests from the 2016 census that I had overlooked **Illaunmore** accessed at low tide from Kilbrackan on the mainland and **Inchaghaun** with further low tide access from **Lettermore**. **Crappagh** was not listed as inhabited. Clearly fine tuning is necessary, but the dynamics of island populations ensures some islands will escape even the most detailed scrutiny.

Gorumna has an unnamed monastery as do many of these remote islands. The landscape is so wild one wonders what on earth, apart from fish, the monks lived on. The attraction to bleak locations on the edge of Europe, the edge of the World to Medieval monks, was the search for solitude and meditation. We should not judge with the benefit of hindsight that their lives were less fulfilling than our own. This is the arrogance of the "First World's" consumer society where possessions are of more importance than experiences or, in the case of the chaste Irish monks, Spirituality and a dedication to higher ethereal matters.

23. The Outer Hebrides, Scotland

By the end of May 2018 my health was rapidly worsening, both mentally and physically to the point where, though unable to walk easily, I found myself wandering aimlessly around Birmingham city centre or sitting in weak sunshine in Moseley alongside the alcoholics who camp on the site of the former underground toilets opposite the *Bull's Head*, now a transformed pseudo–Latin American bar, *the Cuban Embassy*. I just didn't want to go home. I'd experienced people with mental health difficulties, but a first-hand introduction hit hard and made me realise how erosive the effects can be on one's personality.

I'd checked in with *Birmingham Mind,* a vital NHS service and was taking all sorts of anxiety medications. I'd collapsed in the doctor's surgery and again in my Atrial Fibrillation trial ward. I just had to get rid of the beta blockers which I suspected were affecting me, not helping. These were hopeless times and one warm May evening, sitting outside *La Plancha* tapas bar, an old haunt of mine, I found I could no longer easily breath. I was coaxed to Queen Elizabeth A&E, not for the first time, but this time on arrival I was rushed straight for treatment and spent the next five days in a respiratory ward. I was on oxygen much of the time and struggled to understand why my fellow inmates, with similar breathing difficulties spent their time evading the nursing staff to sneak the cigarettes they craved for. Addiction is like that.

I was due to travel to Scotland and meet Paul and Stuart for the Outer Hebrides adventure, but it became increasingly obvious that my trip to Oban to meet them and our hired motor home for the week was in jeopardy. The day I was due to travel I was still in the grips of treatment at the hospital. I pleaded for my release which was reluctantly given, and

THE OUTER HEBRIDES, SCOTLAND

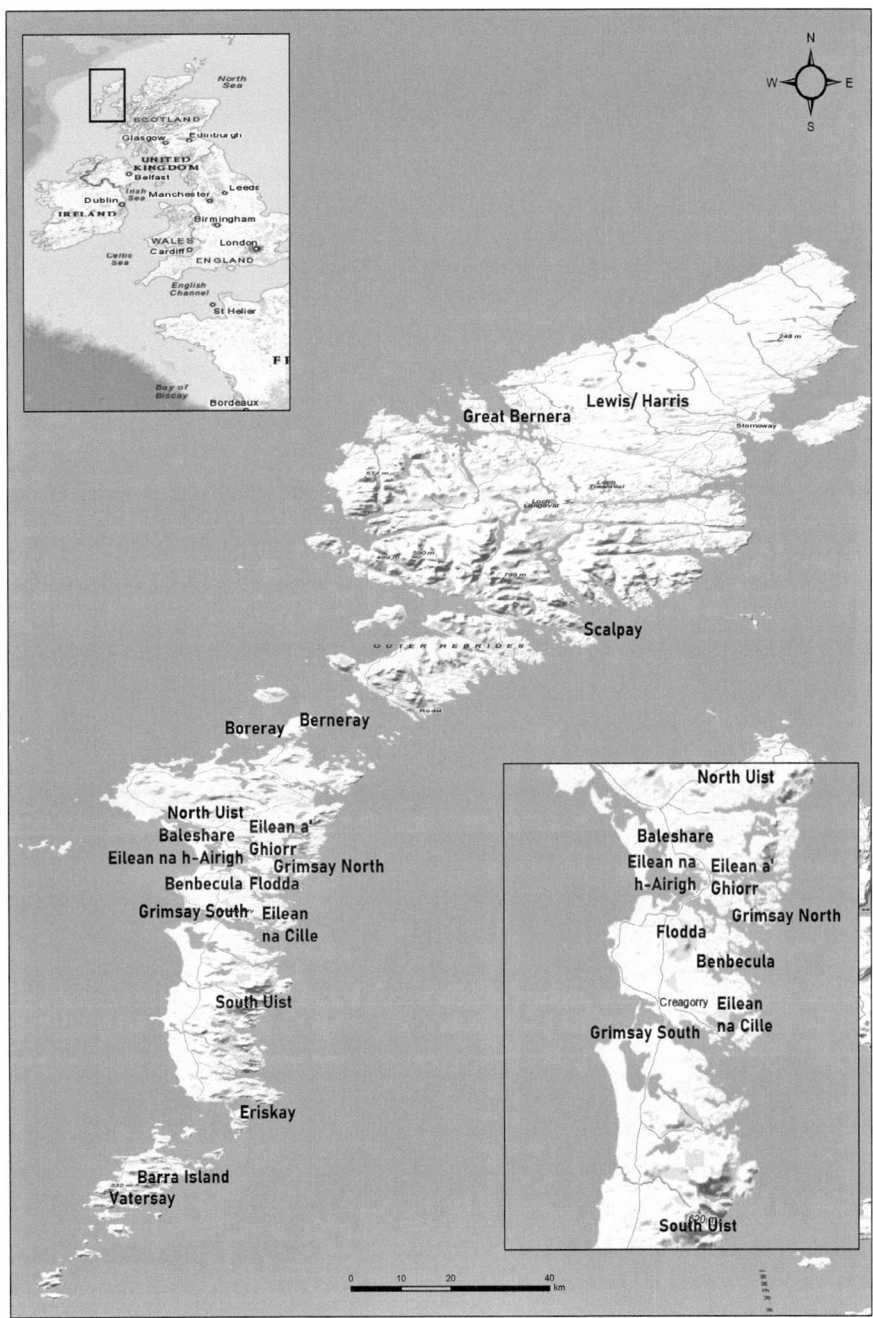

The Outer Hebrides, Scotland

I made New Street station for the three o'clock train to Carlisle to be met my Stuart. All would be well, I mused, as Paul, a retired consultant anaesthetist, would be my personal physician.

The general idea was Paul would drive the camper van, and I would ride shot gun and Stuart would cycle the Hebridean Way, a 185-mile route from **Barra** in the south to the Butt of Lewis in the north, taking in ten of the Outer Hebridean islands. They would sleep in the camper van, and I would attempt to secure accommodation on the route. I hate camping partly because of my irritating nocturia where visits to the loo are at frequent intervals and this exercise is exaggerated in the confines of bunk beds; and partly because of the somewhat negative experience of spending five weeks in June 2004 in a six-berth van whilst negotiating the northwest of Scotland in the *"Walk by the Sea"* odyssey.

We joined the CalMac *Clansman* again and headed for **Barra**, some two and a half hours from Oban. Though summer, the ferry was comfortable with seating amply available but our camp at the bow of the ship had been poached by a rather serious looking woman who was getting stuck into a book on the Greek historian Herodotus. There must be more relaxing literature to take on holiday, but each to their own. The guidebooks promised Minke whales and basking sharks, but these eluded us, and we patiently waited for our adventure to begin.

Arriving at **Barra** with a modicum of apprehension we quickly headed for the bridge crossing to **Vatersay** south of Castle Bay. We passed the impressive war memorial with literally dozens of names from the fallen of the two World Wars. The number of dead seemed totally out of proportion to the sparse populations of **Barra** and neighbouring **Vatersay**. The Isles of **Barra** and **Vatersay** are the most southerly inhabited islands of the Outer Hebrides. **Barra** boasts the only beach runway in the world and is served from Glasgow by Loganair. The de Havilland Canada DHC-6 twin-engine Otter apparently has an under carriage immune from corrosion. Just as well in these stormy climes.

We made the causeway across to **Vatersay** in no time at all and I was ceremonially dumped in the *Isle of Barra beach hotel*, just off the A888 whilst Stuart and Paul (on his newly acquired motorised bike) took on the Hebridean Way at its start point in **Vatersay**. The settlement of Caolas on the north coast of the island is the westernmost permanently inhabited place in Great Britain. We are indeed well out into the Atlantic Ocean with big skies and white beaches the likes of which are usually only seen in the Caribbean or south Pacific islands.

I patiently waited, nursing a Guinness, for the lads to return, noting that the hotel was full but with no signs of life other than a rather bored and inattentive waiter, who explained the hotel was fully booked. The tour bus outside was like the *Marie Celeste* and yet again I was bemused at how there is an inverse relationship between the room occupancy and the profusion of guests. I refer to this as "the pub-car park paradox". Try it yourselves!

After our eventual rendezvous we headed in the direction of the **Eriskay** ferry and found the *Heath Bank* pub for a couple of Skye Gold beers. We acclimatised quickly to our new surroundings and Paul introduced us to '*hygge*' a Danish term with no translation meaning "a sense of wellbeing, the sort of feeling you get as the sun sets sitting by a log fire or candlelight overlooking a calm sea, the sense of being glad to be alive". The Finnish also have a word with no translation for getting drunk just sitting in your underpants. We felt a combination of these emotions sitting in our caravan, parked up for the night in the car park of the **Eriskay** ferry terminal, anticipating the morning ferry. My hospitalisation of the past days seemed in the distant past, with Paul, my personal Florence Nightingale, regularly administering my cocktail of prescription drugs.

Nearly two thirds of the population of **Barra** speak Gaelic and carbon dating of pottery suggests the small island has been inhabited since Neolithic times. The Vikings held sway during their occupation of the Hebrides as 'The Kingdom of The Isles', but Gaelic clans asserted their dominance from the 12th century. The clan McNeil ruled largely unabated until their debt forced the selling of **Barra** with the new Anglo-Scottish owner expelling many of its native population, adding to the diaspora of Scots through the British Empire and the USA. This horrific pattern of greed and neglect is seen throughout the Hebrides.

A century later the McNeil clan were restored as owners with the American Robert Lister MacNeil in charge. They lease Kisimul Castle to Historic Scotland for an annual rent of £1 and a bottle of whisky! With a population of over one thousand, stability seems to have been restored to this wild and windy outpost of The British Isles once a thriving herring port with over 400 boats using the harbour at the end of the 19th Century. The McNeil's have a long, long pedigree with the current owner, the 26th McNeil of **Barra** a distinguished law professor from the prestigious North Western University in Evanston, Illinois.

Vatersay's pedigree is rather more mundane and is owned by the Scottish Government. Its economy is largely based on sheep and cattle and was cut off from its big sister until 1990 when the current causeway was built at a cost of £3.8 million. Before this construction livestock were coaxed to swim the Sound of Vatersay to get to market until the accidental drowning of a prize bull in 1986 led to an outcry for a permanent access with dubious benefits in relation to the costs.

The morning broke after a very restless night and Stuart, already dressed, looked the part in his figure-hugging lycra cycle shorts, though Paul and I were concerned that applying grease to one's anus seemed strangely to be a socially acceptable activity within the long-distance cyclist fraternity. This quaint task accomplished we boarded the ferry to **Eriskay** no thanks to a sarcastic deck hand who when asked by Stuart should he drive onto the ferry was told "No, just drive into the sea".

Eriskay is connected in the north by a causeway to **South Uist** and is the island on which Compton Mackenzie, a **Barra** man, based his novel *'Whisky Galore'*. It was just off **Eriskay** that the *SS Politician,* trying to avoid German U boats, ran aground in February 1941 with its famous cargo of 264,000 bottles of whisky, providing the islanders with a plentiful supply of the amber spirit. What is perplexing is why in the darkest days of the Second World War the cargo of the floundering ship had so much alcohol on board. The great imbiber Winston Churchill clearly saw this as a way to keep wartime spirits high! The irony is that until 1988 **Eriskay** was a 'dry' island. In that year, a pub naturally called *Am Politician* was opened. On further research my Churchill idea was scuppered like the ship as the whisky was bound for the USA. Bottles still occasionally show up on the shores.

Eriksay, along with **South Uist** and **Benbecula** further north were in 2006 the subject of a community buy-out for £4.5 million with management entitlement in perpetuity. It is hoped that this will in some way stem the rapid emigration of past decades. Community buy-outs throughout the Western and Northern Isles seem to be invaluable to maintain future sustainable communities.

Eriskay is a barren island in contrast to its beautiful Gaelic songs with *The Eriskay Love Lilt* its most well-known and brought to a wider audience by Judith Durham's *Seekers* and more recently *The Corries*:

> "Thou'rt the music of my heart;
> Harp of joy, o cruit mo chruidh;
> Moon of guidance by night;
> Strength and light thou'rt to me".

As with **Barra** its population is mainly Catholic and it was here that Bonnie Prince Charlie, the Catholic Young Pretender was sheltered before his legendary, but probably fictitious trip 'over the sea to **Skye**' from a sheltered cove in neighbouring **Benbecula**.

The priest Allan McDonald's valuable collection of Gaelic phrases and poetry was mutilated after his death but rescued by Lorne Campbell of **Canna** (see Small Isles). Many of the indigenous poems and songs were passed down orally and the notation and preservation of Gaelic language and culture owes a lot to **Eriskay's** tradition.

A series of road bridges and causeways links **South Uist** to **Benbecula** and on to **North Uist**. These islands are strongholds of the Gaelic language, with **South Uist** boasting some 82% of the island speaking Gaelic, and like most of the Outer Hebrides the population are largely Roman Catholics. The machair, first encountered on our epic bike ride round **Coll**, dominates the coastal landscape. These are low lying coastal plains leading gently to gleaming white, deserted sandy beaches, and backed by rugged hills composed of Lewisian Gneiss, brought to the surface long ago and shaped by successive ice ages. The rocks are amongst the oldest geological formations in the British Isles.

As a teenager I was into rocks unlike most boys in the nineteen fifties who were into railways, steam trains or rock and roll and the like. I poured over geological maps under my bed covers at night whilst listening to Radio Luxemburg on my crystal set receiver. I could see where the Pre Cambrian igneous rocks changed to Carboniferous and wanted to visit these transitions and collect samples of all geological epochs. I memorised mnemonics to assist my chronological gallop through geological time:

"**A**ll **C**olliers **O**n **S**aturday **D**raw **C**olliery **P**ay" (Archean, Cambrian, Ordovician, Silurian, Devonian, Carboniferous and Permian – the Primary epoch); then "**T**om **J**ones **C**ame" (Triassic, Jurassic, Cretaceous – the secondary epoch; and "**E**very **O**ld **M**aid **P**lays **P**oker **H**opelessly" (Eocene, Oligocene, Pliocene, Pleistocene, Holocene – The tertiary and quaternary epochs)

Just before leaving for London University in 1966, I accompanied my parents and Uncle Eric and Auntie Edna to Scotland, a last holiday as a family. My father indulged my hobby. He was keen I didn't deviate from academic pursuits. He was a mechanical engineer, Chief Engineer of *Hayfield* knitting wools in the small Yorkshire village of Glusburn as was his father before him. He made sure the mundanities of repairing knitting wool making machinery were off limits; the groves of academe were his goal for me.

I sat in the back of our Morris Oxford, geological map open and insisted on stopping whenever the colours on the map changed. We would find a quarry and search at length for a prized rock specimen much to my uncle and aunt's dismay. As we motored through Scotland the car became heavier with my precious loot and Eric became more irascible. I was ruining their holiday, but my dad was proud of my pursuits. A purity of ambition, the last days of innocence before entering the flesh pots of the sixties east London in the days of the Kray twins and Saturday nights watching transvestite drag acts at the *Iron Bridge* or *Bridge House Tavern* on the Commercial Road.

South Uist is the epitome of remote majesty, and the usual tourist hyperbole is, if anything, not strong enough to describe the endless 20 miles of dune and machair running along the Atlantic coast. Stunning endless blue horizons unfold with, if imaginations are stretched, the flight of the golden eagle circling around the peaks of Beinn Mhòr, the 'Big' mountain at pushing 2,000 feet. Over 200 species of flowering plants have been recorded on its Machair Special Protection Area, some of which are nationally scarce. This unique and sensitive habitat could be another casualty of sea level rise following climate change.

In the rugged interior lochs abound with trout. Second of the Outer Hebrides islands in size to **Lewis and Harris**, **South Uist**'s inhabitants are known in Gaelic as *Deasaich* or Southerners; north/south perspectives are relative. For example, Sassenach was not only the name Scottish highlanders gave to the English (derived from a corruption of Saxons) but was a term they used for lowland Scots too. Again, Geordies smile when Yorkshire folk refer to themselves as Northerners. Na Meadhoinean, or Middle District, is the strongest Gaelic-speaking community in the world with 82 per cent fluent in the tongue.

The ancient and the modern are juxtaposed. At Dalliburgh in 2002 the first deliberately mummified prehistoric bodies found anywhere in Britain were discovered. In contrast in nearby Askernish a golf course designed by the fabled Old Tom Morris was rediscovered and restored.

Set in the wild machair golf aficionados (and I certainly am not amongst their number – as Mark Twain remarked "Golf is a good walk spoilt") hail this course as the most natural links course in the world.

In more recent history the Royal Artillery Missile Range sandwiched between the Atlantic and the main road to the causeway to **Benbecula** was built at the height of the Cold war to launch the Corporal missile, Britain and America's first guided nuclear weapon. To parody the emergence of artillery ranges across the Outer Hebrides Compton Mackenzie was inspired to write *Rockets Galore*, as a sequel to his earlier success, *Whisky Galore*.

Whilst Stuart trundled his way north on his high-performance bicycle Paul and I had logistics to contend with, namely planning to get to **Boreray** (population 1), tucked away in the Atlantic Ocean offshore of **North Uist**. We left **South Uist** for **Benbecula**, which though a place I have always wanted to visit was disappointing, a flat nondescript sort of place between the more picturesque and mountainous Uists. With its low-lying geography and remoteness **Benbecula** was an ideal base for nefarious military activity with an airfield to the north, built during the Second World War, which became the control centre for the Hebrides rocket ranges and now reinvented as Benbecula Airport. An army base was established here in 1958 and is still one of the main employers on the island as it is the headquarters for those who service the **South Uist** missile testing range; not the sort of profile that encourages the visitor. Not only is this drab island a steppingstone between **North** and **South Uist** but is symbolically a religious steppingstone between the Catholic south Outer Hebrides and the staunch Protestant north.

We took the coastal scenic road to the **North Uist** causeway, pleased with our progress meeting Stuart in **North Uist**. These trips are plagued with logistical decisions and in our conversations about getting to **Boreray** we totally missed two islands, **Flodda** and **South Grimsay**, which are inhabited but not qualifying within the strict rules of Haswell-Smith's book '*Scottish Islands*'. They would have been easy conquests by causeway but remain for a future, expensive visit, or under the chapter "forgotten islands".

Clan chief Flora MacDonald's altruistic act, securing the Young Pretender's safety contrasts with the atrocities acted out all too often in the Scottish Islands and Highlands. **Benbecula**, like many of its Hebridean neighbours, was sold to a heartless tyrant when its chieftain (we've heard this story so many times before) got into financial difficulties in the 19th century. John Gordon owned 1,383 slaves on Tobago in the Caribbean and was used to treating folk badly. True to form and seeing the financial advantages to livestock farming, Gordon was ruthless, evicting the population with short notice, sometimes even resorting to dragging them to the shore in handcuffs, wearing little more than their underclothes. A repeated pattern right across the Highlands and Islands he replaced the residents with sheep. Despite his behaviour causing a national outcry, this legacy was continued by the widow of his son, well into the early 20th century.

To add insult to injury after the slavery abolition act of 1833, Gordon, like many of his over privileged types, received nearly £25,000 compensation for losing his slaves, equivalent to £3 million or so today. The disparity, arrogance, greed and ruthlessness continue unabated amongst the relatives of these crooks today – the disaster capitalists who invest offshore and resist any attempt at wealth taxation or even any taxation at all. I make no apologies for repeating throughout my travels these stains on our Nation's history. These heinous acts of barbarism should form the mainstream of historical education.

The causeway, with its southern cousin are the lifelines of these islands and effortlessly took Paul and I to **North Uist** with a real urgency to secure a trip to **Boreray** before retreating to Leverburgh on **Harris**. **Boreray** was another island that could have been missed because of my cowardice in making phone calls. I have always had a sort of phobia in confronting strangers. I would rather die than canvas opinion door to door. After a little effort we got the name of a potential boatman and I persuaded Paul to do the sweet talking from a phone box in the ferry port at **Berneray**, the island north of **North Uist** and the terminal for the Leverburgh ferry to **Harris**.

Mobile 4G phone signals often fail in these remote outposts. Entering the red box, rarely seen these days, was indeed a novelty and to find it working was an even greater novelty. Stuart and I later mused we had not used a public phone for nigh on 30 years. Paul did not have my irrational phobia of telephoning strangers and he got hold somehow of the wife of one Jerry Cox who indeed had a boat and as he was due that day to return from a scientific excursion of some sort in France he might be up for a trip. I had become phlegmatic with respect to the crossover between sanity and expense. We had bartered a half day trip from Leverburgh the next day at what seems to be the usual price tag of £350. Sanity seemed to have lost this battle. I could only congratulate my colleagues in their stalwart commitment to duty and arranging my cowardly frame to be transported the next day to **Boreray**.

Whilst waiting for Stuart and retirement for me to the *Orasay Inn* on **South Uist**, we ventured onto **North Uist** a second time and perfunctorily ticked of the tidal islands of **North Grimsay** just across the causeway from **Benbecula** and **Baleshare**, connected in 1963 by a causeway to **North Uist**. I was smug at 'ticking off' five islands in one day, and even smugger to realise with **Boreray** now virtually certain a return journey to the remote Outer Hebrides would not be necessary. I was then, because of yet again appalling planning exacerbated by my recent hospitalisation, unaware that the islands of **South Grimsay** and **Flodda** had eluded me.

Half of **North Uist**'s land area is occupied by lochs. Loch Scadavay alone has an 83km shoreline. The remaining crofters here just about cling to economic viability. The backdrop to **North Uist**'s harsh history is yet more Highland Clearances from heartless, mostly English or at least anglophile landlords. Again, Cape Breton in Nova Scotia was a common migration path.

Grimsay, not to be confused with the illusive **South Grimsay** connects **North Uist** to **South Uist** by yet another causeway and is known for its lobsters, prawns and scallops. We crossed the island with little ceremony on each crossing we made. Causeway crossing had become somewhat of a pastime. At Carinish on **North Uist** is the ruin known as Teampull na Trionaid or Trinity Temple. Like **Iona** off the coast of **Mull** in the Inner Hebrides it was developed as a seat of learning as far back as the 13th Century. It is widely believed to be Scotland's oldest university. Now an interesting historical footnote is worthy of recalling. The Temple was attended by Duns Scotus, renowned for his studies from Oxford to Paris and Cologne. The cornerstone of his philosophy was that religion depended on faith not reason. The more sceptical 'establishment' of the time coined the term 'dunce' for anyone upholding such 'stupid' views.

Just north of Carinish a 350m causeway leads to **Baleshare**, the first Scottish island to see the profitability of harvesting kelp and today it has a thriving population of around 58. It has been suggested that low lying areas adjacent to **Baleshare** were destroyed by the 1607 'tsunami'. This same year saw the Bristol Channel and south Wales similarly devastated with evidence of rushing water inland travelling it was recorded 'at the speed of a greyhound'. The Bristol Channel event was dismissed as an extreme tide surge but its popularity as a tsunami found favour after the devastating tsunamis in Southeast Asia in 2004.

Tsunamis, long since the sole domain of geographical studies, were now mainstream news. The 1607 event was mooted to have been caused by tectonic action off the coast of Ireland but those proposing a tsunami hypothesis underestimate the volume of water and coastal damage involved in storm surges and failed to account both for flooding on the opposite side of the country on the same day. The jury is out on this one but surge storms like the one affecting Europe's North Sea coast in 1953, devastating the Netherlands and the east coast of England, are subject to reasoned statistical probability. Study of tidal records at Avonmouth shows that the 1607 event in Bristol Channel was 'off the scale' based on statistical data records, giving credence to the tsunami theory.

A road bridge links **North Uist** to **Berneray**. If the reader is not already confused as to the location of the satellite islands off **North Uist** we were even more surprised to find that **Berneray**, though geographically linked to **North Uist** is traditionally part of the parish of **Harris**. A combination of fertile topsoil and kelp as fertiliser have led to healthy potato crops over the years as the island slumbered on oblivious to the 20th Century. It was in 1980 that Charles, Prince of Wales and Lord of the Isles (now King Charles III) opted to 'get away from it all' and experience life among 'these gentle, friendly people'. His sustainability credentials are well known but his patronising tone is somewhat grating. He lodged in simple surroundings with 'Splash' McKillop and his wife and the world's press were none the wiser.

I was waiting for a cataract operation and my vision was poor, leaving Paul to do the driving, which he relished, shared with Stuart when not cycling. I was still poorly from my hospital incarceration and still relied on Paul to administer my medication at timely intervals. We never knew where Stuart was on his cycling escapade as despite these islands being small in population there was a veritable spaghetti of roads on which to lose each other. I spied a red figure in the distance. "That'll be Stuart" I gasped. Much to Paul's amusement it turned out to be a post box. Our communication skills were hopeless and rendezvous planning was for 'softies' but in reality, nigh on impossible with hardly any effective mobile phone signals. The harsh reality was that Stuart had no comprehension of short distances and just kept on cycling till we attempted to rein him in. Paul was happy to do bite size motorised cycle rides and we happily leap frogged northwards.

Having had our fill of the Uists and appended islands we took the Caledonian MacBrayne ferry to Leverburgh on **Harris** where we were to meet our boatman the next afternoon for the much-anticipated trip to **Boreray**. On arrival at this busy port, I used my knowledge from a couple of previous trips to **Harris** and we headed for the pub at Rodel, a few miles southeast. My experiences previously had not been good with a sparse clientele of locals supping in a freezing bar with no comforts, but passable food. We arrived to find the pub was being converted into accommodation, with clearly better profit margins and retraced our steps to the crowded harbourside café which offered the only fare available in the village.

After a soulless meal we headed north hoping to 'wild camp'. All available lay by spaces were already taken by an army of motor homes of all shapes and sizes. Miles went by with no room to park comfortably. Unlike in England there is no restriction to parking up for the night on the side of the road. We reached the turn off for Luskentyre beach, a known beauty spot, up there with the beach at Pigeon Point, Tobago in the Caribbean. The nights were still bright and in this 'little slice of heaven' we found a perfect spot to rest for the night. Very little changes here except the intensity of vivid colours and the rhythm of crashing waves on the beach.

We grabbed what was left of the light, sitting outside on a still, warmish evening and reminisced, taking time to recharge. As all accommodation in Leverburgh had been occupied, I had no choice but to join the lads in the camper van and had fitful sleep in the cramped bottom bunk, mercifully close to the 'head'. The morning was bright with the views of the previous evening transformed into new aspects of shade and light. Stuart decided to cover lots of miles on **Harris and Lewis** agreeing to meet us at my hotel for the night, *The Loch Erisort Inn*.

Meanwhile Paul and I passed time breakfasting at the swanky *Hebrides Hotel* in Tarbet, an excellent place I knew well from previous visits. It is a few metres from the ferry terminal for Uig on the Isle of **Skye** and a welcome watering hole on unpleasant 'dreich' evenings as they had always seemed to be.

The road to Tarbet is called the Golden Road so called because of its expense to build, carved out of bare gneiss rock, and carefully avoiding the litany of pock marked lochs along its route. The predominant colours are rich dark browns, greens and greys and the famous Harris tweeds mimic these mixtures. Crofters still manufacture this unique cloth on hand looms in a plethora of cottage industries with retail outlets to entice the buyer. I have many such items of clothing, expensive but, unlike me, will last an eternity. It was the Earl of Dunmore's wife who introduced the world to Harris Tweed in the early 19th Century. *Clo more* or big cloth, though forever associated with **Harris**, has moved its main commercial production north to **Lewis**. At the height of production 650 weavers were producing four and a quarter million yards of cloth per year but with cheaper and lighter weather resistant synthetics now on the market tweed has become a luxury, even a haut couture item of clothing.

Replete we set off to **Scalpay**, north of Tarbet served until recently by ferry only. With the welcome assistance of a 65% grant from the European Union through the Objective One Programme, the island's authorities were able to proceed with the ambitious transport plan they had set themselves to construct the 300m bridge to **Scalpay** which carries road and pedestrian traffic together with the water supply for the island. In December 1997, **Scalpay's** oldest resident, Mrs Kirsty Morrison, aged 103, led the way for the first drive across the bridge.

If only the current swathe of Brexiteers were aware of the myriad infrastructure projects funded by the European Regional Development Fund maybe they wouldn't see our contributions had been a one-way syphon to Europe. Johnson and his Svengali Cummings saw to it that misleading soundbites and downright lies (the £350 million per week contribution to the National Health Service slogan on the side of a bus, if we left the EU) would stick in the minds of those who don't want to know or don't care about what being 'in Europe' actually means to our economy.

In June 2016, and by a 62%/38% majority, Scotland voted to remain in, but their mandate is frustrated by the negativity of the UK Westminster Government led by one charlatan after another. The breakup of the UK is imminent, and maybe a Celtic nation will emerge, containing Scotland, Wales, **Ireland**, the **Isle of Man**, Cornwall and Brittany and maybe Cumbria to boot. Is this wishful thinking? Perhaps not in the distant future as our islands have seen different waves of political rule and language dissemination, from the Romans to the Vikings to the Saxons and to the Normans. Scotland in particular was a sovereign part of Norway for several centuries. Our collective Nation is rich because of these 'conquests'. The xenophobia of Little England makes no sense.

Scalpay a few miles north of Tarbet at least got its independence from a benevolent owner, Mr Fred Taylor in 2012 (now he sounds like a man of the people with no elaborate monikers or noble titles surrounding his name). This close knit, vibrant community is in the middle of a resurgence in its fortunes. It has almost an urban sophistication about it. We drove in no particular hurry to Eilan Glas lighthouse which was the first to be built in the Western Isles, erected in 1789 to serve the busy shipping lanes between the Hebrides and the Baltic states.

We'd made arrangements, well at least Paul and I had (as Stuart had cycling north on his mind) to meet with our boatman, Andy, in the afternoon to travel the few short miles to the isolated island of **Boreray**. We had trouble parking the motorhome in a rather busy Leverburgh as, like all harbours, public access by vehicular transport is strictly forbidden. Luckily, Andy was patient and was waiting. Our verbal agreement over the phone to pay what might to many seem a ludicrous fee for a short journey, may have made him reluctant to prepare and fuel up his sparkling new bright yellow vessel. He had, after all, just returned from a research trip to France studying the carbon sequestration of sea grass and was eager to spend time with his family.

The weather was very fortunately set fair. Andy said we were indeed lucky as the weather in these nether regions of the North Atlantic could be 'cowering'. We set off in his new Cheetah 90 horsepower twin engine craft and he gave us a briefing of the island mentioning many of the Celtic Saints who came to **Iona** were buried there, with evidence of 14 burial mounds at Cladh Manach. It was not clear as to why **Boreray** was a mecca for Saintly burials.

Today the only human presence is a solitary gentleman, Gerry Cox, who owns the Old Schoolhouse and has been eking out a living on 87 acres of the island for several decades. As with many Scottish islands, summer grazing rights are registered to sea shepherds from neighbouring islands, particularly **Berneray**. At its peak the 1841 census indicates that this small island of just 198 acres supported 181 souls, but over-cultivation and the collapse of the kelp trade brought a gradual decline in the population. In 1923, the island was evacuated at the request of the islanders.

We were keen to meet Gerry and from the Robinson Crusoe-esque sandy beach, fringed by low dunes, we could see his self-contained croft powered by green energy. The shallow water was warm and the beach clean as is *de rigueur* for these Scottish islands, a far cry from the plastic infested beaches closer to civilisation. We lunched, or rather snacked, peacefully but were not joined by the incumbent crofter. Self-sufficiency was clearly the top of the list of Gerry's priorities as **Boreray** would be storm bound for large parts of the winter months. A study of the psychology of the human resolve in remote isolation would be certainly worth a PhD thesis but then any invasive probing of coping with loneliness would defeat the object of the research.

We toyed with the idea of walking to the croft, but the distance and terrain got the better of us and instead I lectured Paul and Andy on the importance of dune management. The dunes here had suffered serious 'cliffing' in part, eroding the foredune. This was largely unimportant here but of real concern for coastal golf courses. I had become a bit of an expert on advising Irish golf courses on the need for expedient coastal management.

The 2019 Open golf championship was held in Royal Port Rush across in Northern Ireland and the whole event, bringing incalculable wealth to the region, would have been scuppered if the integrity of the fairways was affected by winter storms. Musings over we headed back to Leverburgh and contemplated a most serendipitous trip. I felt privileged that I could afford such a luxury, which many could only imagine and to me it proved that the elasticity of money in terms of the pleasure derived is incalculable. Andy's fee could in no way be calculated in terms of miles covered.

Our late afternoon mission was to find Stuart, who had no time for communication, this time actually measuring success in miles covered. This could not be hard as there appeared on our tourist map to be only one north/south road. As in **North** and **South Uist** the reality is that there are many spurs off this long and winding road. As we moved forward, we were convinced he had used one of these spurs to visit the coast or was "dead in a ditch", a phrase that would shortly become part of British political folklore, with Prime Minister Johnson uttering in late 2019 that he would rather be dead in said ditch than delay Brexit beyond January 31st, 2020. We reached the turning to the *Loch Erisort inn* and assumed he must have cycled there to await our arrival. Not so and we chased many miles up the A859 to find him eventually blissfully pedalling northwards before returning to the inn, our base for the night.

We drank too much whisky in the camper van to which the grumpy Yorkshire hotelier had granted parking rights and I retired to the bleak but relative comfort of my twin room. Stuart, by his own admission, is not one for sleep and, inquisitive for breakfast the next morning, I found him being chased out of the hotel kitchen by the startled kitchen staff; sent packing in no uncertain terms - Fear and Loathing in Loch Erisort! We breakfasted in haste and vacated the scene.

Our goal was the Butt of Lewis, and we had a leisurely day to pass before our mid evening ferry from Tarbet to Uig on the Isle of **Skye** and then the long journey home, hoping for the third time of asking to take in **Soay** on the *Bella Jane*, a trip that had been called off for bad weather twice already. Sightseeing was on the cards as we journeyed north by campervan and cycle. It was early June though shops were closed with little signs of life.

Our excitement of a leisurely day (no apparent island hopping) made us almost forget **Great Bernera** an island off the west coast of **Lewis** easily accessible by a short road bridge, built in 1953, and the first prestressed concrete bridge in Europe. The island was the location of the Bernera Riot of 1874, when crofters resisted the Highland Clearances. Their stance against the heavy-handed evictions, so successful elsewhere, laid the foundation for much needed land reform in Scotland. At last, this was a success story of the common man resisting the brutality of privilege, power and exceptionalism.

The bridge despite its claim to fame was innocuous and nearly didn't get built until the inhabitants threatened to dynamite the hillside to create their own causeway. It now lays claim to being "The bridge over the Atlantic" which is not only stretching the imagination as to what the Atlantic is but is contested by other small bridges connecting Great Britain to an offshore island. The Clachan bridge connecting mainland Argyll to **Seil Island** is a case in point. The sleepy village of Breacleit just over the bridge offered little of interest so we headed north for the 'Black houses' and the mystical stones of Callanish.

Great Bernera was owned until very recently by an obscure aristocrat and friend of Ian Fleming of James Bond fame who went by the title (deep breath):

> Prince of Coronata, Compte de Lalanne, Freeman of London and patrician of San Marino

For those not up on the minor noble lines of Europe, most descended from Queen Victoria, Coronata is near Genoa and Lalanne is north of Florence. It is unclear how he came to live for 50 years in this bleak outpost off the **Isle of Lewis**.

The famous 'Black houses' at Gearrannan, consist of nine restored traditional thatched cottages. These houses were lived in till 1974 and were the last group of black houses to be inhabited in the Western Isles. Though these stone houses with turf or thatch roofs look old most were less than 150 years old, their interiors blackened as smoke was allowed to seep through their roofs. A museum house (Taigh Thormoid Anna) recreates an authentic 1955 dwelling with animal quarters at one end with living quarters at the other and exudes a feel of real antiquity. However, 'Black houses' were so named not because they were in the early days smoke filled and had small windows, but because they were compared to new houses being built in the late 1800's which were called 'white houses'. The new 'white houses' were designed to separate humans from their livestock and animals. Though the design is centuries old their construction was such that their effective lifespan was limited.

Our 'day out' continued on peaceful country roads unfettered by traffic across terrain more akin to my peaty, boggy Yorkshire Pennines than the rugged **Harris**. The undulating peat blanket was laid down 4,000 years ago and in the current climate crisis is playing a vital part in carbon sequestration absorbing large quantities of carbon dioxide. It is estimated that there are eighty-five million tons of peat on the island, and this is still a preferred fuel with an average family needing 15,000 blocks of peat a year. Some fifteen-man days a year are required to cut, dry and stack the precious fuel. The sides of the roads are littered with the evidence of these activities.

Lewisian Gneiss, the bedrock beneath the peat layers, is a metamorphic rock which is astonishingly up to 3 billion years old, making it the oldest rock in Britain, two thirds the age of the Earth The contrast in the geomorphology between north and south of **Lewis and Harris** is stark. **Lewis and Harris** are regarded as one island forming the largest island in the British Isles excluding Great Britain and the island of Ireland. **Harris** is not restricted to south of Tarbet located on the narrow isthmus separating West Loch Tarbet from East Loch Tarbet but extends some distance north encroaching on land that the uninitiated assume to be part of **Lewis**. Tarbet is the Gaelic for narrow isthmus and is a popular village name throughout Scotland.

Lewis/Harris was the last outpost of the Western Isles to break away from Norwegian rule and adopt the Gaelic language though Old Norse dialect still prevails. As late as the early 17th century James VI of Scotland (to become James I of England) was no lover of its people. His loathing went far beyond prejudice verging on genocide, setting up the Fife Adventurers to plunder **Lewis,** if need be, with:

"slauchter, mutilation, fyre raising, or utheris inconvenieties"

I've never heard inconvenience as a euphemism for murder before.

The remote, treeless moors led us to Callanish, a real treasure of antiquity. The Neolithic standing stones are built in a cruciform around a central stone circle, comprising 13 stones and are of similar age to Stonehenge. They are perceived to be the best-preserved examples of standings stones of the many sites in the immediate area. The stones are mystical and hypnotic with, unlike Stonehenge, access unhindered. Their remoteness sets them apart from the standing stones of England which have become segregated theme parks cancelling out any sense of spiritual connectivity.

Having absorbed this remarkable prehistoric spectacle, we headed for our northern most destination of this trip, the Butt of Lewis. Thoughts became trivial as our time together had been, as it always is, more than convivial. I am a tad older than Paul and Stuart and I mused that I am the same age as the National Health Service, the State of Israel and the founding by Henry Walker of Walkers crisps. We wondered who would last the longest. Our money was on the latter as the NHS, after around 13 years of unnecessary austerity and under investment in this vital public service, was not only on its knees but in 2022 in the grubby hands of vulture capitalists.

Post Brexit Atlee and Bevan's political flagship would soon be open for sale to private health providers from across the Atlantic as part of the brave new world of trade negotiations. I had worked for 13 years for Severn Trent Water, privatised under Thatcher in 1989, and refused to take free preferential share options on offer as an employee. Public health like essential infrastructure services is a public, not private good. I hope my greedy former colleagues rest easy in their Spanish second homes in the knowledge that their share dividend profits are more important than the health of the Nation. Conversation had turned serious. The continued pollution of our seas and rivers by greedy water companies to bolster the pockets of their shareholders at the expense of infrastructure investment is still alive and well under Rishi Sunak's Government.

As expected, it was windy at the Butt of Lewis and our sojourn was short, with just time to explore the pre-Cambrian geology around the lighthouse. We were walking on some of the oldest rocks in Europe and looking out to sea north to….. nowhere. The sea boiled as it crashed between the chasms and crevices of this ancient, gnarled rock. Apart from the small uninhabited islands of Sula Sgeir and Rona over forty miles away the next inhabited landfall is the Faroe Islands. Every August Lewis men make the dangerous journey to Sula Sgeir in search of guga or young gannets which are considered a delicacy.

Satisfied and filled with emotion we headed south with ample time to catch the evening ferry from Tarbet to Uig on the Isle of **Skye** and a layover till the morning, anticipating a trip on the *Bella Jane* to the elusive **Soay**. I was woken by a phone trill. The *Bella Jane* would not be sailing, yet again. Will I ever get to this island? Disappointed we breakfasted at the pleasant *Uig hotel* and headed for home with anticipation of more island adventures together.

24. The Islands of Ynys Mons, Wales

My long time and dear friend Sue lives with her playwright husband, Bob, a published author of not inconsiderable talent, in the charming village of Rowen near Conwy in North Wales, just inside the Snowdonia National Park. We have now known each other since 1986 having been introduced by my cousin Dick at a New Zealand versus England cricket Test match at Nottingham's Trent Bridge. She is not in the least interested in cricket but was using this as an excuse to extricate herself from the boredom that her life with her first husband had become. After the game we went 'out on the town' with Sue flirting with England's premier fast bowler, the late Bob Willis and wicket keeper, Bruce French. Dick and I were apocalyptically jealous as we wanted to discuss cricket with these icons of the game!

After Dick's untimely death in 1995 we continued our friendship to the extent that I became *in loco parentis* to Sue at her wedding in Liverpool to Bob. Rowen was their second home, bought to ease the daily journey from Liverpool to her job as an ambitious consultant psychiatrist in north Wales. Their beautiful, though modest, cottage was next door to *Ty Gwyn*, the village pub and I have spent many happy times there supping their excellent Robinson's Manchester ales. On one such trip we decided to 'tick off' **Anglesey** and its smaller sister, **Holy Island** (one of three islands with this moniker in the British Isles).

I had not ventured onto any of Wales's inhabited islands on this round of visits. As a purist I felt that even if I had visited islands in the past, they should be re-traced. I'd walked around **Anglesey** and **Holy Island** on the designated long-distance path of 124 miles taking two weeks. This was in the wake of my successful navigation of Great Britain, completed on my 60th birthday.

THE ISLANDS OF YNYS MONS, WALES

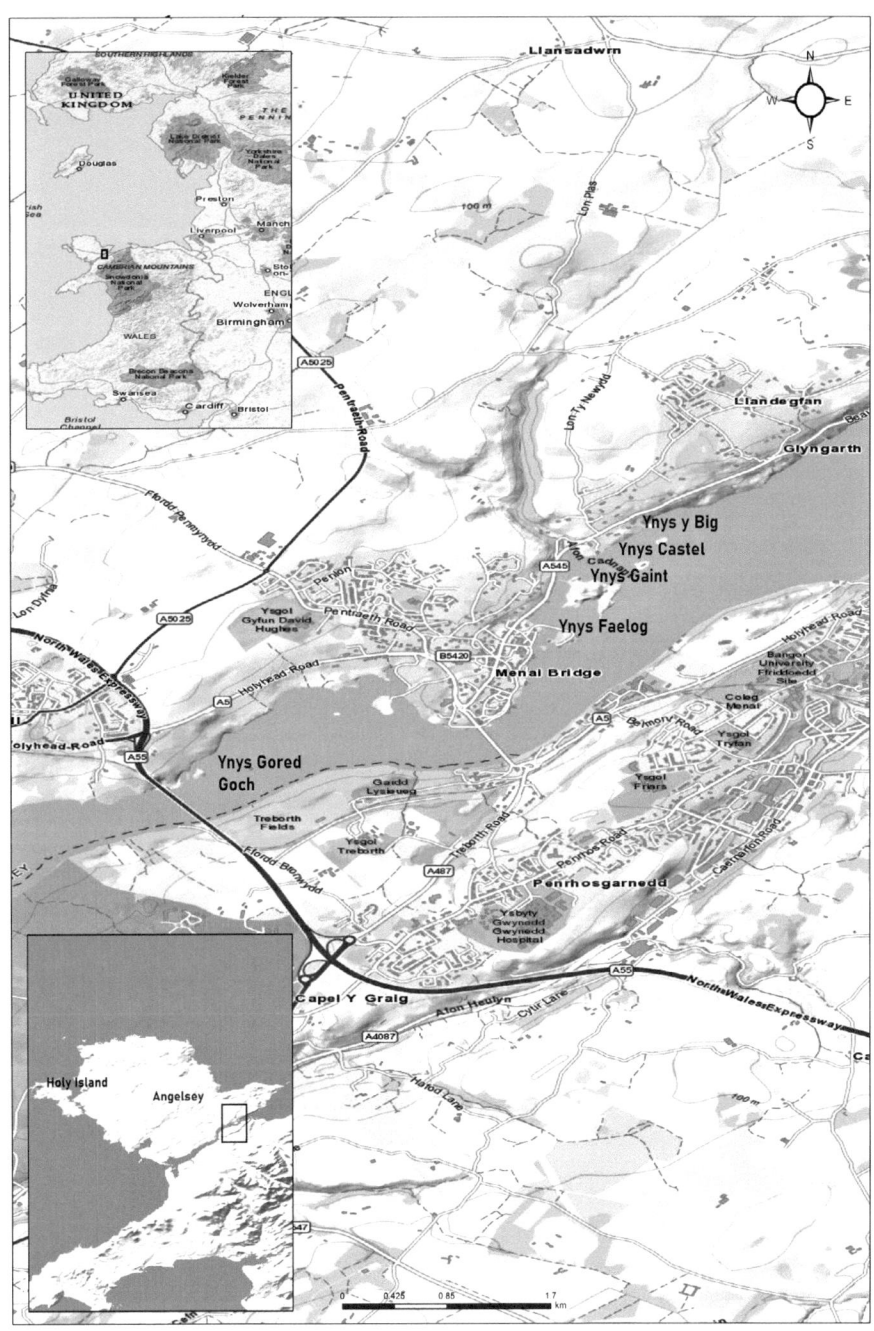

The islands of Ynys Mons, Wales

I needed to keep a semblance of fitness and endeavoured successfully to do so on a number of other long-distance paths: circumnavigating the **Isle of Wight**, following the Thames Path and the Severn Way to their respective sources and finally Hadrian's Wall, before my arthritic infirmity scuppered any further ambitions of long-distance walking.

Attempting the Ribble Way in Lancashire in Spring 2013 with Geoff, a fit walking partner from the latter days of my *"Walk by the Sea"*, I became incapacitated and never walked significant distances in the countryside again. I was devastated as walking had been quite simply the only pastime I enjoyed. My decision to attempt the islands of the British Isles, the inhabited ones at least, was as a result of this affliction and would keep up my interest in quirky geographical pursuits.

After **Lewis and Harris** (combined), **Skye**, **Mainland Shetland** and **Mull**, **Anglesey** (including **Holy Island**) is the 5th largest island by size in the British Isles (well actually 7th if you include Great Britain and Ireland). It is 7th in size by population too. It is larger than the **Isle of Wight** by a massive 333 square kilometres. You see, the **Isle of Wight** is English and therefore in Little Englanders' eyes must be bigger. With the Brexit charade dragging on I was getting a tad tired of Little Englanders and their sense of entitlement. Britain is not the best at everything but part of a collective global ambition.

I'd researched a list of Wales's inhabited islands, and this is not easy to establish, unlike those of Scotland embedded authoritatively in the Annexes of the 2011 Scottish census and scholarly analysed by Hamish Haswell-Smith in his seminal work *"Scottish Islands"*. After extensive research there appears to be 52 islands off the Welsh coast, though source material is confused as some are duplicated as referred to by their English and Welsh names, sometimes as if they are separate islands. No matter, only two exceed three square kilometres (**Holy Island** and **Anglesey**) and only about 14 have some semblance of permanent population, whatever permanent should mean. A dubious Wikipedia reference simplifies this to six inhabited islands.

As usual my spur of the moment trip to **Anglesey** was devoid of any planning and, again, as usual my impetuosity got the better of me. On post trip research it appears that there are five small isles within the confines of the Menai Straits that harbour permanent residences, four of which are attached to **Anglesey** by causeways and bridges. It was appropriate for future sorties into Wales to get at least a basic understanding of which islands form part of this adventure.

My start of the *"Walk by the Sea"* venture was delayed by about six months because the 2001 foot and mouth epidemic closed the British countryside. When writing this we were in total indefinite lockdown because of the COVID 19 pandemic so there was plenty of time, due to the Government incompetence and ineptitude, to complete detailed research and planning of future trips. Trips to Wales in the summer of 2020 seemed only a distant hope. All non-essential travel was forbidden as this terrible disease took its grip on hundreds of thousands of people causing death and terror at worst and long-term family separations at best.

So, which of Wales's islands did I suppose are inhabited?:
- **Anglesey** (Irish Sea) with 69,961 population (2017)
- **Bardsey Island** (Gwynedd) with 11 population (2019)
- **Caldey Island** (Pembrokeshire) with an estimated 40 population including a long-standing monastic community.
- **Flat Holm** (Bristol Channel) with 1 person, probably a warden
- **Holy Island** (**Anglesey**) with 13,659 population (2011) comprising the Port of Holyhead and joined to Anglesey by causeway (A5)
- **Ramsay Island** (Pembrokeshire) with a population of 2, probably wardens
- **St Tudwal's Island** east (Llyn peninsular, south of Abersoch), owned until her death in 2016 by Carla Lane, that great Liverpudlian playwright, most famous for the classic British comedies *Bread* and *Butterflies*
- **St Tudwal's Island** west (Llyn peninsular, south of Abersoch), owned by Bear Grylls the explorer. However, it was uncertain at

the time of this research to ascertain the permanence of the two St Tudwal's occupation.
- **Skokholm** (Pembrokeshire) with a population of two, probably wardens
- **Skomer** (Pembrokeshire) with a warden and probably seasonal occupation only
- **Ynys Faelog** (Menai Strait) with two houses connected at Menai Bridge village by a causeway to Anglesey.
- **Ynys Gaint** (Menai Strait) with two houses connected to Menai Bridge village.
- **Ynys Gored Goch** (Menai Strait) a private island only accessible by boat with one house, situated between the Menai suspension bridge and the Britannia Bridge
- **Ynys y Big** (Menai Strait) a private island connected by a wooden bridge to one house.

Barry Island in south Wales is no longer an island and has been connected to the former industrial port of Barry since the 1880's.

It was always a delight crossing the Menai Strait via the suspension bridge completed by Thomas Telford in 1826. A Grade 1 listed structure, in 2005 the bridge was promoted by UNESCO as a candidate World Heritage Site.

We were on a 'smash and grab' visit and after an amble down the High Street in Beaumaris, where Christmas paraphernalia were on sale on 6th September, we made a leisurely café stop. Views east to Snowdon were truly inspiring on that clear day as we headed back to the A5, hell bent on crossing the causeway to **Holy Island** and Holyhead. On our way we were oblivious to the very existence of the five small and inhabited islands in the Menai Straits. They would in hindsight have to be visited on another occasion, when the COVID 19 lockdown ended and a 'return' to the "new normal" whatever that meant.

Our route took us past the village with the longest place name of any settlement in the UK, or anywhere else for that matter, (except a Maori settlement in New Zealand which sounds equally contrived):

Llanfairpwllgwyngyllgogerychwyrndrobwllllantysiliogogogoch

Shortened to Llanfair PG this linear village straddles the A5, proudly emblazoning its name on any wall long enough to accept its 58 letters but the quadruple 'llll' is surely as eccentric as any spelling gets in any language. I concluded that translation was pointless and felt Liverpool might be better known as:

> "The port by the Mersey that gave rise to those loveable mopheads, John, George, Paul and Ringo, the former dying tragically after being shot by Mark Chapman in 1980, George dying of cancer in 2001 and I can't be bothered to tell you what happened to the other two".

I like languages though, except for a decent smattering of French (I did achieve an A level in 1966) and a couple of dozen Russian phrases, I have never mastered them. There are only 14 scripts in current usage by all world languages and Georgian is one. I have been visiting Georgia since 2013 on many wonderful trips, working for the United Nations Development Programme attempting to make natural hazard prone communities more resilient to climate change. Its ancient script is more akin to the Aramaic of Jesus' Palestine than any other language. It is exotic and cursive: დილა მშვიდობისა or Good Morning!

Like Welsh it is an ancient functioning language of little international use, but which must be preserved as part of our cultural heritage. Most Georgians I meet speak Georgian, Russian and English fluently, which puts me to shame. I knew a bar manager, Tea Sharikadze, in my favourite pub on Erikele street in Tbilisi Old town who can write in 5 scripts (Latin, as we use, Cyrillic, as the Russians use, Georgian, Greek and Japanese). There can be few, other than rare etymological scholars, that can beat that. Popularism, as personified by Brexit has a lot to answer for, narrowing the importance of cultural inclusiveness and breeding suspicion and xenophobia of anything that doesn't fit the gnarled 'norm' of Little England.

In 1901 91% of the residents of **Anglesey** (Ynys Mons in Welsh) spoke Welsh, but the 2011 census reported a decline to 57%, though still a veritable stronghold of Welsh language and culture. There are five schools in **Anglesey** and apart from Ysgol Uwchradd Caergybi in Holyhead the vast majority of children, speak, study and have the choice of taking exams in Welsh. The future of the language appears safe, for now at least.

We crossed largely flat and fertile land making the journey to the **Holy Island** causeway in quick time. From an inhabited island perspective, the Welsh **Holy Island** should not be confused with **Holy Island** (or Lindisfarne), the tidal island off the coast of Northumberland, nor for that matter the **Holy Island** occupied by a Buddhist community off the coast of **Arran** in Scotland.

The ferry port of Holyhead handles more than two million passengers each year with Stena Line and Irish Ferries sailing to Dublin. I have made this journey to **Ireland** on many occasions. In the late eighties Dick and I decided to venture to all points **Ireland**. For some reason that escapes me we journeyed to Holyhead separately. Dick was impossibly unreliable, and he missed the ferry. I boarded alone, angry, but I knew Dick was resourceful. On entering Dun Laoghaire (or King's town to the English colonists, renamed after George IV's 1821 visit), the former port connecting **Ireland** to Holyhead, I received a message on the ship's tannoy saying I was not to worry as Dick had caught the next boat due to arrive in the wee small hours of the following morning. Sure enough 'your man' arrived clutching only a bottle of whisky with no luggage and singing rebel songs. I still miss that colossus of a man almost 30 years since his untimely death.

Sue and I escaped the hustle and bustle of the port and headed for a quiet refuge above the town, which incidentally is exposed to potentially the highest coastal flood risk in all of Wales, to watch the ferry traffic ply its ceaseless journeys backwards and forwards across the Irish Sea. I recalled an amusing tale. Some years previously I helped my good friend John Lawlor with his move back to the sleepy backwater of Abbeyleix in County Laois, Ireland. He had inherited from his Irish father a run-down cottage, the antithesis of the neat modern bungalows built across the country during the 'Celtic Tiger' period of unsustainable growth around the turn of the century. John felt a loyal duty to take up his father's mantle, whatever the cost to his mental state of mind, let alone his meagre finances. John had played 'supporting artist' in *'Game of Thrones'*, *'Vikings'* and Wilkie Collins *'The Woman in White'* and enjoyed his sword collection and swords in general, as did my wife, Lily.

Passing through Conwy on one of many trips to transport John's possessions across the Irish Sea, the trips in many cases being more expensive than the contents within the hired Mercedes Sprinter or my Freelander, we stopped at *The Knight* Shop, which stocked all things medieval. In a mood of impetuosity rather than generosity I bought, for Lily, a hand-and-a half sword. She was enamoured with John's sword and would, and does, love it. On arriving at Abbeyleix and unloading John's sentimental treasures, I realised I had left behind my overnight bag.

After a night in *The Manor*, then Abbeyleix's only hotel – John had a lot of work to do before making his ancestral home fit for guests – I realised that I would be driving back with the sword as my only possession. On my return, I arrived at police checks at Holyhead to the consternation of the Hedlu (police). After all, before the 1998 Good Friday agreement this route would have been common for the Provisional IRA. Indeed, the Birmingham six, wrongly convicted for the atrocious Birmingham pub bombings on 21st November 1974, killing 21 people, had used the port to return home to attend a funeral. My situation seemed so unlikely (who travels with no luggage but just a sword for goodness' sake) that I was waved on my way without further interrogation.

We chatted amiably but with always a frisson of interrogation by Sue before heading back to Rowen. On my walk around **Anglesey**, I had sat overlooking South Stack lighthouse contemplating similarly when my phone trilled. "Welcome to Ireland" a message from O2 implored. Mobile telephony is mystifying. On a trip from Tbilisi to Batumi on Georgia's Black Sea my driver, who hated Russians, stopped on the Tehran to Istanbul highway just outside Gori, Stalin's birthplace. Now Georgia has in recent years been invaded by Putin's Russia; first occupying in 1992 the semi-autonomous republic of Abkhazia on the Black Sea coast, displacing around 250,000 people who took refuge in Georgia. I have friends who were forced to evacuate; second occupying south Ossetia in 2008.

We had stopped at the southernmost extremity of the occupation by stealth of this second illegal invasion. In subsequent years, the border of the occupation was slowly but surely moved south until it is now only 200 metres from the International Highway. My driver gave me binoculars and there in Russian was a sign demarking the start of Russian territory. It is a dangerous cat and mouse game played out, just as in Ukraine, to show the former Soviet Republics who could be their boss again to restore the historic 'Kievan Rus' empire at whatever cost. The modern nations of Belarus, Russia, and Ukraine all claim Kievan Rus as their cultural ancestor. Georgia has eschewed all political contact with Russia looking westwards to the European Union and NATO membership. Again, my phone trilled: O2 informed me, again with hopeless geographical inexactitude, this time "Welcome to Russia". Russia's geographical boundary is over 100km away on the summit of the Caucasian peaks, *"the snow-capped mountains way down south"* made famous by the Beatles song *'Back in the USSR'*.

Geopolitics was on hold during the COVID 19 global pandemic, but on the plus side nature, with its own agenda, was starting to redress the damage done by humanity. Maybe the Reverend Thomas Malthus got it right in his 1798 book *An Essay on the Principle of Population*. Agrarian lifestyles turn to industrial lifestyles which in turn smash through another glass ceiling as population increases. The floods, plagues and pestilences becoming all too frequent and debilitating may lead us to a better and globally responsible lifestyle. Pandemics are swift acting and all too real, but the stealth of climate change defies acceptance by neo liberals who see the greed of mammon above compassion and humility. Pollution was noticeably reducing after weeks of 'lockdown' but reversal is certain under a political system based on entitlement and global capitalism at the expense of natural order.

I looked forward to completing the remaining and eclectic Welsh islands after the pandemic had subsided, but it wasn't until total lockdown was eased in August 2020 that a trip could be arranged safely to the Menai Strait islands and Bob and Sue were eager to join me on this quirky expedition. We planned the trip in *Ty Gwyn* now open for business (well at least the garden was under ramshackle tents, which were reminiscent of shelter provided at early seventies rock festivals). Our lovely hosts Lisa, John and Jean were providing COVID 19 safety to the letter of the law with military precision. Entry into the pub bars was strictly forbidden and the three of them were wearing full PPE (masks, visors and aprons) that would not have seemed out of place in a COVID hospital ward let alone serving beer in a quiet country pub.

Low tide was around 10:00 and Menai bridge village is 40 minutes' drive from Rowen. We set off to conquer at least four islands knowing that **Ynys Gored Goch** would have to be planned at a later date when boat transport and permission to land could be obtained. We decided to park the car and walk to all four islands once access could be discovered to each in a warren of the driveways of expensive properties leading to the shore. From north to south **Ynys y Big** was connected by a wooden bridge; **Ynys Castell** by a low tide causeway; **Ynys Gaint** by a low tide causeway/road and **Ynys Faelog** by another low tide causeway.

The distance from the first to last island was around a kilometre as the crow flies with each access no more than two to three hundred metres from the road. This short stretch of coastline was designated in 2003 as the Glannau Porthaethwy Site of Special Scientific Interest (SSSI), as the most extensive sheltered rock shore between **Bardsey** Island (off the Llyn peninsular) and Great Orme's Head, Llandudno.

We expected obstacles to our progress with perhaps locked gates or menacing *'private access – no entry'* notices. These we agreed to ignore. **Ynys y Big** is owned by a Flintshire business family and after much controversy they were allowed to rebuild the utterly dilapidated bridge to the island in 2019. It is a magnificent and no doubt expensive structure built from Welsh larch felled and milled in Wales, delivered by Welsh carriers and built largely by Welsh people. This 'made in Wales' stamp of approval clearly placated the locals and environmental objectors concerned about either temporary or even permanent displacement of the egrets, herons and oyster catchers prevalent in this biodiverse shoreline. Our way was not barred, and we walked this fine bridge in a welcome cooling breeze. Residents or otherwise were not encountered.

The tide was somewhere close to full ebb, and we spied a suitable shoreline route to the **Ynys Castell** a couple of hundred metres to the southwest. It proved deceptively dangerous but avoided returning to the A545 Menai Bridge to Beaumaris road. The dangers of walking this busy road were balanced by the dangers of the slippery, uneven shoreline composed of very sharp Pre-Cambrian schist. A twisted ankle here would have without doubt spoiled the day. The road causeway crossing was uneventful and leads to a seven-bedroom self-catering mansion with a tantalising tourist blurb:

> "With the backdrop of the mountains of Snowdonia in addition to the historic Menai Suspension Bridge, Bangor Pier and the Great Orme, it will be hard to know where to direct your gaze.
> "**Ynys Castel** (Castle Island) is a unique and exciting holiday experience that starts as soon as you drive onto the causeway!"

They were certainly not wrong with the house hidden from view in dense woodland.

Ynys Gaint is the biggest of the four islands and its access by road was ominously signed as PRIVATE with not even pedestrian access allowed. We hadn't come this far to be put off by tin pot officialdom and I strode off, with Sue and Bob tentatively following in my wake. The island was owned in the 1930's by Sir William Guy Fison of the fertiliser family. Between 1942 and 1944 it housed an air sea rescue unit of the RAF and still has a military presence in the form of an Army Cadet unit and the Maritime Volunteer Service. Though past its former glory one of the houses had a garden designed by Sir Clough Williams-Ellis famous for his Italianate gardens in Portmeirion a short distance down the Welsh coast.

I didn't outstay my non-existent welcome and returned shoreward to find the last of the quartet, **Ynys Faelog** and its access causeway, also marked private. By now we were old hands at breaking civil law if such a law of trespass exists. I nostalgically longed for Scotland where no land is off limits to the careful traveller, not even Trump's golf courses. I was reminded of walking on the 18th Green of the Old Course of St Andrew's golf course just before the 2005 Open (won by Tiger Woods). Not a head was turned. Try this at the Royal St George's at Sandwich, Kent and watch the gammon faced majors and colonels turn apoplectic with rage.

Ynys Faelog is right on the outskirts of Menai Bridge village and part was for sale as recently as 2019, with the estate agents Williams and Goodwin putting a one million pounds price tag on this "slice of paradise". Just like all half decent new flats are pre-fixed by their agents with the word 'luxury', islands for sale are 'unique, once in a lifetime opportunity for peace and tranquillity'. Much of the island was owned by Bangor University but as with all higher education establishments strapped for cash it needed its assets realising.

Mission accomplished with Bob and Sue very content with this short but quirky interlude we made the short walk to Cafi Aethwy for coffee and croissants.

25. The rest of the Small Isles (Rum, Canna and Sanday), Scotland

I'd ticked off two of the four (five, if you count **Sanday**) Small Isles on my return from the Shetland Isles in a vain attempt to sweep up sporadically the remaining islands off northwest Scotland that were part of my master list. **Eigg** and **Muck** had been thus unceremoniously conquered, leaving **Rum**, **Canna** and **Sanday**. These could be accessed on a trusty CalMac ferry from Mallaig though limited time and ferry logistics meant that **Rum** could only be 'stepped on' as turnaround to **Canna** was swift. This was unfortunate as **Rum** is a fascinating, rugged island, in fact the 15th largest island in Scotland.

I assembled my old friends Stuart and Paul, driving up to join Stuart from New Abbey in Dumfries and Galloway. Paul was coming from his own home in a place near Callander I can never remember, but close to the fabled *Gleneagles hotel*. I'd opted for accommodation at *The Marine Hotel* close to the ferry terminal, an unremarkable, cold hotel with little comfort.

I've stayed in worse hotels around the world but the flop house in Dade County, Miami takes the accolade for horror and discomfort. In the early eighties I'd been to a flood management conference in Dallas, Texas and decided to explore more of the southern United States by *Driveaway* car. You pick up somebody's car (they invariably fly home) and simply pay for fuel and return it to its owner, often at the other side of the country.

It was a hot, dusty journey and on arrival I found a hotel room which, from the state of its door lock, had been broken into many times. I found an unkempt, filthy bed (reception had thankfully given me a clean

The rest of the small isles (Rum, Canna and Sanday), Scotland

pillowcase) illuminated by a single, dull shade-less light bulb. I hid my wallet the best I could and disappeared to take solace in the bar with an assortment of undesirables who weaved their way around my personal space. Uncomfortable at this faux and unwelcome attention I tried to leave but found the 20-dollar bill, I had secreted in my jeans pocket, was no longer there. I snarled at the bar tender who was obviously part of the scam and walked off unchecked. Back in the desultory silence of my airless, stifling room I wrote my postcards home. These read *"when your week-old underpants are cleaner than your hotel bed sheets it's about time to reassess the American Dream"*.

We arrived in Mallaig late and after confusing the eastern European receptionist about our room requirements, headed for the *Marine bar* to reminisce and muse on our long weekend together in **Canna**. We will miss these invaluable service staff after our exit from the European Union, we mused. At least they will "no longer be taking our jobs". How fallacious this would turn out to be. The COVID 19 outbreak in 2020 saw fruit and vegetables rotting in the fields and despite pleas for brave Little Englanders to adopt a 'blitz spirit' and 'dig for Victory', they were having none of it. To avoid food chain disaster the supermarkets and farmers were chartering planes to fly Eastern European and other farther afield foreign workers to try to make up the shortfall of farm workers. Meanwhile, furloughed workers were sitting on their sofas watching re-runs of classic FA cup finals.

Two words had become prominent in 2019 and 2020: Prorogue and Furlough. The former means to *"discontinue a session of a parliament or other legislative assembly without dissolving it"*. The latter means *"to grant absence of leave from employment"* (whilst guaranteed protection of said employment). The former was invoked by Johnson to avoid Parliamentary scrutiny during the tortured Brexit debates. The latter was proclaimed to enable payment of wages during the COVID 19 crisis.

Our visit to **Canna** was just before these troubled times. Before boarding the ferry, the *Lochnevis*, I believe, we stocked up on whisky in case the only accommodation on **Canna** had insufficient supplies. After all the permanent population was only 12 in number with a further six across the bridge in **Sanday**. We'd been lucky to book three rooms at the *Tighard* (meaning High House) guest house, a charming, cosy Edwardian detached house with 'awesome' views across the waters of the Inner Hebrides. Fiona, the young owner and only incumbent was charm personified. She had left her home and friends in Glasgow to run this charming B&B single handed.

I generally hate the word awesome as used in modern parlance it tends to exaggerate excessively. Language changes, so in street slang/youth speak 'good' becomes 'bad' and 'sick' means 'cool'. But there is no excuse for using awesome out of context. Whilst dining in Cottonwood, northern Arizona with my dear friend Leonard in Summer 2012 we ordered steaks, a natural thing to do in cowboy country. Having delivered the steaks with impossibly excessive side orders of everything, the waitress asked how our steaks were. We responded to the affirmative that these were indeed to our tastes. "Awesome" she squealed. Leonard looked at her with some disdain "Jesus turning water to wine is awesome" he said, "not the quality of our steaks". The views from *Tighard* were without doubt awesome.

Before docking at **Canna**, I had to disembark and re-embark at **Rum** and undergo the ritual of running to solid ground to prove I had set foot on the island. Seeing an unfit elderly man wheeze his way to a grassy knoll, touch it and run back on board before pontoons were raised amused passers-by here and indeed all across the Scottish Isles.

The origins of the island's name are speculative, but it is known for certain that Sir George Bullough, a former owner, changed the spelling to Rhum to avoid the association with the alcoholic drink. I imagine he must have been a devout Presbyterian who would have associated alcohol with the devil. There are few descendants of the ancestors of **Rum** living there today and most of the residents are involved in research or employed by Scottish Heritage. Just like in most of the Islands and Highlands, the Clearances saw the demise of native populations. In 1825 the inhabitants of **Rum** (then numbering some 450 people) were given a year's notice to quit their homes. The inhabitants had simply been tenant farmers, paying rent to the laird; they owned neither the land they worked, nor the houses in which they lived. On 11th July 1826, about 300 of the inhabitants boarded two overcrowded ships bound for Cape Breton in Nova Scotia. The laird in an act of mind-numbing hypocrisy is said to have paid for their passage.

I had the pleasure of travelling to Cape Breton a year or so earlier with Trevor, meeting Leonard in Halifax, Nova Scotia. We'd been told on a previous visit to Canada that Cape Breton was worth a visit, so we booked a few nights in a modest motel in Sydney, the largest town on the island. The post-industrial town was on its knees though the Scottish legacy was always present throughout the island.

A story about Sydney amused us. A British honeymoon couple had booked a trip to Sydney and were surprised at the cheapness of the flights which were routed through Toronto, and they surmised that flying the 'long way' round to Australia explained the modest price. Inconvenience clearly came at a discounted price. Their leg from Toronto to 'Sydney' worried them as the plane was smaller than expected. They landed in Sydney, Cape Breton with no accommodation and the local newspaper heralded their story with the mayor granting them free board and lodgings. Not quite the holiday they expected and from our experience, apart from the coal mine tours and the Marconi Museum (see **Rathlin** Island), there is little to keep young tourists occupied. In between whale watching we took much solace in one or more of the town's rather unimpressive taverns.

The somewhat eccentric Lancashire mill owning family, the Burroughs, owned **Rum** until midway through the 20th century and used the estate for sport. George Burroughs was responsible for building Kinloch castle, an example of opulent Edwardian grandeur. He imported Lancashire stonemasons for its construction who were paid a premium to work if dressed in kilts and given tuppence (about a modern penny) a day extra for tobacco to ward of the plague of summertime midges. His extravagance knew no bounds and he installed heated tanks for turtles and alligators, with grapes and all manner of citrus grown in the conservatories. Today the castle with its unique collection of objects d'art collected by George, who had sailed around the world, is fast deteriorating.

Fiona met us off the ferry at **Canna** and drove us the very short distance to *Tighard*. The accommodation was splendid as was Fiona's cooking. She did have a modest bar but after dinner in front of a roaring fire in the lounge, occupied only by us, we smuggled our whisky in for late night imbibing. Fiona would not have been happy as her profit margins were being eroded significantly. Stuart is the fittest amongst us and proved to be abstemious as he was in constant training for mammoth bike rides and his honed body was testament to disciplined exercise.

As it turned out exercise was not excessive on **Canna** with few paths but after a delicious 'full Scottish' breakfast we made the mile or so trek to **Sanday** across a recently constructed bridge, built after the previous bridge was destroyed by storm in 2005. Just like **Canna** the island was bequeathed to the National Trust for Scotland by the Gaelic folklorists and scholars John Lorne Campbell and Margaret Fay Shaw in 1981 who had lived in **Canna**'s only other large house, Canna House. Therein is contained the world's largest library of Celtic language and literature.

These days the community are responsible for management and tourism on the two islands. There is hardly any crime with police only visiting sporadically to check on gun licences. Until recently all, and I mean all, commodities had to be brought in by CalMac and this ferry service still provides a vital lifeline. A recent addition to the community is an honesty shop selling basics, which as the name suggests is unmanned with the shoppers' conscience the only means of securing payment. We were not sure this business model would be appropriate elsewhere!

Casual sorties across **Canna**, which after all is only one mile wide, provided views seen from a high vantage point to the elusive (to me) island of **Soay**, tantalisingly close but as yet inaccessible. Unfortunately, the small population is difficult to sustain and a call for 'settlers' was instigated in 2006 with a modicum of success, though by 2011 many of the 'incomers' had left, and the school closed. It appeared that rats and rabbits were more adept at colonialization than people with brown rats estimated broadly at 10,000 in number at the turn of the century. These were a threat to wildlife and in particular the Manx shearwater, and a drastic cull was organised. Unlike the Pied Piper of Hamelin legend, where the rats were piped away using his beguiling magical powers, the Canna rats were unceremoniously despatched by rodenticide. Though the island was rat free by 2006, rabbits replaced them in large numbers, rising to an estimated 13,000 in 2013. Rabbit stew, actually on the only cafe's menus, was an inadequate method of cull and traditional methods were introduced to establish a rabbit free environment.

26. Many more Orkney Islands, Scotland

I had enjoyed the two previous summers visiting islands in Shetland and the Outer Hebrides. In 2019 it was time to complete the Orkney Islands, some sporadically visited on the way to and from the Shetlands trip. A 2019 survey presented in *The Guardian* newspaper suggested Orkney was the best place to live for quality of life in the whole of the UK. Like all these surveys the local tourist board might have had a hand in the promotion of this boast, though Trevor, my dear friend for 50 years, and I were eager to test this claim. Many secrets unfold within the many islands within this archipelago. Orkney is regarded by archaeologists as the Stone Age capital of Ancient Britain and the source of Britain's first common culture that swept throughout what is now Great Britain and culminated in Stonehenge. Stonehenge gets all the popular plaudits (it is in southern England after all), but our civilisation started in these far Northern Isles.

This time planning was essential as lessons were learnt from the 2018 mission to the Outer Hebrides where a couple of small but inhabited islands were missed by paying too close attention to Haswell-Smith's *Scottish Islands* book, which ignores any island below 40 hectares. All but two of the remaining 13 islands were accessible by Orkney's subsidised ferry services or road bridges. **Gairsay** was only about a mile from **Orkney Mainland** so a lift from a kindly local boatman we were sure could be arranged. The rogue remaining island was a worry as **Auskerry** was way out 15 miles in the North Sea and access would need imaginative planning. Would this be the Achilles heel of the trip, as even securing passage could not guarantee success in the wildest of maritime environments? We were in the lap of the, sometimes very angry, North Sea Gods.

As with my Shetland trip with Ian in 2017, my work coincidentally took

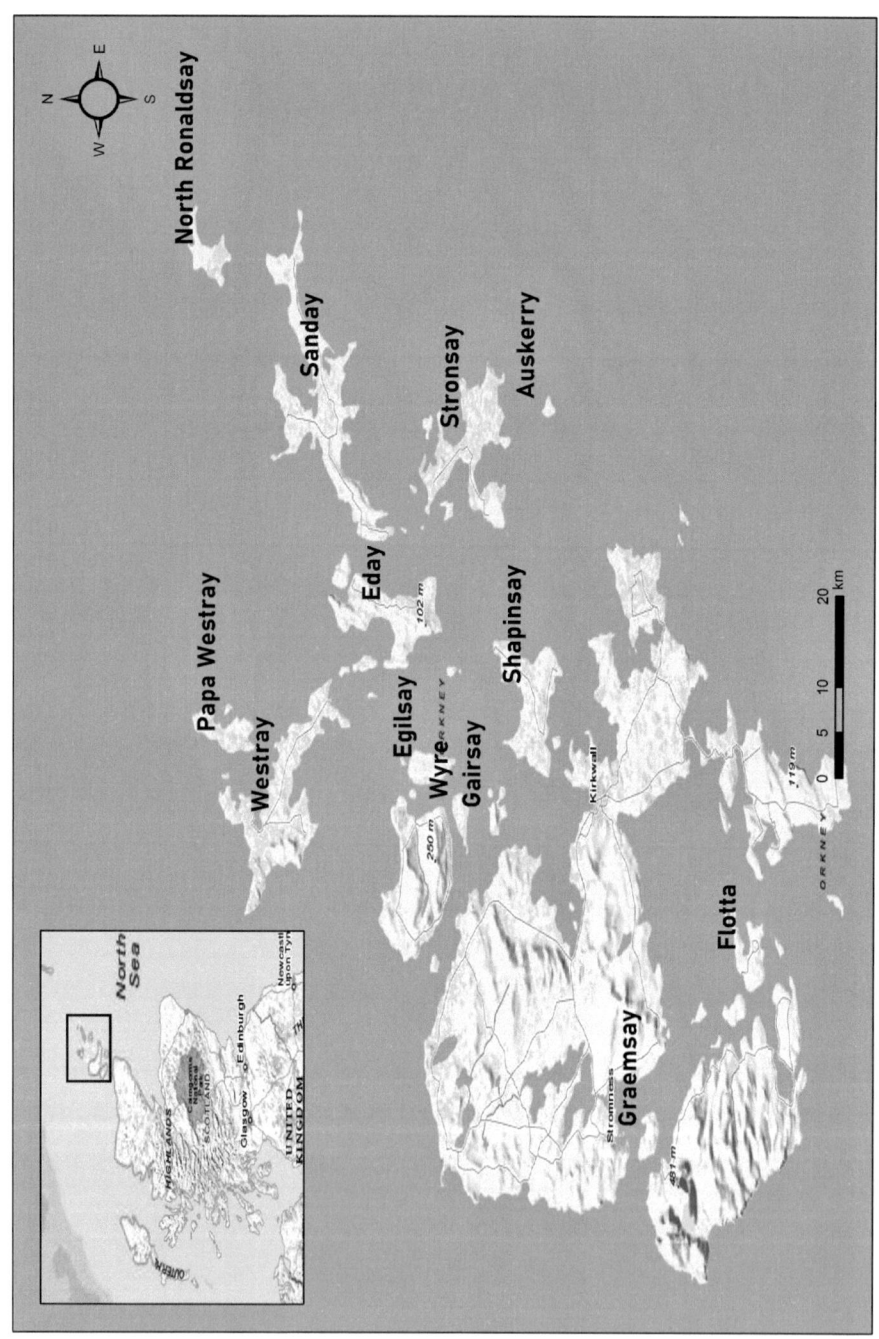

Many more Orkney Islands, Scotland

me to Edinburgh the week prior to my scheduled visit to Orkney. Trevor, who had had a terrible time fighting bowel cancer and clumsy surgery to boot, took the welcome opportunity to accompany me. He has been an almost lifelong friend. We met in London in 1970. I was doing my PhD at London University and Trevor, a school friend of a university friend, John, decided to seek his fortune in the Capital. Now John, who became a very successful premiership football club chairman with Blackburn Rovers, was fussy. No, fussy does not cut it. His fastidiousness knew no bounds. He entrusted me in getting a four-bedroom detached property with all the comforts a seventies London suburban house could offer: central heating, colour TV, fitted carpets, walk-in shower etc., not the typical student accommodation.

By luck more than judgment I came across such a house owned by a Greek family in Corbett Road, Wanstead, just off the noisy Eastern Avenue. It ticked all of John's boxes with an additional feature, a fully stocked bar donated freely by our landlords. All this was on offer for the princely sum of £35 per week or about £450 in today's money, close to £2,000 per calendar month, not typical student prices either! £35 was way more than the average weekly pre-tax salary in those days. I signed the lease for a year surmising if I persuaded six friends to join me then a round fiver each a week should cover the rent. This was never going to work.

The day came when Trevor and John were arriving from their respective parent's homes in Totton, Hampshire. I was ordered to meet them at Waterloo station in my father's racing green Morris Oxford. Before I left I gave instructions that Gloria and Vicky, two east-end girls attached to John Sellen one of the new inmates, should wear their shortest miniskirts (different times, different times!) and sit on the bar stools coolly sipping cocktails from the well-stocked bar with my new roommate Rob as acting barman in full livery. John complained for the entire journey through the congested London streets. He liked complaining. On arrival, he fell into a stunned silence and Trevor thought Metro life had always been like this.

Trevor met me in Edinburgh worse for wear, after downing copious free gin and tonics courtesy of Virgin first class. Booking in advance ensured great bargains. We headed as was usual for me on trips to the Scottish capital to the *Café Royal* on West Register Street for oysters in my favourite Edinburgh restaurant. This had been the very place where Princess Margaret had met Roddy Llewellyn, her 17-years younger beau. Their very public affair scandalised the Nation's 'Red Top' tabloid readers in the mid-seventies.

We needed to be at Gills Bay on Scotland's north coast early the next evening. This made for a leisurely drive and a catch up on our chaotic lives. The journey to St Margaret's Hope on **South Ronaldsay** was on time and uneventful but we needed to hurry to make our first night's accommodation in Kirkwall, and more importantly we didn't want to miss last orders. It was still light when we arrived at the *Kirkwall Hotel*, opposite the islands ferry terminal. "Sorry sir, we don't have a booking for you, and we are totally full", the receptionist sighed. I looked startled; Trevor looked displeased. It had surely been a mix-up but on further investigation it concluded that my booking had been not for the *Kirkwall hotel* but the *Orkney hotel*, a few hundred yards away, an easy mistake to make I thought. Our receptionist rang the said hotel and had some disappointing news as our booking there too was apparently bogus.

It was, on 21st June, later that week, the 100th anniversary of the scuppering of the German fleet in 1919 after the fleet had been held there after the end of the First World War, awaiting further orders from the Admiralty. The scuttling took place at the Royal Navy's base at Scapa Flow. What was left of the German High Seas Fleet had been interned there under the terms of the Armistice whilst negotiations took place over the fate of the ships. Fearing that all the ships would be seized and divided amongst the Allies, Admiral Ludwig von Reuter decided to scuttle the fleet. Some 52 of the 74 ships were destroyed and the remains from decades of salvage are still visible.

There was to be a top brass style ceremony to mark the anniversary and all hotels were full. This explained why I had to struggle to book any hotels in Kirkwall for the remaining seven days of our trip. As usually happens under these circumstances, persistence, politeness and fortitude bought us a room in the attic of the *Orkney Hotel* but sleep despite a long week of seminars for me, and a long journey north for us both, was denied. Our first ferry, this time on a tortuous round robin to **Stronsay, Eday** and, on that Saturday only, **Westray**, was due to sail at 07:00. I tossed and turned for what appeared to be for the rest of the night hoping I'd got the ferry times right and also the exact location of the ferry in what appeared to be a busy harbour.

After a meagre cornflake and toast breakfast but glad to be back in harness, so to speak, we headed the couple of hundred metres to the ferry terminal. I was too eager and overshot the departure gate, making the surprisingly busy ferry in the nick of time. Trevor was amused as he, Mr calm personified, had discovered the correct boarding procedure. On arrival in the passenger lounge we settled down for a long sea voyage first to **Stronsay** and then to **Eday**, but with no time to explore them. Our slumbers, induced by an early start and the throbbing of the ship's engines, were well and truly disturbed when, on arrival at **Stronsay** all hell broke loose with everyone and their wives (and children and dogs) boarding the ferry. These were not tourists, but locals headed for the Northern Isles sports day held each year since 1949. The event alternated between **Sanday**, **Stronsay**, **Eday** and **Westray**, which explained why our day was lengthened with an unscheduled stop in **Westray**. This year was **Westray**'s turn to host the eagerly anticipated event.

The mood was jolly with serious islander rivalry going on between the prospective rival combatants. We wondered why **North Ronaldsay** hadn't been allowed into the jollities. Maybe they'd fallen out, been banned for drug taking or, more likely, with the smallest population of these northern Orkney Isles, couldn't fairly compete.

The packed lounge was filled with anticipatory chatter and fond thoughts of previous meetings. We picked up a copy of the games' programme, filled with details from all manner of sporting events to be held. There were to be nine individual events for boys, men, women and men's and women's veterans ranging from 100 metres, the standing long jump to the gruelling 1,500 metres. Football, netball and tug o' war were also on offer. The programme also listed the Northern Isles Sports records with Billy Harcus from **Sanday** holding the 100 metres record since 1984 in a creditable 11.09 seconds. No other record had been set for so long. Of the 28 records listed 19 were held by **Sanday** residents. **Sanday** was clearly the Soviet Union of the championships!

The day was set fair. This happy, optimistic crowd reminded me of my Yorkshire childhood, when on successive weekends throughout the summer, first one village and then another would hold their Galas with floats and processions and dressing up with copious tea and homemade cakes. Alcohol was forbidden in these strict Baptist and Methodist villages across the Pennines. I still have a photograph of ten village boys including my brother, Philip, dressed in pyjamas their faces blacked with the excruciating caption 'Ten little nigger boys', alluding to the Agatha Christie mystery written on **Burgh island**. How times have changed, from overt racism to 'Black Lives Matter' in a generation.

These Galas were held across the Yorkshire Dales and Lake District with bigger sporting festivals in places like Burnsall on the River Wharfe and Grasmere on the shore of Lake Windermere. These annual events have been taking place since Elizabethan times. The highlight was always the fell run with combatants descending at breakneck speeds quite literally. The legendary fell runner, Josh Naylor, had been, along with Yorkshire cricketer Fred Truman, my childhood hero. The Northern Isles sports day was in this timeless annual tradition.

Our trip to Orkney would be all too short with 13 islands to be visited in seven short days limiting exploration with appreciation of complex timetable logistics at a premium. **Sanday**, like its neighbouring islands, is a vibrant farming community with sufficient population to sustain the economy and provide schooling. It is interesting that most of the Orkney Islands are served by Loganair, significantly subsidised to allow access to **Mainland Orkney** through several flights each day. Without this necessity, an aberration in the age of expensive and carbon hungry leisure, or unnecessary business flights, the cohesion of Orkney could not be managed. We were impressed when in the days of overt capitalism, where profits are more important than people, the Scottish Government, as ever, take an enlightened view. Without Scottish Government intervention, as is also increasingly seen in the Hebrides, depopulation would run unfettered. The tragedy of Highland Clearances runs deep in the psyche of these Northern Scotland islanders.

At the beginning of the 20th Century **Stronsay** was the centre of the herring fishing industry first exploited by the Dutch. At its height Whitehall the largest settlement had fifteen fish curing sheds and forty pubs or about one for about every 25 persons, though bolstered daily by sailors from all around the North Sea with anything up to 300 boats anchored in the Papa Sound. Cured and salted herring were exported mainly to the Baltic States, fond to this day of their fishy delicacies. The stinking fermented herring *sustromming* is a staple delicacy in Sweden. Be warned!

My next 'hop on, hop off' island of the day was **Eday** and like **Sanday** to the north and **Stronsay** to the south survive by the promotion of strong grass roots community partnerships. **Eday** Partnership has instigated numerous projects, including Eday Heritage Centre, and the purchase of a new diesel tank for the island. **Eday's** various community projects contributed £380,000 to the island's economy from 2005-7 and a 900-kW community-owned wind turbine is planned. The income that this asset will generate is expected to reduce fuel poverty on the island, support new community enterprises and create affordable housing. As a result of these very direct investments the population of **Eday** grew by 30% between the 2001 and 2011 censuses. During the same period the population of all Scottish islands combined grew by only 4%. The decline through prior poor investment and inadequate infrastructure is slowly but surely reversing.

Eday can be dark and bleak, but its hills are cloaked with thick peat, absent from other islands. Prosperity in the 18th and 19th centuries came from extracting this for fuel supplying the other nearby islands until cheaper imported coal stifled this trade. Its slate and old red sandstone quarries helped its fragile economy with St Magnus cathedral in Kirkwall built from this fine yellow, stratified stone.

Leaving **Eday** we passed close by the prominent sandstone cliffs of Red Head with large populations of fulmar and puffins nesting on the precipitous cliffs. The 'haar', a local name for a cold sea mist or fog coming off the North Sea, akin to the sea frets experienced in the Yorkshire holiday resorts of my childhood, was with us for much of the day. I was used to these from interminable days out in Scarborough in the 1950's when land ladies would throw out their 'guests' after breakfast and would not contemplate their return under any circumstances until the evening meal at six o'clock sharp. We spent many a long hour huddled in bus shelters, our gaberdine mackintoshes belted tight against the chill North Sea wind that usually accompanied the sea fret. Flasks of weak, milky boarding house coffee and curled up ham sandwiches were our only solace and sustenance with the lure of warm promenade cafes out of bounds to frugal Yorkshire folk. Ice creams were a far-off fantasy.

We docked back at Kirkwall at around 13:00 after disgorging most of our fellow passengers on **Westray**. I chose not to 'hop off-hop on' at **Westray** as this island with its sister **Papa Westray** was reserved for another day. The journey back from **Westray** was devoid of passengers. All were now ensconced in the merriment of the Northern Isles sports day. It is not often one embarks on a five-hour ferry trip before lunch.

We were to meet our landlord for the week at the Bridge Street apartment directly and conveniently adjacent to the entry to the ferry port. He was a charming beef farmer who had made a very good fist of converting a small first floor property behind the *Kirkwall Hotel* into a very comfortable and well-appointed one bedroom flat for his daughter to let. It had been the only available property on Booking.com in all of central Kirkwall so we were anxious to discover its comfort and suitability. Our fears were allayed. I was quick to point out that Trevor and I were not to share the only bed, but that he had brought a sturdy blow up affair to inflate at night in the small lounge/kitchenette.

This beautiful and practically furnished flat was to be our home for the week and within 100 metres of several licensed premises. We were to favour the *Kirkwall Hotel* and *The Shore* with excellent ales and a wide selection of single malts. Our 'office' became the *Highland Park* bar in the rather opulent *Kirkwall Hotel,* though the juxtaposition of the gentlemen's toilet and the kitchen were a little worrisome. Trevor's electronically operated air bed burst during the first night, but this calamity did not detract from an excellent base camp for our brief island visits.

Once settled, we had the afternoon to explore some of **Mainland Orkney**. We chose the southwest corner, past the famous Highland Park distillery, one of a growing number of whisky, and more recently gin, distilleries in Orkney. We skirted the airport and onto the coastal fringe beyond. Highland Park prides itself as a single malt with a Viking soul. Further reflecting the boldness of Orkney's Norse heritage, Kirkjuvagr, or Church Bay, Orkney gin was launched in 2016, with an angelica plant of Scandinavian origin one of its defining ingredients brought to the islands by Norsemen centuries ago.

As we drove, we noticed that all houses were built with windows facing south to maximise daylight in winter which can be as little as five or six hours in these northern latitudes. We were as far north as southern Norway, 530 miles from London as the crow flies. Before electricity was installed in the islands many Orcadians moved to mainland Scotland, lured by the flashing of electric lights in the homes on Caithness just across the Pentland Firth.

We were tracking down a standing stone without realising that these were indeed ubiquitous throughout Orkney, but stoically came across a bedraggled specimen in a farmer's field. The farmer kept beef cattle and regaled us with his misplaced views on climate change and I for once managed to bite my tongue. We looked out over the North Sea to uninhabited Copinsay marvelling in the tranquillity of a late but chilly June afternoon. Disorientated pilot whales had been spotted the previous week and locals had formed a ring of boats around them to help with their sonar to achieve open sea. The explanation for their misguided adventure seemed to be that the female lead of the school had become injured and as the males ventured out to sea the other females stayed behind with her until human intervention directed them appropriately. Well, this was Trevor's theory, or was it the farmer's? Either way Sir David Attenborough would have been very impressed at our perceived knowledge!

The ferry to **Shapinsay** on the following day had its separate berth in the Kirkwall harbour. We decided, as fares were heavily subsidised, to take the car over and spend the day exploring, a luxury not afforded to us much that busy week. As usual Trevor had 'ferry fever' wanting to give ample time between arriving at the ferry and leaving the harbour. I have always been more nonchalant liking a frisson of danger. However, since yesterday, when the ferry to the Northern Isles set off a full 15 minutes before its scheduled departure, maybe Trevor's angst was justified. The ferry was empty save for a couple of farmers and their trailers. Leaving Kirkwall Bay, we passed Thieves Holm, a small isle where, according to legend, witches and thieves were exiled to fend for themselves. Before disembarking at Elwick Bay, the ferry enters the String, a foreboding narrow and deep stretch of water linking the North Sea to the Atlantic Ocean.

Shapinsay boasts the magnificent warm stone colours of Balfour castle built by the self-appointed 'Colonel' David Balfour, from the spoils of the fortunes his family made in imperial India. His father, John, the MP for Orkney and Shetland, had received colossal compensation from the British Government to offset loans by rich colonialists to the Rajah of Tanjore which were never repaid. History is littered with stories of the wealthy elite feathering their own already bloated nests. A 'No Deal' or even a poor deal Brexit was to massively increase the wealth of privileged politicians like Jacob Rees-Mogg, born with self-entitlement running through their blue-blooded veins.

Island of Mist (Eilean a Cheo) leaving for Soay, Highland
(Photo Steve White)

Early morning mist Inishbiggle, Mayo
(Photo John Lawlor)

'Teal', a Norwegian Poiner, transport to Auskerry, Orkney Islands
(Photo Trevor Masterson)

*Inishnakillew,
Clew Bay, Mayo*
(Photo John Lawlor)

*Causeway to Lithou,
Channel Islands*
(Photo Steve White)

*Crossing to Oronsay
at low tide, Argyll
and Bute*

Sark, Channel Islands
(Photo Steve White)

South Stack, Holy Island, Ynys Mons
(Photo Karolina Szczerkowska

Brecqhou from Sark, Channel Islands
(Photo Steve White)

Lynott's pub, Achill island, Mayo
(Photo John Lawlor)

George Martin's House, Alderney, Channel Islands (Photo Steve White)

Holy Island (Lindisfarne) Causeway Northumberland

Floating bridge to Dry island, Gairloch, Highland

Spinnaker Tower, Portsea Island, Hampshire
(Photo Craig Lucas-O'Brien)

Portsmouth Harbour, Hampshire (Photo Craig Lucas-O_Brien)

Northern Lights, Callanish stones, Lewis, Eilean Siar

Longhope, South Walls, Hoy, Orkney Islands (Photo Daniel McNeil)

Marvig Boatyard, Lewis, Eilean Siar (Photo Mark Tywang)

Compton MacKenzie's hut, Jethou, Channel Islands (Photo Steve White)

Bridge over the Atlantic, Seil, Argyll & Bute

Springtime in Gigh, Scilly Isles

Wakering stairs, Thames estuary, Essex at high and low tide (Photo Ian Vesey)

Asplin Stairs, Foulness, Essex (Photo Ian Vesey)

Deserted village, Inishkea south, Mayo (Photo John Lawlor)

Old Man of Hoy, Orkney Islands

Cruit Island, Donegal looking to Omey island

Beach, Inishkea south, Mayo (Photo John Lawlor)

Karst landscape, Inishmaan, Aran islands, Galway (Photo John Lawlor)

Eilean Donan, Highland

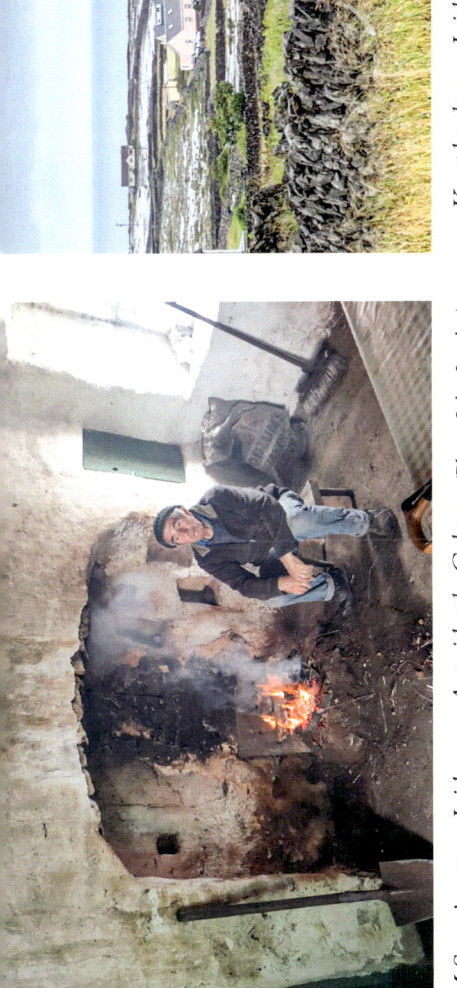

JM Synge's cottage, Inishmaan, Aran islands, Galway (Photo John Lawlor)

Eilean na Cille, Eilean Siar

Low tide crossing, to Coney island, Sligo (Photo John Lawlor)

Rosbarnargh. Clew bay. Mayo (Photo John Lawlor)

Arriving on Jethou, Channel Islands on amphibious RIB (Photo Steve White)

Garinish island, Kenmare Estuary, Kerry

Island tranquility, Northern Isles
(Photo Daniel McNeil)

Northern Isles Car Ferry

Loading CalMac ferry, North Ronaldsway, Orkney Islands

Vaila sea arches, Shetland Islands
(Photo Ian Vesey)

Car Ferry to Jura from Islay, Argylle & Bute

Nuclear subs and rotting tubs, Vickers Barrow from Walney island, Cumbria

Aurigny airlines flight to Guernsey (Photo Steve White)

St Michael's Mount, Marazion, Cornwall

Tresco to Bryher, Scilly Isles at low spring tide

CalMac Ferry: Wemys Bay to Rothsey, Isle of Bute

Dinghy to Eilean da Mheinn, Argylle & Bute (Photo Steve White)

Cable car to Dursey Island, West Cork

Bear Grylls arriving on jetski from St Tudwal's West, North Wales (Photo Craig Lucas-O'Brien)

Lundy Landing stage, Bristol Channel

At least the colonel had a modicum of conscience as following the decline of the kelp industry he set about reforming agriculture on **Shapinsay** dividing land into 10-acre units with appropriate drainage. Despite his good auspices the islanders still regarded him as a petty tyrant. It is always difficult to expunge the stains of tyranny. So impressive is the colonel's baronial edifice that it is visible from St Magnus cathedral in Kirkwall.

We had time to make a complete reconnaissance of the island before choosing places of particular interest. We stopped awhile on a deserted pollution free beach in the far north of the island to admire the firths and islands around us. As usual we had not poured over guidebooks and any quirky find would be serendipitous. Standing stones provide evidence of the island's human occupation since Neolithic times, but our choice of pre-history architecture was one of the Iron Age brochs which abound throughout Orkney.

We followed the rough path to the Broch of Burroughston. Only the interior of this partially buried building has been excavated, allowing us to look down into the broch from the surrounding mound. The surviving dry-stone walls rise to about three metres and are more than four metres thick in some places. These brochs were built, some archaeologists say, as forts or protective round houses and are prolific in their distribution around the Hebrides, Orkney and Shetland and also on the mainland of northeast Scotland. Another theory is that they were the 'stately homes' of their time though their proliferation in clusters makes this theory unlikely.

Shapinsay has always been fertile for agriculture but during the 18th century its fortunes were greatly helped by the kelp industry (seaweed). Some 3,000 tons were harvested annually for fertiliser worth £20,000 to the islanders, with some 70 boats in action. Assuming in 1798 with a population of 740, more than twice that of today, this was spread across all 199 households then the income for each would be £13,000 in today's money; a tidy sum not including fishing or agriculture.

We headed back to the harbour near Balfour castle and spied a café in what was Balfour's old blacksmith shop. This was a disappointing 'honesty café' with kettles, tea bags and instant coffee with a limited selection of Kit Kat chocolate biscuits. We had heard that crab sandwiches would be on offer, but no sign of humanity made this delightful local delicacy improbable. Instead, we availed ourselves of the alternative meagre fare in this dank, airless tomb of a place. With more time to kill we tried to locate the *Gatehouse* 'pub' but soon gave up as hope triumphed over experience. If it does exist, it is well hidden and was almost certainly closed on that quiet Sunday afternoon. Back on the ferry we learnt that our adventure to **Auskerry** later in the week might be jeopardised by poor weather, a common theme throughout my adventures. Obscure and inaccessible islands are the bane of the island hopping 'anorak'.

Graemsay and **Flotta** were our next island goals with embarkation for the former island from the delightful, almost quirky, town of Stromness, perched on the edge of Hamnavoe Bay under the shelter of Brinkies Brae. Its winding, stone flagged thoroughfares and tourist outlets are frequented by travellers passing time before boarding the Northlink ferry back to Scrabster on Scotland's north coast. Embarkation to **Flotta** was from a much more utilitarian commercial harbour at Houton a couple of dozen miles away, so efficiency of travel was at a premium to meet our schedule. I felt smug that even I have resorted to planning.

We breakfasted at *Julia's* café on the dock side with passengers for the later and longer journey heading for mainland, Scotland on *MV Hamnavoe*, idling away time with cups of tea and bacon sandwiches. Stromness's prosperity was built on herring and whaling and in 1841 there were four inns, 34 pubs, a parish church, post office, library, three schools, a town hall, museum and three banks in the town. Northlink ferries had stemmed the decline, perhaps bolstered by the oil boom in the 1970's, though helicopter and company planes were a preferred mode of transport for workers and executives alike rather than the humble ferry.

We boarded our passenger boat, the *MV Graemsay*, to its namesake island with fellow travellers largely bound for **Hoy**, which I had conquered already with Ian before my Shetland trip. The trip was for outdoor types and cyclists taking advantage of the rugged mountainous terrain of **Hoy** in stark contrast with the pastoral, bucolic aspects of most of Orkney's other islands. I was jealous of their seaming fitness as my own health was rapidly deteriorating. **Graemsay** with a population of 28 was merely a staging post on this scheduled trip to Moaness on **Hoy**, mainly we suspected for islanders.

Graemsay is sometimes referred to locally, as 'Orkney's green isle' due to its lush vegetation cover. We settled down patiently and noticed amongst the public notices an Old Testament, presumably in case of rough seas and the need to commune with the Almighty. It is interesting that chain hotels are now supplementing the ubiquitous Gideon's Bible with copies of the Koran or the Hindu Veda. At last, our multi-faith society is getting a tad of recognition.

Nothing goes to plan it would seem on our adventures. I had requested two tickets to **Graemsay** and paid the appropriate fee but was told we wouldn't be stopping at the island if nobody requested a stop. I said, "But I am requesting a stop" and explained my plan to set foot on the turf and regain the boat on its way to Moaness and then back to Stromness. "Then you are not going to **Graemsay**" the ticket collector said firmly. "We will only stop for genuine passengers leaving at **Graemsay**". He was becoming more and more irritated and as people know I have a short fuse and explosion was imminent. Trevor calmed me. I implored my fellow passengers to declare any intention of leaving at **Graemsay** and to my relief a lady indicated that this was her plan. I glared through gritted teeth at the officious purser knowing that he must now make this intermediate stop. I asked the lady in a hushed whisper if I could get off first thus giving me more time to stand on solid ground and get back to the boat before officialdom left me to my own devices stranded until the next boat.

On reaching the quay I waddled off and came back a little like a naughty schoolboy only to be greeted by said purser whose mood had done a 180-degree turn. He was now 'hail fellow, well met' and invited Trevor and I onto the bridge to meet the captain. They were mildly captivated by my exploits, and I attempted small talk asking how often the boat scraped the steel sheet piles of the dock. "Once a week" he said without hesitation. I now see why the Old Testament scriptures were on prominent display. His mate mischievously quipped that the ropes would last a lot longer if his navigation skills were improved. We docked without further incident both in Moaness and back at Stromness and bade our new sea faring friends *adieu*. The whole trip had cost us £4.40p each thanks to the subsidies provided by the Orkney Islands Council.

An innocent journey maybe but the tide in the Hoy sound, we were told by the mischievous captain, can run so fast that the surface of the sea forms high ridges with whirlpools in the troughs, The ridges apparently move like sandstorms in a desert. These areas of massive turbulence are known as 'roosts' from the Old Norse 'rost' or maelstrom.

Trevor, it would seem, has replaced my previous companion, Richard Crace, very often present on my 5,003 mile walk around the coast of Great Britain. He fetches and carries for me at will, is compliant to my demands and rarely complains, even in the face of adversity or when my piques of temper call him a bastard. Still, I miss Richard who in his later years became a recluse and he died in Summer 2019. I had hardly seen him, maybe once or twice at most, since 2006 and was full of remorse for my behaviour to him and barbed jibes for all to read in *'A Walk by the Sea'*. His brother, the world-renowned author, Jim Crace, invited me to Richard's outdoor woodland funeral in Moseley Bog, opposite my house, and to the wake after in the *Covered Wagon* pub. I last saw Richard on Christmas day 2018, sat outside the *Wagon*, hunched over a slowly drunk pint of Timothy Taylor's Landlord, still profusely smoking his Benson and Hedges cigarettes. I gave him my book, but doubt he had the stomach to read it. I regret mistreating him; he meant well.

We needed to get to Hooton to avoid missing the only ferry which not only would take us to **Flotta** but would get us back again to **Mainland Orkney**. Ian and I had tried to do this trip on a sleepy Sunday a couple of years before. On arrival on my second attempt that Sunday, the terminal was deserted as Hooton was essentially a terminal for oil workers billeted on **Mainland Orkney** who made the daily commute to this nondescript little island in the middle of Scapa Flow. The bored attendant at the check in desk looked up from her novel and offered the rather unhelpful advice that there was little point in taking the ferry anyway as there was nothing to do or see on **Flotta** for the discerning tourist.

With some difficulty we found a parking space amongst the parked commuter vehicles and trusted our luck to buying a ticket this time. Until the First World War **Flotta** had been a quiet rural idyll with agriculture at its heart but in both wars had become a military base before becoming silent again, with its elderly population declining to extinction despite in 1970 being connected to mains water. Then came oil.

In 1974, Occidental Petroleum started construction of the island's oil terminal linked by a 230km pipeline to the Piper and Claymore oil fields in the North Sea. This became the second largest major oil terminal serving the UK North Sea's vast reserves. Delivering around 10% of Britain's oil production it is outstripped in size only by Sullom Voe on Shetland. The flare at the tip of its 223 feet stack can be seen all around Orkney and as far as Scotland's north coast. It represents the symbol of modern Orkney in the same way as the Old Man of Hoy sea stack represents its heritage. Thousands were involved in the terminal's construction which is a business on a gigantic scale with accommodation and restaurants for staff in the nick named *"Flotta Hilton"*. With its own airport oil executives come and go at will.

It was opened in January 1977 by the then energy minister, Tony Benn. How times have changed. The socialist firebrand, taking successive Conservative Governments to task, was committed to Maynard Keynes economic policies. These included nationalising infrastructure for the common good but in those far off days was then also pioneering fossil fuels as the future of UK's prosperity. These were the days before the objectives of Global sustainability and the strive for renewable energy, and long before Greta Thunberg and Extinction Rebellion. In hindsight it is fair to say that increasing the Nation's prosperity was low on the agenda of the oil companies and it was corporate greed that was driving the vast investments bolstered by massive Government subsidies. Today, almost as lip service to environmentally driven policies, a 2.3MW wind turbine on **Flotta** was connected to the National Grid in 2010.

Despite the God to fossil fuel that **Flotta** has become, Orkney now prides itself with energy sustainability with 100% of all Orcadians electricity needs met from local renewable sources, with 1 in 10 of the population generating their own power. Electric cars are a common sight with by far the highest per head of population in Scotland. On reflection this is hardly surprising as journeys between charges are short by dint of the islands' sizes. What is more surprising is that often charging is via home-built wind turbines. Since the 18th Century enlightenment movement Scotland has always pioneered inventions from the likes of James Watt to Alexander Graham Bell. This is continuing in Orkney at the European Marine Energy Centre, initiating wave and tidal energy converters for a further sustainable clean energy generation.

As usual the turnaround at **Flotta** was efficient and I felt this would be another Achilles heel of my ventures, just like crossing the Corran narrows on Loch Linnhe near Fort William. This 200-metre journey, the only time in 5,003 miles of the *Walk by the Sea* odyssey when a ferry was taken, was a 'bete noir' indelibly etched on my conscience. The pier at **Flotta** was much longer than usual and involved a breathless 'sprint' to touch the natural sod, my own indicator that I had actually stood on an island. As I left the ferry, I blurted out some fanciful story to the deck hands that I was just delivering a package to a friend and would be back. I felt like a sleazy drug runner but didn't want the confrontation I had had with crew earlier in the day on *MV Graemsay*. I made the long dash to and from naturally firm ground, but only just.

In contrast to **Flotta** the next island trip was to **North Ronaldsay**, the most northerly and farthest (from Kirkwall) of the Orkney Islands, further north than Norway's southern tip. Avoiding its daily flight from Kirkwall involved a two hours and forty minutes ferry journey each way. My job was to sit on a ferry for most of the day with a 30-minute turn around to unload cargo and indeed vehicles as this was not a Roll-on-Roll-off vessel. Of course, the island had an airport as all the larger inhabited islands have, operated by Loganair, and subsidised by the Orkney Islands Council but both the price and journey times, door to door, were similar. The ferry was on our doorstep whilst the flight involved, taxis to and from the airport, check in and waiting around. I opted for the ferry whilst Trevor wisely stayed ashore and thus avoided the tedium of sitting most of the day on uncomfortable moulded fixed plastic seats drinking the sort of coffee usually only reserved for hospital visitors. Eyeing up passengers, who on this trip were sparse in number, was the only entertainment.

We arrived on time, and I had a short walk to the bird observatory where a wee dram would have been on offer, but I elected to watch a rather unsafe looking hoist lifting vehicles from deck to quay and vice versa. This was precarious to say the least and certainly not done according to any Health and Safety Executive Manual of best practice. I wasn't the only returning passenger, but we never struck up more than a modicum of polite conversation. Just another sad old man along for the ride.

North Ronaldsay is world famous for its indigenous sheep, which thrive on seaweed. A 20-mile sheep dyke (or wall) has been built to keep the sheep shore side. In 1993 the worst storm for years flattened three kilometres of dyke and the Royal Navy financed by the Prince's Trust were commandeered to rebuild it thus preserving this unique part of the island's livelihood and heritage. The two oldest dykes, Matches and Gerstsy, are thought to be 3,000 years old. Following the announcement at the Island Conference in June 2019 the **North Ronaldsay** Trust began the recruitment process for a Sheep Dyke Warden, funded by the North Isles Landscape Partnership. An ancient assembly, the ancient sheep court, is elected by the traditional townships of the island to manage these hardy sheep.

The island is low lying with no ground higher than twenty metres. Its isolation has led to the development of a very close-knit population living in a wide scattering of cottages. They apparently read a lot in these dark northern winters with the Orkney library service finding it difficult to keep up with supplies for these insatiable book worms. Their dialect contains similarities with Norn, native to southwest Norway and until 1870 spoken throughout the Orkneys. I was reminded of a trip to Iceland.

I have been fascinated by Norse, or more correctly Old Norse, since a child growing up in the Yorkshire Dales. My mother and father's dialect was peppered with words and expressions derived from Norse. We used to 'lek' or 'laik' out meaning to play. In 1995 when my two-year sojourn in New York was over, I had cause to return to collect some possessions. My beloved cousin Dick had just died, and his grieving partner wanted to go with me. She was a very heavy smoker and couldn't contemplate a transatlantic flight of more than seven hours without a cigarette, so she found a travel package with Iceland air which included an overnight stopover in Reykjavik and a short tour. The price was right, so we booked. Iceland is in reality and metaphorically just a giant ash tray.

It was June and the sun never sets. We enjoyed the experience and the short tour. After the tour the guide asked for questions. Instead of the usual banal ones about temperatures of geysers and whether Iceland really had by head of population the most published authors in the world, I asked what the Icelandic was for 'to play'. The guide ignored me thinking I was some strange eccentric but when I pressed him, he replied 'lek'. The mystery of the connection between Yorkshire Dales dialect and the Nordic language was unravelled and I spent some 30 minutes in discussion with him exchanging other words familiar to us both.

The return journey was about to commence, and I retired to the stark, dreary café in the bowels of the ship where I was the only customer. This was another example of essential subsidisation to keep services viable. The takings in the café would be meagre but then so would the fare revenue with barely 10 passengers on each leg of the journey. After my desultory trip to the café, I took up position in the deserted lounge, staring at the clock in front of me for two and a half hours. It was a Zen like experience watching time tick by minute by minute and hour by hour on the ancient analogue clock. Since my operations for retinal detachment following a cataract operation in 2018, I could no longer read comfortably unless direct bright light was involved. In this dingy cabin therefore, reading was not an option and sitting on deck for too long was bracing to say the least.

Docking was as usual like clockwork and stiff and bored I made the short walk to meet Trevor in the *Highland Park* bar for much needed libation and an evening of unbridled fun on a cold June evening. I once remarked to Ian when we were walking through Lerwick "It would be nice here in Summer" when I realised it was Summer!

The monotony of ferry travel the previous days was forgotten with journeys to **Westray** and **Papa Westray**. I'd heard of the shortest scheduled commercial flight in the World (and this was not the usual tourist hyperbole) was routed between **Papa Westray** and its much larger neighbour **Westray**. *The Guinness Book of Records* endorsed this claim with the journey time on the Loganair flight around 90 seconds, yes, 90 seconds from take-off to landing. More time would be taken taxiing than in the air! Experiencing this was too good an opportunity to miss and I booked Trevor and I a one-way flight some months earlier at the princely sum of £17 each, or just over £11 per minute. Applying this rate to a 20-hour flight to Sydney from Heathrow would cost £13,600 one way!

Of course, we needed to get to the 'airport' so we set out on what should have been, had fate not intervened, a 12-hour return journey from Kirkwall. The Kirkwall ferry docks at Rapness in the south of **Westray** where an island bus was waiting to despatch us to Pierowall some 10 or so kilometres north. As time was well on our side we elected to be dropped at the beginning of the village and, in the hope of acquiring breakfast, stumbled on a delightful café, Groatie Buckie's, run by Stewart and Marian Groat. Now, a Groatie Buckie is a cowrie shell (*Trivia arctica*), apparently found on nearby beaches. Trivium was a Roman word for anything common place, but these little gems of shells were far from common on adjacent beaches, but proudly on display in the café.

Westray, affectionately known as the 'Queen of the North Isles' because of its diverse scenery, is a thriving community of around 600 islanders. It has vibrancy, charm and genuine island spirit of pride and self-sufficiency. Wedding celebrations are legendary in **Westray** with apparently the longest on record reputedly to have been held at Noltland castle which continued from Martinmas on the 11th November to Candlemas on the 2nd February without a break. Now this is a perfect way to while away the dark winter nights.

Refreshed we walked to the Pierowall harbour waiting out of a chill wind in a perfunctory waiting room for the passenger ferry, *Golden Mariana*, to **Papa Westray** to arrive. The short trip took us to the pier on **Papa Westray** and we walked in pouring rain the couple of miles to the tiny settlement of Holland. Just before the village we saw a sign to the Knap of Howar and curiosity got the better of us, so we followed the footpath to the shore. On arrival we stumbled on a Neolithic farmstead which was billed as the oldest preserved stone house in northern Europe, occupied from 3,700 BC to 2,800 BC. Farmers were busy here well before the pyramids were built in Egypt. The site was first excavated in the 1930's and its preservation is quite remarkable. Amongst the artefacts discovered were the bones of the now extinct Great Auk, whose oil was a useful source of energy for light and cooking. The last breeding pair in Scotland was killed on **Papa Westray** in 1813.

There is evidence from artefacts that the farmers who lived in the building left quickly though it is uncertain why. I suggested to Trevor it might have been a tsunami like the much earlier Storegga land slide in Norway when 3,500 cubic *kilometres* of displaced rock triggered the largest tsunami in history, some 3,000 years earlier. I can't help but wonder if there was geological proof that such an event might have repeated during the Iron Age. Even today the scale of these huge displays of nature cannot be predicted, just like the timing of the consequences of climate change or the scale and timing of future pandemics like the 2020 COVID 19 worldwide outbreak.

Suitably impressed we sheltered in the open 24-hour museum that is part of Holland Farm with a bothy recreating the spartan lifestyle of 19th and early 20th Century tenants. Rested, we needed to get to the airport some short distance north to catch the plane to **Westray**. From the oldest house in northern Europe to an airport, all in the space of a mile or so. We could see the windsock from afar and then the 'airport terminal' which was essentially a single storey brick building. We gingerly entered expecting a hive of activity; check in, security, duty free (we were being fanciful!). The place was deserted with radios and phones unmanned and flight logs and manuals left unattended. We had an hour or so to kill and I slept or at least tried to sleep on an uncomfortable bench seat whilst Trevor explored the adjacent windswept terrain.

I was awoken from my fitful sleep by a lady who was frantically organising the next flight, closely followed by two firemen kitted out in their full-length fireproof outfits, a necessary obligation insisted on by the Civil Aviation Authorities. Within seconds the whir of the incoming aircraft, a Britten-Norman BN2B-26 Islander, well suited to Orkney weather, could be heard and without further delay Trevor and I were bundled (the only passengers) into the plane and off it set for the 1.7-mile journey. No security drill seemed necessary with only the briefest of preparatory instructions. Once in the air the airstrip on **Westray** was clearly visible and before any pleasantries were exchanged by the captain we landed safely. The distance between the two airstrips across the Papa Sound is less than the length of Glasgow airport's main runway. To attract tourists an 18-hole golf course has been developed with nine holes on **Westray** and a further nine on **Papa Westray**, with Loganair linking both.

The captain indicated the journey time was not exceptional and boasted that he has done the journey, take off to touch down, in under 60 seconds. We taxied to a building similar to the departure lounge that we had left a couple of minutes earlier and made as to leave the plane. "Where are you going" the captain enquired. "Oh, we'll get a taxi to Rapness and the ferry," I replied. We were unaware that this short hop was part of a round robin of island flights, and he offered us a lift back to Kirkwall. This was a glorious 15-minute flight above the isolated lush beauty of **Eday** and **Shapinsay** below and the majestic grey-blue ocean caressing their shores.

We landed at the rather business-like Kirkwall airport, a far cry from its sister satellites we had just left. The captain bade us farewell and as an afterthought I asked, "Who do we pay the excess fare to?". Nonchalantly he suggested we went to the Loganair check in desk. On finding this we asked the Polish clerk if we could pay our dues. He tapped his keys and thought for a moment and then said, "That'll be £1 each". We were flabbergasted, not a word to use lightly. Apparently, the maximum daily fare to fly between the islands of Orkney was £18 per passenger. I had already paid £17 for each of us so I dug into my trouser pocket and proffered two coins. The, by now, bored Pole said, "We only take cards!".

The lounge was busy with flights to Sumburgh on Shetland, Aberdeen and Edinburgh. Loganair is after all known as Scotland's airline. We called for a taxi to return us to our 'office' in the *Highland Park* bar of the *Kirkwall Hotel*. This cost was £10. The economics of travel never ceases to bewilder.

The day we were due to go to **Auskerry** dawned and we were assured that, though the trip would be 'bumpy' a euphemistic nautical expression if ever there was one, the 15-mile trip across the open North Sea was on as scheduled. We drove to our appointed rendezvous with Richard Zawadski, who despite his name, was a fine Orcadian man with excesses of local knowledge. Trevor had somehow sourced him through a friend of a friend. We donned the suitable footwear and clothing he provided in preparation for any weather the North Sea could throw at us and headed for a unique sailing vessel call *'Teal'*, a Norwegian Poiner made of polyurethane. It was like a mini-Roll-on-Roll-off ferry with the stern able to lower to make contact with the ground on landing. This was essential for my several embarkations and disembarkations as my arthritic body can no longer easily make the contortions necessary to board a conventional small boat.

The boat was just of sufficient size for the three of us with Captain Richard at the helm and we set out at a great pace towards an invisible **Auskerry**, whose highest point is a mere eighteen metres above sea level. The island has been inhabited for over 30 years by a family who keep a flock of 300 strong rare **North Ronaldsay** sheep. The owners of this 250-acre island raised their two children there, but who no longer live on the island. Indeed, Simon Brogan and his partner Teressa Probert in more recent years vacate the island at Christmas to return in March in time for lambing.

Explanation of permanency of occupation within the definition of my rules, seems blurred. However, this is not a twee holiday home but an actual working farm and the Scottish census in 2011 saw fit to enumerate the population as four. That was good enough for me. Clearly the hardy native sheep look after themselves in winter. Sheep farming on the surface is hardly lucrative, but the couple have made a decent living hand spinning yarn and, in particular, curing sheep skins which sell as artisan fleeces for upwards of £200.

We had arranged to meet Simon and learn more about this isolated life. Little did we know that in just under a year the whole country, indeed world, would be self-isolating in the wake of the COVID 19 scourge. It seems digging peat to sustain the round the clock fires necessary summer and winter in this bleak and utterly exposed environment, and engaging in all manner of crafts and cottage industries alleviates any hint of boredom. We could learn a lot from this self-contentment. The journey, which Trevor, ever the imaginary sailor, enjoyed immensely took about an hour.

On arrival the weather was against us, and we had to dock, or at least moor the boat against very slippery rocks, near the lighthouse at Baa Taking in the south of the island some distance from the farmstead. Our scheduled visit to Simon and Teresa was sadly abandoned. Richard mentioned that his house was more akin to that of Scott's (of the Antarctic) base camp than a Scottish croft. They rely on a combination of wind turbines, solar panels and peat and driftwood for electricity and heat but have no plumbing. Before he settled on **Auskerry** Simon was tour manager for Ian Anderson's 'prog rock' outfit *Jethro Tull*. His boys, born on the island, were obviously self-educated but interestingly were now following various media careers in England. Rory has a First-Class BA Honours degree in media production from the University of Sunderland and hosted the weekly Route 66 show on Stockport's Pure 107.8 FM, a far cry from his humble upbringing.

After stretching my aching legs close to the lighthouse with the weather apparently getting 'fresh', another nautical euphemism, we set off back to the safety of **Mainland Orkney**. Apart from Trevor's obvious aptitude for sea travel in small boats, he seemed to be able to identify every bird on the planet. **Auskerry** is designated a Special Protection Area due to its importance as a nesting area for Arctic tern and storm petrel with 4.2% of the breeding population of storm petrel in Great Britain nesting on the island. The pair (Trevor and Richard) not the passing Arctic terns not only knew the size, shape and colour of the birds we encountered but what sounds they made. I am not fond of birds and their attraction passes me by. Give me the grandeur of geology and the geomorphological mantle which shapes it, and I am mesmeric.

We had time to spare on the half day budget for our trip, which at £100 was a modest payment for both the trip and Richard's enthusiasm and unparalleled knowledge. Our original intention was to attempt to understand the unfathomable timetable that would efficiently get Trevor and I to two of our four remaining inhabited islands; **Egilsay** and **Wyre**. Ian and I, with time to spare before our Shetland trip two years earlier, had visited **Rousay**. **Egilsay** and **Wyre** were on the same ferry route, and it became obvious that to achieve both of these islands we would have to route through **Rousay**, but no service from Tingwall, using *Eynhallow* ferry, ever connected all four islands on a single round trip. Planning for these visits, I was losing the very will to live trying to unlock the mysteries of the timetables. At least two separate trips to **Rousay** seemed unavoidable. As for **Gairsay**, with a population of three we would have to rely on *Teal* and Richard's good auspices as no public ferry service connected this small island to **Mainland Orkney**.

With this in mind and realising *Teal* would pass close to all three islands on our way back I persuaded Richard to anchor for a short while on each and ease, what would have been otherwise, hopeless logistics to fit in before our pre-booked *Clansman* ferry off of Orkney. Richard was more than happy to oblige and I'm not sure whether a supplement was charged. The weather was improving and my angst receding on what was becoming a pearl of a day's island hopping. Richard found idyllic, deserted beaches on both **Egilsay** and **Wyre** and in deference to my aging limbs accommodated me with simple embarkations and disembarkations on soft sandy beaches.

Egilsay is a low-lying island with its highest point just over 35m above sea level. Even at this low level we enjoyed great views of the outlying islands, **Westray** to the North, **Eday**, the Green Holms and **Stronsay** to the East, and **Wyre**, **Shapinsay** and Kirkwall to the South not forgetting its hilly neighbour **Rousay** to the West. It is an agricultural island with about half owned by the RSPB where the elusive corncrake breeds. Farmers and conservationists work together to preserve the natural order. It was on **Egilsay** that St Magnus, an Orkney earl was martyred some 900 years ago, his legacy remembered in his namesake cathedral in Kirkwall and the well-preserved 12th Century church on the island. The two cousins Magnus and Hakon entered into a bitter feud over control of Orkney but agreed to discuss peace terms until the duplicitous Hakon had a more sinister intention.

Wyre is one of the smallest inhabited islands in the Orkney archipelago and like its neighbour is flat. We didn't as ever have time to explore. The Viking legacy is particularly evident on **Wyre**. The most famous landmark is Cubbie Roo's castle, a thick-walled fortress, built in 1150 by the Viking Kolbein Hruga. It is most probably the earliest stone castle to have survived in Scotland. It is known to have withstood at least one remarkable siege and is one of the best-preserved castles in Scotland for its age. Bishop Bjarni grew up on **Wyre**, and was the son of Kolbein Hruga, who composed the legend of Jomsviknigs, the only Norse poetry to survive in the Orkneys. Scandinavian heritage is rich in these small islands.

Our whistle-stop round finally took us onto **Gairsay** and a chance meeting with the island's owner, David McGill who was living alone in splendid isolation (his mother was then in hospital) in a magnificent 16th Century manor house, only about a mile from **Mainland Orkney**. He hails from Cornwall and his family has farmed **Gairsay** since 1971. We talked for some time in what was now bright sunshine. We were told not to believe the Viking history documented in Haswell-Smith's *Scottish Islands*. I hate the concept of fake news which is usually used by right wing chancers who object to anything to which the liberal media allude. Their motives are mainly to be controversial but also because their intellect is too lazy or poorly developed to confer with research from primary sources. I was not disrespecting our host on **Gairsay** but just generally frustrated about any mistrust of scholarly and scientific endeavour.

Haswell-Smith tells an absorbing story of the boisterous Sweyn Asleifsson one of the last great Vikings who lived in **Gairsay** in the 12th century. Its melodrama is fit for an opera by Wagner or an epic TV production like *Game of Thrones*. He was a swash buckling buccaneer in the true Errol Flynn tradition with raids as far away as **St Mary's** in the Scilly Islands. In between his pillaging he farmed **Gairsay** in summer and drank the winter away with an entourage of eighty men at arms. In 1171 on one of their raids they sailed to Dublin and captured two English ships carrying wine and cloth. They drank the wine and could not remember returning to Orkney. Folklore perhaps, or an oft told and embellished saga which is imaginative in its telling. His end came on one last raid to Dublin, which he originally captured, but was later ambushed and killed. The McGill's farm is probably built on the site of Sweyn's *langskaill*, the Viking for drinking hall.

Trevor and Richard talked 'boats' with our host for an excruciatingly long time. I was like a small child, tugging on his parent's coat tails wanting to be off and being ignored. Eventually the exchange of 'boat facts' was exhausted, and we made for home, Richard's home that is where his wife had cooked a nutritious courgette soup with crusty bread and a splendid Orkney cheese. Politics, as ever, reared its ugly head over lunch with Richard's immigration views making the then Home Secretary, Priti Patel's policies seem enlightened. She is the daughter of immigrants escaping from the tyranny of Idi Amin's Uganda but like so many who take on the political mantle of the elite of their adopted country become more extreme. Trevor could see me itching for a show down. He is used to mixing in business with unyielding neoliberal conservatives with their gnarled views of self-entitlement and exceptionalism and he deftly and in his inimical way moved the conversation to more benign topics. We bade farewell before any harm was done or resentment felt in what had been a sublime four-hour trip. The afternoon was ours to slumber, watching *Countdown* in our flat back in Kirkwall. Only one island was left to complete the Orkney full house.

As usual I made a mad dash to catch the ferry to **Sanday,** the last island of a very successful mission and like Shetland a full complement of islands completed. **Sanday** was a labour of love and Trevor decided to sit this one out, an unfortunate phrase as I was the one sitting it out on the trip to and from the island, with no time to sight-see with ferry timetables as intransigent as ever. The ferry was busy; it was after all just like the local bus service.

Sanday, known as the "jewel of the isles" is the largest of Orkney's North Isles with a population of 494 (2011 census) with net immigration buoyant. It takes its Norse name from the plethora of spectacular, sandy beaches that grace its long coastline. The magic of "the merry dancers" or Northern Lights are often visible in its clear unpolluted atmosphere. Like on many of the Orkney Islands local development groups have burgeoned organically in recent years to preserve the character of vibrant communities. Their admirable vision is to:

"create an economically prosperous, sustainable community

that is connected with the wider world, but remains a safe, clean environment, where we are proud to live, able to work, to bring up and educate our children, to fulfil our own hopes and ambitions, and to grow old gracefully, enjoying a quality of life that is second to none".

A utopian objective indeed; if only these laudable sentiments could be replicated in our own but very different societies.

It is said that from the safety of the Loganair scheduled flights **Sanday** looks like a gigantic, fossilised bat. At ground level this is a low sprawling island and in dark, misty weather is almost invisible from the sea with the Wart its high spot at only 65m. Devoid of peat for fuel it is said that in times gone by islanders in a sort of mawkish way asked the Lord's assistance to deliver shipwrecks so they could use the wooden hulls as firewood. Amongst the more interesting shipwrecks was that discovered in 1991, a Viking ship burial with the skeletal remains of a man, a woman and a child along with their worldly possessions.

Our last night on this all too brief visit saw us wending in and out of our favourite watering holes with a fine meal at *the Shore*. Our ferry was not until the next evening and at last allowed us some relaxation and sight-seeing and an opportunity to explore west **Mainland Orkney**, which after all is the 7th largest of Great Britain's island after **Islay**. We snaked our way northwest to find a suitable scenic breakfast location. I'd remembered a fine café, when last in Orkney with Ian with fine panoramic views overlooking the Brough of Birsay and towards Marwick Head. We found it more by luck than judgement after visiting the Brough, a tidal island (uninhabited) settled by the Norse in the 9th Century. A large posse of middle-aged German bikers were circumnavigating **Mainland Orkney** and had rested there a while but blighted our peaceful journey all day. We decided not to cross the causeway to the remnants of the Norse houses as we both agreed that stones were indeed stones and I'd stumbled across many of these historic but ruinous symbols of pre-historic civilisation across both the Orkneys and Shetlands.

After a modest breakfast we headed in a random direction to pass more time until our ferry embarkation at Stromness. We had our eye on the Scapa Distillery visitor centre in the small village of St Ola but were distracted by the UNESCO world heritage site of Skara Brae, known as the Scottish Pompeii and older that either Stonehenge or the Great Egyptian pyramids. The International recognition includes three other sites in **Mainland Orkney**: Maeshowe, the Ring of Brodgar, the Standing Stones of Stenness and other nearby sites. The Ring of Brodgar is the oldest henge site in the British Isles (including the island of Ireland). A henge is basically a ring-shaped Neolithic earthwork sometimes though not often graced with stone circles.

The statement of significance by Historic Scotland, indicates just how much Skara Brae and its magnificent neighbours are important in pre-history:

> "The monuments at the heart of Neolithic Orkney and Skara Brae proclaim the triumphs of the human spirit in early ages and isolated places. They were approximately contemporary with the mastabas of the archaic period of Egypt (first and second dynasties), the brick temples of Sumeria, and the first cities of the Harappa culture in India, and a century or two earlier than the Golden Age of China. Unusually fine for their early date, and with a remarkably rich survival of evidence, these sites stand as a visible symbol of the achievements of early peoples away from the traditional centres of civilisation".

As should have been expected the car park was crammed with no legitimate space for parking so we left, a bit like going to Cairo and omitting to see the Pyramids of Gaza and the Sphinx. Having had the fortune to visit these inscrutable monuments to man's ingenuity it is disappointing to find that urban sprawl and its attendant tacky tourism has crept within 100 metres of these heritage icons. I was reminded of the time, as a student, leading the London University speleological expedition to the Yugoslavian Julian Alps in what is now Slovenia. We'd tired of discovering underground passages and headed for the flesh pots of the Adriatic. On stopping at Florence on our return we stumbled across the Uffizi Gallery, the doyen of renaissance art. We had enough spare money for a beer or the admission fee. We chose beer!

Undeterred by our disappointment we made for its sister World Heritage sites, passing the village of Twatt on the way, a delight for those of us with more than a modicum of schoolboy humour. The road sign identifying the start and end of the village had been removed, maybe stolen, since Ian and I were there two years previously so there would not be a naughty photo opportunity for Trevor. The sign on the village kirk was the only evidence remaining of the village name. There is a settlement of the same name in Shetland and in translation from Old Norse Twatt means 'small parcel of land'. I recoiled at our childishness on a day where attention to the wonders of ancient civilisations should have elevated our spirits.

The Ring of Brodgar was also a veritable honey pot, with visitors in profusion, but we just could not resist its lure. Brodgar is one of the many examples in the Northern Isles indicating the sophistication of early civilisation in northern Europe, with a density of Neolithic treasures unsurpassed elsewhere. The ring, with 27 of its original 60 stones still standing, is the third largest in the British Isles and its historic significance is right up there with Avebury and Stonehenge in England and Newgrange in Ireland.

There was a stern sign on prominent display saying that in recent years due to climate change causing heavier rain, the path had become seriously eroded. I do wish there was an understanding between cycles of bad weather and climate change. Weather is short term, climate change is steady and progressive with in some cases almost imperceptible change, until it is too late - the tipping point. We strolled around the stones on the emergency path. Climate change is, like a pandemic, certain but it is the timing that is uncertain. The Neolithic populations in Orkney and Shetland existed when temperatures were higher and more suited to agriculture, sustaining populations higher than expected today. I mused that uncertainty is inevitable.

We noted the advertisements for meetings of the local pagan society, complete with the modern trend of risk assessments to avoid blame deflection. A cheery volunteer accosted us, admiring my tweed waistcoat and jacket, bought in **Harris** on several visits over the years. We stopped and chatted, and I taped her knowledgeable discourse for posterity and this book, so much more edifying than endless Google searches. The wind obliterated all but my own booming Yorkshire questions and interjections so any pearls of wisdom not in the plethora of guidebooks were lost forever. We made a slow and thoughtful circumnavigation of the site, eagerly photographing from every conceivable angle for both artistry and general record. Two weeks later my camera was stolen whilst I was sleeping at home and not a single Orkney photograph had been downloaded.

Our last stop before heading for the Northlink ferry was Stenness, a smaller less crowded site but nonetheless stunning. Four out of an original 12 stones, some five metres high, remain. These are thin slabs about a foot in thickness but cannot be missed from the nearby public road. We had. On a previous day we were looking for sustenance and spied the *Hotel Stenness*, a mediocre establishment that served delicious scones and cakes but with no indication of the magnificent pre-historic standing stones but a few metres away.

The return to Scrabster took us as close as is possible to the Old Man of Hoy, especially enjoyed by Trevor who like me had had his imagination captured during Chris Bonnington's first climbing attempt many years ago. Bonnington re-climbed the Old Man on his 80th birthday and in June 2019 this 450-foot iconic sea stack was lead-climbed by Jesse Dufton who is blind. The breadth of human endeavour never ceases to amaze and enthral.

On arrival, instead of taking the quickest way home we took the *North Coast 500* through northwest Scotland. This modern tourist enticement is a travesty in my opinion as it is used by motorcycle speed merchants and sports car enthusiasts as a racetrack on dangerous single-track roads with limited passing places. We'd booked into the stuffy and expensive

Altnaharra Hotel in Sutherland to fulfil my ambition of having a quiet pint in probably the most remote hotel in Scotland. I'd passed its twinkling lights on a bleak October night whilst driving from Inverness airport to Bettyhill some years earlier. An oft applied adage of mine 'never go back' was indeed true, as the establishment suffered from limited food with clipped conversations and misunderstood exorbitant tariffs.

We left early, as breakfast was not included, hoping to 'tick off' two of the three remaining islands off the northwest coast: **Isle of Ewe**, just offshore from Altbea in Highland and **Soay** just offshore from Elgol in the Isle of **Skye**. Sadly, we had no time to organise these trips and for the 3rd or 4th time (I have simply lost count) an organised trip to **Soay** on the *Bella Jane*, already paid for, eluded me. We cut our losses and made the long journey back to Birmingham leaving these for another time, or perhaps never.

27. Ten more islands in Galway and Mayo, Republic of Ireland

It was fine weather in July 2019 for any part of northern Europe, let alone Ireland contrasting with its normal round of dark, dank, windy days with landscapes of deep emerald green and glowering skies. Recent storms had been beating a regular path across the Atlantic with increased ferocity; named storms like Dennis or Desmond which gave them a sinister, almost anthropomorphic character.

A trek with John Lawlor from his Midland home in Abbeyleix, County Laois was always pleasurable but tinged with the anticipation of certain poorer weather challenging our endeavours. John was his usual effusive self but somewhat reticent about a recent tryst he had been having with a woman in Dublin that summer. It had been a long-distance affair with several added complications.

We trod our usual route to Galway city, stopping once more to buy Ordnance Survey maps in a convenient outdoor store on the city's ring road. In case the weather changed I bought a light anorak as my own waterproof clothing had disappeared with my camera in my recent house burglary. Planning, and planning with good maps, was essential as inhabited islands are aplenty on Ireland's west coast but have, to the English ear, unpronounceable Irish names and are alien to me both historically and geographically. Who has ever heard of **Inishnakillew** or **Rusheennacholla** in Irish except those who live there? Chasing Ireland's islands was like a crazy treasure hunt.

I seemed to escape randomly to Ireland to visit John and explore the little-

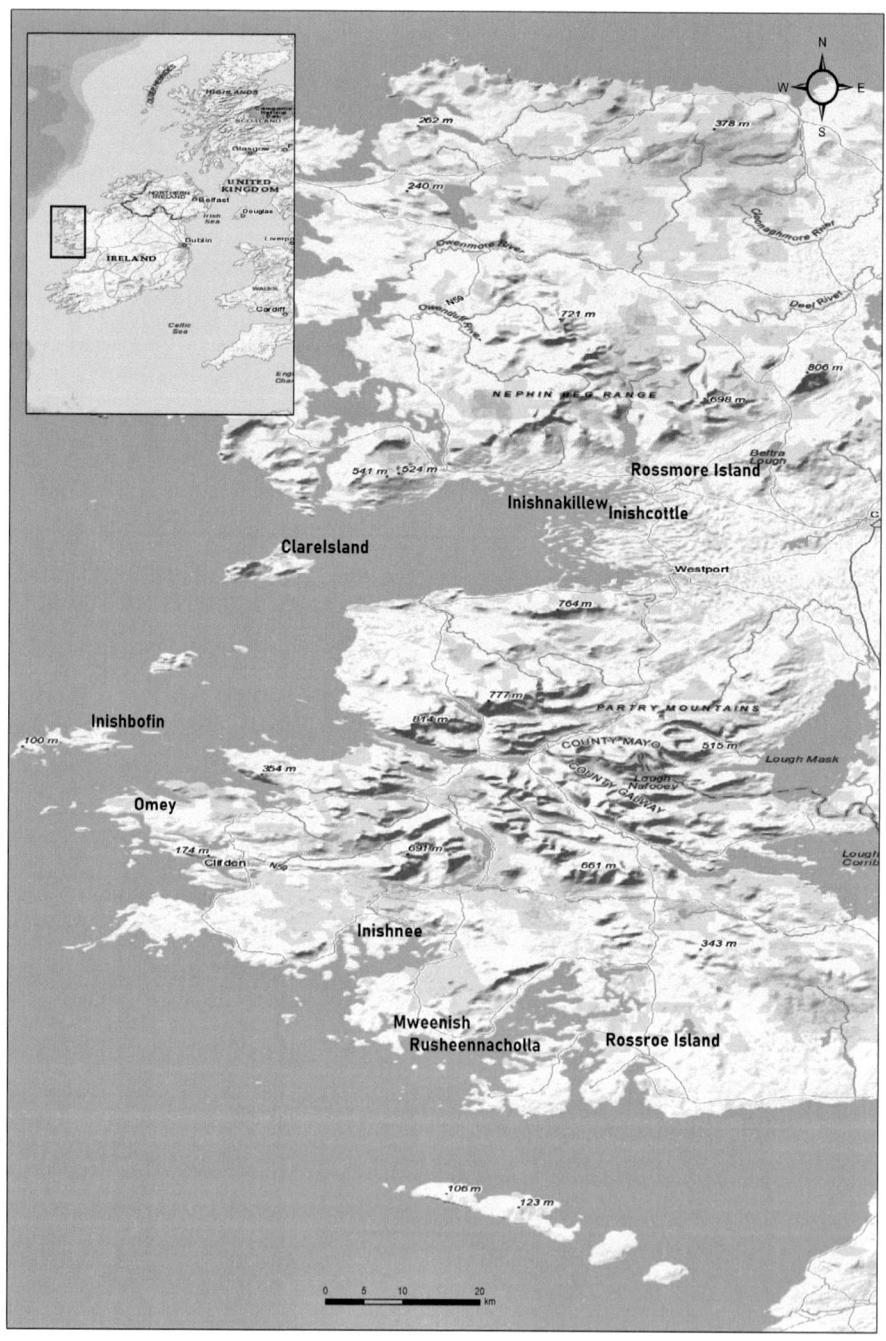

Ten more islands in Galway and Mayo, Republic of Ireland

known islands off its dramatic and beautiful west coast. July 2019 was no exception. There are dozens of small, inhabited islands from Cork to Donegal. A better planner would have created a spreadsheet of probable logistics. I just went where the fancy took me. Inefficient, yes, but full of surprises and travel to parts I would not ever be likely to go again. We swerved the Aran islands yet again and, not because of weather this time, which was set fair, but because I felt it more efficient at some stage in the future to fly there from the little Connemara airport at Inverin west of Galway using Aer Arann.

After securing the appropriate maps, and what turned out to be on this occasion unnecessary outer wear, we headed through a crowded Galway and onto the R336 to Spiddle for refreshment and supplies and, to John Lawlor's relief, a modicum of planning. This sounded like the lyrics to Van Morrison's classic Coney Island:

> "Coming down from Downpatrick
> Stopping off at St. John's Point
> Out all-day birdwatching
> And the craic was good
> Stopped off at Strangford Lough
> Early in the morning
> Drove through Shrigley taking pictures
> And on to Killyleagh
> Stopped off for Sunday papers at the
> Lecale District, just before Coney Island…."

I'd followed Van's route around County Down some years earlier and the song always makes me happy with the simple narrative evoking the inexplicable feeling when in love with life and friends. Thoughts of past love indeed

Refreshed after a long journey from County Laois we headed for Carna, past the **Gorumna** Islands most of which we had visited on our last sortie. **Rusheennacholla** was the first of ten islands we were to bag this trip, linked by road to the mainland and onto **Mweenish Island**, linked by the same road. The detail of the Irish census for this small island in 1911 is remarkable, and probably a legacy of Imperial Great Britain keeping tabs on, or rather spying on, communities. After all, the 1911 census was only five years before the Easter uprising and in the Irish speaking west the population were likely to be at best alienated from the British or at worst troublesome. Pádraig Pearse, one of the key insurgents on the assault on Dublin Post Office in Easter 1916, was a Connemara man. Connemara is neither a province nor a county, but rather a cultural region with a significant Irish language identity or *Gaeltacht*, where Irish language predominates, and this alone sets it aside from much of the rest of Ireland. It stretches from Loch Corrib in the east with the Atlantic and its many islands to the west.

According to the 1911 census there were a total of only five houses in the townland of **Rusheennacholla**. All were occupied and were listed as being private dwellings. All were built of stone, brick or concrete and had thatch, wood or other perishable material for roofing. They were all third-class dwellings (whatever that meant) with house #1 having two rooms and three windows, house #2 had three rooms and one window and the other three had two rooms and two windows each. The out-offices and farm-steadings return shows that there were a total of three outbuildings all of which were cow houses. These were the types of property so graphically featured in Martin McDonagh's 2022 award winning film *The Banshees of Inisherin* starring the inimitable pairing of Colin Farrell and Brendan Gleason.

The enumerator's abstract return shows that there were a total of 33 people living in the townland at that time and consisted of 14 males and 19 females. The enumerator for the area was Constable John Gallagher. The details of all five families, the Greens, Wards, two family Gorhams and the Barrett's were pinpoint in detail that the Stasi of the former East Germany would have been proud of:

> "House #3 was home to the Gorham family and the head of the family was the widow Bridget (50) and she shared the house with 5 of her children, Matt (21), John (18), Norah (15), Bridget

(13) and Mary (10). All were born in County Galway and were Roman Catholic. All spoke both Irish and English. Bridget (50) and Mary could not read but the others could all read and write. Bridget (50) was a farmer, Matt and John were farmer's sons and Norah, Bridget (13) and Mary were scholars. The house they all shared was a 2 roomed, 3rd class dwelling with a cow house. Bridget Gorham was the landholder."

Mweenish, a far larger island, was well known for the building of traditional sailing boats known as Galway Hookers. One such boat carried Pádraig Pearse, Thomas McDonagh and Joseph and Mary Plunkett out to the Aran islands where they attempted to organise the Irish Volunteers but with mediocre success. This was the seedbed for the 1916 Easter Uprising. We had little chance to admire its isolation and rugged beauty, suspended in timeless animation in Galway Bay. I can't think of Galway Bay without humming the seminal Christmas song *Fairy Tale of New York* by the the late Shane McGowan's Pogues and the late and peerless Kirsty McCall:

> "The boys of the NYPD choir
> Were singing "Galway Bay"
> And the bells were ringing out
> For Christmas day"

New York's Police and Fire departments have always had a connection with Irish ancestry. Whilst on my "honeymoon" in New York on my third marriage we stayed in Anoushka Hempel's *chi chi* hotel somewhere around Manhattan's 42nd Street. This former Bond girl from *On Her Majesty's Secret Service* had become something of a style guru and my wife, an up-and-coming designer herself, had favoured her boutique hotel *Blakes* in South Kensington on her frequent trips to London. High up on the umpteenth floor we changed into matching Chinese silk dressing gowns and opened a bottle of Veuve Clicquot to toast our wedding.

I spied an open fireplace, charged with fuel, and proceeded to light it. This might be the height of design chic but not a particularly safe accoutrement in a skyscraper. Before our first sip of champagne smoke was bellowing into the room and the smoke alarm triggered. I stood on a Hempel three-legged chair, which was more stylistic than utilitarian, and tried unsuccessfully to disarm the alarm, collapsing in a heap on the lush pile carpet under a broken piece of useless furniture. With smoke billowing I resorted to opening the door to the corridor and within minutes the FDNY were felling the semi open door down with their pikes. Fire under control we spent our first evening of married life sharing our drinks with three burly, handsome firemen. No wonder the marriage didn't last!

Mweenish is another world altogether and John Lawlor and I were enjoying the very soul of our haphazard journey with no real idea of where it would take us next. We opted to stay in Roundstone, a typical small Irish town on the coast like the one used as a backdrop to David Lean's *Ryan's Daughter* with an unforgettable cast; Trevor Howard as the priest, John Mills, as a disabled mute (and the only actor to win an Oscar without speaking), Sarah Miles and Robert Mitchum, completely out of his hell raising character. It was high summer holidays but bed and breakfast sign 'vacancies' were still on display touting for business, and we opted for *Wits End* and the redoubtable landlady, Eileen Coyne. Pleasantries dispensed with we hit the pubs and, as this is Ireland, we were spoiled for choice. We opted for the *Shamrock*, run by an English landlord, who was dispensing excellent sea food as fast as the clientele were ordering it. The Guinness flowed, but we escaped the turmoil of the holiday drinkers to *O'Dowd's* down the hill, an altogether more sedate establishment. I was tired after all my driving and retired after one last Paddy's whiskey to *Wits End*, leaving John to enjoy his usual nocturnal Baileys night cap before last orders were called.

The weather was still set fair the next day and **Inishnee** was our first port of call, with access by a narrow bridge a couple of miles east of town. We discovered a quiet, unremarkable island of breath-taking stillness on that early morning. With a tight agenda, having discovered at least seven more islands within easy grasp we left in search of **Inishbofin** or 'Island of the white cow' in the Atlantic Ocean, reached from the pier at Cleggan. The road via Clifden was quiet and in bright sunshine with every hue of green and spectacular panoramas around each bend on the long and winding road, we made the harbour honeypot. The car parks were seething with day trippers eager to sample the delights of the island.

The ferry was packed with tourists hoping to make the most of the fine day and the five-mile trip into the Atlantic was edifying with most passengers on deck luxuriating in the fresh zephyr-like breeze, a far cry from the storms that batter this coast much of the year. The partial destruction of the rock armour coastal protection was all too evident, and by chance the subject of a consultancy project I became involved with for Galway County after the second wave of the Covid pandemic. We docked and headed straight for the *Beach Day's* bar a couple of minutes' walk from the harbour.

Irish monks, the Spanish and Oliver Cromwell had all settled on **Inishbofin** at some point in history and relics of these incursions were evident throughout the island. Cromwell's 17th Century barracks were used as a prison for Catholic priests from all over Ireland after the English statute of 1585 declared them guilty of high treason. It is no wonder that Cromwell gets a very bad press in Ireland, largely because of his continued intransigence against Roman Catholics, culminating in the 1649 massacre at Drogheda. The Lord Protector was angered by the murder of a number of his parliamentarian troops there and in his own words ordered the carnage:

> "In the heat of the action, I forbade my soldiers to spare any that were in arms in the town…and, that night they put to the sword about two thousand men".

Recent historians have sanitised the massacre but there is still deep-seated hatred for the man. Sadly, bloody territorial conquests have not been confined to history as witnessed in February 2022 with Putin's invasion of Ukraine. We talk of historical wars in years or even decades, for example the Hundred Years War, and who is to say that Russian imperialism won't dog the continent for years to come.

The delights of the island would not avail themselves to us as we needed to catch a return ferry within the hour, leaving the day trippers to enjoy an idyllic afternoon on the many looped walks and beaches across the island. Sensible tourists do not return to Cleggan within the hour, but we had many other islands to discover (and many rivers to cross – with apologies to Jimmy Cliff!). We were the only passengers returning but the trip alone will live long in our collective memories with the hills and mountains of Connemara creating an unforgettable backdrop to our journey. The experience was similar to that on **Rathlin Island**, Northern Ireland's only inhabited coastal island. During my coastal erosion research project John and I were able to return and experience the whole island courtesy of resident and Galway Council employee, John Daye.

We travelled north through what can only be described as a mythical landscape of quiet glens and precipitous mountains disgorging their twinkling, glistening streams to the languid rivers below. It would not be an exaggeration to describe the journey as ecstatic. On the way, my eagle eye had spied to the south of Cleggan, **Omey** to be accessed at low tide from Claddaghduff. More by luck than judgement the tide was at its lowest and we drove recklessly across a half mile of flat sand to the island following marker posts. We must have caught the very ebb of the tide as on the way back we sensed that within a very short time we would have been stranded as the flow from the Atlantic performed its twice daily cycle. We were told that at high tide the water is deep enough to cover a car! The flat, firm sands host a horse race in late summer, a long-held tradition which was resurrected in 2001.

Though my compendium of Irish islands indicated a population of two, research indicated that the last permanent inhabitant, the Holywood stuntman, Pascal Whelan, died in February 2017, aged 75. He was born on **Omey** but returned on retirement in 1962. At its zenith in 1841 some 341 people called this featureless island home. The Protestant Church of Ireland minister John MacNeice, who became the Bishop of Down, was born on **Omey**. MacNeice was well known for his symbolic opposition to the partition of Ireland, and though accepted as a political reality refused to allow the Union flag to be laid on Edward Carson's grave at his funeral in St Anne's Cathedral, Belfast in 1935. Carson, whose statue stands proud in front of Northern Ireland's Stormont Assembly is celebrated by the Province's Protestants for securing a continued place in the United Kingdom for the 'six counties' of Ulster.

It is always interesting to find that even the most innocuous of islands often have associations with poets, playwrights, musicians and politicians who have shaped our Treasured Islands. The slow pace of life and timelessness must ignite their collective muse. This is hardly surprising with WB Yeats, George Bernard Shaw, Samuel Beckett and Seamus Heaney, all Irish and all awarded the Nobel prize for literature. Bishop John's son was the celebrated poet and writer Louis MacNeice.

John was convinced that there was a connection with John Ford's epic 1952 film *The Quiet Man* starring John Wayne and Maureen O'Hara. Although set in the west of Ireland, and most of the scenes were indeed set in Connemara, the focus for filming was around the village of Cong, straddling the border of County Galway and County Mayo to the north. John's observations, though somewhat unfounded, were the product of the repetition of the sights, sounds and even smells of the interlocked far west in both culture and geography. A subsequent trip in summer 2021 would take us to Cong.

This hitherto unheard-of island, like most we would visit on our trips around Ireland, proved to be serendipitous. Feeling satisfied, even though **Omey** was probably uninhabited now (though there is still self-catering accommodation on the island) we headed for Louisburgh whose name sounds like a town in Middle America. The route followed the virtually deserted Dhulough Pass road, between the Sheeffry hills to the east and the Mweel Rea Mountains, rising to 814 metres, to the west. This is the very essence of Connemara. The tranquillity and beautiful, rugged desolation towards the end of a hot afternoon was close to scenic perfection, the equal of Snowdonia and the Lake District with the added bonus of complete isolation and little traffic. Mundanity was soon to kick in as we needed beds for the night. Unbeknown to us then we were to achieve five islands the next day.

Louisburgh, with an 'h', not to be confused with its American cousin in Pennsylvania, is an attractive town built on the Bunowen River. We had left Galway behind for the time being and crossed the county line to Mayo. The town has nothing to do with its American namesake and was named by the town's founder in 1795, John Denis Browne of Westport, to commemorate the battle of Louisburg (with no 'h') in Cape Breton, Nova Scotia where his uncle had fought the French. It seems on my journey through Scotland and Ireland allusions to Cape Breton and Nova Scotia were seemingly everywhere. The town had a more profound purpose, built to shelter Catholic refugees escaping sectarian conflict in the north of Ireland. The Battle of the Boyne in 1690 had promoted the Protestant cause in the north with sectarianism to smoulder and erupt there until the 1998 Good Friday Agreement.

The UK's abandonment of its EU membership will undoubtedly set sparks of division flying again to satisfy Little Englanders and their political masters who champion their grotesque entitlement with pride. The ludicrous Internal Market bill, in contravention of the EU withdrawal agreement and defying international law, was enacted by Prime Minister Johnson in 2020 to replace the compromised customs barrier in the Irish Sea with a potential hard border between the six counties and their Irish Republic neighbours. The return to 'The Troubles' would for sure be imminent after the politics of Brexit were set in motion on 1st January 2021. The dispute as to the free trade border festers on and on, with inept British negotiators picking at the scabs of their agreements and counter agreements.

On arrival in the outskirts of town we decided to head for Roonagh pier and investigate tickets for **Clare Island** and **Inishturk** the next day. Planning was not our forte as the reader may have already guessed but we didn't want to miss whatever ferries that were available. We reached the quiet car park which contained two booking offices: one the fast O'Malley service and the other the more sedate O'Grady service. There appeared to be a turf war between the two companies, and this wasn't helped by my jokes deriding this serious long-term feud. To ease any tension, we booked our passage to **Clare** and fled back to Louisburgh. Complex logistics could have got us to **Inishturk**, some distance in the opposite direction but still on the same day. Discretion being the better part of valour we agreed to postpone this longer trip for another time.

Back in Louisburgh we attempted to find rooms for the night. The most likely venue, the *West View hotel* in Chapel Street, was full and John set off on a mission to secure an alternative. Angela's *Louisburgh Lodge* was a charming out of town B&B and suited both our pockets and aesthetics. Its only other guest was a Dubliner who was hoping to retire in the vicinity, and we could indeed see why. I was suspicious at first about its remoteness from the flesh pots of the town, but John assured me it was no further than the distance between the *Prince of Wales* and *The Village* pubs where I lived back in Moseley. This sense of relative scale gave me some comfort. We settled into our digs and headed across the river to source a suitable watering hole and dinner. A Fleetwood Mac tribute band was playing at one venue but overcome with fatigue, we stuck to more mundane pursuits: eating and drinking Guinness at pubs more reasonable in price.

Clare Island is a mountainous island guarding the entrance to Clew Bay. It is infamous as the home of the warrior, or more glamorously the pirate queen Gráinne O'Malley, clearly a distant relative of the ferry boat owners. Gráinne or Grace was ruling a successful dynasty in the west of Ireland, especially Iar Connacht (roughly the Connemara of today) during the reign of the English Queen Elizabeth the First. Grace, like Boudica in East Anglia, was a formidable adversary. She even went to Greenwich in London to negotiate the release of her two sons with the virgin Queen. Discussions were in Latin as she had no knowledge of English. I suspect, as a powerful woman herself, Elizabeth had a sneaking admiration for Grace. An interesting footnote to this charming story is that far from the British ruled territory around Dublin known as The Pale, "beyond the Pale" its tribes were not the Barbarians history makes them out to be with

Latin seemingly spoken not only by priests but also by their educated rulers.

Our busy schedule meant we had only 15 minutes on the island and John, like me, was getting sick of these rapid assaults on beautiful islands that it was unlikely we would ever see again. We were in the wrong generation and needed to, like Boswell and Johnson, on their grand tours, travel sedately on horseback. A brief squint of Grace's castle near the pier was all we had time for. Again, our return journey was idyllic with no other fools wishing to waste the glorious day by returning to the mainland early.

Looking west were the most magnificent, drowned drumlin islands in Clew Bay. This is a beguiling world of water and land unlike anywhere else in the British Isles. Drumlins are earth mounds or lateral moraines sculpted by slow moving ice during the last ice age 20,000 years ago and then drowned by rising sea levels as the blanket of continental ice retreated. These dramatically sculptured features are prolific in my own Yorkshire Dales, and this 'basket of eggs' topography west of Skipton fired my imagination and a lifetime's interest in earth science. In Clew Bay there are 365 islands, though thankfully for my adventures few are now inhabited. The word drumlin, known to all GCSE geography students, is actually Gaelic for 'small hill'. This makes sense. Bathymetry exposes twice as many submerged and although protecting the mainland against severe gales, these underwater features make navigation treacherous.

I'd been working in Nepal with the International Centre for Integrated Mountain Development, a multi-disciplinary research institute in Kathmandu embracing both physical and human issues within the Hindu Kush, an 800-kilometre-long mountain range that stretches through Afghanistan, from its centre to northern Pakistan, India, Nepal and China and into Tajikistan. The Himalaya mountain ranges are prominent. There are some 21,000 glacial lakes in this region, shored up by terminal moraine, the sort of material that drumlins are made of. Scientists recognise the probability of an eight-degree centigrade rise in temperature in these high-altitude regions by the end of the century. Just like 20,000 years ago when the last ice age retreated in northern Europe shaping the landscape of Clew Bay, glaciers will melt, and lake levels will rise either breaching or overtopping the fragile moraine dams that contain today's lakes. The resultant GLOF's (Glacial Lake Outburst Floods) will wreak havoc on the densely populated valleys of Nepal, with death and destruction beyond into India. People get in the way of nature's wonderment, but ironically it is man's disrespect for nature that creates these devastating triggers in the first place. The devastating floods covering one third of Pakistan in 2022 were partly caused by the 'GLOF' effect.

Leaving the four or five inhabited Clew Bay Islands requiring a private boat hire for another trip we made for three 'easier' inhabited islands, **Inishnakillew, Inishcottle** and **Rosmore** in Westport Bay to the north, joined precariously to the mainland. Heading through Westport the task of finding these islands amongst a myriad of rural byways was not easy with map reading not really John's thing, though out of utter frustration and to avoid my uncalled-for criticism, he became quite adept. **Inishnakillew**, an island of 0.1 square mile or 62 acres (and two roods and 35 perches to be exact!) is recorded as 55,653rd largest townland in Ireland with 35 residents recorded in the 1911 census. It is no surprise it was like finding a needle in a haystack. We left the N59 and headed for the sleepy village of Kilmeena, the scene of a defeat for the local Irish Republican Army during the Irish War of Independence on the 19th May 1921.

At Ardkeen a 500m tidal causeway leads to **Inishnakillew**. The weather and tides were favourable and beyond the causeway the badly made road roller-coastered across the island to **Inishcottle**, the two islands connected by a further perilous causeway. Once across we realised that turning round might not be an option on this tiny island but John, ever patient, guided me on what became a seven-point turn with disaster averted. We saw not a soul as I crashed hopelessly through the gears. At 26 acres according to townland records this was the 59,112th largest townland in the Republic, but with a population of 45 from the 1911 census. This really is the end of Europe with these islands attracting tourists looking for 'nowhere else to go'. We sat in our car relaxing after a traumatic and potentially disastrous manoeuvre on the narrowest of quays, wondering why we were putting ourselves in danger accessing potentially uninhabited islands.

This could only be resolved thorough research and during the 2020 Covid lockdown I set about to check from census records just which of Ireland's islands were inhabited and needed a future coordinated effort to visit efficiently without the random efforts so far made. The Irish Central Statistics Office (latest 2006) – *CN17 Population of offshore islands* - is the best source, or most reliable source of data. Some 132 islands are listed as having been inhabited in the past though this has reduced to around 69 inhabited islands in the most recent census. Here is the conclusion of my research, based on the Department of Culture and Heritage and the *Gaeltacht*:

County	Island	Population 2011	Population 2016
Co. Donegal	Árainn Mhór★ (Arranmore)	514	469
	Inis Bó Finne★	11	2
	Inis Fraoigh★	2	0
	Toraigh★	144	119
	Gabhla★	15	5
Co. Sligo	Coney	2	3
Co. Mayo	Clare Island	168	159
	Inis Bigil★	25	18
	Inishcottle	5	0
	Inishlyre	4	4
	Inisturk	53	51
	Clynish	4	4
Co. Galway	Inishbofin	160	175
	Árainn★	845	762
	Inis Oírr★	249	281
	Inis Meáin★	157	183
	Inis Bearacháin★	1	0
	Inis Treabhair★	1	0
	Inse Ghainimh★	2	2

	Omey	1	2
Co. Cork	Bere	216	167
	Cléire★	124	147
	Dursey	3	4
	Heir	29	28
	Long	10	20
	Sherkin	114	111
	Whiddy	20	18
Total		2,879	2,734

★Gaeltacht Islands (using Irish names)

Well, that made things a little clearer and a goal to aim for though this list is at odds with the 'comprehensive' list found on Wikipedia and I was more confused than ever. More research created a *eureka* moment when I came across the official Irish census of inhabited islands for 2016. A brief email to the Irish Census Office in Swords, Dublin provided me in response with the latest 2016 up to date population estimates. It would appear **Inishcottle** was indeed unpopulated, which could explain its total desolation, but **Inishnakillew** has had a population explosion since 2006 with six inhabitants.

The appendix at the end of this book attempts to be definitive, though populations are very much a moving feast. As we will see later owners of holiday lets fill in census forms to fool the census enumerators into believing occupancy is permanent. In truth this is a ruse for funds to be made available from the Gaeltacht to maintain piers and jetties without which access would be impossible and the lucrative holiday let business of island owners scuppered.

Our next island, **Rosmore**, had a solitary soul identified in the 2016 census. What was frustrating was that the tantalisingly close **Clynish**, and other nearby islands accessible only by boat, also had tiny populations, but inaccessible on our present timetable. A modicum of forethought would have been useful instead of my all-pervading hubris, impetuosity and bravado. I fear these may be some of the handful of 'forgotten islands', like the unattainable **Soay** off the Isle of **Skye**, or the impregnable **Osea** island in Essex, perhaps never to be visited.

Overshadowing the landscape is the holy mountain of Croagh Patrick, where St Patrick is said to have fasted for 40 days. Pilgrims, once a year, make the spiritual journey up this 662m peak, many doing penance in bare feet. Catholics certainly know how to repent for their sins.

Travelling north to Newport, Newport Bay is deeply indented. Here there are long, narrow peninsulas of land that in several cases are barely connected to the mainland by ancient bridges or causeways. Although several of these fractured pieces of land are not specifically identified as 'islands', they retain a tenuous relationship with the mainland. We headed for one such island **Rosmore** divided from the mainland by a 20-foot-wide channel, which is crossed by a narrow bridge. Though so close to Newport it was frustrating to find even given the detail of our 1:50,000 scale maps. One single track two-kilometre-long very narrow road leads to Rosmore point and spectacular views of the drumlin phenomenon in Clew Bay. Many of these 'mainland islands' had significant populations in the 19th century but even the long tentacle that is **Rosmore** may not be inhabited today despite its registration in the latest 2016 Irish census.

Elated but confused about our island acquisition we headed for refreshment in Newport. I was anxious to watch the final of the World Cup one-day cricket match which England had miraculously squeezed into to challenge the in-form New Zealand. The pub was crowded, and forgetting I was in Ireland anticipated cricket would be on offer on the flickering screen. Mayo was playing Gaelic football and despite the English captain, Eoin Morgan, born in Dublin to an English mother, the huddled drinkers were not in the least interested in cricket. I retired to find a suitable radio station in the car, whilst John finished his pint.

The Irish are totally reverential to what many consider to be their national sport (Gaelic football), with rugby union and football of much lower status. GAA (Gaelic Athletic Association) sports clubs are to be found in even the smallest of towns. I was once assisting the Northern Irish Rivers Agency with their flood alleviation strategies and wondered why around a million pounds had been spent on substantial floods walls, embankments and expensive flood gates to protect a GAA sports ground and facilities. This was surely not cost beneficial. The almost religious significance of these was quickly explained to me and I kept my English mouth shut tight.

Eager to head south to attempt our tenth island of the weekend on the way back to Galway, and distracted by the cricket, which was getting tense, I took a wrong turn at Clifden, and time was now against us. **Rossroe**, in Greatman's Bay and accessed by bridge beyond Casla was our goal with an apparent population of 12. Naturally, our map reading was appalling and my driving becoming reckless. The game, thanks to the imperious Ben Stokes, had ended in a tie and a 'golden over' was required to separate the teams. I couldn't stand the tension. We found the island, got out, span the car around and headed for Galway City. The radio signal failed. The so called golden over lasted at least 20 minutes and my nerves were fraying all the way to Spiddal. John, who hates cricket and indeed any team sport, was idly thumping his smart phone and with total indifference uttered two words 'England won'. Ben Stokes was yet again the hero of the hour.

It was at least 24 degrees centigrade as we drove along Galway's busy promenade with glamorous couples enjoying the rare evening summer sun. These pleasures were denied to us, and it wasn't till eleven in the evening that we made the *Abbeyleix Manor* hotel. We drank our Guinness in silence watching Ireland's annual commemoration day spectacle on TV which seemed, in this politically correct inclusive society, to consist of faiths of every hue, including a humanist to please the atheists. They each in turn recited words of inspiration or consolation depending on the listeners' points of view. Leo Varadkar, the Taoiseach was present with the little guy, the President, Michael D Higgins, whose sole duty, in British eyes, appears to be shaking hands with rugby players during six nations matches at Dublin's Aviva stadium. Cynicism apart Higgins, an ex-senator, has used his time in office to address issues concerning justice, social equality, social inclusion, anti-sectarianism, anti-racism and reconciliation. A rare pedigree for a politician these days and a National treasure in Ireland.

I was hoping to complete my *Treasured Islands* in 2020 with trips to the Channel Islands, and Ireland again high on the agenda but the COVID 19 lockdown prevented any further island hopping for a year and a day from that sublime weekend in Connemara.

28. Lindisfarne (Holy Island) and Piel Island, England

The start of my walk around Great Britain was delayed until August 2002 because of the outbreak of Foot and Mouth disease across the United Kingdom and the countryside was effectively out of bounds. COVID 19 had effectively suspended all my trips planned for spring and summer 2020 with my ambition to complete the Irish islands and the eight inhabited Channel Islands. A bold plan was wholly in tatters. The tedium of virtual meetings in far flung corners of the World and writing drafts for *Treasured Islands* filled my waking hours with lock down an unfortunate necessity to stem the spread of COVID 19's virulence. My Shetland companion Ian had succumbed to the horrors of the disease and spent uncomfortable long days in hospital gasping for oxygen. I stayed home alone with Lily and Maxim marooned in southern Russia. Weekly food rations were brought to me by my thoughtful nephew Simon, and I hunkered down for the duration.

The Government's wholly shambolic response to dealing with the pandemic gave me no real hope that we as a country would ever return to normal and the phrase 'new normal' was coined; a life where with precautions and sensible personal risk assessments we could cautiously go about our business again. Apart from a short trip with Lily to Tenerife to visit Rob a university friend and his wife Joan, in November 2019, I had not been to any island other than my own since 14th July 2019. Ancient punishments were often banishment for a year and a day following a misdemeanour (see **Oronsay**). This had been my punishment now but with lockdown easing a little I headed for Lindisfarne or **Holy Island** on 15th July 2020. I was apprehensive at leaving my home fortress to enter the new world of COVID 19 compliance. At motorway service stations I

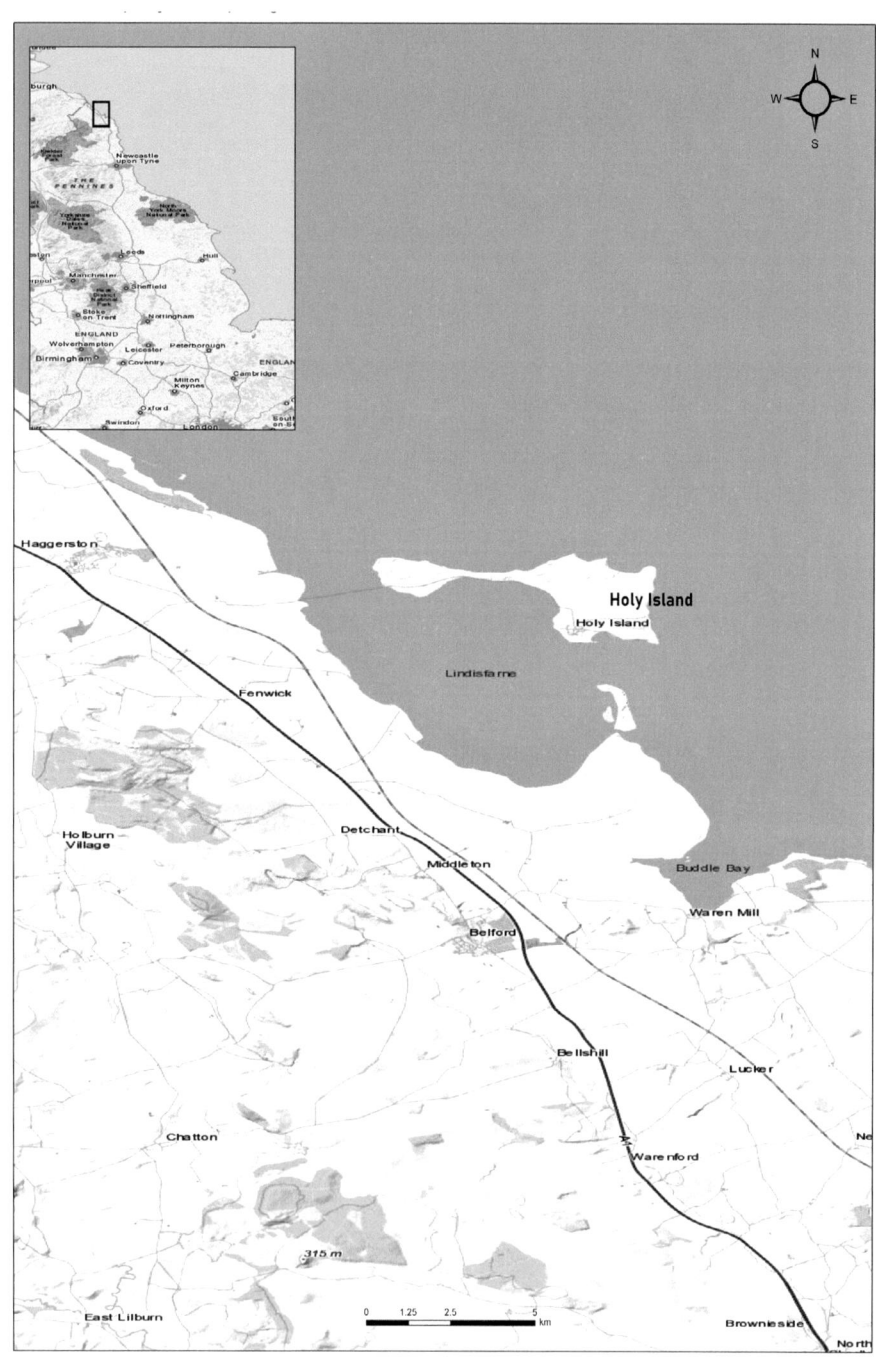

Lindisfarne (Holy Island), England

was like a small child attempting to become acquainted with the new one-way systems, social distancing, mask wearing and the ultra-politeness the disease was necessitating.

On the long journey north, I reminisced about that glorious July day in County Galway having just visited **Rossroe** in Greatman's Bay, with the stoical Ben Stokes about to win the Cricket World Cup for England. I had arranged to meet with my trusted companions from Scotland, Stuart and Paul, a reunion overdue with our last trip together to **Canna** in October 2018.

I drove across the three-mile causeway over Goswick Sands, and we met in the Lindisfarne car park. Many other visitors were also making the most of a random release of lockdown despite deaths still in three figures per day, though our mendacious, incompetent Government had long since stopped publishing official figures or having daily press briefings. We stretched our legs around the ancient ruins of the priory with Paul, whose nautical and technical knowledge knows no bounds, educating us about shipping lanes and safe access out in the North Sea. It was an unseasonal July day with annoying drizzle and glowering views to Lindisfarne castle sitting proudly on its igneous windstone perch, once the home to Sir Edwin Lutyens, described as the greatest architect of the twentieth century.

The interchangeable **Holy Island** and Lindisfarne can confuse the casual visitor as Lindisfarne is reserved usually for the castle, built in the mid-16th Century. **Holy Island**, centred on the priory has deeper historic roots founded around 634 by an Irish monk Saint Aidan, who had been sent from Iona, off the isle of **Mull**, to Northumbria at the request of King Oswald. **Holy Island** became the base for Christian evangelism in the north of England with connections to the Venerable Bede and Saint Cuthbert. Scholarly works by these revered early pilgrims are amongst the earliest in English historical writings including the earliest surviving Old English copies of the New Testament Gospels. It is fitting that both Stuart and Paul had accompanied me to both **Iona** and **Holy Island**.

It is generally accepted that the Viking raid on Lindisfarne in 793 is the start of the Viking age in Great Britain. Alcuin a Northumbrian scholar in Holy Roman Emperor Charlemagne's court at the time, wrote:

> "Never before has such terror appeared in Britain as we have now suffered from a pagan race ... The heathens poured out the blood of Saints around the altar and trampled on the bodies of Saints in the temple of God, like dung in the streets."

Following the terror waged on the tiny saintly island the Vikings turned their attention north to Scotland with the Danes being England's main adversaries in subsequent centuries.

We crossed back over the causeway which at high tide gives the islanders a sense of proud isolation. They are resisting moves to create a 24-hour permanent crossing. Our overnight destination before the long trek over to Cumbria and **Piel Island** was the *Blue Bell hotel*, Belford, a few miles inland. It was an internet booking with a seemingly modest reputation. On arrival the dismal looking hotel which dominated the market square of this picturesque village was firmly shut, with no sign of activity. Hotels had only just been allowed to re-open post lockdown and we surmised some miscommunication between *Booking.com* and the hotel had muddied the waters of my booking. Phoning the owner resulted in a disconnected phone signal. I saw across the square a pub, *The Black Swan,* and went to attempt to solve the mystery of Northumberland's *Marie Celeste.* The charming incumbents confirmed our fears. COVID or otherwise the hotel had been disappointing pre-booked customers for some time.

The Welsh landlord was keen to show us his refurbished apartments at the rear of the pub. He'd done the work himself he proudly boasted but his workmanship would never be a candidate for Kevin Mcleod's *Grand Designs.* We negotiated a price and then drove to Seahouses for Fish 'n Chips. This was the first time I had eaten out since mid-March and the COVID protocol was bemusing. Businesses were being jeopardised through months of enforced closure and the economy was fragile. Small businesses like *The Neptune* fish bar may be lucky to survive. Back at our home for the night we were treated like mystical travellers sent to bolster their non-existent trade; a modern-day Cargo Cult where Pacific Islanders built infrastructure in the usually vain hope that this would attract distant visitors. We were those visitors; my pockets brim full of cash after the sale of my Freelander and inconsequential expenditure during months of lockdown. No request was too much for our fawning hosts.

Ask anybody who is a little geographically savvy about how far it is from Northumberland to Cumbria. They will think for a few moments and say, "100 miles tops". They'd be wrong. From Belford to Snab Point on **Walney Island**, the starting point for our low tide walk to **Piel Island**, is 189 miles taking with stops the thick end of four hours along the A1, A69, M6 and finally the A509 to Barrow-in-Furness. **Piel Island** was my last of the four inhabited Furness islands. The fifth, Foulney Island is a low sandy island and uninhabited.

Piel Island had thwarted me earlier in my excursions when the boatman offering trips for £5 cancelled my booking at the last minute. I was unwilling to be left stranded again, so I decided on the risky option of a low tide crossing from Snab Point. For once in my life, knowing the potential dangers of crossing the tidal sands in and around Morecambe Bay, I consulted the tide tables. Low tide on Thursday 16th July was at 15:14. The journey of around 2 kilometres each way was estimated to take about 45 minutes.

I deduced three things:

- Time and tide wait for no man.
- The perfect sinusoidal curves of rising and falling tides are unfaltering and one hundred percent predictable; it's the moon you see.
- Drowning whilst crossing on a falling or ebb tide was nigh on impossible unless deep tidal channels were encountered, and their depth misunderstood.

I reckoned that starting the crossing before 13:30 would give us plenty of leeway to cross, rest and return safely. Paul was unconvinced. Stuart was more worried about the pandemic than drowning. We travelled in separate cars and Paul, looking for an alternative, had telephoned John Cleasby who organised the boat trips from Roa Island near Rampside on the opposite mainland. A combination of COVID 19 and family illness meant no crossings were being organised. The tidal crossing became the only option, safe or otherwise.

Paul was circumspect at the Snab Point car park, worried about my ability to cross the sands without detailed knowledge of deep channels or quick sands. It was just around the bay in February 2004 that twenty-one undocumented Chinese immigrant labourers lost their lives on an incoming tide. This was a national scandal etched in our collective memories. My father, in the mid-seventies retired with my mother to Grange-over-Sands overlooking Morecambe Bay. He was friends with Cedric Robinson, the Duchy of Lancaster's ceremonial guide to the sands. Crossing without a knowledgeable guide was not recommended, though on my epic coastal walk I had foolishly crossed the sands on a bright summer's day from Silverdale to Grange, getting very wet in the process. Official web sites suggested that under NO CIRCUMSTANCES should the **Piel Island** crossing be attempted without an official guide.

I am not a risk seeker and generally risk averse. After all I had not ventured out other than for short walks for over 16 weeks of the Lockdown, not even for shopping. I am however impatient and attempt foolish things when impetuosity takes over common sense, like:

- Climbing Mount Cotopaxi in Ecuador, at 5,895 metres two metres higher than Mount Kilimanjaro, Africa's highest mountain. I'd hired two young guys and a cook in 1991 for the princely sum of $US100 to guide me to the summit. On the Altiplano (a high, barren plain at around 3,750 metres) our female cook vanished fearing the so-called Quito rapist was at large close to her tent. The final ascent on steep snow-covered slopes from the mountain hut built at an altitude higher than Mont Blanc, Europe's highest mountain, was done without food. The cook had taken the food with her. But for a chance hook up with two experienced high-altitude climbers, a Swiss national and a Columbian, my life could have been in serious jeopardy.

- In the summer of 1992, I journeyed alone to the south rim of the Grand Canyon, reflecting on the embers of my third impetuous marriage. I saw a sign which read: "Do not attempt to hike to the Colorado River in one day. Many have tried and many have died". This seemed like a challenge! I picked up two (American) gallons of water and set off down the seven-and-a-half-mile trail to the river. On retracing my steps in the blistering 100-degree Fahrenheit heat I reached the south rim, past the carnage of dehydrated tourists who had ventured the much shorter distance to Indian Plains. Helicopters were bringing out casualties and park rangers administering electrolyte. I spied a McDonald's, the bastion of capitalism in the midst of Nature's wonderland. I desperately needed salt and sugar. Large fries and a 20 ounce Coke would do the trick, I thought. I consumed these avariciously and promptly threw up over the floor of the hallowed Golden Arches. I couldn't pee for two days.

- In early 1998 I was working in Trinidad and decided to climb El Tucuche, at 986 metres the second highest mountain in the country's Northern range mountains, a continuation of the Andes. A path took me into primary rain forest covering the top of this magnificent conical peak with a clearing at the highest point affording perfect views of Venezuela and the Orinoco delta. Now climbing up a conical mountain is one thing: descending quite another. In the gathering gloom (darkness comes quickly at six o'clock sharp) I fell down a ravine into a scour pool and realised my best chance of survival was climbing to a safe ledge and sitting out the night trying to avoid any insects or predators that might take a fancy to me. I had no food and little water. At first light I continued down the mountain until I came across a hut hidden in the jungle occupied by the unlikely combination of Rastafarian men and two beautiful young Danish women. I knocked on the door and refusing their 'weed' the head man gave me his son to guide me back to safety, with army rescue helicopters hovering above me.

Paul looked subdued as we got our boots on but knew I was determined to cross. He had brought ropes (in case of quick sands) and a compass and marker sticks to guide our return. He had even thought of bringing flares! We set off in light drizzle but good vision with the foreshortened Piel Castle looking enticingly close. The sloping path to the sand was very muddy and slippery and Paul's apprehension and anxiety was palpable. However, once on the flat sand the going was firm with no sinking sands or hidden channels to thwart our progress. Elated we arrived on the island and were greeted by Karen and Keith the only two permanent residents. I was nervous as Karen had been shielding there during the pandemic and our intrusion may have been unwelcome. Quite the reverse, she offered coffee and we chatted about their isolated life and misadventures of those, mostly motor vehicles, trapped by the tides. Residents must now pay £36 per year for the privilege of driving across the sands via a robust locked gate.

Keith's grandfather had run the *Ship Inn* on **Piel Island** and after retiring from the police he had now made one of the cottages their home. Keith convinced us that we had several hours before safety would be compromised and even offered us a lift back to Snab Point. Tempting as this was, we declined in order to make the visit more memorable. In high spirits we followed vehicle tracks. The dangerous 'Gutter', which catches many crossers by surprise, was still not filled with water, and we reached our cars with no mishaps and feelings of great elation. After over four years since visiting the other Furness islands, **Piel Island** had at last been conquered.

Piel Island was given to the people of Barrow-in-Furness in 1920 as a First World War memorial by the Duke of Buccleuch, an obscure Scottish peer. A quaint duty the good burghers of Barrow also perform is the election of the King of Piel, who doubles up as the pub landlord. The island was originally known as Fowdray or Fodder Island in Old Norse and was used as a store house by the Cistercian monks of nearby Furness Abbey, presumably as a safe haven from the countless waves of marauders during the Middle Ages. In 1327 they commenced the building of a motte and bailey fort for further security (also known as a "peel" - hence the island's modern name).

The origin of the king of Piel dates back to one Lambert Simnel a pretender to the throne of England. His claim in 1487 to be Edward Plantagenet, 17th Earl of Warwick, led to the Yorkists, during the war of the Roses, using him as a figurehead. Simnel was crowned as 'Edward VII' in Dublin and led an army of mainly Irish and Flemish troops landing on **Piel Island** as king. Entering the pub today you can become a "Knight of Piel" serving the king as long as you buy a round of drinks for all present. A new king is anointed in a ceremony of uncertain origin, in which the chosen candidate sits in an ancient chair, wearing a helmet and holding a sword while alcohol is poured over his head. By the 19th Century it had become an important aspect of the island's history to such an extent that responsibility for looking after the helmet and chair fell within the tenancy agreement. At the time of our visit a new king had yet to be appointed.

We returned through Barrow's grimness to **Roa Island** and sat by the lifeboat station watching workers returning from their wind farm travails in a rapid succession of boats plying through the Piel channel. William Wordsworth is known to have frequented nearby Rampside and his enjoyment of our view to Piel castle is recorded in his 1805 poem *Rampside:*

> 'I was thy neighbour once, thou rugged Pile!
> Four summer weeks I dwelt in sight of thee:
> I saw thee every day, and all the while,
> Thy form was sleeping on a glassy sea'.

The early evening was warm, and the tides imperceptibly but slowly and surely drowning out Snab sands obliterating our afternoon footsteps. A drink to our success was called for and we retreated to the *Clarke's Hotel* in Rampside where the regimen of social distancing was in full swing.

29. More Essex islands and The Broomway, England

With lockdown restrictions further easing I suggested to Ian a tentative trip to complete the eight Essex islands with habitation. I'd actually increased the tally by two having discovered that **Horsey** Island in Walton Naze and **Wallasea** adjacent to **Foulness** were also permanently populated. I'm sure other obscure islands will come to light at a later date. My tally for England has now grown to 28 with **Whale** Island, home to Royal Navy Command Headquarters in Portsmouth harbour also added to the list. Permission to visit there will be fun.

The mysterious **Osea** Island in the River Blackwater was still an enigma and **Foulness**, occupied by the clandestine Ministry of Defence, was still to be conquered. The blurb I received on my previously attempted visit from Quinetic, who manage the island on behalf of the MoD, suggested that access to **Foulness** was only possible, unless you are a resident in Churchend or Courtsend in the north of the island, on the first Sunday of the month between 12:00 and 16:00 from April to October. This allowed access to the Heritage Centre for a nostalgia tour and jam and scones made by the insular locals, now reduced to 131 in number. No other access was permitted via the only road from Great Wakering. It was coming up to the first Sunday in August 2020, so I called the Centre and as expected was told that these visits had been suspended until April 2021 because of the pandemic.

I scratched my head to devise my Plan B, previously considered outrageous with my fitness and health impediments. I would walk The Broomway along "a designated public right of way', a six-mile walk from Wakering Stairs to Fisherman's Head, the ancient access to Courtsend before the current road to **Foulness** was built in 1922. Drovers, carters and even the postman on horseback plied this route back in the day. Before the

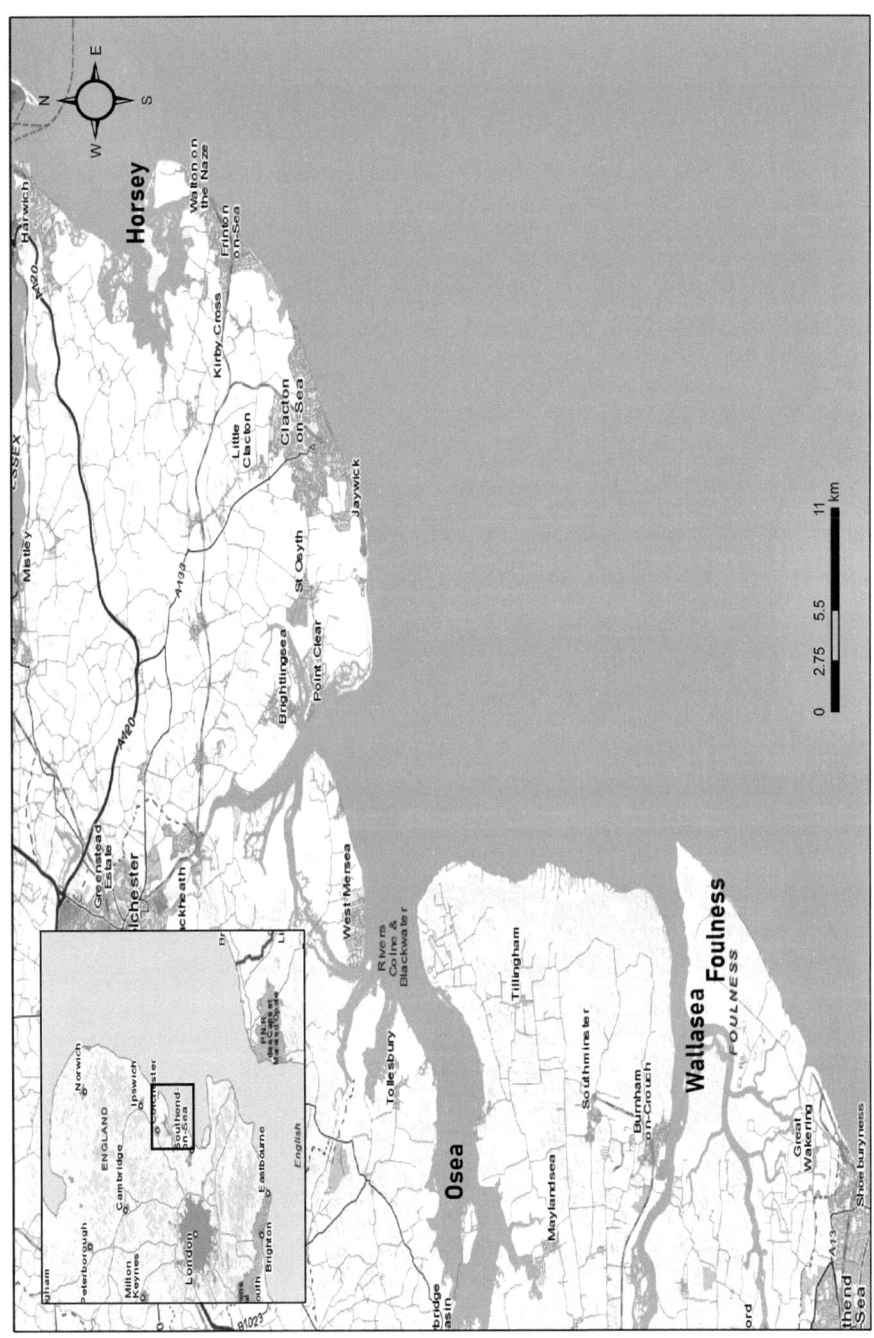

The remaining Essex islands

current road bridge was built, villagers too could only enter or leave **Foulness** via this route. Research indicated that this walk was considered to be the most perilous path in Great Britain and had taken the lives of countless hapless travellers cut off by the unpredictable tides on Maplin Sands. This was where the exposed Thames estuary meets the North Sea and although tides are sinusoidal, rising and falling at predicted times, the vagaries of the wind and the tidal influences from the rivers Roach and Crouch can produce rising tides and fulminating whirlpools from unexpected directions at unpredictable times.

This was not the only danger as artillery fire by the MoD onto the wastes of Maplin Sands could leave flooded craters in the sand where drowning would be certain. If drowning was avoided unexploded munitions could crop up randomly as the firing ranges were in use most days except weekends. The final literal nail in the coffin was the presence of quicksands. These were generally sited close to the shore which meant the Broomway ancient causeway had been built at least a quarter mile from shore, following firmer sand. The walk was largely featureless and, this far from shore, a sudden mist or change of weather would obscure the shoreline and disorientate the traveller, who could easily walk out in the direction of the sea to their certain death.

This was not going to be a repeat of **Piel Island**, which was literally like a walk to the pub. My foolish ventures have taken me ill supplied to the top of Cotopaxi in Ecuador, a mountain higher than anywhere in Africa; to the bottom of the Grand Canyon with insufficient water in the sweltering heat of the Arizona Summer but attempting Broomway was even by my ambitious standards, a step too far. Then I discovered Tom Bennett, an outdoor guide who specialised in guiding the Broomway. I would as often I do throw money at the problem and hire Tom. He returned my email and regretted that the daytime trip he had organised on 2nd August was fully subscribed by a private party, but he could, for a cut price of £150, take me and Ian on an earlier trip to coincide with the morning low tide, starting at four in the morning with the first hour in darkness – as if I needed another hazard.

Tom was a little suspicious of the enthusiasm of an elderly man, but I charmed him into thinking all would be fine. He was leader and would order the return at any time he saw my efforts fading. I agreed. I had not told him that I had arrythmia nor that Ian, though 15 years younger than me, had been hospitalised and on oxygen with COVID 19 in April. I knew I could be caught out, but I wanted to at least try. Days before the trip I walked a mile or two close to my suburban house and returned exhausted. This was not auspicious.

I transferred my money to Tom, confirmed the logistics, booked into the *Holiday Inn*, Southend some six miles from our rendezvous at the MoD guard post and waited for the day to arrive with great fear and trepidation. We would drive via **Horsey** Island and **Wallasea** before an early night at our hotel.

I'd been to Kirby le Soken on my walk around Great Britain and been aware of **Horsey Island** without knowing it was inhabited. It lies in Hamford Water and is part of the Hamford Water National Nature Reserve, co-managed by Natural England and the Essex Wildlife Trust. It has recorded habitation since at least the mid-16th century and though a cornucopia for wildlife it is still stoically farmed and takes the accolade as the most easterly inhabited island in Great Britain, not **Mersea** as is so often thought. There is now a rather splendid holiday home on **Horsey**, perfect for isolationists willing to tackle the rough one-kilometre causeway across the Wade at low tide, amidst the inhospitable mud and salt marsh.

We found the entrance to the road leading to the causeway off the B1304 east of Kirby only to find a locked gate barring our way. I was deeply annoyed, but Ian discovered the lock was easily unravelled and we drove triumphantly to the head of the causeway. Discretion being the better part of valour we opted to walk across as even with a four-by-four vehicle skidding off the causeway would result in entrapment in thick mud with little hope of extrication. Meeting another vehicle would be unthinkable. Freddie Flintoff and his *Top Gear* pals had attempted (and failed) to cross on a rising tide on one of their TV escapades.

Our feet were soon soaked with residual sea water from the falling tide, and we had till 17:02 before the tide turned and indeed the gates, so a notice warned, would be locked properly. The weather was pleasant, and we became immersed in the solitude of the marsh away from the frenetic traffic that had plagued our long journey from Birmingham. I for one after weeks of isolation at home was not used to the big, bad plague-ridden world. The container docks of Felixstowe with a myriad of cranes, acting as sentinels to World trade, dominated the distant landscape allowing shipments to and from Rotterdam and China and the Far East beyond. The world was shrinking and oases like **Horsey** were special. We rested on the largely abandoned sea wall on the island and passed a few words with the brusque farmer on his way to some assignment off the island.

The phrase "Time and tide wait for no man" is in common parlance but its origin is uncertain and is thought to pre-date modern English. The earliest known record is from St. Marher in 1225:

"And te tide and te time þat tu iboren were, schal beon iblescet."

Our return off island was uneventful except for assisting a family heading for the self-catering accommodation to negotiate the apparently locked gates. We worried about their transit across the causeway as they had been filled with optimism when booking regarding its comfort and safety. Surely this was a selling point of the pros of a holiday on this remote island.

We had a 65-mile journey to **Wallasea** avoiding the rivers Blackwater and Crouch, whose estuaries carve westwards from the North Sea. The island nestles between the Crouch to the north and the Roach to the south and is a featureless landscape with an altitude rarely rising above four metres, with the sea wall surrounding the island its highest point.

This featureless island was drained by Dutch settlers in the 15th century and its fertility gave rise to wheat production with a peak population of

135 in the late 19th century. There is now only a small clutch of houses and a pub – *The Lighthouse* – servicing the *Riverside* caravan park at the western extremity of the island. The island's demise coincided with the cheap imports of American wheat and the island's economy, as with **Foulness**, reverted to grazing. This is a stark warning as following a 'No deal' Brexit Great Britain could be bombarded with cheap and largely unregulated American food imports, following the abandonment of the safety of EU food standards.

As the saying goes, "What goes around comes around" and on July 4th, 2006, a £7.5 million project to convert part of the island's farmland back into mudflats and salt marsh was completed by bulldozing 300m of the sea defence wall, at the points of maximum pressure on the estuary. This was an attempt to offset 'coastal squeeze' to help to relieve coastal flooding as sea levels rise through the century. The **Wallasea** Island Wild Coast Project is an extension of this pilot with the construction of the London Crossrail tunnel providing four and a half million tonnes of earth, equal to 2,400 ship loads, to sculpture a Nature Reserve managed by the RSPB. The contradiction of the carbon footprint of importing the spoil versus environmental gain would have given some environmental economists a headache.

We stood on the massive residual sea wall overlooking Burnham on Crouch with our next intrepid goal, **Foulness** glowering menacingly in the distance. It was time for an early night as our mission would begin at four o'clock the next morning. At the *Holiday inn* we sanitised, obeyed social distancing and had a drink in the so-called 'Sky lounge' overlooking the forlorn Southend airport managed by Stobart haulage (or logistics as they now euphemistically like to be called). An array of easy Jet planes was going nowhere, and the airport car park was deserted. Dinner was fully booked because of reduced numbers allowed in the dining area and an awkward meal was our only alternative at the McDonalds opposite.

Our sleep was fitful and almost non-existent. I hate sleeping in the same room as male snorers and I am sure the feeling is reciprocated. The alarm was set for three twenty and after its trill I felt strangely energised, perhaps the adrenalin of the adventure ahead. We had had the foresight to trial the 15-minute journey to our meeting point the night before so we were confident our rendezvous with Tom would not be delayed.

After perfunctory introductions we donned our unnecessary waterproofs and very necessary head torches (it was still pitch black) and headed down the slippery and uneven Wakering Stairs to the eery gloom of an empty estuary and the 400 metres or so journey over the 'Black Grounds' to meet the path of the former causeway. It is now non-existent but was once waymarked by bunches of broom (think witches broom sticks) every thirty metres or so, set into the sands and replenished as tides washed them constantly away. This is how the Broomway got its name.

We were transported into a dystopian nightmare like something out of a Mad Max movie, the darkness only making things worse. Care had to be taken at every step of the way and feet were soon drenched. Our goal was Asplins Head, about three miles away, the only causeway exit to **Foulness** that is now kept open, largely for military purposes. It is here that the shore is set on fire just to see what happens and the samphire growing in profusion on the foreshore, for which you'll pay a small fortune in Waitrose, is toxic from the smouldering chemicals frequently set alight.

The 'path' goes back to pre-Roman times and like **Horsey** and **Wallasea**, **Foulness** has been flooded on numerous occasions most recently in 1953, from the catastrophic tidal surge that devastated much of the Netherlands and the east of England. It seemed crazy therefore to even think of siting the third London airport on Maplin Sands adjacent to the island. The Roskill Commission published a report in 1971 recommending the airport siting in Oxfordshire, but this was rejected in favour of a site at **Foulness** despite huge environmental protests. The Maplin Development Act received Royal Assent in October 1973 with proposals for not only the airport but a deep-water port and a new town to accommodate 600,000 people. The project would have cost over £10 billion at 2020 prices but was summarily abandoned when Harold

Wilson was elected as Prime Minister in 1974. The same common sense should apply to the HS2 railway project today.

The notoriety of the Broomway is legend. In 1769, a guidebook stated that:

> "the passage into [**Foulness**] is at low water, and on horseback, insomuch that many, either in negligence, or being in liquor, have been overtaken by the tide and drowned".

At least we were neither negligent nor drunk! It is estimated that in excess of 100 victims succumbed to the tide with around 65 graves marked in the Churchend graveyard. I asked Tom why we couldn't shorten our journey at Shelford Head just beyond the uninhabited Havengore Island and he mentioned that after the quicksand had sucked the life out of returning **Foulness** residents that Head was abandoned to its lost souls. We had no choice but to continue to Asplins Head to gain access to **Foulness**.

I kept my spirits up as dawn broke telling my many idiosyncratic anecdotes to my captive audience, but this kept my mind from both my fears and infirmities. The only navigational aid is the 'Maypole' whose beacon marks the entrance to Havengore Creek. From then onwards progress is by knowledge of the sands helped these days in bad weather by GPS. How the carters and postmen would have enjoyed this modern device. The weather was perfect and less than two hours after we set off the Kentish ragstone and gravel headway leading to Asplins Head was reached. I crossed the sea wall and touched the turf of the island: mission accomplished.

After a cup of tea and chocolate biscuits, Tom insisted we left to return to safety retracing the route. He wanted to complete the walk before the lowest point of the morning tide giving extra safety. I was tired through exertion and lack of sleep, lagging behind Tom and Ian. Further stories and conversation bucked my spirits, and we arrived back at Wakering Stairs at seven forty-five amongst early morning dog walkers making the most of early Sunday sunshine. We left Tom and headed back to the *Holiday Inn* for sleep, sweet sleep, returning at high tide luckily only to imagine the terrors of being swept away by the inevitable diurnal onslaught of the filling and emptying of the Thames estuary. Truly, Time and tide wait for no man.

Southend-on-Sea promenade was buzzing with at last some responsibility regarding social distancing. We didn't stop but headed north around the Crouch and Blackwater estuaries again to Goldhanger and the access by causeway to **Osea Island**, one of my last English islands. Just as on the last time I visited the road to the causeway was barred. Ian is a consummate dreamer with money making ideas changing on a weekly basis. With his lawyer bravado he had contacted the island owner with a plausible if not convoluted story asking if he could visit with a view to potentially bringing a party of Vietnam businessmen to their luxury accommodation next year. The management seemed receptive but could not meet with us that Sunday, but intimated that we were free to cross the causeway.

On arrival, Ian phoned the island and our request to gain access was rejected on the basis that the island was closed for a private function. The mind boggled. Was this a cult meeting or some form of disreputable gathering away from prying eyes? We would never know. Suddenly the barrier opened, and we were on the foreshore in a flash with residents of the nearby Osea caravan site happily enjoying their beach activities on a warm afternoon. We will just drive across the mile causeway cocking a snoop at our rejected request. To my utter consternation it would be two hours before the causeway was passable, so we turned for home. Another time; another time! **Osea** was joining the ranks of **Soay** off **Skye** and the **Isle of Ewe** as impregnable islands.

Once a treatment centre for alcoholics including the ill-fated Amy Winehouse, **Osea** had been resurrected as a luxury and very expensive idyll of peace and tranquillity suiting visitors wishing privacy and solitude. It catered for the likes of Olly Murs and another ill-fated celebrity, Caroline Flack at outlandish prices and its advertising blurb suggested a warm welcome for all those who might afford a minimum two-night stay:

"Surrounded by 550 acres of rustic gardens, orchards, meadows and salt marsh the island has an eclectic mix of accommodation. Its charming cottages, apartments and grand houses are available for holidays and family get togethers. Exclusive hire of the whole island is also possible for private events".

I will visit one day even if I have to pay to stay there. It appears to be rather exclusive for musicians as it is owned by music producer, Nigel Frieda and hosts recording artists in a fully equipped studio. The likes of Rihanna and Stormzy recorded there. Maybe I should form a band to gain exclusive access! My deflation however was easily mitigated by the previously impossible belief that I would never attempt let alone conquer the glorious Broomway.

30. Lundy Island, England

For some inexplicable reason I had forgotten about **Lundy Island** situated in the Bristol Channel about twelve miles off the Devon coast. There are some ten islands with allegiances to either England or Wales in the Bristol Channel but only three, **Lundy**, **Flat Holm** and **Caldey** [3] are permanently occupied with **Lundy** affiliated to the Torridge district of Devon. I had attempted in vain to get a trip to **Flat Holm** from Cardiff marina, but COVID 19 thwarted me. Although we live in the 'United' Kingdom, this small Kingdom is anything but united and COVID rules in Wales differed from those in England, Scotland and Northern Ireland.

With jurisdiction for **Lundy** in England COVID rules had been relaxed and trips on the *MS Oldenburg* from Ilfracombe had kick started albeit in a socially distanced manner. The *Oldenburg* would normally accept up to 267 passengers but a maximum of a third that number were allowed to ensure that new phrase in our lexicon – social distancing. Booking a trip was nigh on impossible and reminded me of trying to book tickets for Bob Dylan concerts in the seventies. After two hours perseverance I connected with the shore station and managed the last seat on a late August trip.

My recent island trips had taken me to literally all corners of England (Northumberland, Cumbria, Essex and now Devon) as well as **Anglesey** in Wales. My lockdown was well and truly over, well temporarily at least. The day trip necessitated an overnight stay, and I chose the *Imperial Hotel*, the sort of down at heel three-star establishment that caters for pensioners' coach trips. Although their COVID rules were impeccable the underlying décor was grubby and outdated, and I was glad my time there would be brief. I have a theory after staying in random seaside hotels the length and breadth of the UK that there is an inverse relationship between the

---

3   See Chapter 32

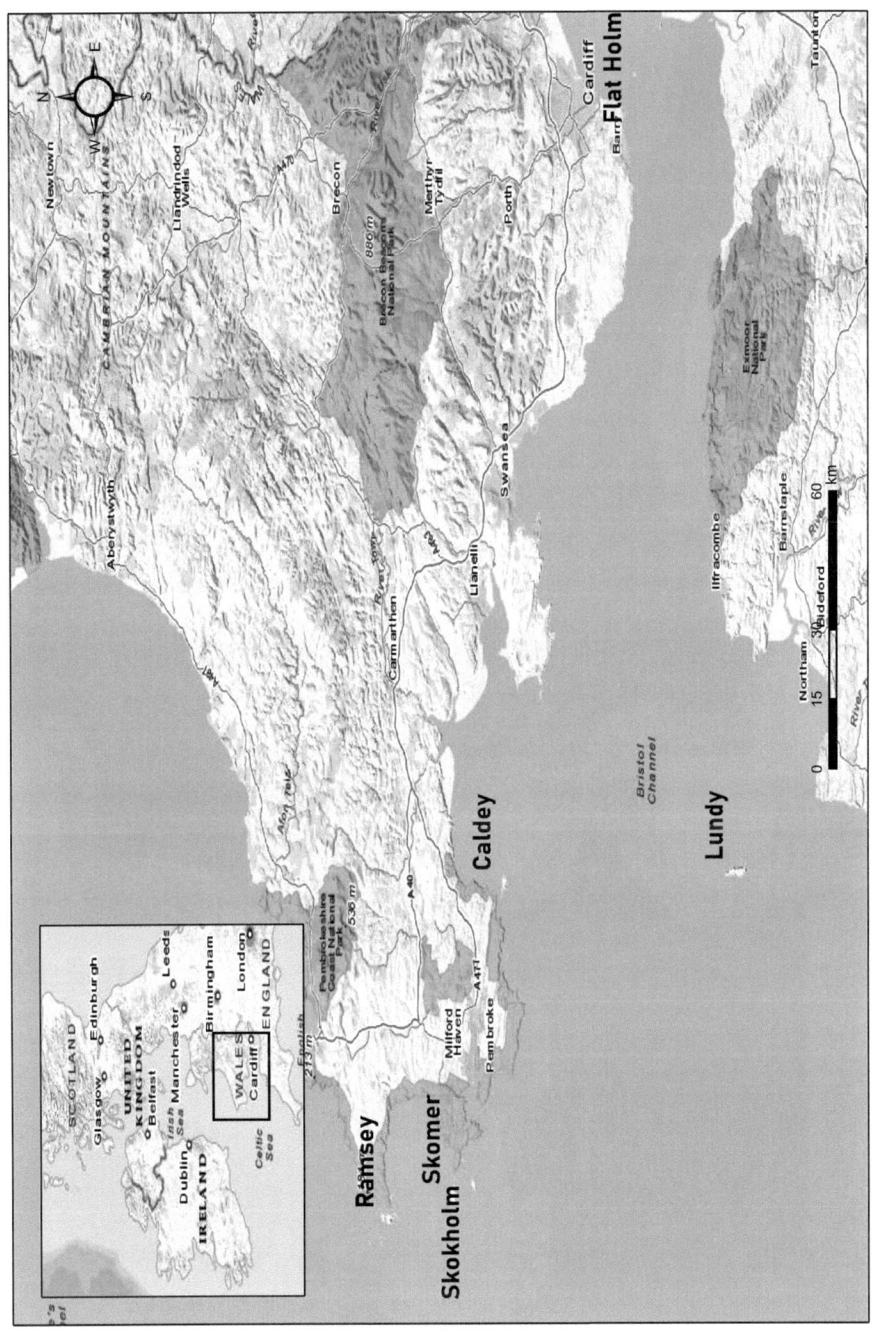

The islands of the Bristol Channel, England and Wales

grandness of their name and the quality of accommodation. The *Imperial* certainly lived up to this rule. Brexiteers who lament the loss of Empire would feel right at home in this down at heel establishment with decaying shades of its past glory.

Ilfracombe is billed as the jewel of the north Devon coast, though the information centre is a concrete carbuncle on an otherwise genteel town, then awakening from post lock down slumbers with a good smattering of holiday makers. Peter Sellers first appeared on stage in Ilfracombe and the Collins sisters, Joan and Jackie, attended stage school there whilst escaping the Blitz. I munched on my fish and chips supper *al fresco* before retiring early hoping for fair weather as gales earlier in the week had made day trips to **Lundy** impossible.

The harbour is dominated by *Verity* a colossal 20m high stainless steel and bronze statue by Damien Hirst who lives in nearby Coombe Martin. To give context to this magnificent artwork, depicting a heavily pregnant naked woman holding aloft a sword while carrying the scales of justice and standing on a pile of law books, it is about 30cms higher than Anthony Gormley's *Angel of the North* in Gateshead. As one might have expected many locals were not amused, objecting to its prominence in this sedate Victorian town. *Verity*, meaning truth, is something in short supply in post Brexit Britain and its symbolism ironic, though probably lost on the passengers waiting to board the passenger ferry enduring an early morning autumn-esque chill.

MS Oldenburg is a German ship built in 1958 in Bremen and requisitioned as **Lundy**'s lifeline in 1986 when the previous ferry, *the Polar Bear*, was decommissioned. With a speed of 12.5 knots, it takes two hours to reach **Lundy** and I took up my position below deck only to be joined by an, at first, affable guy about my age but who just wanted to spill his knowledge of photography *ad infinitum* in my general direction. I was a captive audience and his monotone spewed shutter speeds, focal lengths and the like until I could take no more. I started to sweat profusely and realised the rolling of this old German tub was giving me sea sickness, so I politely explained my predicament and sank into an acute torpid state for the remainder of the journey.

The jetty to **Lundy** village is over half a mile up a steep incline rising to 114m. It rained and rained hard and soon my out of shape body was drenched. I had optimistically thought of walking the 6km to North End and back, but I lost the will to continue and headed instead for the *Marisco Tavern* to dry out with a couple of pints of delicious Lundy Light. COVID distancing and sanitising were upheld with military precision; passing the virus amongst the 28 Landmark Trust staff who looked after **Lundy** for the National Trust, was unimaginable. The community has 23 cottage lets for around 93 people all year round and with tourism put on hold for four or more months further disruption would have been the last straw in an already fragile industry.

Lundy is England's first Marine Nature Reserve and Britain's first Marine Conservation zone and though primarily remembered for its puffin population, from its iconic stamp design beloved of philatelists, a staggering 317 species of birds have been recorded on what is a traditional flight path for migratory birds. The puffin pink and blue stamps are still accepted as legal postage tender but in quirky English tradition have to be affixed on the left top corner of the envelope rather than the right top corner reserved for stamps bearing the monarch's head!

Located strategically in the Bristol Channel **Lundy** has throughout history been a hotbed of smuggling and piracy with a quixotic past. Barbary pirates were in occupancy for five years at the beginning of the 17th century and a self-contained Irish community held sway for a while at the beginning of the 19th Century. The Marisco family (hence the tavern's name) were prominent in **Lundy**'s history and partaking in various nefarious activities. Ships were forced to navigate close to **Lundy** because of the dangerous shingle banks in the fast-flowing estuary with its extraordinary tidal range (second only in the World to Canada's Bay of Fundy).

Bristol was the epicentre for the infamous 'Triangular Trade' and rich pickings were easy for those in control of the island. Of course, **Lundy** too, like many estates throughout the UK owes its prosperity to the spoils of the slave trade with William Heaven buying the island for £9,870 (well over one million pounds today) in 1836 and building Millcombe House from his compensation for losing his Jamaican slaves.

After a brief visit to St Helen's church which doubled as a museum, I ambled back to the jetty in bright sunshine with the Devon coastline snaking along the late afternoon's glistening horizon. On spotting me a steward, remembering my wretchedness on the outward journey, offered me ginger biscuits, a remedy for sea sickness of which I was wholly unaware. Too late, the sea was by now flat calm and the return journey a delight with my photographic friend no doubt boring some other unsuspecting soul in the *Marisco Tavern*.

31. Remaining islands in the Highlands, Scotland

Three islands remained a mystery to me in the Scottish Highlands. These had been elusive and unattainable either because of weather conditions or my inability to source a boat when nearby. I am good with people but hopeless at the initiation of contact with strangers to the point of paranoia. It is almost as if I should really just stand on the shore looking longingly out to sea and expect a well-wisher to read my mind and offer me a lift on their boat which was conveniently moored nearby. This was never going to happen. I had booked a passage on *Bella Jayne* a tourist boat operating out of the village of Elgol at the southeast end of **Skye** during my Easter 2017 trip to the Isle of **Skye**, but weather put paid to my aspiration of getting to **Soay**. In subsequent years on returning from Shetland, Outer Hebrides and Orkney I had contacted her skipper, David to claim my £55 trip. Each time bad weather intervened and **Soay** was destined to be "the one that got away".

I'd passed the **Isle of Ewe** in Loch Ewe north of Gairloch also on my return from the Northern Isles, but I had not the courage to cold call the Grants whose family had lived on and farmed the island for many years. On similar trips I had diverted to Crinan to attempt to access **Eilean da Mheinn** a tantalising hundred or so metres across Loch Crinan from the busy Crinan harbour. Each time I stood looking forlornly out to sea hoping for divine intervention and a friendly tap on the shoulder by a passing sailor who could read my thoughts.

Dry Island or Eilean Tioram was altogether a different matter. I'd misread the Scottish Census of inhabited islands, 2011 and assumed this island, not more than a dozen miles from Gairloch, was actually the island in Loch Moidart on which stands Dorlin castle. Both are in the

Remaining islands in the Highlands, Scotland

Highland administrative area but many miles apart. I was ignorant to this fact until, during our eventually successful attempt to access the **Isle of Ewe**, our boatman asked nonchalantly whether I had 'done' **Dry Island**. I confidently replied to the affirmative and was utterly confused by his conflicting description of 'his' **Dry Island** as against 'my' **Dry Island**. To resolve confusion, we elected to visit the mystery island for ourselves as Dry/Tioram is a common Scottish island name. Our investigations were surprising to say the least.

The trip was initiated by my island-hopping dear friends Stuart and Paul, and we were to be joined by another friend, Steve, from our London University days caving club or 'Cave Soc'. He had left for California in 1976 and was still resident in Sacramento, California, having made rich pickings developing software used by the oil industry. He had for a few dollars been 'ordained' into the Universal Life Church so he could legally marry two friends on the top of Half Dome, Yosemite; only in America. These three were adventures personified. Not for them sitting in cosy pubs reminiscing but with the mind set of teenagers wanted alternative and challenging pursuits. Nobody but they would have eagerly anticipated a 650 mile plus jaunt across the Highlands to visit what in reality are four obscure Scottish islands. The distances covered would be jaw dropping even by Californian standards.

I was to meet Steve and Stuart at Stirling station and make the 217 miles journey to Aultbea to meet Paul armed with a small inflatable dinghy and a sturdy outboard. Crazy does not cover this. Having conquered the one-kilometre sea journey to the **isle of Ewe** we were to make the 81-mile journey to **Skye** to conquer **Soay** and then the 150-mile journey to Crinan, all in three days. At the time of planning, I had no idea about the newly discovered **Dry Island**.

After a four-hour drive from Stirling through stunning if not moody scenery we made it to the jetty at Aultbea where Alisdair Grant had arranged a courtesy trip to his island. He was an accomplished craftsman of traditionally built clinker boats, and we were very lucky to avail ourselves of his service. We had constantly worried about the weather, which was on the cusp of Beaufort scale five, or a fresh breeze, which would have certainly prevented our original intention of using Paul's cramped two man blow up dinghy. Though only about a kilometre from the jetty the reality of travel in this wholly unseaworthy contraption was far from advisable. Alisdair had been Plan B and even his journey in filthy weather was far from pleasant. We got very wet.

The **Isle of Ewe** (say it out loud) is apparently a magnet for young marrieds who liked to circumnavigate the island as part of sealing their troth. In popular culture, the island's name also came up in *'The Goon Show'*, during a November 1954 episode *"Lurgi Strikes Britain."* Neddie Seagoon (Harry Secombe) is informed that the "dreaded lurgi" has appeared on the **Isle of Ewe**, to which he replies, "I love you too. Shall we dance"? As COVID 19 still raged how appropriate was this reference from over sixty years ago.

On arrival on this dot of an island Alisdair returned to his boat workshop, and we idled around the island for an acceptable time admiring the stone craftmanship of ruined buildings, but for most of the time Paul and I sat stoically on Torridonian sandstone rocks patiently awaiting our return journey, thankful that plan A had not been invoked. Unlike neighbouring and uninhabited Gruinard Island which was used by scientists from Porton Down in 1942 to test anthrax as part of chemical warfare experiments and whose access is ill advised, **Ewe** had a population peaking at 43 in 1881. During the Second World War 19 of the Arctic convoys to Russia left from Loch Ewe and NATO manoeuvres are still carried out there.

Cold and wet but elated we left the jetty after giving our boatman a well-deserved generous tip 'for the fuel' and headed for the *Gairloch Hotel* for the night. As it had been a logistical nightmare to get four single rooms in a hotel popular with the motor cyclists riding the 'North Coast 500' I left the others and decamped to the *Old Inn*, a charming over-priced hostelry last frequented on my circumnavigation of Great Britain. My vision of *the Gairloch Hotel,* based on an earlier and failed visit to the **Isle of Ewe**, was of pensioner bus tours, with tea dances and DJ's specialising in Matt Munroe and music of the fifties. COVID had seen off these coach tour holidays to be replaced by leather clad bikers and sports car enthusiasts.

The 'North Coast 500' attempts to emulate the great Wild Atlantic Way on the west coast of Ireland. It is a circular trip up the west Highland coast and along the north coast to John O'Groats and down the east coast to Inverness before joining the west coast at Applecross. The latter village was favoured as an unlikely holiday destination during the pandemic by then Prime Minister Johnson for his apparent camping holiday! There are two schools of thought on 'North Coast 500'; the first that it is a travesty ruining the tranquillity of the far north, and second a much-needed boost to the fragile Highland economy. A major accident is waiting to happen with gangs of twenty or more bikers emulating the **Isle of Man** TT races on often twisty single-track roads.

We were inquisitive about a trip to **Dry Island** or **Eilean Tioram** in a sheltered bay near Badachro only twenty minutes' drive from the hotel. It turned out that this was indeed the island listed in the Scottish 2011 census and was indeed populated, by the McWhinney family, though we were oblivious to this on arrival at Aird via a track from the B8056. Google had suggested that self-catering accommodation was on offer on the island, but access was a mystery with the only possible route to the island firmly labelled PRIVATE. We were intrigued and despite Paul's reticence we opened the gate bedecked with a gay pride rainbow flag and descended a reasonably well-maintained steep path with a board walk along much of its length.

At sea level the path turned west parallel to the shore and there in front of us was **Dry Island** accessed by a floating walkway. We were about to cross when a large figure on the opposite shore caught our eye. He approached. Paul stood back. Our first exchanges were cautious and the guy of about fifty berated us. I stood firm and spluttered on weakly about my island mission. His face was stern. "Why didn't you phone?" he scowled. I squirmed with no satisfactory answer. Then his scowl turned to a cheeky grin, and he asked us to wait until he had gone to collect his post at the main road.

On his return he invited us to his island and offered coffee and chocolate biscuits in his cosy kitchen. This was Ian, who announced himself as 'King Ian the First' of Islonia, claiming independence from both Scotland and the UK since 2010. His three princesses and prince were at school and Queen Jesse, his wife, was nowhere to be seen, though the scruffy terrier Dubh was on hand to repel invaders. His family had fished the local waters for shellfish for years. Now in most circumstances when someone announces that he is 'a king' the urge would be to get away as quickly as possible, but Ian was immensely likeable with captivating stories to match.

As with many Scottish fisheries salted fish has been and still is an economic staple with for centuries preserved fish headed for the Caribbean colonies as food for slaves with salt brought in from Scandinavia. Salt fish delicacies are still favoured throughout the West Indies today. Much of the soil on the island and surroundings was brought in as ballast, instead of rocks, with the salt cargo from Europe. Today Ian was proud of his exports of langoustines to Spain and Portugal insisting that he caught prawns and sold langoustines to ramp up the market price of what is essentially the same sea food.

We were presented with our personal passport to the Kingdom and inaugurated as citizens. I am proud citizen number 13,161 and swore to uphold the Kingdom Constitution:

- All visitors must smile.
- All children must obey their parents.
- All memories should be stored securely.
- If your footsteps be big or small, may they always lead you back to Islonia.

This was a quaint master stroke by Ian to ensure his shellfish safaris and mackerel fishing trips were too good a draw to miss. Islonia rather overstates the hype calling the Kingdom "The jewel of the Northern hemisphere". This continues the rich vein (or should it be vain!) of British exceptionalism in the world, though in this case King Ian's tongue is firmly in his cheek. This truly was a serendipitous experience.

With no time to lose we headed for our overnight stay on **Skye** at Kyleakin, just over the Skye bridge to our B&B for the night, Glenarroch, which was in reality not the chintzy place we'd imagined but a down at heel establishment with all the charm of a rather expensive bail hostel. It was a place to rest our heads in preparation for the elusive trip to **Soay**, fourth or was it fifth time lucky. I'd found the *Misty Isles* charter out of Elgol and unlike *Bella Jayne's* crew the MacKinnans agreed to take us, weather permitting.

Paul's pessimism makes my grumpy fatalism sound positive. He studied the weather forecast and felt postponement was the likely outcome. I phoned Anne, the matriarch of the business that is reputed to have taken Bonnie Prince Charlie and Flora MacDonald from Elgol to the mainland on his well-documented escape to France. These stretches of imagination were fuel to the tourist industry and reminded us of the time at London University when Stuart made up stories for gullible Americans on our stint as summer holiday guides in London. I'm sure the grandchildren of these folk, when visiting London, are being told to this day of the exact spot where the apple landed on Sir Isaac Newton's head!

Anne indicated that if we arrived at nine the next morning the trip would be more than likely on. We slept well and after breakfast headed past the glowering Black Cuillins, a primeval landscape where the weather and light change from minute to minute, to Elgol to board the vessel *Eilean a Cheo or The Isle of Mist* crewed by Sandy and his son Seamus. I had paid a king's ransom for the two-hour trip, seizing the day, *carpe diem*, as a return trip from Birmingham with the necessary accommodation would have involved similar costs. We huddled in the cuddy (Paul, an experienced nautical man, introduced us to this term as the shelter offered by the cover adjacent to the skipper's 'bridge'). A tender was on board for Seamus to row us two by two, like a latter-day Noah, to shore on **Soay**.

On our arrival we made for several abandoned cottages, one previously lived in by Tex Geddes, harpoonist for Gavin Maxwell's basking shark oil business, set up after the Second World War. Maxwell will be forever remembered for his book *Ring of Bright Water* written in 1960 about how he brought an otter back from Iraq and raised it in Scotland. It surprised us that, as an assumed conservationist, he was responsible for harvesting around 4,000 sharks and processing them on **Soay**. The processing plant now lies forlorn and derelict, overtaken by the healing powers of nature. His crazy exploits are recorded in a fascinating read: *"Harpoon at a venture."*

In 1953 because of poor communications the Government presided over the evacuation of 27 islanders to new homes on **Mull**. Only Geddes and his family remained but subsequently a tiny community grew up 'on the verge of viability'. Sandy our boatman had a friend who was schooled on the island, but the schoolhouse now lies derelict, and its teacher is long since gone. Today two houses are occupied, one by an old fisherman and the other by an enterprising English couple who saw an advert for the property in an estate agent's window in Portree. The image was burnt into Anne Cholawo's memory and her challenge renovating the property and adjusting to life away from the Home Counties and the bustle of her job in London led to her book *'Island on the Edge: A Life on* **Soay***'*.

We headed back to the jetty in, as anticipated, worsening weather with descending mist obliterating the views to the Black Cuillins. Stuart reminded us of the words of Laurence McBride writing about the poverty endemic at one time on **Skye**: "These hills are misery". Stuart's namesake John Arnott MacCulloch in his 1904 epic *The Misty Isles* put my three and a half years of effort to get to **Soay** in context (though perhaps a tad melodramatic):

> "It seems that everything is near its ending
> — existence and the universe itself. You perceive

sharply the dreadful misery of life, the isolation of everyone, the nothingness of all things, and the black loneliness of the heart which nurses itself and deceives itself with dreams until the hour of death. So it is, sometimes, in **Skye**; until there comes a day of sunshine, and all is forgotten, and the desolation passes away as if it had never been".

Islands unlock a kind of spirituality not attained anywhere else, with elusive tranquillity the backdrop to an ever-changing land and seascape with the ever-changing weather beguiling both visitor and resident alike. It is the permanence of change that beguiles.

Elated by at last reaching the elusive **Soay** we set off on the route march down the west coast to Crinan, first stopping at **Eilean Donan**, the quintessential, photogenic Scottish castle adorning all the 'Visit Scotland' tourist guides. It wasn't in the 2011 Scottish Islands census, but I wanted to check its permanent occupancy. As usual tourists abounded and the custodians of the bridge leading to this picture book castle indeed confirmed its owners only made occasional use of its facilities. This was enough for me and saved the £10 entry fee. On my very last island reconnaissance to Scotland, I did cross over the bridge mainly so I could use one of the many photographs of the castle in this book.

We reached Crinan harbour at around five and Paul having driven his Toyota Landcruiser solo was exhausted and suggested that we reserved the 'onslaught' onto the island by his precarious dinghy until the morning. Stuart and Steve were distraught. Paul pondered and realised that the flat calm conditions were perfect for the crossing and what is more the rain had largely stopped. The next day would not be any better, so Paul made the executive decision that the crossing was on. Now I like walking as this involved little 'faff' other than donning boots and outer wear and setting off. Not so with a dinghy crossing. The vessel had to be inflated, accoutrements attached, and the very heavy engine secured to the stern without dropping into the drink.

Paul leading the mini expedition morphed into a cross between Herman Melville's Captain Ahab in *Moby Dick*, the monomaniacal captain of the whaling ship *Pequod,* and Captain Bligh the irascible captain of the *Bounty* whose mutineers in 1789, led by Fletcher Christian, set him and 23 loyal sailors adrift in the Pacific in a seven-metre launch. As lead mariner Paul always demanded silence and absolute obedience during the tricky manoeuvres of embarkation on and landing from this ludicrously unstable tender on our attempt to secure **Eilean da Mheinn**. He had studied aerial photographs and picked a muddy beach to the southwest of the island on which to land well away from the house occupied by Richard and Sally Stein the new owners. He and Stuart set off and steadily but surely Steve and then me were also safely escorted across this 200-metre millpond. Obligatory selfies were taken, and the reverse journey was undertaken just before light faded.

We headed for the *Lochgair Hotel* and celebrated the night away with Old Poultney malt. I like going away with male companions as splitting bills is simple. Despite modest drinking by Steve and Stuart all bills for the trip were split four ways unlike especially female teachers who dissect and scrutinise the bills precisely and largely spoil the pleasure of the meal. Many is the time I've heard the cry "I didn't have the popadums" when payment was due.

The weather the next morning was foul and without Paul's quick-thinking the evening before **Eilean da Mheinn** would still be unconquered. We travelled home with a great sense of achievement and adventure. I love travelling with those boys. I drove back to Chesterfield with Steve reminiscing all the way. He had just bought a flat in Derbyshire's Peak District to get away from the California heat in summer and I hope to see much more of him on future island adventures. We suggested a trip to the west coast of Ireland in July 2021 to compete my Irish islands but with COVID 19 entering wave after wave this was hope triumphing over experience.

32. The remaining Welsh islands

COVID 19 lockdowns were a necessary affliction as cases and more importantly deaths soared through the early part of 2021. I had meticulously prepared an itinerary to complete my inhabited Irish islands, reserving the whole of July for this task. I'd even begun to source fishing boats to transport me and my adventurers to obscure islands with sparse populations but no regular transport. The planning itself was anticipatory of what would be a magnificent trip. Hopes of pulling this off faded rapidly as national restrictions became fierce and ever more convoluted to understand. Even if restrictions were lifted then accommodation would either be non-existent or at a premium as 'staycations' were becoming the new norm with foreign holiday traffic largely stifled.

My thoughts turned to completion of the sporadic remaining Welsh islands. I had never been keen on these as adventure would be limited as the majority left to visit were tourist islands. These were mostly visited by enthusiastic twitchers and naturalists keen on sightings of puffins, manx shearwaters and other sea birds too numerous to mention or simply to soak up the natural majesty of these wildlife reserves. The exception and by contrast the antithesis of nature watching was **Caldey Island**, off Tenby and a veritable mecca for tourist hoards out for a day trip.

Two islands were privately owned, **St Tudwal's West** off the coast of Abersoch and owned by the media adventurer Bear Grylls and his family, and **Gared Goch** with a solitary occupied house nestled underneath Pont Britannia in the Menai Straits. I froze at the thought of getting permission for these trips as my temerity was in overdrive. Should I really make the effort to get to **St Tudwal**'s at all? After all it did not register on the list of populated Welsh islands from the Office of National Statistics (ONS). But

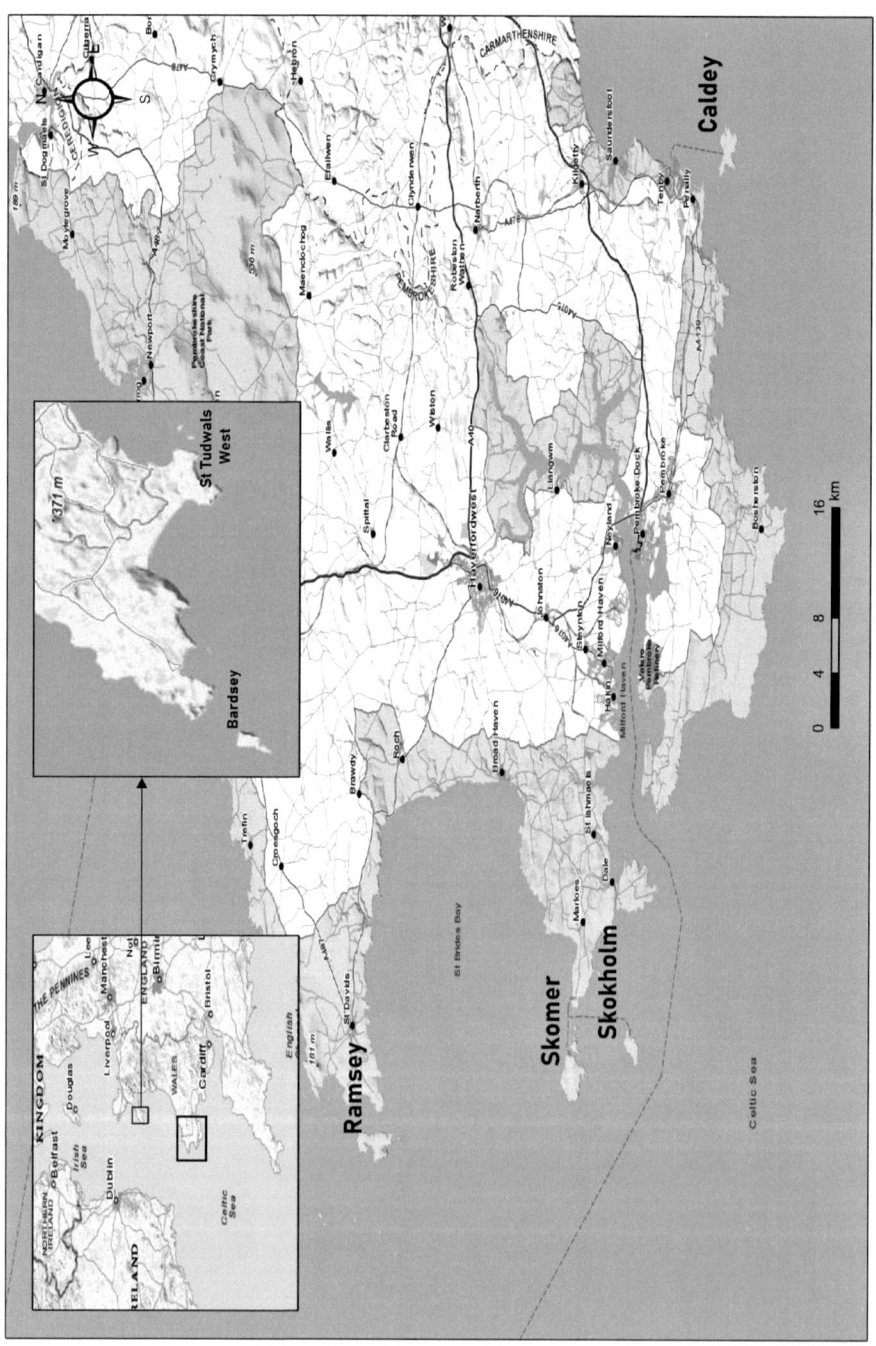

The remaining Welsh islands

then neither did **Skomer** owned by the Royal Society for the Protection of Birds, and I'd already arranged this trip. **Gared Goch** was however mentioned by ONS.

What would seem to be a simple question: just what does 'inhabited' mean is far from simple. Is it the occupants living there on each census day? Well, **Bardsey** is definitely populated all year round and this is missing from ONS data. Does 'permanent' occupancy most of the year by wardens as on **Skokholm** and **Ramsey** count? Well, ONS seem to think so as farming communities had long gone. Nobody lives anywhere permanently if one wants to be really facetious. To make matters more complex, unlike Scottish and Irish censuses, Welsh (and English) censuses do not separate island populations from the census Output Areas which include adjacent mainland parishioners.

Only 10 Welsh islands are recognised as 'inhabited' by ONS:

Island
Anglesey (*Ynys Môn*)
Caldey Island (*Ynys Bŷr*)
Flat Holm (*Ynys Echni*)
Holy Island (*Ynys Gybi*)
Ramsey Island (*Ynys Dewi*)
Skokholm (*Ynys Sgoc-holm*)
Ynys Castell
Ynys Faelog
Ynys Gaint
Ynys Gored Goch

The omission of **Bardsey** and the inclusion of **Skokholm**, **Ramsey** and **Flat Holm** but not **Skomer** are perplexing, so I have therefore nominated 14 islands as having signs of frequent habitation. Included in addition to the list above are **St Tudwal's West**, **Ynys y Big** (Menai Straits), **Skomer** and **Bardsey**. St Tudwal's East was once owned by Carla

Lane, the Liverpool born writer of the popular *'Liver Birds'* and *'Butterflies'* sitcoms which she bought in 1991 to protect its wildlife but was never occupied except by the hermit St Tudwal in the 6th century. Only the ruins of a priory remain.

My last island trip was back in September 2020 completing all but three of the Scottish islands and as soon as COVID restrictions were eased in June 2021 I couldn't wait to get to **Flat Holm** in the Bristol Channel close to Mermaid Quay, Cardiff and then to **Bardsey** about two miles off the Llyn peninsular near Aberdaron. This would leave the four Pembrokeshire islands and the two elusive private islands.

On a fine June morning I drove to Cardiff to take advantage of a journey to **Flat Holm**. Landing visits were still forbidden because of the pandemic so I 'threw money at the problem' and chartered a RIB to 'land' me there and return. Arriving at Mermaid Quay, a bustling thoroughfare waking up from the emergent relaxation of COVID 19 restrictions, I made for the Bay Island Voyage pontoon to await my exclusive carriage. I hate exceptionalism so it was with shame and embarrassment that I had to deny envious onlookers the opportunity to join me. I mumbled something about 'doing research' and we headed off to await the opening of the tide lock through the Cardiff barrage. At 1.1km in length and one of Wales's major civil engineering projects the £220 million plan, which commenced in 1994 and was completed in 1999, was the catalyst for the £2 billion regeneration of the old docklands areas of Cardiff and Penarth, making historic flood defences redundant.

Once through the complex system of locks managing the massive 15 metre tidal ranges in the Bristol Channel we were speeding fast to **Flat Holm**, which the tourist blurb lauds as 'The jewel in the Bristol Channel'. I could have sworn that this accolade had been given to **Lundy**! This nature reserve, which is managed by Cardiff City Council, and explains the tight COVID 19 security, is the southernmost land fall of Wales with fine views to its English sister uninhabited island Steep Holm which is, err, steeper! When day trips are allowed it even has its own pub *'The Gull* *and Leek'* paying tribute I assume to Wales's favourite vegetable. Overnight stays are possible. Occupation of **Flat Holm** has been sporadic since the Bronze Age with three principal groups requiring isolation; those seeking religious solitude; those requiring physical isolation and those wanting to be away from the prying eyes of authority.

Those with religious retreat foremost on their minds were the followers of St Cadoc in the 5th and 6th centuries. This Norman era monk is of particular relevance in being one of seven monks making a case for the authenticity of King Arthur other than in Geoffrey of Monmouth's *Historia Regum Britanniae* whose 'inventions' of Arthur have been regarded as a flight of fancy to spice up the history of the times.

The second group of residents occupied a cholera sanatorium built in 1896 to service those caught up with the disease in the then crowded and unsanitary port that was Cardiff. On Mermaid Quay is an engraved plaque of John Masefield's alliterative poem *Cargoes* evocative of Cardiff's maritime past:

> Quinquireme of Nineveh from distant Ophir,
> Rowing home to haven in sunny Palestine,
> With a cargo of ivory,
> And apes and peacocks,
> Sandalwood, cedarwood, and sweet white wine.
>
> Stately Spanish galleon coming from the Isthmus,
> Dipping through the Tropics by the palm-green shores,
> With a cargo of diamonds,
> Emeralds, amethysts,
> Topazes, and cinnamon, and gold moidores.
>
> Dirty British coaster with a salt-caked smokestack,
> Butting through the Channel in the mad March days,
> With a cargo of Tyne coal,
> Road-rails, pig-lead, firewood, ironware, and cheap tin trays.

The islanders were none too pleased at being joined by sailors requiring isolation (initially being confined to canvass tents) as this 'plague island' detracted visitors and prevented the sale of vegetables grown on **Flat Holm** from being sold in Cardiff markets. The Marquis of Bute, Cardiff's coal baron, thus leased land to Cardiff City Council to build the sanatorium which was in use until its closure in 1935.

Although a military battery was built in the 1860's as part of a line of defences known as the Palmerston Forts because of the concern of the burgeoning French navy, the third group were smugglers and pirates, just as on neighbouring **Lundy**, with the Bristol Channel ideal for access to Bristol and beyond to dispose of contraband, largely tea and brandy. Although **Flat Holm** was in full view of both the Welsh and English coasts, customs authorities were powerless to act as they had no boat to take them to the island.

Of further strategic importance, Guglielmo Marconi transmitted the first wireless signals over open sea from **Flat Holm** to Lavernock on 13th May 1897 a distance of 3.7 miles with the message "Are you ready?", predating the transmission from Ballycastle to another of my islands, **Rathlin** in Northern Ireland. The island made communication history again on 8th October 2002, by becoming one of the first areas of south Wales to link to the Internet through a wireless connection deployed by Cardiff Council as part of the Flat Holm Project.

My visit complete I returned to Mermaid Quay transformed out of all recognition from the docklands of Bute Town that I remembered fifty years ago. Of course, until the gentrification of Cardiff the dock area was the infamous Tiger Bay, birthplace to the magnificent diva that is Dame Shirley *'hey big spender'* Bassey whose father was an immigrant from Nigeria. I settled down to a cappuccino at one of the many cafes on the quay side to prepare for my journey home and mused that in a generation the coal ports of Cardiff and Barry servicing the long-gone mining communities had made way for a brave new world of Nando's, Starbucks and Pret a Manger. The week I wrote this Prime Minister Johnson had the audacity to suggest that the closure of Britain's coal mines by Margaret Thatcher was her early attempt to combat climate change through abandoning fossil fuels. His attempts to falsify reality and hide behind unscrupulous lies and mistruths became daily more unfathomable.

The affable Colin runs the boat trips to **Bardsey** leaving from Porth Meudwy a couple of miles from Aberdaron. I arranged a trip soon after securing **Flat Holm** travelling with Bob and Sue from their home in Rowen above the Conwy valley. The boat is unceremoniously pulled from the small bay by tractor and the intrepid visitors, about 12 of them including us, clambered aboard socially distancing as best we could. It became obvious that we English (well to be accurate Sue is from Northern Ireland) were in the minority with Welsh being the language of choice for both Colin and the other day trippers enjoying an enervating day out from Carnarvon. Rightly so Colin dispensed with English after his rudimentary bilingual safety messages, obligatory to comply with maritime authority regulations. Safety is paramount on pleasure trips since the disaster on the Thames in August 1989 when 54 passengers enjoying a birthday party on the *Marchioness* died after colliding with the *Bowbelle,* a Thames dredger.

Porth Meudwy is close to a place, Whistling Sands, evocative of my childhood when my father booked a cottage from an advertisement in the *Manchester Guardian* (before it became *The Guardian* we know today). Our excitement was dashed on arrival when the cottage, whose name I forget but translates to pig sty in English, turned out to be as dirty as its name suggests. My poor mother whose middle name was cleanliness scrubbed and scrubbed but eventually threw in the towel quite literally and we scraped together a few pounds (no cash points in those days) to seek out modest B&B's for our week's stay. The disappointment has stayed with me always and I hoped **Bardsey** would help to dispel my bad childhood memories of the Llyn peninsular.

We had about four hours to explore the island which, despite ONS 'official' statistics, is permanently occupied by about a dozen people with four resolutely remaining in the winter. Despite my walking infirmity we strolled for over three miles on the island with a coffee stop at Ty Pellaf and souvenir shops in makeshift 'galleries' or rather abandoned cowsheds. The old school was abandoned in 1953 but the chapel still appears functional with the Bible open at Jeremiah 48, verses 42 to 44:

> "And Moab shall be destroyed from being a people, because he hath magnified himself against the Lord.
>
> Fear, and the pit, and the snare, shall be upon thee, O inhabitant of Moab, saith the Lord.
>
> He that fleeth from the fear shall fall into the pit; and he that getteth up out of the pit shall be taken in the snare: for I will bring upon it, even upon Moab, the year of their visitation, saith the Lord".

The Old Testament must have put the fear of God into the insular folk of **Bardsey**. My paternal great grandfather went by the name Jabez, a biblical name meaning "he makes sorrowful" from 1 Chronicles 4:9-10. Victorian churchgoing didn't seem much fun!

At the end of the 18th Century **Bardsey** had a king. It is uncertain as to why a monarchy was established. One possibility is so that the inhabitants (as many as 132 in 1881) could feel part of an independent state or members of the owner, Lord Newborough's 'colony' and they were free from having to pay tax or rent. The last king was the enigmatic Love Pritchard who died on the island in 1926 after famously aligning his kingdom on the side of the Kaiser in the First World War! He was aggrieved at being rejected for military duty by the British at the age of 71.

Bardsey, known as the legendary burial site for 20,000 Saints, is Wales's 4th largest island but its etymology is confused as the English name refers to the island of the Bards, though as with many place names alternative interpretations are alluded to. In **Bardsey**'s case the name could derive from the Viking chieftain Barda. In the 6th Century the Breton Saint,

Cadfan oversaw the building of St Mary's Abbey in the north of the island. For centuries, the island was important as "the holy place of burial for all the bravest and best in the land" and in medieval times a pilgrimage to **Bardsey** was the equivalent of one to Rome; it was regarded as the gate to Heaven and Paradise.

The island is also claimed as the burial site of King Arthur's wizard Merlin, though that presupposes that, as with King Arthur himself, Geoffrey of Monmouth did not fabricate the legend. Geoffrey was good at making up stories to spice up the Dark Ages. He went to great lengths to suggest that the Anglo-Saxon/Danish invasion of Eastern England was a bloody affair. However, recent archaeological excavations using state-of-the-art imaging showed little signs of violence inflicted on the several thousand skeletons discovered. The truth seems to be that the 'invaders' largely co-existed with the resident population and integrated freely with providing food and shelter of more importance than warfare. These seemed socially more enlightened times than today with the current wave of Brexit xenophobia.

As we look towards self-discovery we become deeply introverted; globalisation and parochialism - a strange paradox in the modern world. It is fascinating that waves of immigrants through history used to blend into the landscape and townscape of their adopted countries, borrowing a section of the country before becoming part of it in culture and dress. The persecuted Jews of Eastern Europe or the dispossessed Irish would all congregate in East London or Lower Manhattan before blending imperceptibly into new environments farther afield as they became more settled and affluent. The Pilgrim Fathers morphed into American citizens. 'God Bless America' was the clarion call. Often just the surname gave away their origin and even these were often camouflaged, changed to make the integration complete. In contrast today, urban ghettoes persist, culture and language of adopted countries are resisted, and opinions polarise. Neighbours are suspicious of neighbours. It is as if cultural identity must win over the common good. These suspicions became more and more complex and entrenched post 9/11 and in the UK post Brexit.

The Pembrokeshire islands, **Skokholm, Skomer, Ramsey** and **Caldey** beckoned and in June provision had been made to book the leisure boats that took tourists to these offshore islands. On trying to book suitable accommodation I was shocked to find that all possible choices had been reserved for weeks as 'staycations' were the only means of summer holidays. Foreign travel had been jeopardised by the Government traffic light system with post-holiday quarantining for 10 days essential and, for those returning from 'red list' countries, a self-paid incarceration into a sub-standard hotel costing the traveller a couple of thousand pounds or more.

Of the remaining very limited choice, 'an exceptional yacht with two bedrooms in west Wales' caught my eye as a quirky alternative posted on Booking.com and I quickly booked and paid for this, snared by the adjective 'exceptional'. Like all new build flats are called 'luxury', these adjectives lure us into a web of deceit, and we should know better. The yacht was moored in Milford Haven and about an hour's drive equidistant from each of our four islands.

The day before our trip (with Bob and Sue again) the owner of the yacht telephoned, explaining that the accommodation was no longer available due to an irreparable electrical fault. The trip and our bookings to the islands lay in tatters. I could only think back to my desultory childhood memories in Wales. Our only option was to book into an eye-wateringly expensive but exclusive 5 star converted priory (Penrhiw) in St David's.

St David's, as with all tourist locations in Pembrokeshire and coastal resorts throughout the United Kingdom, was crammed to the rafters with the residents of 'plague island' unable or unwilling to seek sanctuary in the usual Mediterranean resorts. Getting a simple pub meal involved tortuous lengthy queuing just to eat in gardens. Ordering food had changed with bar service not allowed and the downloading of tortuous QR code-based apps to gain access to menus and payments. If this is the post COVID 19 future I want no part of it. The surly waiter indicated if we didn't like the new system we could go elsewhere, an impossibility with queues for the fish and chip shop snaking around the block along the main thoroughfare, Nun Street.

Penrhiw was a steepish (for me) climb about half a mile from the cathedral but was, as one might expect from a former priory, a tranquil rural idyll with a modern airy lounge where we could sit undisturbed by fussy hotel staff who did not occupy the building overnight. I was excited about my early morning trip to **Skokholm**, and we needed to leave the hotel around seven to meet the boat carrying staying visitors to the island.

Skokholm was essentially a closed island nature reserve owned by the Wildlife Trust of south and west Wales not allowing day visitors, so I had to plead for special dispensation from the warden to step on the island and return on the boat. As with the **Skomer** boat it leaves from a precarious mooring at Martin's Haven about an hour's drive from St David's. The skipper was James Hedley Phillips or young Jim whose agility belied his 73 years. He was just 22 days older than me but an impressive, fit seaman whose personality lit up the trip. His business card indicated he was a 'shipwreck and maritime researcher' and was fascinated by my odyssey. He had dived the wrecks coming to grief on the jagged rocks around **Skokholm** and **Skomer** and though in his seventies has even renewed his diving licence. I was put to shame.

Skokholm (together with **Skomer**) is home to the largest concentration of Manx shearwaters in the world, with an estimated 45,000 breeding pairs on this island alone. Together with up to 5,000 puffins during the breeding season and razorbills, guillemots and fulmars along with an estimated 20% of Europe's storm petrels, this island is a veritable cornucopia for the twitcher. The Atlantic grey seal is omnipresent and if you are lucky schools of dolphins and harbour porpoises skim through the near shore waters. Whilst waiting for our departure in Martin's Haven a lugubrious seal clambered on rocks beside us to take in the heat of the early morning sun.

Its great value as an exceptional sanctuary for sea birds was recognised by the pioneering ornithologist Ronald Lockley who moved to **Skokholm** in November 1927. Living till the age of 96 he wrote 50 natural history books, best known for the book *'The private life of the rabbit'* which must go down as one of the page turners of the 20th Century. Joking aside it was this publication that inspired Richard Adams to write *'Watership Down'*. His notable scientific monograph *'Shearwaters'* is a result of a twelve years' study and remarkably he made a successful living from his publications. But there is more; in 1934 his documentary *'The private lives of gannets'* won him a Holywood Oscar!

We were joined by two solitary regulars to the island and in fine weather made the landing in around 30 minutes greeted by the warden and an array of returning guests. Unlike my **Caldey** visit later that day these guys were hardened naturalists toughened by many experiences on islands and reserves like this where creature comforts were sparse. For some reason they were praising my 'achievements' and photo opportunities were centre stage. Photo calls complete we boarded the boat to return to Martin's Haven and I chatted animatedly to a young Finnish woman from Oxford University who had been researching the guts of mice on **Skokholm** and was laden down with traps and other paraphernalia. This was not a tourist excursion. Jim fed the tame seagull perched on the stern of the boat, a party trick he must have repeated a thousand times. On arrival back on the mainland I bade farewell to young Jim happy in the knowledge that he would be entertaining us the next day on our trip to **Skomer**.

An hour's drive took us to Tenby whose claim to fame was its prowess as the stag/hen capital of Britain for a few short years at the turn of the Century. This was before cheap Ryanair and easy Jet flights to the likes of Prague, Tallinn and Riga and all points Eastern European, where booze was plentiful and cheap, moved the revellers to these more quixotic destinations. I was expecting the worst and wasn't disappointed. The streets were throng with holiday makers and the car parks heaving with traffic. This wasn't going to be pleasant, and with little chance of parking close to the harbour Bob and Sue dropped me off to fend for myself and run the gauntlet down to the beach where I was reliable informed that the **Caldey** leisure trips embarked. These trips were production line in their efficiency with long lines of tourists queuing up on the beach for departures every 15 minutes.

Any attempt at social distancing or mask wearing had long been abandoned with profit motive triumphing over health and welfare. There was not a twitcher in site, only families and their grumpy teenage charges and a buzz of excitement for anyone aged in single figures. I paid the princely 'senior' concession sum of £12 and waited patiently for my turn to board. Summer wear was 'de rigueur' despite the chilling breeze at sea in mid-afternoon and this elderly man looked out of character with his outer wear and walking pole. Older people become invisible and although nature lovers going to **Skokholm**, **Skomer** and **Ramsey** engaged me in erudite conversation about lengths of puffin breeding seasons and the gestation period of Atlantic grey seals, my **Caldey** compatriots ignored me enthralled as they were in a series of never ending self-indulgent 'selfies'.

The trip is about 15 minutes and on disembarkation whilst my shipmates were headed for the cafes, souvenir shops and ice cream parlours on offer I made a brief cursory incursion inland reading about the delights of the island. Ironically **Caldey** is, like **Iona** in the Inner Hebrides, **Holy Island** in Northumberland, and **Bardsey** Island off the Llyn Peninsular, one of Britain's Holy islands. The Cistercian monks of **Caldey** continue a tradition which began there in Celtic times. "More than a thousand years of prayer and quiet living have made this remote and beautiful island a haven of tranquillity and peace", so the tourist blurb offers in complete contrast to the objectives of the daily tourists.

Monks across Europe have had a long tradition of creating craft products like the Trappist monks in Belgium famed for their full-strength beers. **Caldey** monks are no exception doing a roaring trade in lavender, perfume products and chocolate, sold at sky-high prices. Their lavender perfume is said to be "simply the best lavender soliflore on earth". The **Caldey** monk's predecessors indeed originated from the Trappist monasteries in Belgium, coming to the island in the early 20th Century taking over from the Anglican Benedictines who after building their monastery got into financial difficulties. The canny Trappists embraced commercialism and the 40 or so residents rely on the burgeoning tourist trade confirming the inextricable link between God and mammon, a chaotic juxtaposition of pleasure and spiritual retreat with trips forbidden on Sunday's.

I boarded a return boat with little fuss sitting cramped next to a lady with a nosegay of lavender - a fitting accoutrement, like in the times of the plagues of yesteryear where sweet smells might attempt to block out the nausea of decaying plague victims. COVID 19 had not yet got that grim! Tenby was still in full throttle with industrial consumption of ice creams and fish 'n chips. I had a contemplative pint in a harbour tavern before my rendezvous with my companions and thoughts of a wholly different trip to **Skomer** the following day.

We were now old hands at getting to Martin's Haven and the anticipated trip to **Skomer** with the effervescent 'Young Jim'. He was in his tourist guide mode today as all on board were to enjoy a 4-hour stay on this National Nature Reserve which is one of the most important wildlife sites in northwest Europe with the usual array of sea birds. In 2020 the puffin population increased to 34,796 birds (how ludicrously precise is that!), making it one of Britain's premier sites for this iconic bird. About 87 steep steps lead to the start of a number of trails all across the island and briefing over we set off to enjoy a short stay. Jim had arranged for us to curtail the normal 4-hour trip.

There is a large rabbit population surviving a number of waves of myxomatosis most recently in 2006. There is a symbiosis between rabbits and puffins as although puffins are perfectly capable of digging their own burrows they often utilise rabbit holes for breeding. Without the rabbit population coastal slopes would become overgrown and not ideal as habitats for these cute birds. It was the end of the season for puffins, which mate for life but have no interest in their young once they hatch. The vagaries of the lifestyles and habits of fauna across the hundreds of thousands of species around the world is truly awe inspiring.

We walked the 15 minutes to the farm complex where volunteers and enthusiastic self-catering visitors are based bringing all their food and belongings for their stays. It was a fine day and whilst Bob and Sue ventured farther afield, I sat and mused on nature's wonderland in the week that the most recent Intergovernmental Panel on Climate Change (IPCC) Report was published with stark warning of irreversible damage to our planet unless zero carbon is achieved. The UN Secretary-General António Guterres said the IPCC Working Group's report distilling thousands of peer reviewed scientific papers was nothing less than "a code red for humanity. The alarm bells are deafening, and the evidence is irrefutable". July and August 2021 saw unprecedented temperatures across Europe with 48C recorded in Italy, wildfires throughout North America and in Europe from Greece to Algeria with Biblical flooding in Germany and the Low Countries killing hundreds.

Contemplating such Armageddon cheerily dismissed by right wing climate deniers I strolled the half mile to the embarkation point in a reflective mood shuddering at what will be left for future generations. We are borrowing the earth and cannot in any sense change the fact that beyond man's tenancy it will revert to its original design purpose as an integrated biosphere, atmosphere, lithosphere and hydrosphere that will shape life in another form, hopefully more peaceful and civilised than currently exists. James Lovelock's 'The *Revenge of Gaia'*, predicted that man's lack of respect for the Earth will produce a runaway effect, accelerating climate change and if unchecked will ultimately lead to our demise. Whatever the outcome of the checks and balances to eliminate our rape of natural resources and our endless inabilities to get on with each other, even without humans, the Earth will last again for a time well beyond our brief sojourn. The beauty of **Skomer** is testament to that.

Jim's smile brought me back to the present and he used his charm to dispel any of my residual fears with his oft used joke "All aboard, this boat is for the **Isle of Wight**". We had a reflective trip to the shore station, and I promised to keep in touch with Jim, who was genuinely interested in my island project, but knowing I never would.

The leisure boat to **Ramsey** leaves from St Justinian's former RNLI lifeboat station about two miles out of St David's. I was to go on my own for the four-hour visit. The RNLI had just been slandered by that arch Brexiteer racist Nigel Farage who is fuelled with hatred and xenophobia. Brexit had already been called out as a disaster with, amongst a litany of other negative effects, empty supermarket shelves because of the lack of tens of thousands of lorry drivers which Johnson's Government blamed on COVID 19. In reality all sectors of the economy were suffering because of the newly introduced draconian rules on immigration driving nurses, doctors and vets and many other essential workers away from the UK.

Recent legislation had put strict restrictions on refugees seeking sanctuary from their unstable nations either as a result of war, politics or famine. Many hundreds are attempting the treacherous voyage across the English Channel in flimsy, overcrowded dinghies which would often flounder. Farage suggested that RNLI was just a taxi service for 'illegal' immigrants. His crass stupidity knows no bounds and appeals to ill-informed flag waving popularists, the so called 'Red wall' of labour voters who brought Johnson to power in December 2019 by flipping their voting preference.

RLNI is run largely on voluntary donations and is a vital support to HM Coastguards. To think that legislation might make their efforts to rescue vulnerable asylum seekers illegal is beyond the pale of right-wing political agendas. That week saw a huge surge of donations to RNLI, outraged by this foolish man's comments.

Getting to the boat involved descending about 30 concrete steps to the base of the RNLI station, climbing a further 30 or so wooden steps to the launch ramp and then a steep descent to the boat. The journey to **Ramsey** is about 15 minutes and after the introductory drill my fellow passengers deserted me to make the best of their 4 hours stay. Two ladies lagged behind and one of them proudly announced that her grandfather had farmed the island. Today only the warden and deputy warden live on the island year-round, but the legacy of habitation goes back to the 5th Century when the hermit St Justinian lived there. Justinian was the confessor to David or Dewi, the patron Saint of Wales and this island, Ynys Dewi, in Welsh, takes its name from him.

I have trouble walking distances now, so I found a suitable vantage point and sat by myself in tepid sunshine on a remote headland for 3 hours looking out to St David's Head and the western most landfall of Wales contemplating nature's strength and man's fragility. RIBs carried exhilarated tourists and along with skilful kayakers made there precarious way through the tidal races off the island. These phenomena known as 'The Bitches' can reach speeds of up to 4 metres per second on a flood tide and prove challenging to cross.

Like on **Skomer** puffins had now fled for the season but peregrine falcons and choughs rule the roost with a herd of wild deer cavorting the hills and dales of this diverse island. **Ramsey** has the most important grey seal breeding colony in southern Britain, with over 400 seal pups born each autumn. In October 2017 the remnant storm of hurricane Ophelia was responsible for some 90 seal pup deaths. Life and death are fragile in the periphery of our islands.

The final Welsh islands of **Ynys Gored Goch** in the Menai Strait and **St Tudwal's West** off the coast of Abersoch would be a challenge as both are private islands with no public access. Although outward going in work and socialising I am weak when it comes to the logistics of dealing with the unknown. I brought the subject up with an old friend Adrian and he relished the idea of helping me gain access to both islands. **Ynys Gored Goch** is the home of a property developer and his wife and **St Tudwal's West** the Welsh home each summer to the adventure Bear Grylls, whose exploits with the likes of US president Barack Obama are sold to TV companies around the world.

Without breaking sweat Ade had contacted a chain of likely candidates from whom to charter boats and who to gain permission for visits. He had been a big shot in recruitment in the eighties and cold calling was of no concern to him. My fragile ego would not let me make such contacts for fear of rejection like a gawky student asking for a dance at a fresher's ball.

We were to base ourselves at *Ty Mawr* in Llanbedr just south of Harlech, now owned by Jane, an old flame of Ade's from his youth. Only two dates were available at the hotel in 2021's COVID summer so efficient logistics were of the essence. Ade elected to be called my 'logistics manager' and within 24 hours of requesting visits green lights were given. His charm and possibly bullshit, making me out to be a 'famous' travel writer, may have helped but in an age when even Government cannot function without torrid lying as its principal strategy these exaggerations as to my prowess paid off.

Firstly, we were to tackle Ynys Gored Goch. We drove from Birmingham stopping at Carreg Bran Hotel, Ffordd Caergybi, before meeting our ferryman Bryn and his assistant Mark at the shore station underneath Pont Britannia, Thomas Telford's magnificent 1826 suspension bridge. Bryn was charm personified and had brought a functional work boat to ferry us the few hundred metres to **Ynys Gored Goch** across the swirling strait. The depth of the channel reaches 15 metres in places, and the current can exceed 7 knots (13 km/hour). We were entering treacherous waters. One of the most dangerous areas of the strait is known as the 'Swellies' (or Swillies – Welsh Pwll Ceris) between the two bridges connecting **Anglesey** to the mainland and this is where we were heading.

The island can be cut in two during high spring tides and the sense of exposure on arrival at the island was palpable. Efficient pumping systems prevent serious flooding today. Bryn said living there was like living in a fishbowl with RIB laden tourists and adventuring kayakers testing their skills on the Swellies ignoring the privacy of the island retreat. The island had been used since the 16th century as a fish trap with the two fishing weirs still prominent on the **Anglesey** side of the island. These weirs would trap fish as the tide retreated. Gored means tidal fish trap. A smoking chamber was built in 1842 and tourists in the early 20th Century would take a boat to the island to enjoy a 'Gored whitebait tea'.

The island garden is tiny, though graced with a hot tub, but the views to both Telford's and Stevenson's bridges are spectacular and a rare opportunity to see the strait from sea level. Bryn was proud to be associated with the island and his nonchalance and good humour and offer of a free passage was humbling. We bade farewell at the shore station and set off to conquer my last Welsh island, or would we?

St Tudwal's East and West, just off the Llyn Peninsular near Abersoch, were mysteries and after grappling with the Office of National Statistics census data it appeared that neither was permanently occupied. St Tudwal's East had been bought some years ago by the Liverpool comedy playwright Carla Lane, the writer of '*Bread*' which ran for five or so years in the late eighties starring the indefatigable Boswell family under the strict control of matriarch Nellie played by Jean Boht. Sue and Bob owned a terraced house identical to the Boswell's overlooking the Mersey where the tight knit families congregate to gossip on summer evenings around their interconnecting alleyways.

She did not buy the island for occupation as only the ruins of a 13th Century abbey remain with the island having been occupied by St Tudwal, one of the seven founding Saints of Brittany. Her aim was to preserve the island as a conservation project as she was a passionate environmentalist until her death in 2016. Under the rules of combat no visit was necessary and access without a solid pier would have been treacherous.

I could have also chosen to omit its sister island **St Tudwal's West** but as its owners and temporary occupiers were the Grylls family an opportunity to visit was too good to miss. They had taken over the island and converted the lighthouse complex into a holiday home, a place of tranquillity for Bear when not chasing around the World as one of the modern breed of adventures, filming for Netflix or acting in his capacity as Chief Scout.

Ade, 'the master of logistical planning', had sourced a number of alternatives to get to the island including a RIB from Pwllheli but settled on a sedate tourist fishing boat, *Jenny Two* from Abersoch skippered by yet another affable character called Bryn. This Bryn sported an array of tattoos and piercings that would not have disgraced an 18th Century pirate. We were accompanied by Ade's son James, both he and his father veterans of Atlantic crossings by yacht and Craig my young colleague working with me as a flood risk asset management consultant.

We were to meet on Abersoch beach with Bryn driving a home-made tender which had seen better days with a bow wheel for ease of access to the beach. Nobody had told me that we had to climb aboard the tender and then negotiate boarding *Jenny Two* in what Bryn referred to as 'choppy' seas. Choppy is clearly a nautical expression for anything not flat calm. Luckily my young and burly compatriots were able to hoist me from tender to fishing boat unceremoniously and with little finesse, each vessel moving in different directions both horizontally and vertically. Worse was to come.

"Look at the horizon" Ade offered as he saw a pallid, frightened look on my face with my stomach becoming queasier with every slap of the hull on each successive wave with conditions worsening all the while. Bryn was in communication with Bear perched on his new access jetty waiting on our arrival. This had been built at enormous expense to take his military style amphibious hydraulic RIB at all states of the weather. Bryn could not use this as his conventional craft needed a traditional jetty.

Bryn then broke the news. It would have been foolhardy to land on the old jetty built to service the lighthouse and to my dismay less than a hundred metres from shore we were forced to return. My plans were in tatters though Bear had agreed in true adventurer style to jet ski over to Abersoch yacht club to meet us.

The return was a little smoother but by then my stomach lost the will to digest and the excellent breakfast cooked for me at *Ty Mawr* was soon 'food for the fishes'. The ordeal was far from over. The return transition from *Jenny Two* to the tender proved to be hazardous yet again compounded by the fact I just wanted to die. This time the differential height between the boats was in my favour and I dumped my arthritic body over the side and onto the tender with little finesse. The tender hit the beach at speed, and I felt as if I had been part of the 'D day' landings.

Obstacles were still not over, this time human obstacles. Yacht clubs by definition are class ridden affairs. After all yachts are neither cheap to buy, moor or maintain as Ade will testify. Ade had kept his yacht, *Hercules*, in Palma, Majorca marina and with a wry smile had repeated to me the oft used adage: The two best moments of a yachtsman's life are on buying a yacht and on selling it!

I was looking wretched, and my 'crew' were somewhat dishevelled though I had donned my Helly Hansen over jacket to provide a semblance of reality as one of the yachting fraternity. This didn't work and stares from the blazer clad club members and their well-heeled wives were accompanied by mutters of "How the hell do they know Bear" as we were warmly greeted by him at the boat club jetty looking the true adventurer after a swashbuckling trip across Tremadog Bay to meet us. We exchanged pleasantries and he kindly signed his autobiography *'Mud, sweat and tears'* for my son Maxim. I offered him a signed copy of my book *'A walk by the Sea'* which he graciously accepted and sped off back to his island, inviting us back when the weather was calmer.

In July 2022 a year later, Ade sought permission from Bear's people to make a return visit though this time the man himself would not be there. I had been invited to my friends Andy and Tara's wedding in the very up market surroundings of Portmeirion, the Italianate village designed by Sir Clough Williams Ellis in the early 20th Century. Portmeirion was made famous in the 1960s as the location of the cult TV series *The Prisoner* starring Patrick McGoohan, playing an unnamed British intelligence agent who is abducted and imprisoned in a mysterious coastal village, where his captors designate him as Number Six. My room for the wedding was in the green dome where prisoner Number Two had resided. The series had passed me by, so I was rather underwhelmed though impressed by the setting.

This luxurious and intriguing wedding venue was less than three miles from Porthmadog harbour where Ade's power boat instructor Jonno was based. He had agreed to take us on his brand new £90,000 RIB the 45 minutes to **St Tudwal's West**. The weather for both the wedding and our trip, prior to the ceremony, could not have been different from the previous year. Ade and his son James joined us again with Joe, a young friend from Moseley and like me a wedding guest. Joe had been an adventurer with snowboarding and white-water rafting instruction credentials. He seemed non-plussed about the boat ride I had promised, and we set off out of the harbour at a languid pace in flat calm waters. Without warning Jonno, a thrill seeker par excellence, ramped up the speed to 45 knots nearly throwing us from the vessel. Joe's attitude to this gentle old man's trip did a 180-degree U-turn and we were met at the ramshackle old jetty by one of Bear's workers to set foot on the island at last. They hoisted my ungainly body ashore. This second trip was well worth the wait and Jonno wouldn't accept any money for his impeccable efforts. Wales was now complete.

33. The remaining islands of County Mayo, Sligo and Donegal, Republic of Ireland

It had been a little over two years since July 2019 when I'd last travelled to Ireland to continue the Irish odyssey. Many of the Galway islands had been 'ticked' off and some in Mayo. I remembered with great satisfaction driving back to Galway City after a glorious trip through Connemara. England had just beaten New Zealand in the one-day world cup international and John Lawlor and I drove happily into the city with the evening sun reflecting on the iconic bay with couples languidly strolling down the promenade above Grattan Beach. The Irish island ventures were taking shape. I was planning a month's trip in July 2020 to complete the challenge.

I took the decision to be a little more meticulous in my planning as so far on the three trips from Cork to Mayo I had just selected islands at random with little in the way of planning. With, according to the 2016 Census, upwards of 60 inhabited islands I needed a precise plan. All would be well but as the world now knows the pandemic struck putting paid to any Irish island adventures throughout 2020 and much of 2021. Covid 19 travel protocol was daunting to say the least and booking a passage and accommodation would have been foolish. I had to weather the storm, sit tight, and wait for the release from plague. The more I planned my route the more frustrated I became.

Quite by chance I became involved with two coastal erosion projects on Ireland's west coast, and I was asked by my client in Belfast to visit in August 2021. The succession of Atlantic storms during the last decade, especially in 2013/14 has left the fragile coastal defences – rock armour,

TREASURED ISLANDS

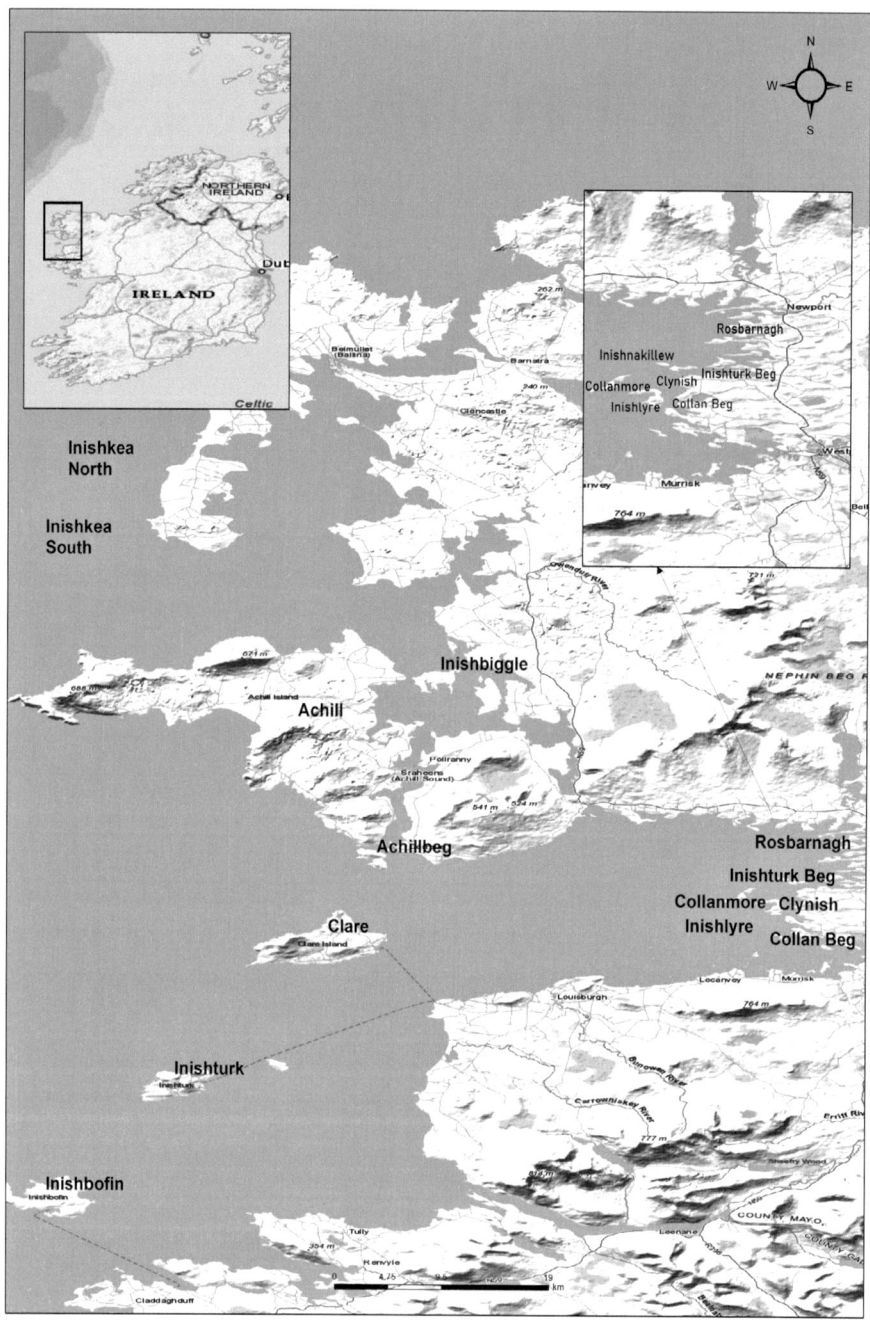

The remaining islands of County Mayo, Sligo and Donegal, Republic of Ireland – South

natural dune systems, jetties and sea walls – ravaged exposing long tracts of the coast vulnerable to both flooding and erosion as climate change marches relentlessly on. Any work organised and funded by the Office of Public Works will be merely a sticking plaster. Nature will be supreme assisted by man's dereliction of his custodial role in sustainably managing the earth's resources.

One of my coast erosion inspection visits was to **Inishbofin**, Galway which, ironically, I had already visited but this time I was, through the courtesy of Galway County's John Daye, a lifetime islander, able to drive around the island and see the cumulative devastation of this succession of Atlantic storms. The island depends on tourism with even at the end of the Covid ridden summer season over 300 visitors crammed on each boat. The future for the island without significant injections of Euros for coastal protection is bleak with beaches destroyed, access to holiday hotels and other property severed and shingle banks breached permanently changing the fragile ecosystems of the natural hinterland.

The other site was the tourist destination of Strandhill, Sligo a honeypot for surfers and boarders waking up out of the extended lockdowns which had crippled the local economy. Strandhill was a mere dozen kilometres from my first island, one of only two in the County – **Coney Island** a tidal island some two kilometres offshore.

I'd been working for the same consultants in Largs, Scotland and I took the ferry from Cairn Ryan to Larne in Northern Ireland. After a briefing by the consultants, I picked up John Lawlor in Belfast on the hottest day of the year. He was just off the coach from Abbeyleix and had been desperate for a pint of English real ale after a long sweaty journey and had almost run into the *Crown* across from the bus station. Crestfallen he was denied entry due to the Covid booking restrictions. With no other choice we drove directly to our accommodation in Enniskillen; both now gagging for a cold pint.

We stayed overnight near Enniskillen in one of over a dozen spontaneously

TREASURED ISLANDS

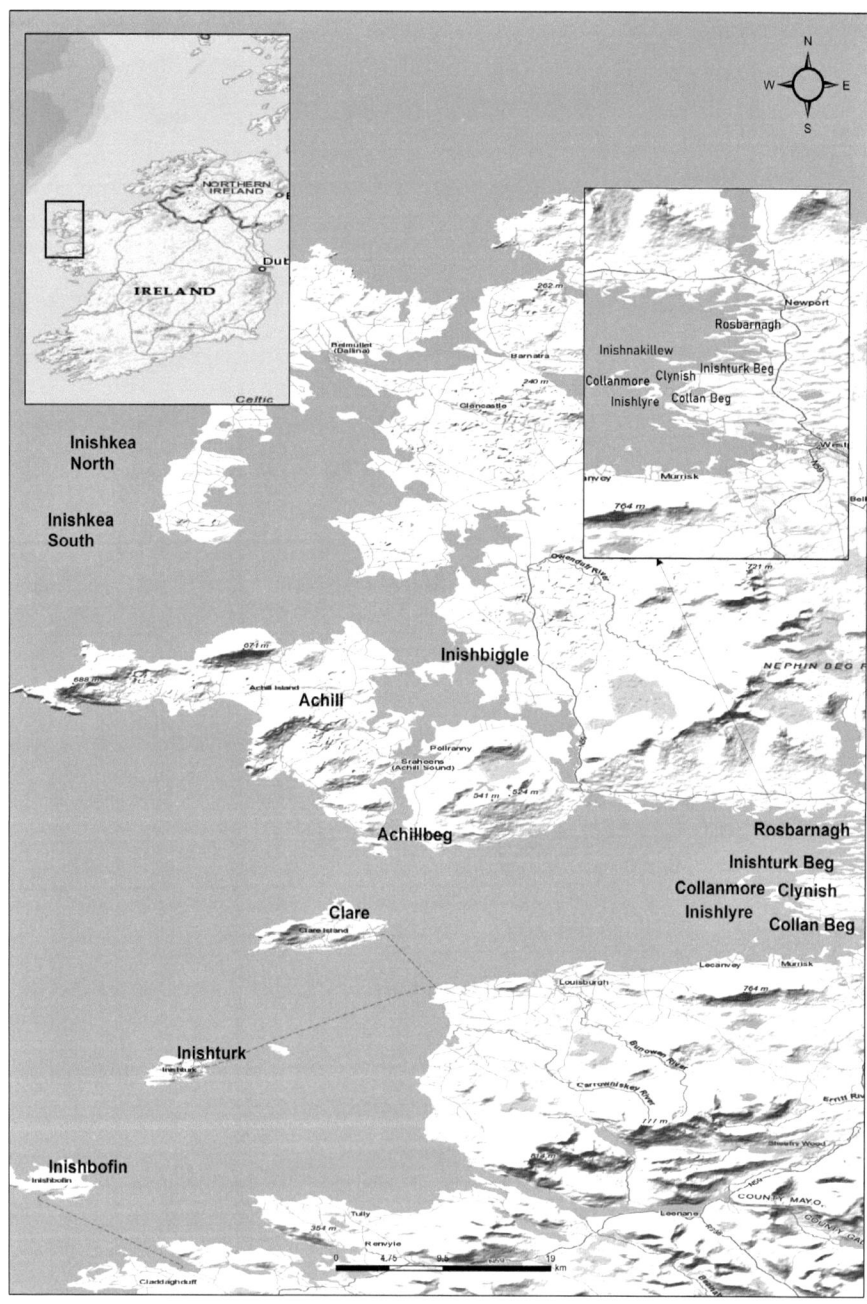

The remaining islands of County Mayo, Sligo and Donegal, Republic of Ireland – North

booked establishments only discovered each morning using the joys of web searching and taking potluck with the limited available accommodation. As in Wales earlier in the Summer 'staycationing' had swallowed up most accommodation leaving only very limited expensive hotels, unappealing B&B's and down at heel pubs, often not near our island destination so we would zig zag across west Ireland like mad dervishes to visit our island goals. The sequential planning of the previous year was thrown out and extemporising became our only option.

That first night I had booked a private house directly across the road from the only pub in a small village about twenty minutes from Enniskillen and I felt this juxtaposition of pub and accommodation was fortuitous for the rest of the trip. Upon arrival though we found the pub was closed, possibly forever. We had no other choice but to search for sustenance in a wide network of villages that eventually led us to Enniskillen via a drive-in off licence the like of which I had not experienced since visiting Australia.

John was keen that we didn't just tick islands off in the cold, frantic and cynical fashion of previous hurried visits so a little tourism was imbibed into our schedule. We crossed the border with Northern Ireland the subject of idiotic post Brexit debate where the hapless and inadequate Johnson Government had decided to create a border down the Irish Sea. This would effectively keep Northern Ireland in the EU Customs Union as the alternative was to destroy the hard-won Good Friday Agreement of 1998, re-creating a border within the island of Ireland and risking an upsurge of sectarian violence largely abated for almost a quarter of a century.

We crossed the border at the bustling town of Belcoo without a heartbeat of delay. The redundancy of my apparently obligatory Lateral Flow Covid 19 test, my Green Card to allow driving my Discovery Sport in the EU and my passport (which I had actually forgotten!) were all too evident. Before heading for **Coney Island**, we detoured to Drumcliffe churchyard beneath the towering Ben Bulben Mountain to pay respects to William

Butler Yeats amongst the more notable of the feast of Irish poets and writers and a pillar of both the Irish and English literary establishments. The day was warm, weather which lasted all our stay. Thankfully we were not to be subjected to the trials of 'choppy' water or abandoned ferry timetables.

Yeats' grave is marked with a simple headstone with the inscription, *"cast a cold eye on life, on death, horseman, pass by."* This was his self-penned epitaph together with the instructions that the grave consist of "no marble, no conventional phrase". Amongst 11 Nobel Prize winners from Ireland including Samuel Beckett, George Bernard Shaw, and Seamus Heaney for literature the Nobel committee described his work as "inspired poetry, which in a highly artistic form gives expression to the spirit of a whole nation." His poem 'the lake island of Innisfree', though not a coastal island exemplifies the start of modern Celtic poetry. It is printed in Irish passports and exemplifies the spirit of the Nation. Visiting Drumcliffe was a fitting start to the continuation of my Irish journey.

> I will arise and go now, and go to Innisfree,
> And a small cabin built there, of clay and wattles made;
> Nine bean rows will I have there, a hive for the honeybee,
> And live alone in the bee-loud glade.

In a reflective mood we headed for **Coney Island** and the low tide route across Cummeen sand. An SMS messaging service told us it was safe to cross, and we toyed with walking the kilometre or so. An enthusiastic sturdy and determined woman of a certain age was ahead of us and was picking her way through residual pools left by the fast-retreating tide. Not wanting to get our feet wet (my swollen feet would only let me fit into a size 12 CAT work boot, and I had no more shoes) discretion became the better part of valour and we opted for access in our car; after all it was 4-wheel drive, and the route was waymarked by 14 evenly spaced pillars. The foreshortening of distance beguiles the potential walker.

It was an obstacle race through shore side tidal puddles and a brave decision to drive needing careful navigation with first use of the 4WD settings after two years of driving my Land Rover Discovery Sport. Behind us was now a steady convoy of vehicles crossing the sand and crunching mussel beds without a care. On arrival we expected desertion with the census indicating only one permanent family in occupation but as with most islands off the west coast neatly trimmed and painted holiday homes had sprung up. At its mid-19th Century population peak 124 people lived on **Coney** and even today a pub remains in 'the village'. As on our many island trips up and down the west coast the small but functionally beautiful pub was shut. It felt incongruous to tour the narrow lanes by car and we made a swift retreat.

The merchant ship *Arethusa* used to sail between Sligo and New York City. Folklore has it that the captain of the ship, Peter O'Connor, observing many rabbits (the Irish for rabbit is *Coinín*) on a New York island, apparently then named Coney Island, New York, after his own **Coney Island** in Sligo Bay. I've been to Coney Island, New York with its tacky funfairs and boardwalks and still even in the late 20th century those 'freak' side shows of bearded women and deformed wretches now assigned to the dustbin of history in most civilised nations. Worlds apart does not begin to contrast the differences between the two namesake islands. Neither should the Sligo pastoral paradise be confused with the County Down 'island' of the same name made famous by Van Morrison's evocative narrative in his broad Northern Irish brogue about a lost time and bygone memories of lost love. I too reflected on lost personal memories swept away as easily as the tide:

> "I look at the side of your face as the sunlight comes
> Streaming through the window in the autumn sunshine
> And all the time going to Coney Island I'm thinking,
> Wouldn't it be great if it was like this all the time".

Following a fairly straight forward visit to **Coney** my reflections of the past were jolted into the complex logistics of securing passage to those islands in Mayo and Donegal only accessible by private boat. Looking at the Irish census for 2016 there appeared to be about 25 of these in these two counties alone. My experiences of private boat hire in Scotland suggested improbably steep prices would ensue to persuade the many local boatmen to charter their services. I was intrigued however that a fair number of these islands including Dernish (Sligo's only other offshore island) had populations of two or less. Yes, I had come across isolates living in Scottish islands and suspected that similar folk in Ireland seeking tranquillity and solace were happy to live alone.

As John attempted to secure passages from successive boatmen it became clear that the census officials had often been misled and we were met with derision from locals in the know at suggestions that certain islands were permanently inhabited. The truth is that the Garda have an obligation to visit offshore islands during census night to deliver official forms and return with them in their ballot boxes. Part time residents often using these beautiful islands for holiday homes either for themselves or commercial gain travel with the Garda, fill in the forms and return with them on completion. This ensures evidence of *permanence*. We enquired why this practice continued and were told that this was a necessity to ensure vital infrastructure on each island, especially piers and jetties, was maintained by the respective local county authorities or Gaeltacht. Infrastructure would not be maintained at public expense on islands with no permanent population.

Thus, houses visible from distant shores were quite often spic and span holiday homes interspersed with the ruins of long abandoned settlements. As I was to visit only offshore largely permanently *inhabited* islands then the following were ceremoniously ditched as part of this venture:

- Dernish (Sligo)
- Duvillaun (Mayo)
- Owey (Donegal)
- Inishirrer (Donegal)
- Eadarrinis (Donegal)
- Croaghan Island (Donegal)

Dernish Island close to Streedagh Point, overlooked from the N15 road to Donegal near Moneygold, was tantalising close. Yeats's brooding beauty of Ben Bulben watches over the island, an inescapable form. Research suggested the island could be accessed with extreme care from a spit of land (Connor's Island) leaving access of about 150 metres at low tide, but we arrived at mid tide and the 45-minute walk from Streedagh Point meant any attempt would be foolhardy.

The west coast of Ireland is notorious for the loss of ships and men fleeing from the defeated Spanish Armada. Dernish holds a dark secret, not just as yet another island where unscrupulous landlords, mostly English, evicted residents at will forcing them to emigrate and often succumbing to famine. This is one location where survivors from the remnants of the retreating Armada who had got ashore nearby were first stripped naked and robbed of all their possessions before the English arrived and murdered the remaining sailors demanding ransoms for the wealthier officers. I write this on the 20th Anniversary of the 9/11 attacks on the World Trade Center. Man's inhumanity to man through the ages is and always was a stain on so-called civilisation.

The archipelago of islands in Clew Bay between the attractive coastal towns of Westport and Newport were to prove a logistical challenge as four or five of the 365 islands were very definitely permanently inhabited, but first we tackled the 'low hanging fruit' of **Rosbarnagh** an island of similar characteristics to the offshore Clew Bay Islands but still precariously attached to the mainland by a narrow causeway in a treacherous condition. We'd missed this island during our mad dash visit to Mayo in July 2019. It was accessed via sedate country lanes south of Newport at Rosentubble and was remarkably similar in its approach as those nearby islands already secured on that July trip. John was convinced we had been before, but our trusty SatNav (now an essential tool with maps largely dispensed with) thought otherwise and a brief visit by car ensued across the causeway, on not the sort of surface a more faint-hearted visitor would have ventured. Information on this small island rising to 37 metres was elusive and remains an enigma as does the status of its solitary occupant.

I have been fortunate to travel the world to over 80 countries both for work and pleasure and witnessed the spectacular natural wonders of our planet. I have woken up to the glowing dawn of Arizona's Painted Desert with ever changing hues of colour as the sun welcomes the day transitioning from vermillion red to shades of lavender. I'd stood on Ecuador's Mount Cotapaxi, again at dawn, with the sweep of the Andes Cordillera, an almost infinite vista of peaks and valleys, bombarding my vision. I'd broken through into virgin passages in the Postojna cave system in what is now Slovenia with the crystalline sparkle of translucent stalactites never before seen.

To me the sunken drumlin seascape of Clew Bay is right up there in the premier league of nature's wonderland. They formed under melting glaciers at the end of the last ice age about 10,000 years ago. Similar to the 'basket of egg' topography of my native Yorkshire Dales these are even more majestic as rising sea levels as the ice melted left them semi drowned and seen from the air are breath taking in their form and symmetry.

We tentatively made enquiries with local boatmen as to arranging a trip to visit **Collan Beg, Collanmore, Clynish, Inishlyre** and **Inishturk Beg** and were passed from pillar to post with no positive responses, just blind alleys of enquiry or vague possibilities. This was to become a *cause celebre*. I would not give up until passage was secured. Whilst waiting for responses we set off to **Achill Island** accessed from the mainland by the Michael Davit Bridge west of Newport with a view to staying the night there and attempting access to **Achillbeg**, a small island off **Achill**'s southern tip and **Inishbiggle** to the north of the island just off the coast at Dooniver. The former required a friendly boatman and the latter a local ferryman who made on demand trips at just a few Euros per trip.

Achill is the largest of the Irish islands with a healthy population of over two and a half thousand and part of the Gaeltacht though tourism ensures that English is spoken in daily parlance. We'd booked a neat B&B, Monastery View, close to the Achill distillery, *Irish American*, a name conjured to appeal to the many American Irish who visit these parts to confront and discover their ancestry. The monastery in question in Bunnacurry, now ruined, was as elusive as its neat namesake bungalow.

This was the summer of 'staycationning' and as my visit was impromptu no bookings had been made so we had a daily ritual of deciding our day's itinerary of island hopping (or island hoping!) interspersed with trips to reconnoitre the ravaged coastline laid bare by successive Atlantic storms. There were only two types of accommodation in the very limited lists still vacant: the exclusive and obscenely expensive or the basic, cheap down at heel pub accommodation. We alternated between pricey and cheap and cheerful. Occasionally like with Monastery View 'must needs' and we were forced to frequent the clipped but 'boutique' private houses superficially glamorous but restored on tight budgets.

Scratching beneath the surface of many islands are the dark secrets of either heartless landlords or religious zealots, neither with little regard for wider humanity. Edward Nangle is notorious in the history of **Achill** when in the mid-19th Century at the height of the potato famine, which quite simple ravaged Ireland's population, he set up a Mission to feed those wretches who had fallen foul of the famine. Nangle was a Protestant in a largely Catholic community and though setting up soup kitchens he would only feed those who converted to his own form of Christianity. Those who accepted his bribe, (and in desperation who wouldn't), were known as 'soupers' a pejorative term used across Ireland to this day.

With time on our side for once John my 'logistical consultant' managed to secure the services of a boatman to **Achillbeg**. We were to meet Paddy Kilbahn at the jetty on the southernmost tip of **Achill**. Arriving well in time we were met by Paddy, a spritely 80-year-old and his son and granddaughter, Luscilla, visiting from Italy. Paddy had been born on the island and it is interesting how quickly the generations disperse spreading the diaspora far and wide. The son had lost the sea faring skills of his 'da' and slipped hip deep into the sea on the gradient of the aptly named slipway with the octogenarian to my embarrassment helping me in and out of the currach.

Paddy and three score of the remaining inhabitants had left the island in 1965 at about the time the school closed and apart from a couple of hardy residents all that is left is the abandoned village in the lee of the island. Like many Irishmen Paddy had gone to London (Cricklewood) to work as a chippy and like some had returned to live out his life in the contentment of **Achill Island**. He told first-hand stories of life on **Achillbeg** attending Sunday Mass on **Achill** by currach, and weekly crossings by some to the *George* pub to fritter away their 5 shillings (25 pence) dole money. Memories of distant times but on reflection these 'distant times' were in my own lifetime. We returned after a brief inspection of the abandoned village, a haven for kayakers and his request for a twenty Euros fee was raised by me to fifty after a scowl of incredulity by John at my meanness. The cost of experiences is priceless.

We headed north to find 'Monastery View' which had no discernible signage and, in our confusion, to locate the clipped, neat bungalow, we came across *M.P. Lynott's* pub and made a mental note to visit later that evening. The pub was enticing with a peat fire, a genuine traditional Irish pub in contrast to the roadhouse a couple of kilometres down the road, *Ted's* a tourist bacchanalia with 'Blasta' mobile cafe doing a roaring trade in cheap stodgy food.

Midges were out in force on that sultry evening and inside seating was a necessity. Phil Lynott's mother Philomena had visited to see whether there had been any connection with her son, the front man of Thin Lizzy. The bar staff were unaware of any association though some suggest the pub was owned by his uncle. Likewise, I expect there was no direct connection with John Fitzgerald Kennedy whose picture along with first lady Jackie also adorned the smoky walls of this excellent establishment, one of the most westerly bars in Europe. After JFK's visit in 1963 his portrait would have been as prominent in Irish households as Pope Paul VI.

After an unfortunate altercation with a cheap armchair in my 'boutique' suite at Monastery View costing me one hundred Euros in recompense, enforcing a trip by the landlady to Castlebar to source a replacement, we headed for **Inishbiggle**. John had arranged the previous evening a 10-minute ride by currach with the ferryman Joe O' Malley. At 10 Euros each Joe was never going to be a wealthy man though every end of August holiday thousands take over the island for the **Inishbiggle** Festival / Féile Inis Bigil. The event is a celebration of the traditional island life and focuses on the wildlife and natural beauty of **Inishbiggle** and its heritage and culture. This is Joe's pay day but sadly abandoned in recent Covid plague years. There had been long forgotten plans to build a cable car across the Bullsmouth Channel, but this was rejected quite rightly as a blight on an area of outstanding natural beauty. The journey across one of Europe's most treacherous tidal races is left to Joe O'Malley's very capable navigational skills.

The tranquil journey on a flat calm day belied this apparent danger and took us through the mist and midges at the start of one of the west coast's rarest of dawn to dusk sunny days. With a population of 18 from the 2016 census, mostly old folks who toil as fishermen and by working the flat, fertile land with hand scythes, this Irish speaking buoyant population of the mid-19th century had also suffered at the dastardly hands of the proselytising Edward Nangle. Its school lasted until 1998 and the island which traditionally looked to **Achill** for its communications now looks eastwards to Ballycroy where crossings in winter months are more benign and now boasts a pier after the ambitious attempts at an aerial crossing failed. Intriguingly vehicular access is also possible at low tides from Claggan on the mainland to the uninhabited island of Annagh. After traversing the width of the island vehicles can slice through the compacted sand to **Inishbiggle**'s eastern side. This innovative route is largely reserved for the tenacious islanders.

Thoughts now turned to the five plucky inhabited Clew Bay Islands and a boat to get us there. This was not going to be easy. Yes, there were boat trips galore cruising the exquisite bay at 30 Euros per passenger, but none were likely to manoeuvre onto and off jetties. These boats were commercial ventures dedicated to fishing trips or wildlife spotting. A trip like the one I was proposing would have to be a full personal charter at sky high prices. But this had to be done and John was awarded the task of sourcing a suitable candidate not already booked, very unlikely on this glorious flat calm weekend.

Like all small island communities in Ireland with tiny populations it is difficult to gain precision as to the permanency of occupation as even the Irish census of 2016 is not definitively authoritative. The rich and the eccentric love islands for privacy and seclusion but the novelty of this hard life and logistics of access via ever dilapidating infrastructure soon wears thin with the purchase becoming a millstone. John Lennon once owned one of the Clew Bay Islands, Dorinish, purchased in 1967. Had Lennon not been shot by Mark Chapman outside his Dakota building in New York in 1980 he planned to build a house there for him and Yoko and had hoped to revive his plans with full planning permission. In 1970 Lennon handed the island over to a commune of hippies, who made it their summer camp. After John's murder Yoko sold the island to a local farmer named Michael Gavin, who still grazes sheep there. She gave US$50,000 of the proceeds from the sale to a local orphanage.

We retired to Westport with logistics firmly in our minds. Leads were sought and channelled to other leads who promised to return our calls but never did. John deplored my huge scepticism and accused me of sucking the energy out of the afternoon even after a last-minute offer of a vessel and skipper. My cynicism was not assuaged, and I continued to pour negativity upon the whole venture coming together, taking myself off for a sleep in the marina park. Fruitless leads had set the tone of the whole hot afternoon and finding the requisite RIB or boat became a 'mission impossible' and though cutting a dash as a supporting actor in "Game of Thrones" John was no Tom Cruise.

Late that evening whilst drinking a pint or two of Guinness in Louisburgh as a desperate consolation to what seemed an aborted mission Reg phoned. We were to meet him at Rosmoney pier at 09:30 the next morning. He had had a cancellation and for two hundred and fifty Euros he would captain our trip, so long as we gained permission from the assortment of residents on the five Clew Bay inhabited islands. I lied that we would, and my desolation turned to celebration.

Weather set fair we met Reg our boatman a genial fellow, a Jack Sparrow lookalike with long flowing dreadlocks, an incongruity for an Irish seafarer. He was accompanied by his 9-month-old pup Molly secure in her doggy lifesaving vest. Reg had already secured visits for 4 of the 5 islands to be visited and we met the owner of **Collanmore** at the pier who insisted we didn't go up to his 22-bed lodge, a veritable island paradise with private bar, hot tub suitable for 9 and the perfect hideaway for a hedonistic weekend. He expressly forbade us to take photographs.

The myriad of islands was confusing, but Reg navigated effortlessly through the still waters landing briefly on the smaller **Collan Beg** which appeared uninhabited though with a sturdy, well-kept pier to service the well-kept summer home. We didn't stay long, and our adventures were already beginning. Reg, who had inherited his boat, *Lady Helen*, from his father, didn't look the sort of free spirit who would be fazed by anything, but he kept nagging me about my attempts to secure landing on **Inishturk Beg**. I dismissed this saying we only needed to step ashore. Reg made calls and became more and more anxious. "I live here", he said under a weak smile. "We shouldn't go". I became inquisitive and left my imploring until we had visited **Clynish**.

Clynish had been farmed for centuries and its present incumbents, father and son Patrick and Pádraig and his mother Helen (who stayed indoors) were hospitable and very welcoming. The island was intensively farmed and mechanised and the family hardly ventured to the mainland save for provisioning and selling and buying stock. Though Clew Bay is in the Gaeltacht the family did not speak Irish and Irish speaking is the key to obtaining vital grants from the Department of the Gaeltacht. They had no choice but to carry on without support which seemed to be a benign, social apartheid, sinister in character. Not only has the Irish Government seemingly washed its hands of **Clynish** but the 2nd edition of *Oileain: The Irish islands* guide describes the island rather unfairly as "No real attraction to the passing recreational user". Reminiscent I thought again of the entry for Earth in Douglas Adams' *Hitchhikers Guide to the Galaxy*: 'Mostly harmless', though later edited for lack of space to 'Harmless'. I liked the island and its industrious and laid-back inhabitants.

We waved goodbye from the jetty and Reg became serious, very serious. We were headed for **Inishturk Beg**. He had been advised by colleagues that under no circumstances was he to dock at the jetty. I was intrigued and nudged him to attempt a landing as I was not prepared to try again another time. Reg was not happy and gingerly pulled up to the stone jetty. As we prepared for a brief landing a pack of about 30 mongrel dogs came out of nowhere, snarling and barking at us followed by a surly brute of a man in a tracksuit cursing us in an indiscernible foreign accent. "Get off this island", he barked with the same threat as his dog pack. I implored for a brief visit and his booming voice became more menacing. Reg was eager to obey and get the hell out of a position he never wanted to be in, in the first place. I poked my walking stick at the jetty as a weak gesture of success and we sped away.

Inishturk Beg had provided me with a litany of intrigue during my planning of these island trips. It had been billed in my searches as Ireland's 'poshest island'. Between 2003 and 2013, it was owned by Nadim Sadek, an Irish-Egyptian marketing entrepreneur who transformed this deserted island into an exclusive holiday complex and cultural centre with a working farm showcasing boars, as after all the translation of **Inishturk Beg** means 'island of the wild boar'. More than this the island became a centre for whiskey distilling and fish smoking. Live Irish music gigs were organised featuring the Westport flautist Matt Malloy of The Chieftains fame.

The island is now intensely private with various rumours of occupancy and ownership whispered around Westport. Getting information on its current status and use was impossible and it can only be imagined that the island either protects exclusivity or is the centre of nefarious activities. Probing as to its status resulted in rapid changes of subject. The gruff Eastern European who ordered our swift departure was seen as the caretaker, but the caretaker of what? The locals referred to him as the 'Turk'. The Irish have a gift for ascribing nicknames. The island's name could be one of the reasons for giving this moody fellow that moniker. As we headed for our next island, **Inishlyre**, I surmised fancifully that this was the centre for gun or drug running with the Atlantic Ocean and beyond a short journey west out of the tranquillity of Clew Bay. We will never know but Reg's body language suggested that sinister activities were behind the façade of this once vibrant, exclusive tourist island.

We were met at the jetty of **Inishlyre** by the owner Joe Gibbons who lived there with his wife and another lady. I smiled at Joe and headed for the island proper to be greeted with Joe barring the way in front of a very official notice indicating that beyond was a COVID 19 exclusion area. The ladies had health problems and were therefore vulnerable to infection. It was no use pleading to go further as protecting his kith and kin were paramount.

Joe was the postman for the Clew Bay Islands, so I took the opportunity to ask further about **Inishturk Beg**. He quickly mentioned that although only 5 islands were occupied or partially occupied that my mystery island was not included on his rounds. My, by now ever more convincing, theory of a Russian drug running Mafia cartel owning the island was taking imaginary shape. Joe changed the subject and was interested in my island escapades as his partner Rhonda Twombly is secretary of the 'European Small Island Federation' (ESIN), whose vice chair was from the Inner Hebridean island of **Eigg** and chair from **Bere Island** County Cork.

ESIN is the voice of 359,357 islanders on 1,640 small islands, helping them remain alive and strengthening the islands' cultural identities. Representation by country is given below:

Country	Number of islands	Approximate population
Croatia	48	122,418
Denmark	27	5,300
Estonia	16	47,000
Finland and Aland	431/55	8,700/30,000
France	15	15,000
Greece	29	65,000
Ireland	33	3,000
Italy	29	18,000
Scotland	89	100,000
Sweden	576	32,000

Larger islands of these countries are not always represented but the Irish island list (down to a mere 33) appears to have the lowest average per capita population indicating just how fragile island living is on the west Atlantic seaboard. Ireland's representation is through Comhdhail Oileain nah Eireann (Irish Islands Federation).

We bade farewell and headed for the last island of our Clew Bay tour, **Collanmore**. The well-appointed lodge on this island which we were not to photograph seemed to be the way forward for near shore islands with **Collanmore** not being anything like as ambitious a project as that originally developed on **Inishturk Beg**. Opulently modest I thought, with the accoutrements for an ideal private getaway at affordable prices with vinyl wall prints in the bar replicating the interior of Matt Molloy's pub in Westport. The trip had been successful, maybe not as planned but an insight into very contrasting lifestyles of the few islands still inhabited amongst the 365 of Clew Bay. Paddy, Joe and Reg had uncertain futures with island life ever eroded by the march of modernity, but their present lives were without doubt rewarding as custodians of a bygone age.

We'd booked the early afternoon boat to **Inishturk** (not to be confused with the nightmare island of the same name we'd attempted to visit the day before). The larger island some distance from Roonah pier, set firmly in the Atlantic Ocean contrasted abruptly with its much smaller namesake. One is efficient, informal and tourist friendly; the other mysterious, threatening and enigmatic.

We'd had to stay in Castlebar in a no-frills B&B, Carragh House, with identical but adequately functional rooms, close to what passes for a lively Saturday evening night life in those parts. We idled away our time between a noisy GAA sports bar, a fancy but mediocre restaurant which I insisted eating in, finishing up in John W Hale's, a delightful cool little traditional bar near our digs.

Our route to the Roonagh pier ferry the next morning took us through Cong the setting for John Ford's Oscar winning 1952 film *The Quiet Man* starring John Wayne and Maureen O'Hara. John knows every scene by heart and he and his dad would watch together with their own reminiscences of the homecomings of many an emigre Irishman to these quiet corners of the Emerald Isle.

We whiled away time at Louisburgh's Community Bookshop *'Books at One'* before boarding the lengthy ferry ride to **Inishturk** some 15km offshore. The ferry has only been a commercial venture since 1997. **Inishturk** gained international attention in 2016 after a number of websites claimed that the island would welcome any American "refugees" fleeing a potential Donald Trump presidency. No inward immigration was ever noticed following Trump's election!

The sparse ferry clientele heading from the pier dispersed across the tracks circling the island and we had four hours to enjoy the perfect peace of the place. We chose to head up the steep hill to the community centre pub/restaurant and while away our time overlooking the ocean, the strenuous walk on my tired arthritic legs worth every step of the effort. We soaked up the great view, good food, good beer and good atmosphere. In contrast to its neighbour, **Clare Island**, visited in July 2019, facilities on **Inishturk** were sparse which added to its charm boasting, with 3 pupils the smallest school in Ireland. The history of the island is poorly documented but follows the usual tragic trajectory of population depletion because of famine, eviction or voluntary emigration.

With most of Mayo's islands complete we headed for County Galway, not to salvage the remaining islands there left unvisited in previous trips but to return to **Inishbofin** to meet with John Daye and begin the reconnaissance of the work to be funded by Galway County and the Office of Public Works. The ferry from Cleggan was crammed with late summer tourists. On arrival it was evident that, though the sea will always win the battle against man's attempt to stem the steady onslaught of coastal erosion, there is an immediate need to shore up the battered coastal protection to allow unfettered access for tourists to coastal cycle routes, accommodation and sheltered beaches. The eastern beach in particular would soon be wholly depleted if the jetty/breakwater, almost completely shattered, was allowed to be abandoned. John and his team were fighting a losing but valiant battle to maintain the coastal defences and retain the tourist foothold on this fine island. What the great famine and unscrupulous landlords started in the nineteenth century nature will complete giving Ireland's islands back to nature.

Strategies discussed and photographs taken we headed north for the Mullet peninsular to attempt to get a boat to **Inishkea South and North**. John managed to source a willing boatman leaving from Blacksod pier at the very tip of the peninsular with a gruelling couple of hours or more of driving from our overnight digs. Approaching the Mullet, the wildness of the west coast moderated with much flatter land with wide perspectives across the peat bogs.

We met Micheal Keane owner of Blacksod Bay Sea Safaris. He pulled out the stops for us and it was he who confirmed that the 2016 census of permanency was not to be believed. Irish Ordnance 1:50,000 scale maps show large numbers of buildings on both **Inishkea South** and **Inishkea North**, but we were told these were abandoned with just a smattering of renovations for recent, lucrative holiday cottage businesses. Striking them off the list was an option, but the charm and spirit of the island visits would be diluted without a trip. We were later told that only two islands were now permanently inhabited in Donegal's west coast – **Tory Island** and **Arranmore**.

We were accompanied by Jed whose family had lived on **Inishkea South** and his daughters were now via the internet enticing small groups of people to enjoy the desolation on an island with zero amenities with all provisions meticulously prepared and transported for the duration of their stays. Our 40-minute trip was enriched by first-hand accounts of better times on **Inishkea South** which actually wasn't on the 2016 census unlike its northern neighbour. As access by our fishing boat was not possible to the northern twin transfer to a smaller boat had been arranged which was towed triumphantly behind us.

An *Irish Times* article in May 2022 suggested the **North and South Inishkea Islands** are 'the Nirvana' of north Mayo experiences and lauded the two islands as the remotest in Ireland. The author got it spot on with the journey out on a breathless summer afternoon within sight of the north of **Achill Island.**

We disembarked onto one of the fabled piers maintained to support the 'permanent' population and were entranced by another world of several dozen cottages in various stages of decay and dishevelment. The former village backed onto the sort of beach that would not be out of keeping in the Caribbean and the clear azure blue water on that glorious day contrasted with but complemented the golden deserted beach. Missing out on this trip because of some rigid technicality of population permanence would have been a travesty. Amongst the dereliction is a midden of shells left behind by an ancient monastic industry, extracting valuable purple dye from the shells of dog whelks. Inishkea dye travelled as far as Constantinople. Maybe it swathed a Byzantine king.

The demise of the village was tragic to say the least. It is possible that the remoteness of the islands somehow preserved some form of pre-

Christian Celtic religion. In the early 1900s the islands were populated with more than 350 people, most of whom were probably monolingual Irish speakers, but the inhabitants completely left the islands in 1939 after most of their young men died at sea in a storm. On 26th October 1927, ten young men whilst out fishing were drowned after being tricked into thinking that they were safe in the lull of the storm only to be struck by powerful westerly's. The heart had been ripped out of this fragile community and settlement on the Mullet peninsular swiftly followed. The last survivor of this tragedy Pat Reilly died age 101 in 2018. To this day there is an island melancholy within the re-settled communities into what is now the third generation since the catastrophe. The islands which once sustained so many people are now still visible but forlorn shells of their former self.

Though **North and South Inishkea** are but a short boat journey apart there was always intense rivalry between them. **North Inishkea** was the island of law and order with coastguards stationed there and even three policemen at the height of the population growth to attempt to control illegal distilling and piracy. This came to a head during the Irish Civil War of 1922/23 when the North were Pro-treaty and the South staunch republicans. At one point the two sides stood either side of the 100-metre channel separating the two islands hurling missiles at each other.

Meanwhile our hosts had met two guys known to them who had travelled over on a RIB. They had surmised that my physical condition would have meant a difficult transfer to our accompanying smaller boat. We were transported from North island to the South island in this rather speedier vessel than our outboard boat and spent an hour or so ambling through the dunes and machair (the grassy fringe above the beach) now smothering whatever life was left out of the once proud village. These treasured and tranquil moments have no parallel with the mind engaged wholly with the majesty of nature's wonderland. White beaches, cobalt skies, balmy temperatures of the clean, clear sea water, the warmth of the gneiss rocks we sat on above the silver-grey pebbles, and above all the beautiful desolation; it was quite literally a desert island.

I woke out of a reverie with a start. The RIB was waiting and a couple enjoying the isolation pushed and prodded me back onto it; wading or paddling out to the vessel to power off from an island which no sane person would want to escape, on a day like the day of our visit. Transfer to our mother boat over we enjoyed a smooth return to Blacksod Pier. Money is an inappropriate numeraire to measure the enjoyment and fulfilment trips such as these give.

Donegal beckoned, Ulster but within the Irish Republic. The most northern county of the Republic but located in the 'south' as xenophobic Brits like to refer to Eire. It is not 'the south' of anywhere just as the fabricated 'Northern Ireland' is not 'the north'. The border was a convenient divide during the partition of the island of Ireland as it suited the Protestant majority and the British. Just like the partition of India and Pakistan this divide on religious grounds was to create mayhem and bloodshed on a scale unimagined by the legislators. In Ireland between 1969 and 2001 in what were in crass understatement the years known as 'The Troubles' some 3,500 or more people were killed by military and paramilitary groups. This was a fraction of those killed during the partition of India but within our islands and in our lifetimes.

Donegal is stunning in its beautiful isolation with beaches as wide and glistening as anywhere in the Caribbean or south Pacific. I'd touched the county briefly in 1989 but never explored. Arran Island (or **Arranmore** so as not to confuse with the 3 Aran Islands in Galway Bay) was our first island reached by a regular car ferry from Burtonport. In fact, with a permanent population of around 450 there were two commercial ferries plying their trade hourly to cater for tourists and residents alike. The short journey took us through Rutland Sound with **Rutland** Island to port and Edenish and Inishcoo to starboard. **Rutland** and Edenish were on the 2016 census and scattered with upmarket residences but despite the benign shelter afforded by **Arranmore Island** itself with easy access to Burtonport no truly permanent islanders resided on these pretty onshore islands. It is estimated that two thirds of **Arranmore**'s population speak Ulster Irish which has more in common with Gaelic and Manx than Irish spoken in the rest of the Gaeltacht. Even the two ferries were inherited from Scottish operator Caledonian MacBrayne.

The island is twinned with Beaver Island, an island in northern Lake Michigan where a large number of former residents gathered after being evicted from **Arranmore** in the 19th Century to escape the horrors of famine and eviction. Most famine stories are heartrending. When walking past Liverpool Docks during my round Great Britain walk, I spotted an insignificant plaque on the dock wall above eye level written in Irish and English, almost forgotten amongst the present dereliction. It read:

> "Between the years 1845 to 1852, 1.3 million Irish migrants strode through these gates: Remember the Great Famine".

At the height of the famine **Arranmore** was taken over by a Walter Chorley who ordered all his subtenants to leave the island by 1st March 1848. He marched them to Donegal town and those surviving he put on a ship to USA. Those remaining tenants fared no better as he deprived them of any opportunities to farm or profit from the kelp industry whilst also building himself the usual stylish mansion beloved of self-entitled despots.

In stark contrast we modern day tourists devoured cream scones back in the harbour café before making our way to **Cruit** (pronounced krich) island accessed by road at Kincaslough. We drove the leisurely half dozen miles to the golf course, not that we had any interest in golf, as the road gave us unbridled access to an ecstatic beach deserted other than by a German family making most of the bright afternoon sunshine. This was another 'experience' moment that money cannot buy. I sat on the sand looking out to Owey Island another precious island now deserted except for the summer holiday makers who want solitude over comfort.

We'd booked an afternoon private 'on-off' trip to **Rutland Island** from Burtonport and had time to consider **Gola** which was reputed to have a summer ferry service from Derrybeg pier. Both islands were on the

2016 census, but local knowledge yet again derided the accuracy of these Government 'statistics'. The burgeoning and lucrative holiday let business was ensuring Gaeltacht or other such funding could be assured to keep the landing stages viable. These often-ancient items of vital infrastructure in various states of disrepair from the relentless force of the Atlantic storms were the key to holiday maker access. Irrespective of their permanency status we opted for visits to each.

We arrived at Derrybeg pier after several false attempts to find it with directions muttered that it was right off the main coast road past the GAA. Now the Gaelic Athletic Associations sports grounds are as important to the Irish as their Catholic churches, even more so with secularism rapidly becoming the accepted 'faith'. The sexual scandals of juvenile abuse by priests were still raw. Ireland was the first country ever to legalise same sex marriage and times were changing with the Jesuit Brothers and other Catholic orders no longer holding sway and control over the younger generations. My Irish contemporary friends, including John, lived in fear of their brutal disciplinary tactics to cow their charges into total submission. On the other hand, Gaelic football was the new religion and driving through Mayo virtually every house in the countryside was adorned with the county's team flag. I believe they had just qualified for the all-Ireland 2021 final at the hallowed turf of Dublin's Croke Park. (They lost to Tyrone).

Despite our navigational ineptitude we arrived at the jetty comfortably making the eleven o'clock ferry courtesy (well at a reasonable price) of Michael Curran in his Aquastar fisherman boat joining a number of day trippers. Also on the boat was local artist Fran O'Boyle originally from Lancashire but Irish speaking and with a penchant for Donegal landscapes and who could blame him with its exquisite changes of light and shade and seasonal moods. His latest project was a mural on a house wall on the island. This attractive island largely sheltered in the Gweedore Bay 'see saws' between permanent occupancy and summer holiday lets but the latter are winning the balance. Even at its population zenith of 165 in 1861 **Gola** had no church.

Gola is immortalised for altogether more sinister reasons. Two **Gola** men were in the crew of the *Asgard* the gun running yacht that armed the Irish Volunteers in 1914 under Erskine Childers' command. These clandestine sorties led the way two years later to the Easter uprising leading to the creation of the Irish Free State and the ultimate sacrifice for the English born Childers.

We stayed a while on the island until our rendezvous with our boatman, Jim Muldowney, to **Rutland** who was making a quick 50 Euros having spent the morning fulfilling his stock-in trade, wildlife trips around the uninhabited islands of Gweedore Bay. The late 18th Century saw lucrative herring catches off The Rosses area of Donegal and **Rutland** Island was transformed by Lord Burton Conyngham a Member of Parliament (the British Parliament don't forget in those days) into a town of 'hundreds of people' with a vibrant fish processing industry. His labour was recruited from English speaking outsiders who replaced the Irish Catholic Ulster Plantationists. Burtonport is of course named after him. Natural resources can be fickle and by 1793 the fishery had all but failed with rapid depopulation.

We headed for the remote northwest corner of Donegal, a day ahead of schedule, booking into the very passable *Teach Jack* hotel (or Jack's house) and whiled away time at the mysterious Bloody Foreland evocative to me as a child of remoteness at the end of the world. Cnoc Fola, or 'The Hill of Blood' suggests that this was the site of some ancient Celtic battle. However Bloody Foreland takes its name from the way in which the setting sun enhances the natural red of the granite cliffs. Donegal's highest mountain Errigal dominated our journey with its conical peak and jagged quartzite edges. To John it was evocative of the Lonely Mountain from Peter Jackson's Hobbit films. It captivated our attention and shone out against the other rock scenery.

We found a deserted track and enjoyed the late afternoon moody view to **Tory Island**, the next day's goal and again a place I had wanted to visit since childhood. We were pleased as we had driven along the Wild Atlantic

Way all the way from Galway and the next day would be the end of this iconic route wending its way around coastal crenulations for 1,600 miles from Kinsale, County Cork to the Inishowen Peninsula just shy of Derry or Londonderry (depending on your religious and or national affiliation). It is reputed to be the longest defined coastal route in the world, but this could just be the Irish Tourist Board being imaginative.

Teach Jack was zealously upholding Covid passport verifications with strict table service policy. This amused me as there had been on our two-week journey in late August/early September 2021 three responses to the extraction of my NHS Covid certificate from my wallet (now a ragged scrap of paper). "No, it's fine, in you come", or on presentation a total indifference to its content, or finally, an acknowledgment but without any ID check as to whether I was the true owner. The England World Cup qualifier versus Hungary was on the bar TV but gleaned little interest from the Irish drinkers with England beating Hungary 4 nil. We drank our Guiness quietly; we were becoming punch drunk with our island visits.

In October 2021 it had been two years since the Conservative party conference and the self-styled 'King of the World' otherwise known as Alexander Boris de Pfeffel Johnson, UK's post Brexit glorious leader, wanted to cement his standing with the party faithful in Manchester. His mendacity, bluster and disregard for any democratic rule of law had been backed up by his handpicked cabinet minister sycophants fawning to uphold the 80 or so majority won or rather stolen at the December 2019 General Election. The pandemic had been appallingly managed as an exercise in issuing emergency contracts for PPE and the like to Party donors rather than with a consideration of the Nation's health. As recovery began shortages of food and fuel were further exposing the inadequacies of his shambolic Government as a result largely of EU drivers returning to Poland, Romania, Lithuania or wherever.

Why am I mentioning this in the midst of writing about Ireland's island charm and legacy? Johnson's Tory party derives its name from the Middle

Irish word *tóraidhe*, meaning bandit or outlaw. During the exclusion crisis of 1679 to 1681 the opposition to the Conservative party, the Whigs, akin to the 20th Century Liberal party, used the word Tory as a pejorative term as the 'Tories' were against the exclusion bill barring Charles II's brother James from succession to the British throne. The name has stuck ever since though there is conjecture as to whether the root of **Tory Island's** meaning is from tóraidhe or from toraigh meaning island 'abounding in towers'. I could find no real evidence that through history this isolated island 12 kilometres offshore of mainland Ireland was associated with bandits. Nevertheless, the current **Tory** party in the UK Government seems to deserve the derived name but that association is a slur on the good folk of **Tory Island** today!

As with **Piel Island** off the coast of Barrow-in-Furness or **Bardsey** Island off the Llyn peninsular in Wales **Tory Island** has its own king, though unlike Johnson, elected by consensus. The last king until his death in 2018 was Patsy Dan Rodgers (Patsaí Dan Mac Ruaidhrí) whose role was neither formal nor despotic but largely for the promotion of much needed tourism.

The daily ferry service all year-round leaves from Meenlaragh but, before taking a midday ferry, we arranged to sneak over to **Inishbofin**, another 'island of the white cow' but smaller and far less populace than its namesake in Galway we had visited earlier in this trip. We discovered that Harry Coll's boat, *Saoirse the Mara II* (Freedom of the Sea) had started up a regular summer months ferry service for a return trip of 10 Euros. We didn't have much time on the island though Harry's co-pilot guided us ashore to have obligatory selfies in front of a symbolic object proving our undisputed access to the island.

The Tory ferry was very much a community ferry with islanders greeting each other or waving goodbye as they either left or were returning to 'Ireland' as they referred to the mainland. Tourists were part of the melee but were taking second place to those with a genuine necessity to take the ferry. The main settlements are either side of the pier at West town and East town and a walk between the two was like an intrusion into a community content with its lot at the edge of, or even beyond, the civilised world. The hotel in East town was clipped and urbane though the community hub in West town was an oasis of tranquillity and reflection for walkers, like on many of the islands we had visited, having completed the island's walks.

We were coming to the end of our Donegal island escapades and were headed for the last three or four in Lough Swilly, Broadwater and Mulroy Bay, not exactly coastal but definitely tidal. En route we made an obligatory stop at Malin Head the most northern point of the island of Ireland and on good days with views to Kintyre and **Islay** in Scotland. Before political divides strictured the world as we know it today, geography was the only boundary known to sea farers. There was no Scotland, no Ireland, especially no Northern Ireland. Trade, fishing, exploration and sadly enmity were with those neighbouring lands that could be safely visited or explored for glory and expansion with risk taking not for the faint hearted.

I stood and looked at the menacing wild Atlantic in a stiff late afternoon breeze before heading for the dubious comfort of the *Lennon Lodge* pub in Rathmelton on the sheltered shore of Lough Swilly.

The *Lennon Lodge* was the 'fag end' of the accommodation spectrum, utilitarian rather than comfortable and we settled down to a Guinness with the sort of male age profile expected in this sort of pub. We were joined by a partially sighted guy whose mysterious credentials suggested he was part of the *Moody Blues* band or wider entourage of the 1960's but he would go no further. The clientele referred to him as rock and roll Gerry. Clearly then in his very late 70's and partially blind his rolling lilt was suggestive of a history of adopting mind altering substances.

By absolute coincidence we had rocked up at the very town where one of John's school friends, Colin now lived and he joined us for an interesting evening retiring to a lively pub, *Conway's Bar,* brimming with a bevy of scantily clad young girls fresh from their exam results reminding us of just how stunningly attractive Irish 'colleens' are: think Andrea, Caroline and Sharon of 'The Corrs'. The contrast with *Lennon's Lodge* couldn't have been greater.

The next morning, we set off first for **Roy Island**, a low lying and gravel-based eminence of 100 acres accessed by causeway. It is a bucolic setting with lush green pasture abutting rocky shores with an abundant growth of seaweed. This was definitely not like the wild land and seascapes of islands off the 'Wild Atlantic' but with breath-taking views of Rossapenna's sand-dunes, the surrounding Mulroy coastline and the Donegal hills. Easy pickings I smugly muttered as we left the well-maintained causeway for the tiny **Croaghan Island** a few metres off the coast of Broadwater. This innocuous looking island south of Kindrum is located within the maze of tidal waters but many miles from the sea and Broadwater's only 'inhabited' island.

I'd downloaded a photograph of the island during my lockdown preparations for the trip and it looked as though a causeway connected this pimple of an island to the mainland. We arrived via the R267 high above the island and made for the steep descent to sea level meeting a local farmer on our way who suggested yet again that the census was inaccurate, and the only occasional visitor was the owner from Northern Ireland, who seldom visited with only a solitary shack for shelter.

I wasn't put off and persuaded John we should explore the access. Discretion should have been the better part of valour, but my enthusiasm won over John's rightful scepticism. The causeway was dangerous to say the least and it was only accessed via a jagged rock promontory. My days of scampering across such terrain were long gone and John pleaded with me to think about my folly. As expected, I lost my footing and crashed onto the unforgiving rocks, feeling sure I had inflicted serious injury on myself. I lay in a trance unable to move and but for John's shovels of hands (inherited from his father) there I would have remained in arthritic paralysis.

Licking my wounds, we eventually arrived safely back at the car and headed back to Rathmelton and the penultimate island of the trip, **Aughnish** accessed by farm track across private land off the shore of Lough Swilly. Like **Roy**, **Aughnish** was mainly farmland and secluded with privacy notices giving little welcome to itinerant travellers, so we didn't stay long, just ticked another island off the list like in an I-Spy book of 'whatever' so popular when I was a boy. We returned to Rathmelton and had a farewell coffee with Colin before setting off for our final island of our two-week ramble.

Inch Island also in Lough Swilly was the final prize and easily accessed by an asphalt road crossing a dam from the mainland. The island is noted for its migratory birds. Its population of a healthy 450 or so is dispersed with no village or focal point like a public house, surely unique in Ireland where the focus of rural social life has always been the pub. We drove around the island which offered little of great interest and a terrain reminiscent of the East Anglian coastal belt with quiet lanes, hidden cottages, salt marshes and gluey grey silt estuaries known as 'glar'.

Satisfied with our circumnavigation of **Inch**, demob happy and with time to spare we headed again for the island of Ireland's most northerly point, Malin Head. It was bitterly cold for early September and the view to the Mull of Kyntyre and **Islay** in Scotland was indistinct. Shivering, we didn't stay long, and we were cold and exhausted as we drove the short distance across the border back to the UK. We spent our Saturday night in the flesh pots of Derry within the walled city pubs packed with post pandemic revellers. I'd never been to Derry with the Bloody Sunday massacre of 30th January 1972 in the Bogside my only reference point to this historic city. I'm glad my first and perhaps final memories of the city were the carnage associated with Saturday night drinking not the shots inflicted on 26 unarmed civilians by the British army.

Before leaving our 'boutique' city centre apartment I gave a witheringly scathing review of the newly appointed accommodation with serious 'snagging' issues. As I left the building a burly guy in army fatigues, who I thought was the concierge, verbally accosted me in his frighteningly booming Derry accent and asked if I was John Chatterton. I replied to the affirmative and he challenged me about my review. He turned out to be the owner. I was speechless and tried to back track with pathetic excuses and in my best interests agreed to take down the post. Fear and loathing in Derry! Danger averted we took the Antrim coast road to Belfast and finally got into the *Crown* on Great Victoria Street after making a Covid booking. The journey had gone full circle.

34. The Channel Islands: UK Crown Dependencies

Another winter passed with Atlantic storms mercilessly beating the coasts and islands of the British Isles. The nation was restless to escape COVID 19 which, transmuting to the Omicron variant, had become a fact of life with mass vaccination preventing serious illness. We were living with it. The world was getting more Orwellian, and the Johnson Government mired in unremitting scandal which they weather ignobly like school bullies. The Metropolitan police had proven evidence that Downing Street had broken their own isolation rules time and time again. Johnson and his chancellor Rishi Sunak were fined but resignations were laughed off with the same disdain exhibited by 'Partygate'. They were above the law but beneath contempt. Dead cat strategies like deporting channel crossing refugees to Rwanda for processing would give the greasy piglet Prime Minister currency amongst his ardent Brexiteer fan base and detract from his criminal record.

Things could get worse and worse they got with Vladimir Putin invading and pummelling Ukraine in a misguided attempt to give pay back for apparent but unsubstantiated atrocities by right-wing factions like the Azov battalion on the Russian speakers of the Donbas region of Eastern Ukraine. Putin couldn't back down against the valiant resistance of a well drilled Ukrainian army and destroyed whole cities with heavy artillery, especially Mariupol whose capture would create a land bridge for Russia between Crimea and the Donbas.

It was against this bleak backdrop that I planned a trip to the 8 Channel Islands of **Jersey, Guernsey, Herm, Jethou, Alderney, Sark, Brecqouu** and **Lihou. Jethou** and **Brecqhou** might prove tricky as both were leased from the States of **Guernsey** as private islands. **Lihou** is a tidal island, and the rest are served by commercial boats and planes.

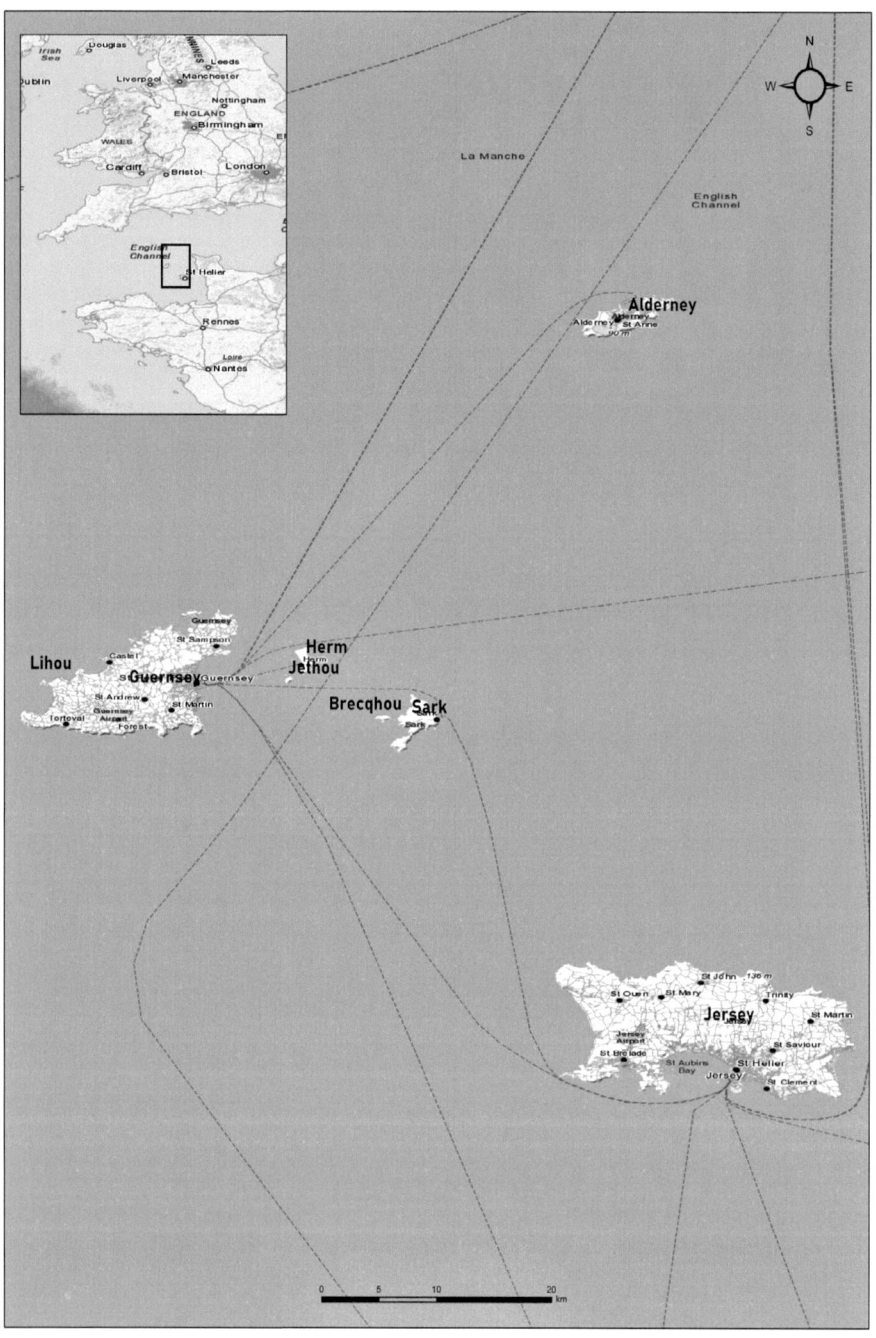

The Channel Islands: UK Crown dependencies

Steve was to join me from California, and we booked a base in *Fleur du Jardin*, a rural idyll of a hotel in the middle of **Guernsey** as inter island services were scheduled from nearby St Peter Port a five- or six-mile taxi journey away. The staff, mainly guys from the Philippines, were charm personified though we could only believe that with no UK minimum wages to adhere to and beyond EU regulations that these poor guys were subject to exploitation, far from home but able to secrete funds beyond their wildest dreams to send to their families.

Steve is an excellent companion who had accompanied me on my final Scottish island adventure but unlike me is agile and athletic. He was on his way to Syria on holiday! Dark tourism was Steve's bag with many trips to places off most travellers' wish lists. He is particularly fond of anywhere ending in 'stan' with the ex-soviet regimes high on his travel agenda. He was looking forward to touring Aleppo, Homs and Damascus and what is left of the ancient Semitic city of Palmyra's archaeology mostly destroyed by ISIS, now expelled via Putin's interventions and no doubt hiding in desert bolt holes to emerge from their own ashes of self-destruction.

Our first (after **Guernsey**) visit was to **Herm** and nearby **Jethou**. I had written to the estate manager Bill Bayley requesting permission to visit Sir Peter Ogden's island expecting to be rebuffed but received a welcoming response and a ringing endorsement from Sir Peter. He is one of the founders of Computacentre one of the UK's largest computer businesses but more importantly a well-known philanthropist with the Ogden trust supporting a wide range of scientific start-ups.

Bill arranged to meet us on **Herm** and right on cue docked in his amphibious RIB, whisking us off to the seclusion of his domain, niftily leaving the water and driving up the slipway to park in a garage. This was a smaller version of Bear Gryll's boat allowing him unfettered access to his island home at **St Tudwal's West** which I had attempted to visit the previous summer.

We were briefed on a clockwise route around the island on neat paths created to give ease of access to his grouse shooting guests on this 18-hectare island. Like much of the 'wetlands' around **Guernsey** and its sister islands **Jethou** is a Ramsar convention site (meaning of international importance providing habitat for waterfowl). It is ironic how on the one hand one species of bird is unceremoniously shot whilst another species protected under international treaty.

The island has had an eclectic range of leasees/owners with a legacy of smuggling and piracy. From 1920 to 1933 **Jethou** and neighbouring **Herm** were leased to Sir Compton Mackenzie, author and island lover, famous for his novel *Whisky Galore*, and also one time resident in **Barra** in the Outer Hebrides. Sir Peter is reconstructing a pub for his guests to replace the original, *Admiral Restald*, once open to the public and notorious for illicit drinking sessions when drinking laws were strict. Sir Peter certainly seems to have a sense of humour as he has preserved a 1940's red phone box with buttons A and B replete with "keep your calls short as there is a war on" and inserted calling cards for 'Sexy Sarah' and 'Busty Brunette' – discretion guaranteed!

Island circumnavigation over we were whisked back to **Herm** by dory courtesy of Giles an intern responsible for ferrying Sir Peter's workforce to and from St Peter Port each day. These days my gait is poor and falling on the Rosaire steps whilst attempting to land I licked my wounds and pride to walk the seven or so minutes to the 'village' and the safety of the *Ship Inn* and its Thatcher's Haze cider, a real thirst quencher on an unseasonal warm spring day.

Herm unlike its commercially overblown neighbour **Sark** is tranquil and unspoilt with quiet, trafficless unmade roads leading to exquisite beaches within a twenty-minute walk, notably Shell Beach. We elected to travel from St Peter Port by the shiny new 'Isle of Herm' ferry which was remarkably empty just before the Easter holidays. The more popular Trident tour boat is £3 cheaper and preferred by families with not insignificant savings for them. As a colleague with 3 children once said to me 'A penny bun costs 5 pence'. Such first and second-class rivalry alluded Steve and I when, on waiting to board the ferry back to **Guernsey**, the shout 'Isle of Herm' fell on our deaf ears. We were here already we joked. None of the hundred or so other waiting passengers stirred until we realised that they were waiting for the Trident ferry. Our mistake corrected we boarded 'first class' and made the 20-minute crossing in virtual isolation.

It had been 40 years or so since I last visited **Guernsey**. Chris my second wife had a sister, Rose, who worked there in some sort of hospitality endeavour, and we had visited her. I remember little of the trip or the island and probably spent most of my time in an alcoholic stupor, reminiscent of a similar trip we had to the **Isle of Man** at the same time. However, I recall being apprehended at customs and interrogated for what seemed hours. We were long haired and strangely dressed (all Afghan coats and leather) and had, for some inexplicable reason, been mistaken for members of the Baader Meinhof gang, anti-fascist terrorists prominent in Europe at the time. We didn't even speak German. Indeed, a spaniel had been elected to sniff me out for drugs at the airport this trip. I was told that to relieve boredom the dog handlers play drug snooker, so a red clothed suspect has to be followed by a yellow, then a green clad suspect etc.

Drug running seems to be an occupational hazard in the Channel Islands. One of our 'go to' taxi drivers, an ex-detective, one time assigned to **Sark**, (though why they needed a detective on this close-knit island where everyone knows each other is anyone's guess), fell on hard times. He contacted known villains to become a gamekeeper turned poacher, keen on making money out of drug smuggling. This seemed a futile and desperate attempt at making a quick buck as, as you might expect, he was 'grassed' by his nefarious contacts who knew him in his previous occupation. He regaled us of his four or so years in a **Guernsey** jail the victim of cons with grudges. This wiry old guy, then 79, insisted he fought his way out of many a charged confrontation and lived to tell the tale. We were suspicious of his fanciful tales, but these were confirmed by another taxi driver. Small islands are, as I have discovered many times, no places to keep dark secrets.

As all prospective citizens applying for 'Leave to Remain' in the United Kingdom appreciate, in preparation for their 'Life in the UK' obligatory examination, the Channel Islands are Crown Dependencies, a rather useless piece of civic knowledge of which only ardent British born constitutionalists are aware. To all intents and purposes, the Channel Islands are British, but they are not.

Furthermore, the scholars mastering this hapless test know that a Crown Dependency is not to be confused with Crown Protectorates. The latter are the rump of the British Empire that is those not having gained independence from their historic masters. These are a motley crew of about 14 territories across the globe. They include Pitcairn Islands in the Pacific Ocean occupied by descendants of Fletcher Christian and his 'Mutiny on the Bounty', and Montserrat in the Caribbean or the better-known Falkland Islands. Crown Dependencies are **Jersey**, **Guernsey** (and its adjacent islands including **Alderney**, the nearest of the Channel Islands to France (a mere 7 miles away) and the **Isle of Man**. They are not in the UK, but the British monarch is Head of State, and they share only foreign policy with the UK, having separate parliamentary legislations.

The two Balliwicks (each headed by a bailiff) of **Guernsey** and **Jersey** are separate administrative entities. Though quaint islands reminiscent of a bygone era in England before motorways and by-passes throttled William Blake's 'green and pleasant land' their main claim to fame is as tax havens for the rich and offshore financial centres away from British financial regulations. They are a European version of the Cayman Islands, another Crown Protectorate, where blatant tax avoiders store their tax-free wealth.

On a more sinister note, the Channel Islands were the only parts of the British Isles to be occupied by the Nazis during the Second World War and the last parts of Europe to be liberated. The occupation museum close to **Guernsey** airport is a chilling reminder of the horrors of Hitler's atrocities. Concrete fortresses and lookouts adorn the coastline for German strategic advantage between the five years of occupation (1940 to 1945). Nazi memorabilia banned almost everywhere else in Europe is on display in the museum as a reminder of the dark days for all the islanders. Those native to the islands not evacuated endured unimaginable deprivation whilst those not native were summarily deported to camps in Germany. The 2018 film *The Guernsey Literary and Potato Peel Pie Society* starring Lily James rather romanticises the horrors of occupation.

Towards the end of our stay, we hired a car and toured the quaint highways and byways where it is legal to mount the pavement to avoid oncoming traffic and stop signs are non-existent with instructions to filter at junctions. Although the islands represent the last remnants of the Duchy of Normandy (still known in France as Isles de Anglo-Normandie) and under the control of William the Conqueror, in 1239 the Treaty of Paris recognised them as part of Henry III's territories. They have been 'English' ever since with few if any French speakers though a few vestiges of the language Guerneslais still exist amongst academics and enthusiasts. The 2001 census suggested that 2% of the population speak this ancient Norman language though 14% suggest having some knowledge.

Even so almost all roads and buildings have French names, so our hotel was on Rue des Grandes Moulins (street of the large windmills). This is bizarre as most modern roads would by no means have existed in medieval times. The clue to French naming comes from the fact that until the 20th Century French was the only official language. All deeds, and the sales or purchase of real estate were in French until 1971. Spoken French virtually died out following wartime evacuation to the UK in 1940. Today French visitors are bemused by the native islanders' almost non-existent command of their language.

Our second trip was to **Alderney** the most northerly of the Channel Islands and some 20 miles from **Guernsey**. Flights are available but maintenance problems suspended flights during our visit. We had elected to pay £80 return for a day trip on the *Salty Blonde* (aka *Ashlin*) a new subsidised franchise between the islands on an 11 metre Storm Force RIB a 275 hp diesel vessel built in Cushendall, Northern Ireland. *Ashlin* is their 50th Storm Force boat. The boat is owned by Julie-Anne Uggla a philanthropic entrepreneur who fell in love with **Alderney** when diverted there on a flight to Cornwall. Her boutique hotel the *Blonde Hedgehog* is a *chi chi* addition to **Alderney**'s eclectic mix of residents and visitors.

The journey is fast and generally less than an hour with room only for an exclusive 8 passengers and 2 crew with only 2 forward facing passenger seats and 6 cramped bench seats in the rear. On the outward journey we were sandwiched in the rear, and I was not happy with my pending sea sickness rearing its ugly head at every lump and bump. Our companions were a jolly bunch with one lady hailing from Steve's hometown of Staveley in Derbyshire. The skipper was an old sea dog with many miles at sea as a tug master. He had semi-retired with a croft in Lyness, **Hoy** on the Orkney Islands which meant serious distances covered from two extremes of the British Isles. We chatted bizarrely but knowledgeably about ferry timetables from **Mainland Orkney** to **Hoy**!

We knew nothing of **Alderney** but Bill Bayley on our visit to **Jethou** had strongly advised we booked a taxi prior to our arrival as we would only have 3 hours on the island. Bill's taxis were found and phoned and Bill who turned out to be an **Alderney** man through and through was instructed to meet us on arrival for an hour's tour at the princely sum of £18 per person. Incidentally, **Guernsey** bank notes still have one-pound denominations.

My sickness subsided on arrival, and we headed off in Bill's taxi to learn about this odd island. His graphic narrative deviated between the horrors of Nazi occupation and occupation by tax avoiding celebrities, an unlikely juxtaposition of bed fellows. **Alderney** was notorious for its slave camps at which forced labour from a mixture of Russian prisoners of war and Auschwitz concentration camps worked on starvation rations and little shelter to build concrete edifices, watchtowers and gun emplacements to gain strategic advantage of the English Channel. This was known as Hitler's Atlantic wall. Before the Nazis arrived, all islanders were evacuated, and they landed on a deserted island and set about building two work camps and two concentration camps. The harsh conditions led to over 6,000 losses of lives with a constant stream of replacements. Bill reckoned that lives following internment could be as short as 10 days. The true human casualty will never be known as this was hushed up by Churchill to prevent any outpouring of outrage which might have jeopardised the war effort.

Since the 1960's occupation has been of a different kind with well-heeled celebrities and sports stars buying up property. Bill's graphic portrayal of the horrors and deprivation of war turned to a Hollywood style tour of the remarkably modest homes bought by amongst others; John Arlott the legendary cricket commentator and wine fanatic; Ian Botham who bought unknowingly a house close to the island's foghorn; George Martin, the Beatles record producer; Elizabeth Beresford, creator of the Wombles, one of which was named **Alderney**; Julie (Mary Poppins and Sound of Music) Andrews and designer Laura Ashley. Ms Ashley was so frightened of falling downstairs she built a house on **Alderney** as an intricate series of ground floor rooms. The irony is that just after her 60th birthday she fell downstairs at her daughter's home in the West Midlands and died of a brain haemorrhage.

We sunned ourselves outside *Jack's bistro* on Victoria Street, St Annes, the pleasant village or 'town' as the natives refer to it before being taxi'd back by Bill to the *Salty Blonde* in good time to get the two front seats for our return. The fog was still allowing limited visibility but free from sea sickness facing the boat's bow I pleasantly dozed.

Sark has in my mind always been regarded as the 'jewel in the Channel Islands crown' with picture post card images of horse drawn carriages ambling along roads where cars are banned. It is billed as a 'do not miss location' some 45 minutes by pleasure ferry from St Peter Port. The island is reputed to have been the smallest independent feudal state in Europe and to have the last feudal constitution in the western world. This archaic system of Government started in 1563 and there have been 23 seigneurs till the present day who report directly to the monarch of the UK. It was not until 2006 that a referendum was held to replace the 'feudal' regime with an elected 'parliament' known as the Chief Pleas with 18 elected members out of a permanent population of close to 500.

We joined a happy band of visitors on Easter Saturday and on yet another fine day. The smart 'Isle of Sark' ferry is a modern vessel charging £25 per head for the return journey. On arrival a couple of dilapidated carriages pulled by antiquated tractors take the unfit or just lazy tourists to the main village. Steve was having none of this idle pampering and walked up the modest hill beating the sluggish tractor and its £1.50 fee paying passengers.

The main street is lined with smart cottages offering the usual tourist trappings with a penchant for locally made silver and jewellery. We had other things on our mind: a trip to **Brecqhou**, the bolt hole of arch capitalists the Barclay twins, Sir David and Sir Frederick, though the former had died in 2021. They were reclusive billionaires with once ownership of London's *Ritz* hotel and the Sunday and Daily Telegraphs, and the Spectator, renowned for their heavy leanings towards the Conservative party. Boris Johnson was once the Spectator's editor-at-large with open season articles often insensitive to common decency. He incurred many Liverpudlian's wrath for outrageously suggesting they 'wallow' in their 'victim status', adding it is part of the 'deeply unattractive psyche' of many in the city. In his outlandish outburst he added the city made a scapegoat of the police in the wake of the Hillsborough disaster, when 97 Liverpool fans were killed at the Sheffield football ground. Blame was deflected onto "the drunken fans at the back of the crowd who mindlessly tried to fight their way into the ground".

The brothers had been notorious for their desire for privacy and an opportunity to visit **Brecqhou** would prove to be one of the biggest challenges of my island adventures. Unlike my request to Sir Peter Ogden my request to **Brecqhou**'s estate manager, Aiden, was ignored and I feared this would be one of the islands that would evade my footfall. We headed for the tourist information centre and our request for suggestions of access were met with the same incredulity as I had experienced from **Guernsey** residents. The brothers had not been in the past and were not popular now with the people of **Sark**. The Guardian has described them as "tax exiles" but Sir Frederick has been quoted before as saying he and his brother left the UK solely for health reasons.

In 1993 they bought the 32-hectare island for almost £3.5m. They built a castle, designed by Quinlan Terry and planted vineyards, an olive grove and an organic market garden. The island could be visited by residents of their hotels in **Sark** but in 2008 they announced they were closing down all their businesses there with the loss of about 100 jobs, a fifth of the island's population. They later reopened the businesses but there had been a long-running dispute with some locals over the brothers' desire to change the island's system of governance. In short, they are not liked either in **Sark** or the wider Channel Islands and I was on a fool's errand to think I could get there with the Barclay family's permission. So tight is their grip on the locals that even RIB companies refused to take me there for a brief visit even though landing below High Water mark 'to pick seaweed' is not illegal.

We could at least look out onto **Brecquou** and walked the mile or so to the Gouliot Headland a Ramsar biodiversity site with spectacular scenery to get an excellent vantage point high up above the Gouliot passage, popular with kayakers braving the tidal currents which race between the two islands. There is little more than 50 metres separating the two islands at this point though a crossing would be suicidal. We stopped and stared across to this inaccessible island, and I snoozed taking in the coconut smelling yellow gorse and wild garlic in all its profusion.

Slightly depressed we headed for the *Bel Air* pub for refreshment with not a tourist in sight, but a public bar frequented by Sky TV watching local males anticipating the Manchester City versus Liverpool FA cup semi-final. The febrile atmosphere in this innocuous venue would be being repeated all over the British Isles. Liverpool won 3-2. It was time to return to **Guernsey** with the happy band of contented day trippers.

Lihou would not cause problems so long as we crossed the causeway on the day of our visit during the 12:22 to 16:00 low tide slot suggested by the **Guernsey** tourist board. We had for once a leisurely breakfast from our attentive southeast Asian waiters who delivered the best soft-boiled eggs I had in any hotel for a very long time. Steve is eager for full coverage of tourism experiences, and we opted for a visit to the Occupation Museum with grizzled Nazi memorabilia and artefacts from the brave resistance movement, a chilling reminder of the horrors of warfare which we had hoped had been left far behind on the European continent. We marched around the exhibits in sombre silence before travelling the perimeter of the island reaching the north of L'Eree bay just as the last vestiges of the ebbing tide were evacuating the causeway.

Lihou like many locations in the Channel Islands is a Ramsar site in full time occupation by a warden. Like **Brecqhou** and **Jethou** the 'hou' suffix is Norman for a small hill or mound. The island is dominated by the ruins of St Mary's abbey which is the most extensive religious relic in **Guernsey**. A self-contained hostel is the only other building of note.

The terrain under my increasingly clumsier feet was pretty good after the uncomfortable cobble stone entry and exit to and from the island though seaweed was a significant obstacle. **Lihou** was once an important location for a commercially significant industry based around the harvesting of seaweed (or vraic in the local Guernésiais language). Sheep enjoying seaweed fodder were imported from the Orkney Islands until the 1980's when soon after the island was bought by the States of **Guernsey**.

I snoozed in the spring sunshine whilst Steve, ever the adventurer, circumnavigated this 15-hectare island returning to complete our own circumnavigation of **Guernsey** taking a late liquid lunch at the *Hotel Jerbourg*, St Martin in the throng of serving its famous carvery Sunday lunch. Steve had a plane to catch as his adventures as a passionate dark tourist were to take him to Beirut and onto the post-civil war devastation of Homs, Aleppo and Palmyra in Syria.

My journey to **Jersey** a couple of days later was not so eclectic (I had left a spare day in case bad weather had delayed any schedule). I boarded the Condor ferry which plies its way between Portsmouth and the Channel Islands, slightly delayed because of what had been referred to in an email message as 'Royal Navy manoeuvres in Portsmouth harbour' which sounded sinister and reminiscent of the gathering of shipping to rescue the Falkland islanders in spring 1982 some 40 years ago. I shuddered to think that we are still engaged in territorial wars but with the stakes now, with the Russia Ukrainian war showing no sign of a peaceful settlement, considerably higher than those days of Thatcherite jingoism.

The lounge of this modern ship was full of families on Easter breaks making use of the utilitarian canteen service of burgers for the kids and miniature bottles of merlot or shiraz for mum or dad and the two-hour passage was pleasant enough. I reflected on the extent of my travels over the last 6 years and realised I was going to my most southerly island. I'd visited Skaw the most northerly settlement in the British Isles on the island of **Unst** in the Shetland Islands and I reckoned the journey by car and boat to **Jersey** would be 1,054 miles taking a continuous 30 hours and 54 minutes.

I checked into the two-star *Norfolk hotel* as a quick pit stop before flying back to East Midlands airport. Its bland desperation and utilitarian modesty were in direct contrast to *Fleur du Jardin*, and I took a brief solace in the equally modest bar where pensioners were enraptured by the resident singer giving passable renditions of Neil Diamond's 'Sweet Caroline' and any number of Elvis hits.

Jersey is 14 miles from the Cotentin Peninsula in Normandy and during my brief stay I felt it had an air of brashness as against the quaintness of **Guernsey**. High performance sports cars with their personalised number plates growled through the central business district representing the tip of the financial iceberg which sustains the **Jersey** economy. Clientele on the Blue Islands airline were fashionably well heeled with not a track suit bottom in sight. These 'ex pats' or rather financial immigrants were making the most of their limited 90 days back in the UK so as not to upset

Her Majesty's Revenue and Customs. Some 40% of **Jersey**'s Gross Value Added comes from financial services and the Crown Dependency has economic output per capita substantially ahead of all of the world's large, developed economies. Gross national income in 2009 was £3.7 billion (approximately £40,000 per head of population). This does not reflect the standard of living of most born and bred islanders with two tier housing and locals priced out of a very competitive and lucrative market, just as in **Guernsey**. However, offshore asset hiding is small fry here with in 2020 the island accounted for only 0.46% of the global offshore finance market, making it a small player in the total market compared with the 'big boys', like the Cayman and British Virgin Islands, where many well-heeled Tory politicians and 'establishment' figures secrete their colossal wealth.

On my way to the airport, I pondered if I should return to explore more of this eccentric island paradise, not French but not really British which gets 95% of its energy from France. By the time the taxi arrived I felt that there were other more eclectic islands worthy of a second visit.

35. South West Ireland – again

I brought my potentially final trip to Ireland forward to June 2022 as I was acutely aware that despite the energy and cost of living crisis brought on, depending on your political stance, by a failed Brexit, the energy crisis as a result of the War in Ukraine or a combination of all these factors, the cost of accommodation was sky rocketing. A single night in a modest Dublin hotel was unavailable for less than 200 euros and often much, much more. The prices would only escalate by the August holiday period.

I contacted John and got his approval for a 10-day visit to sweep up candidate islands in counties Cork, Kerry, Limerick and Galway, an eclectic mix of private islands, bridged and causewayed islands, low tide crossings and passenger ferries. I had no time to contact the owners of the private islands so these would either be in the 'ones that got away' class or left till formal introduction was possible.

At the start of this odyssey, I was hell bent not to leave out any inhabited island, but I was taking a more cavalier attitude now should I wish to ever get my book published. Who would notice, let alone care? I've done my best at incalculable expense, though it is my horrendous carbon footprint that should be of more concern.

My first shock was the ferry fare for myself and my Discovery Sport at a little shy of £450 for a return crossing to Dublin, but I wanted the comfort of my own vehicle. John and I had suffered the discomfort of modest rental cars in the past and my lack of movement brought on by a combination of neuropathy and arthritis and of course old age begged for a modicum of luxury. John too was suffering from mobility problems after falling on rock armour during one of our previous trips.

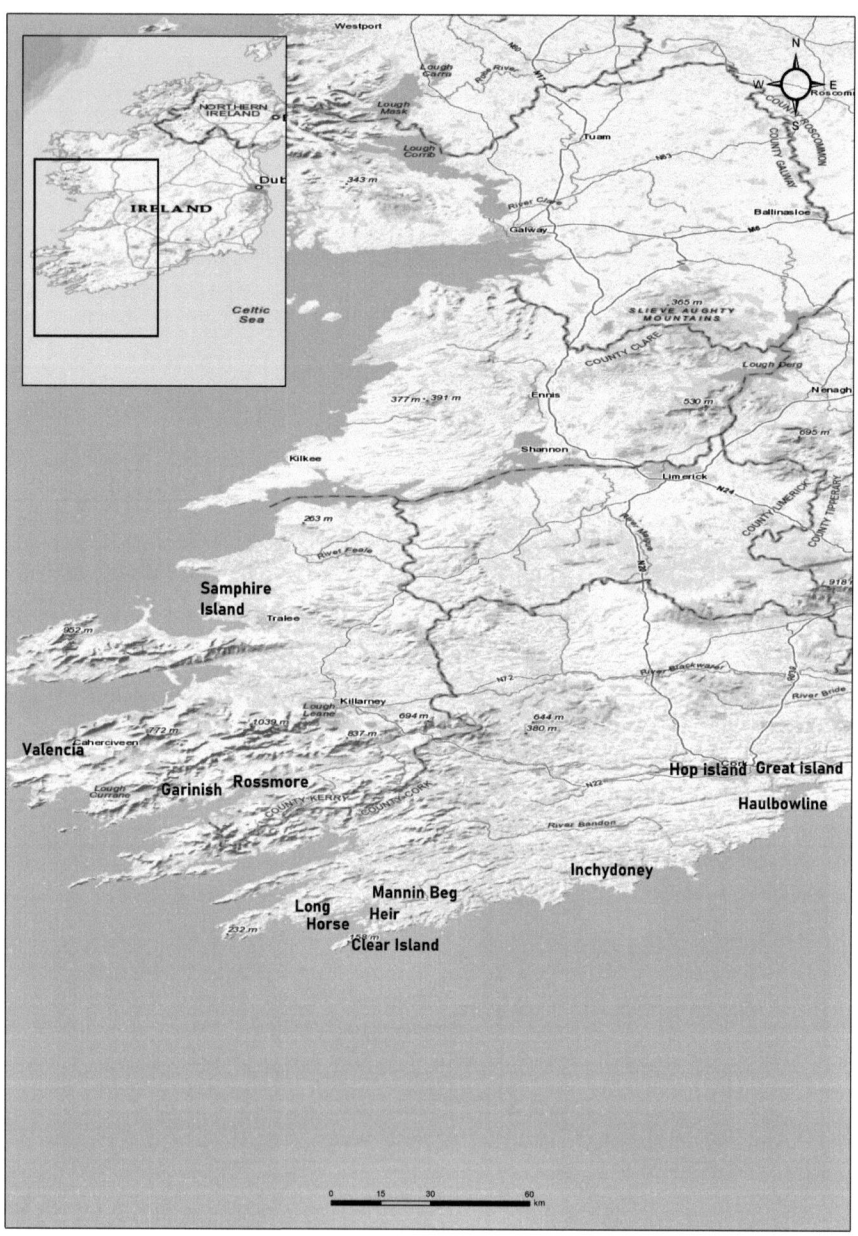

South west Ireland again (South)

I caught the Swift ferry from Holyhead, manned by low wage Nepalese or Filipinos or some such nationalities. Staff on P&O ferries had been summarily dismissed earlier in the year so cheaper foreign labour could replace local staff. I surmised that Irish Ferries were no better with minimum wages being denied so reducing operational costs and boosting shareholder profits, the watchword of modern Capitalism. With thoughts of widening inequality in our laissez-faire world I picked up John in his Abbeyleix home and headed southwest for four easy islands, **Great Island, Haulbowline, Hop Island** and **Inchydoney**, the first three in the environs of Cork City with a fourth further west close to the historic town of Clonakilty, birthplace of the Irish revolutionary and pro treaty leader, Michael Collins.

The 'craic' was good as we sped towards Cork. John and I communicated regularly but had not met since he came to Birmingham earlier in the spring for the funeral of his good friend Keith who, wracked in tortuous pain from degenerative spina bifada and depression, took his own life. John was finding those events difficult to come to terms with and a random trip to 20 or so islands would maybe distract his mind from his understandable sadness. John had been on all my Irish island trips and his company and perspicacity are always welcome. We have the sort of relationship where trading insults is not dwelt upon by either party and enhances healthy debate. Our main contentions in the past were his questionable map reading skills, but 'Google Maps' was enlisted to guide us seamlessly on our whistle stop tour.

Cobh is the main settlement on **Great Island**, a deep-water seaport on the ria coastline, the familiar indented post-glacial drowned valleys of Cork and Kerry. We arrived in Cobh via the dull suburbs of Cork. Cork is to Ireland what Yorkshire is to England or Texas to the USA. I am told the citizens of Cork are brash or arrogant feeling superior to the good folk of Dublin and John warned me that to my ears their accent would be impenetrable; he was not wrong.

Cobh, known as Queenstown until Irish independence, with its steep

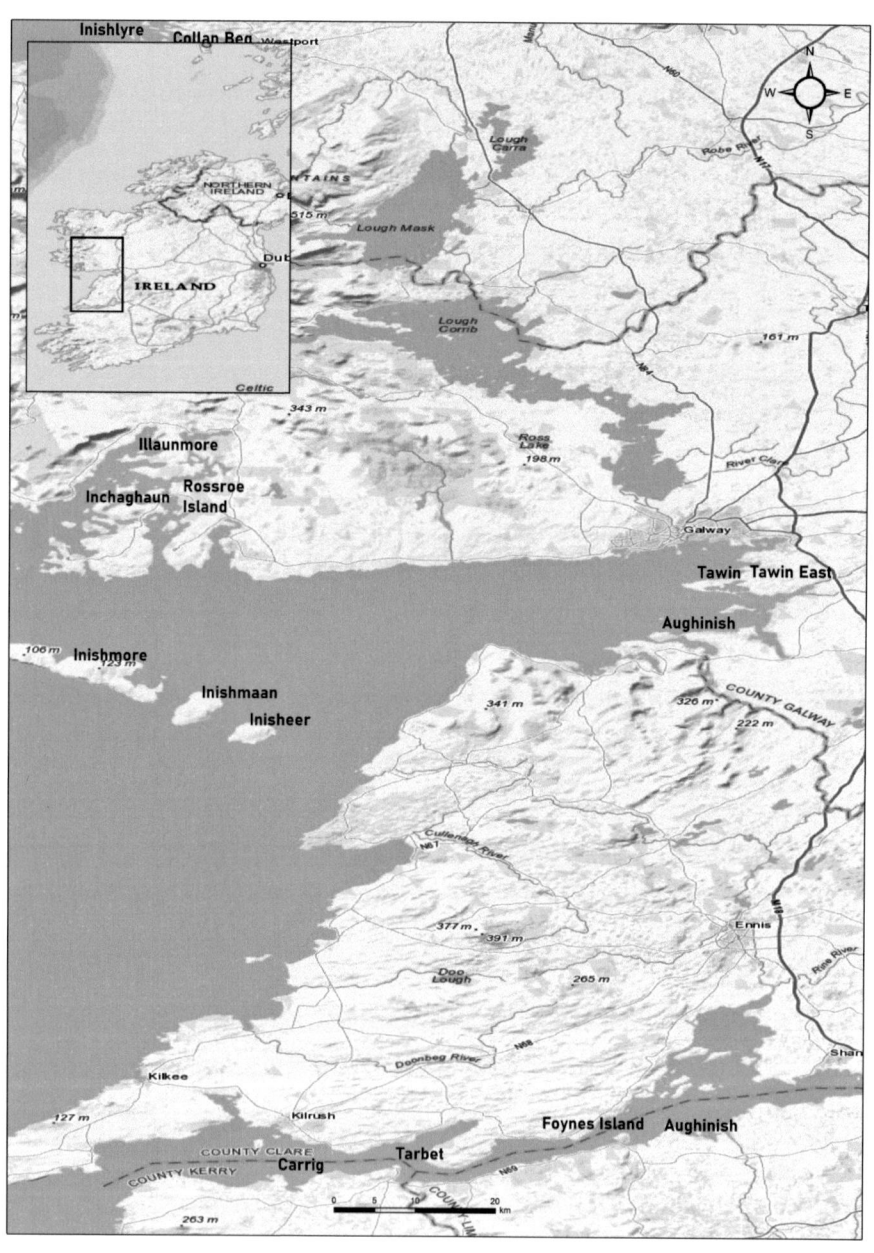

South west Ireland again (North)

streets leading down to the harbour was pleasant enough and is dominated by St Colman's cathedral, the tallest church in Ireland. As usual our 'step-on step off' tactics which I dubbed 'fast food' island trips meant we had no time to explore, picking up a sort of cream scone in a cosy café where though closed we were welcomed in the true Irish hospitality fashion.

Great Island's sea faring credentials are impressive with the predecessor of the Royal Cork yacht club founded in 1720 across the estuary at **Haulbowline**, thought to be the oldest yacht club in the world. However, like all such claims there are counter claims and counter-counter claims. The Russians are adamant that it was Peter the Great who in 1718 founded the River Neva Yacht club in St Petersburg. The Russians seem to want to claim anything that displeases them - records, territory, scientific achievements - like a small child is acquisitive about his toys or an ex-Prime Minister from a certain neighbour of the Irish Republic!

On a more sombre note, the town was the departure point for 2.5 million of the six million Irish people who emigrated to North America between 1848 and 1950 and on 11th April 1912 *RMS Titanic* set out from Cobh with a cargo of expectant passengers hoping for a better life across the Atlantic. Some 123 passengers boarded at Queenstown, with only 44 surviving the sinking. Just as devastatingly momentous, survivors and the 1,198 dead passengers were brought to Queenstown after the sinking of *RMS Lusitania* by German U-boats in May 1914. A dispute as to the formation of the first yacht club palls into insignificance in comparison to these historic landmarks of world beating tragedies.

It was well after five in the evening, and we had three more islands to visit before overnighting in *O'Donovan's* in Clonakilty. We headed to **Haulbowline** via the Cross River Ferry at Rushbrooke (cash only) taking 5 minutes and slicing off time circumnavigating the dreary suburbs of Cork again.

Haulbowline is located at a strategic and deep-water position in the harbour and as such the island is a military base, first fortified in 1602. It is connected to the mainland by a road built in the sixties and thus simple to access. Unaware of its role as HQ for the Irish navy we encountered security detail when approaching and parking the car at the island end of the bridge. I attempted to plant my feet on the island before being gently accosted by a military guard. I spluttered my objective to this tattooed Ross Kemp look alike expecting to be summarily ejected from the base. However, I was able to detect through his thick Cork accent that part of the island was dedicated to parkland and open to the public. I thanked him and we found the largely deserted car park and reflected on the history of the island via the usual information board.

The site of the park had been reclaimed from industrial wasteland where toxic and even radioactive waste had been dumped during steel processing by Irish Steel. Plans for residential and commercial development were shelved because of this toxic legacy and campaigners, including Erin Brockovich, pushed for action by the state, and €61 million was allocated to clean-up the site and to redevelop it as the park which opened to the public in January 2021.

We drove the shortish distance to **Hop Island** feeling smug that access to the restricted **Haulbowline Island** had been possible. The turning to **Hop Island** near Rochestown was indistinct with access via a tarmac causeway across a narrow isthmus, stretching the definition of an island though recognised by the Irish census (the Bible of my Irish island pursuits) as such. It is now largely an equestrian centre and effectively a heap of boulder clay emerging from the surrounds of Lough Mahon, part of Cork's inner harbour.

The island was occupied by a French Huguenot, Laurence De la Main in the 18th Century. He was known for his aptitude for music and dance hence the name given by passing sailors aware of the dancing or hopping from this accomplished teacher of waltzes and quadrilles to the citizens of Cork. A surprising connection to the author was discovered as by the 19th Century the property built by De la Main on the island was leased out for £16 per annum by the Chatterton family who were Cork baronets. The family owned five other homes in County Cork. It seems that my long-lost cousins were part of the British aristocracy throwing their weight around in Ireland. The third baronet James Charles Chatterton was MP for Cork in mid-19th Century, High Sheriff of County Cork in 1851, fought in Waterloo and was a General in the British army. The baronetcy became extinct upon his death in 1874.

It was an easy drive to **Inchydoney** crossing the causeway from Clonakilty. The island was waking up to the short summer season as the Irish school holidays had already begun. A one-way system took us around this neat seaside community. The island's historical significance relates to the succession of skirmishes in what is known as the 11 years' war in the reign of Charles the First. This Irish confederate war was the most destructive conflict in Irish history and caused 200,000–600,000 deaths from fighting as well as war-related famine and disease. English history teaching sanitises at best or ignores at worst these atrocities that beset our closest neighbour, just one of the many unjust struggles between the Irish and the arrogance of England's rulers. In **Inchydoney** in 1642 several hundred Irish soldiers fled the English troops towards the island to take refuge but were caught and drowned in the rising tide before reaching **Inchydoney**.

We drove to our hotel in Clonakilty, a busy neat town attracting tourists or students of the Irish fight for independence following the Easter uprising of 1916. This is the birthplace of Michael Collins, chairman of the Provisional Government of the Irish Free State from January 1922 and commander-in-chief of the National Army from July until his death in an ambush in August 1922, during the Civil War. To commemorate the war many of the streets are named after the freedom fighters for Irish independence – Pearse Street, Connolly Street and Casement Street. The latter was named after Sir Roger Casement, a British diplomat and Irish nationalist executed for treason during the First World War after he made efforts to gain German military aid for the Easter Rising that initiated the fight for Irish independence. One country's terrorist is another country's national hero.

With our usual hurried itinerary, we had no time to visit the Collins museum in the cradle of the revolution. We made do with an Asian street food restaurant opposite our dated but very comfortable hotel which was a warren of memorabilia to Collins. Old Irish towns once known only for their pubs selling the ubiquitous Guinness with Irish stew, bacon and cabbage, boxty, soda bread, coddle, and colcannon as basic fare are rapidly catching up with contemporary tastes. Even **Inchydoney** seemed to be upgrading the bucket and spade beach holiday for Chakra Yoga and healing and restorative therapies at the island lodge and spa.

With four easy islands secured we headed for Baltimore harbour to board the Cape Clear Ferry. Our delays this time were not self-inflicted as we fell foul of some sort of incident involving the fire brigade and but for the kindness of the skipper, we would have missed our pre-booked (yes, a modicum of planning had been done) trip. The weather was bitter and rain, biblically heavy rain, forecast for much of the coming week. When packing for the trip I thought my gloves would be superfluous in June and I was glad that I had inadvertently left them in my car.

Cape Clear Island is the southern most populated island in Ireland and very much part of the Gaeltacht. The official **Cape Clear** website eulogises its "wild romantic scenery, its sparkling harbours, its cliffs, bogs and lake, all contributing to the island's unspoilt charm". Unfortunately our return was to be almost immediate with a stroll around the harbour to stretch our legs our only glimpse. We busied ourselves watching the unloading and loading of local cargo from the passenger ferry supporting its 147 population. This was an eighth of that prior to the potato famine, as like all the Gaeltacht and much of rural Ireland their history is defined by famine and subsequent depopulation.

The Fastnet rock and lighthouse is visible from this southern vantage point evocative of the Fastnet yacht race, one of the world's classic races from Cowes on the **Isle of Wight** to the rock and in the past back to Plymouth but from 2021 returning to Cherbourg. More prosaic and in stark contrast Fastnet was known as Ireland's **Teardrop** as it was the last part of Ireland seen by thousands of Irish emigrants as they sailed away to the New World, most of them never to return again; two very contrasting travellers' worlds colliding.

The trip back, about an hour, was in bright early summer sunshine and we took to the upper deck to take advantage of the brief respite in the weather. Our next objective was **Heir Island** accessed from Cunnamore pier some 40 minutes away around Roaringwater Bay.

The weather had become colder, and John and I and two couples made a hellish 4-minute crossing to the island in biting wind. As usual on our travels this small island had no open café or restaurant for refreshment and we walked slowly up from the jetty to pass the 4 hours before our scheduled return. The island was deserted but with signs of a thriving population of residents and visitors. The advertised 'restaurant' was as dead as the grave and my spirits were low finding shelter by laying on a rough wooden bench and fitfully sleeping. I had been looking forward to the "catch of the day" at the Island Cottage restaurant whose enticing menu varies depending on the season; shrimp, lobster, salmon, crab and a variety of local fish as advertised on the island website.

Oh, how I wished I had brought my gloves, left in the car in our hurry to board the ferry. Stiff with a combination of arthritis and cold I made creaking efforts to return to the jetty. On the way I heard the most sublime chamber music from behind what turned out to be an open door. I gingerly entered to encounter a small group of musicians, an ensemble, playing Dvorjak, probably Wind Serenade in D minor. (I knew this not from my limited knowledge of classical music but from the composer's name on the score). I asked if I could listen more to keep out the cold than enjoy the music. The two bassoon players were captivating, and I soon forgot my cold and all-around misery to become enraptured by these delightful musicians on a summer school on the island. Summer schools either artistic or linguistic (Irish language) seem to be the bread and butter of these small islands whose fight for economic survival is fragile. The fishing industry had disappeared from the island years ago and the island's capital strangely call Paris hosts our summer school tourists and the Roaringwater sailing school.

Replete with an unexpected experience I joined John cowering in the lee of the wind in an inadequate bus shelter until *MV Thresher* arrived to despatch us back to the mainland.

We had booked suitable accommodation near Union Hall, a nondescript town near Skibbereen and had time to conquer an eclectic private island, **Mannin Beg**, owned by the actor Jeremy Irons and his wife Sinead Cusack. Access might be a challenge though John had messaged the actor's agent in anticipation and got a returned message indicating that the Oscar winner, famous for his roles in *Brideshead Revisited* and his first major film *The French Lieutenant's Woman* in 1981 was away in Italy, the vacation of choice of many in the theatrical fraternity. This could be a blessing in disguise as the island supporting the 15th Century Kilcoe castle was easily accessed connected to the mainland by a 50 metres or so bridge.

Our satnav guided us off the main road down meandering lanes until suddenly, around the last bend, a spectacular sight presented itself: Kilcoe, a terra-cotta-coloured edifice composed of two towers, a thick one and a thin one, rising from **Mannin Beg**. Fortunately, the imposing and impenetrable portcullis gate protecting the keep was on the island, so a quick scamper saw me on the island with not a soul in sight.

Kilcoe Castle was the only castle in west Cork to hold out against the Elizabethan English forces. The invading army could not get close enough to aim their cannons at the strong tower walls. After multiple failed attempts, the English returned on foot, starting in 1600, to carry out a series of raids. They first managed to steal cattle but never breached the castle walls. Finally, in 1603, Kilcoe Castle like all other fortifications fell to the English forces.

Jeremy Irons had bought the castle at the head of Roaringwater Bay in a dilapidated state during, as his wife reportedly said, 'a midlife crisis' some 25 years ago. In a *Vanity Fair* magazine interview with Irons its unique transformation suggested that *'Kilcoe is at once stately-home beautiful and slightly mad—a 360-degree immersion in its owner's eccentric psyche'*. It would have been nice to have experienced some of this eccentricity, but we had to be content with catching the late afternoon sunshine on the imposing red tower before heading to Skibbereen for tea at the classy *West Cork Hotel*.

We were pleased to leave our modest self-contained apartment in a complex frequented by those with mindfulness and spiritual connection uppermost on their agendas. A long day ahead we made for Colla pier to catch a ferry to appropriately named **Long Island** beyond the small town of Schull. We were assisted to the ferry by a guy of advanced years who to make himself useful welcomed the boarders. He was probably a sea dog who needed to go through the motions of work to survive the tedium of retirement. I know the feeling and dread the long days ahead when infirmity enforces long winter nights and longer summer days at home with only thoughts as company.

It was cold still and the weather forecast was for torrential rain so staying on this bleak island with no facilities (a common pattern was emerging) for another 4 hours was not an option. *MV Chieftain* arrived skippered by Maurice who welcomed us with the usual Irish charm and warmth in contrast to the harsh day. He agreed for a few extra Euros to take us back at our leisure and after this negotiation the five or so minutes journey (this time not forgetting my gloves) didn't seem so bad.

We disembarked for a stroll around this unremarkable island but were intercepted by Maurice who insisted we drove ourselves around the island in his dilapidated old banger-cum-death trap. It was a generous gesture, but the gear changes were impossible to master. For fear of ending up in the drink Maurice who had witnessed my ineptitude exchanged the creaky saloon for an ancient Land Rover Freelander. Both would have failed their MoT's decades ago.

The island is three miles long and the largest of the Carbery Hundred Islands. It has a single track around the periphery but with no redeeming features to speak of. Some 25 minutes later we were ready to leave but not before a brief chat with Connor, an islander whose only trips off the island were to follow country music bands around the southwest. He was pleased, after COVID isolation to be going to Limerick that day to follow his passion.

The next island, still in the Carbery Hundreds, was to be a private island, **Horse Island**, but with no time to arrange access we asked Maurice for ideas. In his affable no-nonsense manner, he asked us to contact him when next we were in the area so he could arrange a private charter. We would have to leave two other islands, one in Kerry and the other in Limerick for similar reasons. A late breakfast was taken in Schull where the old guy at Colla pier was now sat with his own thoughts slowly supping at a cup of tea.

Refreshed we headed across the Cork and Kerry mountains to find **Rossmore**. The Ring of Kerry is spectacular and draws visitors from all over the world many of whom come to see Skellig Michael, a mystical looking outcrop and site of an ancient monastery off the coast of Kerry, as their ultimate destination. It is now popular not for ecclesiastical reasons but more because scenes from Star Wars film Episode VII "The Force Awakens" and Star Wars Episode VIII "The Last Jedi" were filmed at Skellig islands.

As we climbed up leaving County Cork for County Kerry I couldn't help but hum to myself the Irish traditional folk song. 'Whiskey in the jar", made famous by the Dubliners and Thin Lizzy.

> As I was goin' over the Cork and Kerry mountains.
> I saw Captain Farrell and his money he was countin'.
> I first produced my pistol and then produced my rapier.
> I said stand o'er and deliver or the devil he may take ya.
>
> Musha ring dumb a do dumb a da.
> Whack for my daddy-o,

Whack for my daddy-o.
There's whiskey in the jar-o.

The rain poured all day and views of the spectacular scenery were denied to us. My immediate goal was **Rossmore** connected by a picturesque, small arched stone road bridge from the N70 (Ring of Kerry tourist route) east of Tahilla on the Iveragh peninsula. We were entering the lush verdancy of the very southwest of Ireland on the deeply incised Kenmare estuary, kissed by the Atlantic Gulf Stream. In June the mild humid micro-climate following the rain resulted in rich and prolific flora. Tree ferns and Cordyline Australis (cabbage palms) thrive in this region. This part of southwest Ireland is not subject to winter frosts and well managed private and public gardens are prolific.

We drove through the island hinterland almost reminiscent of the sub tropics with humidity to complement the abundance of plants. Michael Flatley of *Riverdance* fame tried to get planning permission to build a holiday cottage on this sublime island but was refused given the island's Special Area of Conservation status and the scale of his plans. This was an ideal retreat for those lucky enough to live or holiday there but with rain lashing down we headed for **Garinish** Island (not to be confused with Garnish Island in Bantry Bay, Cork) near the local tourist town of Sneem. Access was difficult to find without purchase of an Irish Ordnance Survey 1:50,000 scale map bought in one of Sneem's many souvenir shops and a honey pot for tourists completing the Ring of Kerry. The weather conditions were dire, and John bought a handsome cut-price Aran sweater to stave off the summer cold.

The road to the jetty from Inishkeelach was safely navigated but a visit was hope triumphing over experience as we had not introduced ourselves to the owner of this private island a few hundred metres from the jetty. What did I expect that a random person would accost me and offer a trip over? As with **Horse Island** this was for another time.

From 1900 onwards Windham Wyndham-Quin, 4th Earl of Dunraven developed the island into a subtropical wild garden. It is still in existence today though the house, Garinish Lodge, was burned in September 1922 during the Irish Civil War, but later rebuilt. After years of neglect the gardens were redeveloped and extended to their former glory. Today **Garinish** is the home to a rich Swiss-Lebanese financier, an uber reclusive member of the billionaire Safra family, who is well known for bankrolling a number of Woody Allen films including *Bullets Over Broadway*. Gaining access to what appears to be an exclusive island will take all our collective cunning. Maybe access to this island will defeat me?

Disappointed at the thought of never getting to **Garinish** I consoled myself with the fact that I had managed to gain access to **Jethou** also owned by a billionaire. Hope springs eternal and a suitable letter to the estate manager might just work.

It was onwards to **Valentia Island**, (Ireland's fifth largest island) which I remember going to three decades ago with Cousin Dick. Access is via a bridge (Maurice O'Neill Memorial Bridge) crossing at Portmagee. I had vivid memories of the lushness of the vegetation. By now the rain was well established and attempts to see Skellig Michael were abandoned.

I needed a rest whilst John went for a welcome Guinness, or stout as he prefers to call the elixir of St James Gate, Dublin. On continuing our journey onto the island, as often happens, my past vision of **Valentia** was disappointing and a humdrum seven-mile journey in the gloom of a wet afternoon took us to the ferry at Knightstown for the 5-minute trip to Reenard Point, just west of Cahersiveen. For five Euros this saved us precious time as we needed a hotel for the night, knowing that hotels were expensive and few and far between. The poor woman collecting our ferry fare was wholly exposed to the elements and took on the persona of a very drowned rat but went about her tedious duties with no complaint.

Like many settlement names there is often contradiction as to the origin of the name. Though it is thought not to be associated with Valencia, Spain it is possible the spelling was influenced by Spanish sailors as there is a grave marker to Spanish sailors lost at sea in the Catholic cemetery at Kylemore.

Valentia was the eastern terminus of the first commercially viable transatlantic telegraph cable in 1866. Another landmark communication first was on 21st May 1927, when Charles A. Lindbergh made his first landfall in Europe, flying over Dingle Bay and **Valentia** Island on the first solo flight from New York to Paris in the famous single-engine Ryan monoplane, the *Spirit of St. Louis*. Bringing up a third notable connection to **Valentia** the Valentia Island fossilised tetrapod trackways are among the oldest signs of vertebrate life on land, preserved for some 385 million years.

Our next island was **Samphire Island** north from **Valentia** in Tralee Bay near the town of Fenit. We had no luck finding suitable accommodation on the way and arrived in the town without a place to stay. As often happens late in the evening rooms become vacant and before despair set in with the prospect of sleeping in the car Booking.com came to the rescue with perfect accommodation in the *Bianconi Inn* in Killorglin a retrace of our steps by around 30 miles with the wretched satnav taking us over twisting mountains instead of the direct road towards Tralee.

Killorglin is home to the ancient Puck fair every August. Every year a group of townsfolk go up into the mountains and catch a wild goat. The goat is brought back to the town and the "Queen of Puck", traditionally a young schoolgirl from one of the local primary schools, crowns the goat "King Puck". The goat is held captive in a cage for three days before being released back to the mountains. Tradition is maintained but at the expense of overt animal cruelty. This tradition was stopped in 2023 when the goat was only put on the platform for an hour each day.

A delightful sojourn in the upmarket *Bianconi inn* refreshed our spirits and a renewed assault on **Samphire** Island began. For once my four-wheel Discovery Sport came into its own with a beach approach at low tide and a rough causeway traverse to the heart of the island. Fenit has two islands though the man-made one (Great Samphire because of its prominent height) is an industrial port complex with no overnight population. The populated (though sparse) island is a low lying scrappy agricultural hinterland with little to recommend to visitors who would be well advised to avoid the access road and stay on the expansive sandy beaches. The island is protected by extensive rip rap or rock armour which has seen better days and it is hard to see the economic benefit of continued maintenance. Most islands have some obscure or interesting facts to titillate or intrigue the traveller but not in the case of **Samphire Island**.

The Shannon estuary beckoned with first **Carrig Island** with access gained by a road bridge (St Senan's road) from Ballylongford. The island is named after one of Ireland's most celebrated Saints who settled on the nearby Scattery Island, now uninhabited. In his lifetime he was noted for his learning, utter contempt for any riches and possessions, self-denial and austere asceticism. In the tradition of the good Saint, the second island of the day gave us no pleasure with only a brief comfort stop in the centre of the island where the satnav ceremonially guided us. This is a quiet bucolic island again with few redeeming features with the single exception of the nearby Carrigafoyle tower house adjacent to the island bridge, built in 1490. This imposing castle is referred to as the 'Guardian of the Shannon' because of its strategic location overlooking the shipping lanes that supplied the city of Limerick.

Close by is the isthmus leading to **Tarbet Island** and the ferry crossing the mighty Shannon to Killimer, near Kilrush in County Clare. It is difficult to see that this is still an island in the true sense of the word. Apart from the ferry terminal the island is largely occupied by an electricity plant with four oil-fired turbines and a capacity of 640MW. It was saved from closure in 2009 by Spanish power company Endesa, securing local jobs. Another island visited but with very little glamour or interest. This was all to change further up the coast at Aughinish in Limerick.

First, we made a perfunctory stop at **Foynes Island** knowing that a visit would be out of the question without a formal invitation. Foynes, though a small town, is a major port with six terminals handling 10 million tonnes of cargo each year with **Foynes** Island resplendently isolated from the industrial mayhem some 100 metres away. Of significant further interest is Foynes history of seaplane aviation as before the Second World War land-based planes had insufficient flying range to cross the Atlantic and Foynes was the last port of call for sea planes flying to the USA. These were the glamorous days of flying where Hollywood 'A' listers at the time would frequently use this route. The journey was cold and Irish coffee was invented to take the edge off any discomfort. John made a 'flying' visit to the flying boat museum shop whilst I garnered energy for the journey beyond.

We stopped at the **Foynes Island** lookout to the island and apart from a number of sizeable Victorian houses the circular island of no more than a square kilometre was made up of impenetrable coniferous and deciduous woodland. Permission to set foot might be a challenge. Like most islands sea faring comes hand in hand and in 1923 Conor O'Brien, a resident of the island, was the first in a small boat (the 42-foot *Saoirse*, built in Baltimore, Cork) to go around the Cape of Good Hope, Cape Horn, and Cape Leeuwin in Australia. The feat, paving the way for the likes of Sir Francis Chichester, was all the more impressive as in those days there was no communication at sea. O'Brien was also a fearless mountaineer climbing with the likes of Everest pioneer George Mallory. My 'adventures' look tame by comparison.

On looking at the map I was ambivalent as to county Limerick's **Aughinish** (not to be confused with the island of the same name in County Clare); same name but two islands that could not be different in character and functionality. From our map the former **Aughinish** seemed to be now a peninsular built up from the mudflats of the Shannon. We were intrigued.

We entered a road leading to what appeared to be the peninsular to the island. The road was a wide, empty dual carriageway virtually deserted which continued for a couple of miles with the only turn off to a car park and a nature reserve. Suddenly we were confronted with a welcome sign to 'Rusal' with a bilingual sign (maybe in Irish too), Добро пожаловать. My wife is Russian, and I recognised the greeting. Beyond was a huge aluminium smelter, the second largest in the world. This Russian owned corporation UC Rusal accounts for 6.2% of the world's primary aluminium output and 6.5% of the world's alumina production. It is ultimately controlled by oligarch Oleg Deripaska. With its **Aughinish** smelter on the banks of the Shannon the refinery is ideally placed for bauxite imports from Brazil and Guinea. The plant was completed in 1983 on the reclaimed land around **Aughinish** Island and the current annual capacity of the refinery is in excess of 1.9 million tonnes of alumina.

We proceeded past the welcome sign to the gatehouse with some trepidation. It was like entering the site of a Bond movie, a monolithic group of structures with no sign of life. How far could we get before men in white overalls with sub machine guns came out to meet us? Maybe my imagination was in overdrive but with no sign of life at the barrier we chickened out and headed back along the broad dual carriageway.

Our thoughts turned to the war in Ukraine and the sanctions imposed on Russia and their Putin supporting oligarchs. In March 2022 Irish Ministers were told that while operations continue as normal at the plant (preserving jobs), it had its account suspended on the EU Emissions Trading System (ETS) platform in the wake of a raft of sanctions against Russian companies and individuals imposed by Brussels. However, the then Taoiseach Micheál Martin said **Aughinish** Alumina is not included in sanctions. "They have not been included in the sanctions regime on the basis of their strategic importance to Europe"; a pragmatic case of jobs versus sanctions for the 400 jobs at the site. Glencore of Switzerland, the global metals trader that previously owned the Limerick business has since been in talks to take over the smelting plant.

On the way back we stopped at the site set aside for nature conservation, a sop to environmentalists used by huge industrial polluters to pin their environmental colours to their hypocritical mast. The bright red slurry pits eclipse the attempts at environmental reconciliation. A 50,000 tonne, 450-acre site blights the Shannon estuary. The nature trail and butterfly sanctuary with a carpet of bird's foot trefoil and kidney vetch, the food plants of the dingy skipper and small blue butterfly, are clearly welcome habitats amongst the spoils of heavy industry but I couldn't help feeling this was a cynical ploy to placate Rusal's opponents.

In complete contrast, **Aughinish Island** #2 in County Clare was our next island destination which could only be reached by road bridge from Kinvarra in County Galway. We checked into our hotel at *Doolin Lodge* to allow easy access the next day to the first of our Aran Islands and set off to complete **Aughinish** #2.

The island was originally connected to County Clare, but in 1755 that connection was lost due to the tsunami effect of the massive Portuguese earthquake (9.0 on the Richter scale). It is not the first time we have encountered the effects of historical tsunamis on our islands and remembered stories from the Outer Hebrides and the Orkneys.

I recall passing through Montrose during my epic walk around Britain's coast. Montrose Basin is the largest saltwater lagoon in Britain. The basin was hit by a tsunami in 6,100BC, generated by the massive underwater Storegga Slides, in Norway. The tsunami waves were 70 feet high when they hit the Scottish coast. The three Storegga Slides are considered to be amongst the largest known landslides in pre-history. They occurred under water, at the edge of Norway's continental shelf (Storegga is Norwegian for "Great Edge").

Tectonic plates will continue to move, volcanoes erupt and tides surge. The problem is people get in the way. This is another example of man's arrogance in the belief that he is supreme in nature. Not so, and as the Earth's population rockets to 7, then 8 billion we'd better get used to disasters. They have always been with us. Man has not. The tsunami on the east coast of Scotland 8,000 years ago was even bigger than the 2011 Japanese tsunami. There is, however, one difference: No people, nuclear reactors or possessions to kill or destroy were in its wake. It is a sobering thought but one of the world's "ticking time bombs" that may trigger a tsunami is located in the Atlantic Ocean emanating from the Mid Atlantic Ridge tectonic plate. The effects on large coastal cities in Europe and North America would be off the disaster scale.

Driving across this 2-mile-long featureless island to its north shore on Galway Bay illustrated the exposure of the sporadic houses and the 34 population to surge tide effects. The twisting access causeway to the mainland, after a bleak reconnaissance of this even bleaker coast, was built by British troops to support the construction of a Martello tower during the Napoleonic war.

After a night of traditional music in *Fitzgerald's* pub in Doolin, missing out on food of any kind, we were ready for **Inisheer** the smallest in size and most easterly of the 3 Aran Islands. John was incredulous at my inability to appreciate traditional Irish music as my preference was for mournful laments, rebel songs or contemporary renditions by the likes of the Pogues and the Chieftains. The male half of an innocuous, elderly couple sitting by us got a standing ovation for his interpretation of an early Bob Dylan song. I must never judge anyone from a distance.

We had originally hoped to stay on one of the three islands and 'hop' between them, but accommodation was at an expensive premium (a bed in a 6-bed dormitory in **Inishmore**, the largest Aran Island was 100 Euros per night) with all establishments cashing in on the worldwide inflation as a result of the energy shortage and the Ukraine war.

Our plan 'B' was to go on a day trip with the Doolin Ferry Company express tourist ferry from Doolin pier to **Inisheer**; fly to **Inishmore** from Connemara airport in Inverin again for the day; and take the commercial island ferry to **Inishmaan** from Rossaveel beyond Spiddal 20 or so miles west of Galway City. The plan was hatched, and the tickets purchased.

I'd arrived rather in hope than expectation at Doolin pier on two previous occasions hoping to secure at least one of the islands but each time the extensive car park was reminiscent of the Marie Celeste and the ticket offices of the two rival companies offering their services firmly closed. Winds were howling and clearly sailings had been abandoned. This time there was a buzz of excitement as hundreds of tourists were forming orderly queues to go to the islands or excursions to the famous Cliffs of Mohr nearby which attract seven figure annual tourist numbers plying their way up and down the Wild Atlantic Way. Its distinctive road marker logo deserves a design award:

It is a visual onomatopoeia capturing the mood of this 2,500km driving route which passes through nine counties and three provinces, stretching from County Donegal's Inishowen Peninsula in Ulster to Kinsale, County Cork, in Munster, on the Celtic Sea coast.

The weather was poor, but the winds were lightish and braving the outside deck was not an option for me. On arrival at the island jetty after a choppy crossing we were greeted by about 15 horses and carriages for the grand tour. I climbed into one to take cover (it was too early even by my standards to go to the pub for shelter). John looked on with disdain but succumbed to the charm of Joe the driver and his Irish cob, Black Betty. Once knowing the horses name the African American labour chant resurrected by Leadbelly and made into a rock anthem by the Ram Jam band in 1977 was my ear worm for the rest of the day:

> Whoa, Black Betty (bam-ba-lam)
> Whoa, Black Betty (bam-ba-lam)
> She's from Birmingham (bam-ba-lam)
> Way down in Alabam' (bam-ba-lam)

Often a euphemism for a whip used on prisoners, we were relieved that the poor horse didn't suffer the same fate but ambled along a route she had trodden a thousand times with little coaxing necessary from Joe.

The geology of the islands is Karst limestone with dry stone walls crisis-crossing the whole island demarking tiny plots of barely cultivable land. From higher vantage points these chaotic walls looked like the Yorkshire Dales of my childhood on acid! The Aran Islands are the heart of the Gaeltacht with Irish the ubiquitous language. During the COVID pandemic the islanders were cut off from the rest of Galway for many months with provisions brought from the mainland.

The highlight of the tour seemed to be the shipwreck of a cargo vessel *Plassey* on the 8th March 1960 which has since been thrown above the high tide mark at Carraig na Finise on the island by strong Atlantic waves. Horse drawn tourists flocked to see the wreck not for any historic reason but because the ship features in the opening credits of the TV Show *Father Ted*, showing **Inisheer** from the air. However, it is the larger **Inishmore** that hosts each year the *Ted Fest* probably because of the plentiful accommodation.

The village by the jetty had a couple of pubs and a welcome respite from the continuous rain. We whiled away our remaining time until our return ferry enjoying the company of groups of tourists from around the world, eager to buy traditional knitwear (Aran jumpers) as a mark of their visit to these famous Irish islands. This was the Holy Grail for both *Father Ted* fans and Americans proud of their Irish ancestry.

Back in Doolin we were headed for Spiddal, via Galway, as hotel prices in the city were outrageous. We opted for the pleasant pub/hotel *An Cruiscin Lan*, our base for the rest of our adventures. Our journey passed by two remaining islands in Galway Bay **Tawin Island East** and **Tawin** accessed from the main Galway road at Clannbridge. Two bridges-cum-causeways link the two islands and in turn the mainland. Like **Aughinish** further south the islands are featureless, flat and largely treeless with one small row of houses the main centre of activity.

Like so many of the islands in the Gaeltacht the **Tawin** islands were the haunt of Irish nationalists at the beginning of the 20th Century including Sir Roger Casement. He went in 1904 to support parents who had withdrawn their children from the National school in protest against the withdrawal of Irish as the preferred spoken language in the Gaeltacht. The British were always good at, whether in Ireland, Scotland or Wales and even Cornwall, suppressing historic languages which had been the glue binding together proud Celtic communities.

The revival of Welsh as the official language of Wales stems from a nonviolent protest held on Trefechan Bridge in Aberystwyth on 2nd February 1963, demanding equality for Welsh language. Now, of course, irrespective of the expense Welsh is ubiquitous but more important a legal obligation, from signposting to official documents in the public domain. The recognition of Gaelic and Irish too in recent decades as official languages of Scotland and Ireland has led to an upsurge of grass roots teaching and especially in the Gaeltacht language summer schools for students across Ireland. Interestingly, Scotland now has three official languages with Scots, the language of Robbie Burns, being recently added. The 2011 census suggested over 1.5 million people in Scotland are reported as being able to speak Scots. The best-known example of Scots is Robert Burns' poem Auld Lang Syne (literally, "Old Long Since").

In **Tawin** sympathisers and islanders raised money to build and support an Irish school. Eamon de Valera, founder of Fianna Fail and head of the Irish Republic Government sporadically till 1959 spent three summers prior to the Easter uprising as director of the Gaelic League's (Conradh na Gaeige) summer school. It was on one of these visits that he was introduced to Roger Casement. They may be two small islands but were the seedbed for the Irish Republican movement in eventually escaping the shackles of the British Empire.

We were ready for the largest and most popular of the Aran Islands, **Inishmore** and a tourist paradise. Our mode of transport was one of

Aer Arann's Britten-Norman BN-2 Islander aircraft. The flight is about 8 minutes long and we waited to board with a number of women of a certain age enjoying a few days away. It was unclear whether the short flight was a shuttle service as the 8 passengers on our flight were none of the dozen or so ladies who we magically encountered when we were on the island.

We were both weighed (our bodies not our luggage which was sparse) though security was dispensed with and taken individually to our seats. On arrival I quipped that this was long haul in comparison with the 90 second flight I had taken between **Papa Westray** and **Westray** in the Orkney Islands. The captain gave a wry smile.

A minibus was our means of transport to Kilronan, the main settlement by the jetty for both passenger and commercial vehicles. Crowds were out in force jostling for bargains at the plethora of stores selling all things woollen especially the trademark Aran sweaters. I bought a jaunty scarf which sometimes one winter I will leave in a random pub or restaurant as I do with all my scarves. I do not often wear my expensive Fair Isle scarf bought in Lerwick, Shetland for this very reason. My beautiful grey alpaca scarf bought for five pounds equivalent in an Andean mountain town in Chile was such a sad casualty.

The weather, after many days had brightened and we sat like two invalids (John had popped his knee) in the weak sunshine overlooking the comings and goings of the Rossaveal ferries. Our eight-minute return flight monotonously negotiated by a different captain was faultless. This got me thinking. School children often want to be a pilot or a fireman or some such exciting occupation. The truth is all jobs are monotonous with only in some cases a modicum of excitement or inspiration.

Before tackling the final Aran Island, we opted to secure two low tide islands that we had inadvertently missed on our very first trip to the Gorumna Islands, **Illaunmore** and **Inchaghaun**. These were tidal islands only accessible across the seabed at the lowest of tides, so we had consulted the tide tables and discovered low tide was conveniently poised around midday. This was perfect for our journey from Spiddal.

Illaunmore was accessed following narrow lanes to Kilbrackan which our satnav found effortlessly. On arrival my heart sank as I was foolishly anticipating 100 or so metres of flat sand and an effortless crossing. The opposite was the case with slimy seaweed covering jagged equally slimy granite. Was this going to be an adventure or just a foolish suicide mission? John is risk averse and recalled my near catastrophic fall emulating the same type of journey to one of Donegal's islands the previous year. He reminded me of my adversity and poor walking skills, advising me to abandon the crossing. My stubbornness kicked in and with a steadying hand from John we bumbled our way to above the island's high-water mark. I was ecstatic but then remembered the return journey had to be negotiated.

We met two guys who had crossed over to see the only resident on the island, an 86-year-old who had lived there permanently since 1966. To gain provisions he phones for a taxi to meet him at the jetty and walks across for a trip to the nearest food store. He then returns with his shopping across the dangerous seabed. The tenacity of human endeavour never ceases to surprise me. I was pleased we had conquered this 117-acre island but was disappointed not to meet its only permanent occupant.

Onwards to **Inchaghaun**. Accessing this island would be my only 7th order island as to get there from Great Britain I had to cross to **Anglesey** and **Holy Island** in Wales, the island of **Ireland**, **Annaghvaan**, **Lettermore** before finally making **Inchaghaun**.

We arrived at the jetty and were confronted with an even greater challenge as the shore was protected by large rock armour boulders which even with my optimism, I felt were a step too far for my fragile state of perambulation. John was quiet but through perseverance we found a less perilous passageway through the rip rap. Now old hands at this type of crossing we followed our learnt instincts until we reached the sward above high-water mark, cognisant that our journey was not complete until we had secured the return. Making the few steps through the largely impenetrable rock armour felt good and we deserved a celebration back at our base in Spiddal with our west coast objectives almost complete.

The two tidal islands were a boost to my wrecked body, and I felt an elation I had not experienced for a year. I cannot climb stairs unaided but had patiently negotiated two stretches of treacherous seabed across slippery granite and unstable cobbles. I had started my adventures; first my walk around the British coast, succeeded by this momentous island trip, some two decades ago and soon all I would have would be memories. I was elated but calm and celebrated with a cup of tea in the *Hooker* pub near the **Lettermore** causeway in the company of rheumy eyed Irish speakers sipping their reflective Guinness. My own reflective memories were exhilarating but tinged with sadness that these crazy journeys were almost over.

Inishmaan was our third and final Aran Island and we made the short journey to the Rossaveal ferry terminal to meet the slick, largely commercial passenger ferry for our 50-minute journey. We hadn't researched the island and assumed it would be the same mix of tourist shops and horse drawn carriages as were the other two. We were to be proved very wrong.

I engaged with one of the deck hands and blurted out brief details of my island odyssey. He seemed impressed. We settled down in aircraft style seats and I dozed on a calm but wet day. I was jolted awake as the ferry docked but no one moved so I assumed some disembarkation problems had been encountered by the crew. Suddenly my friendly deck hand rushed up to us enquiring why we weren't leaving as the ferry was shortly taking most of the passengers to Inishsirrer. Had I not befriended the crew our visit to Inishmaan would have been scuppered.

We disembarked well after the other passengers and walked into a squally downpour failing to recognise the shuttle bus which left without us. I was not pleased. The jetty unlike those of the other two islands was some distance from whatever passed for the 'capital' of this small island with tourism strangely limited: no sweater shops and certainly no carriages. We could see properties in the far distance so set off in the murk to find shelter. The bleak limestone Karst landscape took on a sinister appearance, hauntingly beautiful despite the drenching rain and it was heads down for an extended walk. Fortunately, John flagged down a local going about his rural business as both a stonemason and a beekeeper who in that glorious Irish manner 'effed and blinded' but meant no harm. He cheerily despatched us to *Teach Osca* the only pub on the island to await its opening in the pouring rain. To quote from that seminal cult film *Withnail and I* we appeared to have gone on holiday by mistake in a similar downpour to that very scene of the film!

John Millington Synge author of *Playboy of the Western World* spent time in Inishmaan. It was William Butler Yeats who suggested that Synge come to these islands. "Go to Aran," Yeats told his friend. "Live there as if you were one of the people themselves; express a life that has never found expression." His ramshackle house is now being opened as a museum just up the road from the pub. Of all the Aran Islands Synge was most enamoured by Inishmaan quoting "the life is perhaps the most primitive that is left in Europe". He was not wrong.

The pub opened on the dot of midday, and we expected a few dreary hours in the distant company of one or maybe two lunchtime topers. But as the afternoon wore on it became obvious that this was the social heart of the island with local women catching up over coffee with a gentle buzz of earnest conversation. All that was missing was the fug of pipe smoke which would have complemented the peat fires in Synge's day. Calmness was the watchword and even the minibus driver back to the ferry – we had the foresight to book the return journey - seemed little worried about missing the daily ferry as he wound slowly between limestone walls picking up the odd fare heading for the mainland. His final passenger, a garrulous woman, engaged him in fast and furious Irish only for him to reply tá (yes) from time to time in a lazy lilt. Ferry timetables are always published 15 minutes ahead of their actual departure to allow for this carefree attitude to time.

On reaching the mainland in total contentment we headed back to the Midlands unable to find appropriate accommodation until we nearly reached the Slieve Bloom Mountains in Offaly. We overnighted in Kinnitty at a glamping site, the next day crossing over the ancient mountains formed 300 million years ago. They are arguably the oldest mountain range in Europe, weathered to a mere 527 metres at their highest point, though they share this accolade with Massif Central in central France. This gave us time the next day to head to **North Bull Island** in Dublin Bay accessed by a causeway from Dollymount in the lee of Howth. We sat momentarily at a roundabout in the centre of the island catering for golfers and naturalists alike. We watched in silence well-heeled Dubliners strutting their stuff, cycling or power walking before we headed off for a celebratory lunch of mussels at the *Summit Inn* on Howth Hill.

I needed to catch a 08:00 ferry back to Holyhead the next day so I bade farewell to John after returning him to Abbeyleix. To avoid too early a rise, I booked into a modest but comfortable B&B in the heart of the Curragh, a flat open plain of almost 2,000 hectares in County Kildare known for its fabled racehorse breeding and training. On an early July morning the stillness and quiet of this deserted heathland was a fitting end to my Irish island conquests that trip with only four tricky, private islands left in Ireland, but these were for another time.

36. The GB stragglers: Whale Island, Portsmouth harbour and Osea Island, Essex and three small islands of the Outer Hebrides

With the exception of a small number of Irish private islands almost all the permanent inhabited islands of the UK and Ireland had been conquered. Two tiny road causeway islands in the Outer Hebrides, carelessly forgotten on my adventure there (**Flodda** and **Grimsay South**) remained in Scotland; a long way to travel for so little gain.

In England, two remained: the elusive **Osea Island** in the Blackwater estuary in Essex and **Whale Island**, the HQ of the Royal Navy High Command, an island in Portsmouth harbour connected to Portsmouth by a road bridge. **Osea** had eluded me at least twice because of tides swamping the mile long causeway, and officialdom guarding this private island costing up to £40,000 per day to take advantage of its exclusive facilities. Although Ian had made attempts to visit the top security **Whale Island**, 'through a friend of a friend' I held out little hope of securing this bastion of the British navy, the nerve centre of administration and operational command. Faint heart……indeed so the challenge went on.

In July 2022 I was driving down to **Hayling island** to present one of my routine coast protection courses when I realised as I was heading around Portsmouth on the M27 that my hotel in Langstone was only about 15 minutes' drive to **Whale Island**. Excited by an opportunity not to be missed I emailed the Royal Navy Press Office explaining my odyssey but

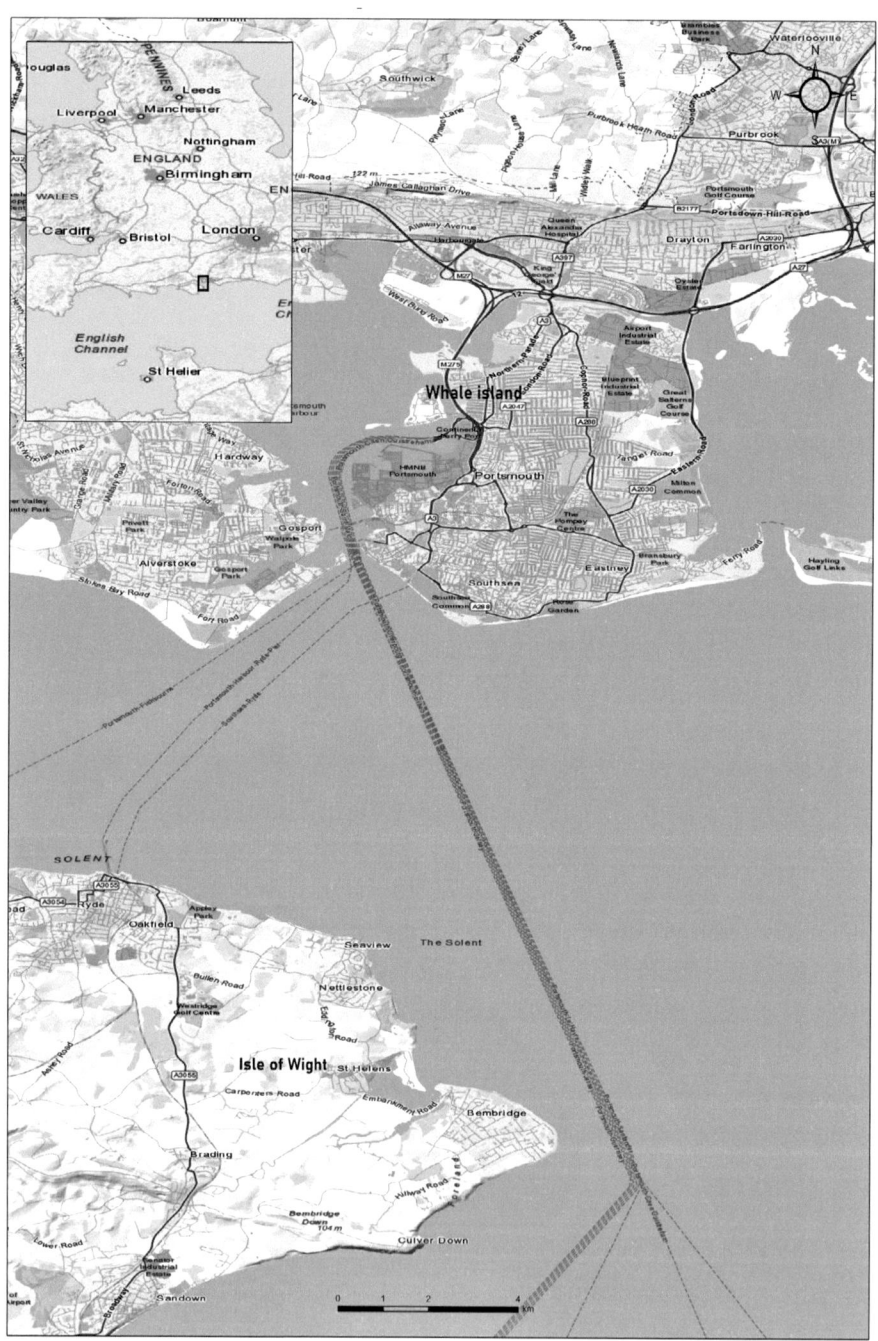

Whale Island, Portsmouth Harbour, England

not expecting a reply. These days the Royal Navy had more on their plate than accommodating the peccadillos of an elderly gentleman.

I was met by my co-workers and at the end of a very hot day evaluating the condition of beaches, groynes, seawalls and the like which protect our coastline, one of these young guys, Craig, always up for a challenge – we had been to visit Dartmoor's 'Dark Sky' earlier in the year to marvel at the many galaxies clearly visible from this vantage point unpolluted by extraneous light – suggested we paid an impromptu visit to **Whale Island.** What could go wrong? We checked on Google Street View which indicated that the security post, heavily guarded we assumed, was on the island, not the mainland.

Craig, his co-worker Mark and I set off with a modicum of trepidation the short distance, passing Nelson's illustrious flagship *HMS Victory* on the way. To paraphrase the Norfolk admiral, we all had roles on arrival at the guard house, "I expected every man to do his duty". I was to stay quiet whilst Craig and Mark would explain my previous battles to conquer my treasured islands, with an explanation that all I wanted was to step on the island's turf. The heavily armed guard looked on unmoved by their pleas. However, the civilian gate keeper cracked a smile directed us to park and we were soon on our way to experience the delights of Wagamama's fusion food in the shadow of Portsmouth's Spinnaker.

The next morning at breakfast whilst idly checking my emails I came across an invitation from the Navy's press office to visit the island with the filming of the visit by naval photographers. This was too good an opportunity to miss, and I accepted the invitation two days hence. I was treated like royalty. Indeed, Princess Anne has a permanent billet on *HMS Excellent* as the island is officially known – all shore bases have an HMS name it appears. Interviews ensued, film footage and photographs were liberally taken, and I was fortunate to have an audience with Lieutenant Commander Ian Pratt, the commanding officer.

The island is home to about 500 staff, many resident and including the

Royal Marines. *HMS Excellent* is also home to the gun carriage used in all State funerals all too vividly remembered at the funeral of Princess Diana. It is the Royal Navy's oldest shore training facility. The original natural island was built up from reclaimed land from the excavation of Portsmouth harbour by prisoners from the Napoleonic wars. Its history and relevance today were meticulously explained to me by Commander Pratt. I felt privileged. Only a few short weeks later the gun carriage would be brought into active service at Queen Elizabeth's State funeral.

Following the visit, the Navy press guys went into overdrive and distributed photographs and footage to a blanket of media outlets across Britain. I had my 15 minutes of fame with BBC radio interviews and articles in all manner of Nationals and local papers too numerous to collect. The Scottish Daily Record had a full page spread and for a couple of weeks my odyssey was the talk of my friends and beyond. Today's news is tomorrow's chip paper (in the days before Health and Safety banned this practice) but the publicity was a fitting end, well nearly, to an ambitious project.

Osea was my final English island. The whole 80-acre island is now owned by music produce Nigel Frieda. Like many of my island visits it was punching above its weight with regards to its fame and fortune.

My friend Steve was sheltering from the Californian sun in his Derbyshire home though 'blighty' too was in the grip of the worst heatwave and drought since 1976 when I enjoyed a holiday with Steve in Death Valley. Steve was always up for adventure no matter how quirky, and he drove me to Maldon, Essex to await low tide and the safe exposure of this snaking one-mile causeway first built by the Romans.

Osea is flat and low lying with little of interest other than to the inquisitive. On arrival at the security barrier by the smart (and also private) Osea caravan park we realised that access would be again difficult, but we chanced our arm and walked stealthily to the dilapidating Blackwater seawall. The tide was out, and the causeway exposed. In twenty minutes we would be above high-water mark and we could return; mission accomplished. However, on our outward journey we met a family who had been caught on CCTV and had been summarily dismissed by the observant island management.

If challenged we concocted a story about my recent fame with both the BBC and the Royal Navy, both worthy credentials. Sure enough a beat-up four-wheel drive vehicle stopped us literally in our tracks ordering us back. My story held no sway. We weren't allowed further. Introducing my story led to an accusation by the agitated driver of threat after I said that refusal would lead to bad publicity for them. One hundred metres from our goal and I was about to run for it (except I can no longer run). For no apparent reason Nina, the Polish island manager did an about turn when Steve suggested in his laid-back way that she took me by vehicle to the island. Her attitude did a 180-degree change and we chatted amiably, mostly about February's storm Eunice destroying the rock armour barrier protecting the causeway. She even gave me a welcome lift back to the mainland and my mission was well and truly accomplished.

I was determined to complete all inhabited islands in UK by the end of Summer 2022 and three errant islands off **Benbecula** in the Outer Hebrides remained, bypassed on my trip there with Paul and Stuart. I was not long out of hospital on that trip and forgot the spreadsheet that I had carefully constructed over the last few years. **Flodda**, North of **Benbecula** and **South Grimsay** connecting to **Eilean na Cille** (actually missed on my elaborate spreadsheet!) to the south of **Benbecula** were outstanding. Now the sensible adventurer would have carefully continued to ignore their contribution as UK inhabited islands, but a nagging voice wouldn't allow me to do this no matter the cost.

There were two options: the first mad, the second madder. I could at vast expense drive the 550 or so miles to Uig on **Skye** and take a CalMac ferry to Lochmaddy on **North Uist** and accomplish securing these islands in 3 days. Or, I could fly as **Benbecula** has a commercial airport served from Glasgow. The extreme expense would be similar.

Whilst planning the second attempt to **St Tudwal's West** (Bear Gryll's island) the chilled-out RIB owner Jonno nonchalantly mentioned he had a pilot's licence and could fly from his North Wales airstrip at Llanbedr to **Benbecula**. He indicated that for insurance reasons he could not charge and computed the cost of fuel at around £700 for the three-and-a-half-hour trip each way. This surprisingly was on a par with my proposed road trip when considering accommodation, fuel, ferry fees and the like. After all I don't need possessions at my time of life, but experiences to treasure. I toyed with each option and as Jonno's schedule prohibited a 'smash and grab' trip in the summer I arranged for the road trip with a couple of friends who wanted to tackle **Skye's** Cuillin ridge.

Hotels and ferries were booked, and a plan cemented. We set off on a fine early autumn day for the journey, a journey past the bonny, bonny banks of Loch Lomond through Rannoch Moor (the backdrop to Daniel Craig's James Bond in the final scenes from '*Skyfall*'), Glencoe, Fort William and Glen Shiel on a route, the A82, that I rate as the finest scenic experience on earth, bar none. My co-driver, Mike, had let us down as he was concerned about the weather. This annoyed me as nobody would set foot in Scotland if they worried about the weather and of course the ubiquitous midges which curse each and every trip. Fortuitously a dear friend Doug offered to co-drive to Dumbarton East and return immediately by train, leaving the rest oif the journey to me. This was beyond the call of anyone's duty, but a 10-hour drive in a single day is not for the faint hearted.

Karolina and I reached **Eilean Donan** the fairy-tale castle on the small tidal island situated at the confluence of three sea lochs (Loch Duich, Loch Long and Loch Alsh). Though this is not inhabited on a permanent basis I decided to pay my concessionary £9 fee to cross to the island as I was rather tired of telling people that I had not visited this universally well-known landmark island and its castle built in the 13th century and named after Saint Donan.

The island's ownership exchanged hands often between feuding clans and fell into disrepair until Lt. Col. John MacRae-Gilstrap rebuilt and restored the castle using the original plans between 1919 and 1932. In 1983 ownership of the castle was transferred to the Conchra Charitable Trust, established by the Macrae family to maintain and manage the castle. Some half a million people visit the castle each year to enjoy this uniquely restored castle. The castle has been a film location for no less than twenty-three movies including *Highlander*, Pierce Brosnan's James Bond in *The World is not Enough*, *Entrapmen*t and *Rob Roy*.

I left Karolina to wild camp above the Old Man of Storr as the sun was setting over the magnificent Black and Red Cuillin mountains, for once not brooding in the mist. The shots she took that evening and at dawn the next morning were clear candidates for the cover and frontispiece of this book.

I like Calmac ferries, and I have been on many on this odyssey. They are in my experience on time, spacious and comfortable with not the usual scrabbling for the best seats experienced on cross channel or Irish Sea ferries. I settled down to a relaxing one- and three-quarter hour crossing and had accomplished visiting all three errant islands by late afternoon before heading for my accommodation in a neat and welcoming residential property '*Hebridean Way*'.

Flodda was reached within a half hour of the ferry terminal, and I was entranced by the treeless landscape of infinite small lakes crossing the causeway from **North Uist** onto the flat terrain of **Benbecula.** The rock armour reinforced causeway attempted to assuage the aggression of the North Atlantic storms. These causeways are the very lifeline of the three main islands with **South Uist** to the south. **Flodda** itself is joined to **Benbecula** by another causeway and my visit was short with a light smattering of houses and crofts and a majestic calm beneath big skies. The end of the road in the middle of the island is a bus turning circle. Rural bus services are mocked for their inadequacy but this island of a population of only 7 has a twice daily service.

My perfunctory visit over I headed the handful of miles to **South Grimsay** and a signpost to Peter's Port on the B891, a commercial fishing terminus at my journey's end. I could find no references to **South Grimsay**, with its burgeoning population of 20 souls and its history remains a mystery. **Grimsay** to the south of **North Uist** is documented but OS maps do not register its southern neighbour. On 1:25,000 maps it is marked as Grimsay too. The road which leads to my final island **Eilean na Cille** was built to service the pier at Peter's Port, which was constructed in 1896 at a cost of £2,000. Though the 'port' showed signs of activity particularly lobster fishing, at the time of my visit it was deserted. Although the island is included in the Scottish census of inhabited islands only one abandoned barn was evident in this undulating landscape between the sea and the sky. I dipped my hand in the water at the southern end of the access pier, thought about the conclusion of my UK island odyssey and headed for my night's stay in the *Hebridean Way*, made memorable by a whisky loving landlord and three affable Swedes of an annual expedition to sample Scottish whisky.

I listened and sang to music with Karolina on my 10-hour journey back to Birmingham in an attempt to stay awake on this final gruelling journey of my UK island visits. I was oblivious to events unfolding in Balmoral. The music tape ended abruptly at 19:00 on 8th September 2022 and the radio news brought me the sad news. I had been alive all of the Queen's reign and the shocking but maybe expected news was the backdrop to the end of my adventures. Queen Elizabeth II had ruled over all the islands of England, Scotland, Wales and Northern Ireland and I felt proud to have visited every one of her inhabited domains.

37. The Ultimate Stragglers

There were always going to be inaccessible islands, not because of physical difficulties but because of either the intransigence of very private and very prickly owners who had bought islands to avoid opening them up to the public and especially busy bodies like me. I was now committed to not getting the 'full set' so to speak but in June 2023 I would have one last gasp try. Stubbornness has always been part of my DNA. It comes with being a Yorkshireman.

I had arranged a trip hopefully in late summer to go to **Brecqhou** in the Channel Islands with Steve on one of his many visits from his home in Sacramento to blighty. This left four legitimate candidates, all in Ireland – **Lambay** off the coast near Dublin, **Garinish** a stone's throw off the Coast of the Kenmare estuary in Kerry, **Horse island** in the Carbery Hundreds in west Cork and **Foynes** in the Foynes harbour in County Limerick. John Lawlor and I had failed to gain access to the last three on our June 2022 trip.

Whilst researching ownership and requesting access Craig my work colleague telephoned me asking if I had been to **Holme Island** in Cumbria. He had been undertaking asset surveys of the railway embankment in south Cumbria which links Lancashire to Barrow-in-Furness and hugs the coast of south Lakeland. This was news to me and rather ironic as I owned land adjacent to the railway not more than 2 miles from the location of this 'new' island. I sighed when I heard the news but realised there would always be some obscure island brought to my attention. I checked the Ordnance Survey map and yes, there it was poking out of the salt marsh beyond the railway line south of the Grange-over-Sands golf club.

I was by coincidence to go to Northern Ireland to conduct my final asset management course after 25 years. My body could no longer stand the

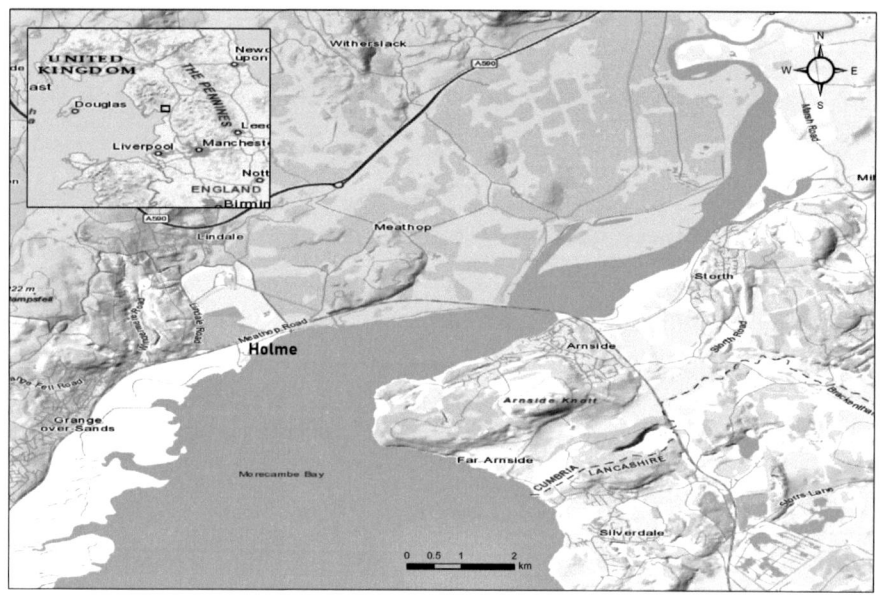

Holme Island, Cumbria, England

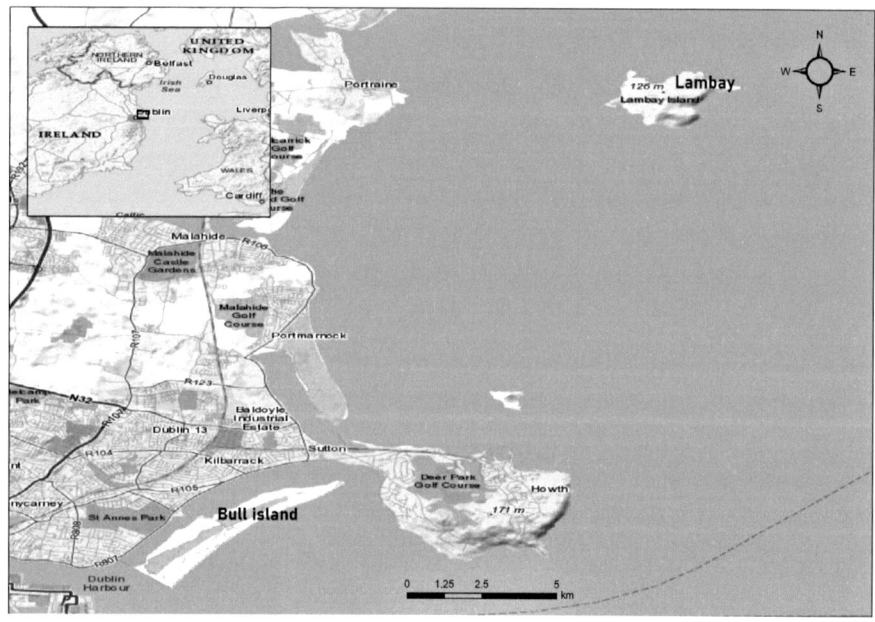

Lambay Island and North Bull Island, Dublin Bay, Ireland

rigours of walking as was required in assessing candidates' competence at understanding the fitness for purpose of our coastal and river flood defences. I chose this trip to visit the island stragglers listed above and opted for a ferry journey via Cairnryan to Larne, a short two hours crossing but the journey north would take me within a handful of miles from **Holme Island**.

I arrived after a journey made tolerable by listening to the first Ashes cricket match with a cocky England using new aggressive tactics (Bazball) against an in-form Australia who had just been declared world Test team champions after beating India. I crossed the railway track on foot to be confronted with iron gates locked firmly to deter intruders along with a large 'strictly private' sign, a further menacing deterrent. The island was on a causeway some 200 metres beyond the gates. A fitter more determined man would have somehow cocked a snoop at this security and managed access. I am determined but with discretion being the better part of valour realised any acrobatics would put me at serious risk.

It was still and overcast and the wild garlic a sensory experience long remembered at this time of year from summer visits to my parents in Grange. I was defeated and stood looking at the majesty of the Morecambe Bay estuary, so familiar to me from ventures at low tide onto the vast expanses of soft white sands when at age 25 reflecting on my future. I had foolishly even crossed the sands from Silversands to Grange on my circumnavigation of Great Britain. The views over to Yorkshire's famous peak, Ingleborough was an impressive backdrop to this peaceful setting. I even contemplated that **Holme Island** was no longer an island as the River Kent estuary had long since moved southwards with the permanent salt marsh surrounding the island never inundated even at the highest of tides.

I was about to leave convincing myself that **Holme** did not fit my definition of an island when I saw an open railway gate leading to the salt marshes covered with the all-pervasive spartina grass adjacent to the west side of the causeway. I opened the unlocked gate and gingerly found a path that I suspected had been created by local youths as beer cans were strewn across the marsh. After 15 minutes of careful negotiation of this uneven tufty surface I reached a rock buttress and climbed triumphantly onto it knowing the island had now been conquered.

Local historian Robin Webster suggested that the island has a connection with the famous legend of England's last wolf being slain on nearby Humphrey Head in the 14th century. The island, so legend has it, was given to the man who killed the wolf as a reward for his bravery. The causeway was built by the Brogden family when they lived on the island in the mid-nineteenth century. They helped to build the railway which runs right past the island. Some say the causeway was built as a little "extra" when the railway was built, if you know what I mean! The fake Roman temple called the Temple of Vesta was obscured from view on my visit, hidden by lush undergrowth. It is a replica of the temple near the Forum in Rome. English families with grand homes often copied buildings they'd seen on their Grand Tour of Europe. Obscure islands encountered on my travels never cease to surprise me with their eclectic history.

After my return to County Tyrone for my last hurrah as a river inspector and after a nostalgic 'goodbye' to a part of my life that had been centre stage for almost a quarter of a century, I headed across the border to pick up John Lawlor, my constant companion for trips to all Irish islands.

I'd done my homework having gingerly made requests, helped by John, to gain access to the remaining islands. We had been told that **Lambay Island** was impossible to get to for mere mortals. The island had been bought at the beginning of the 20th Century by Cecil Baring, later 3rd Baron Revelstoke, a member of the Baring banking family, and a director in the New York office. He brought in Edwin Lutyens the architect who designed the Whitehall Cenotaph and Indian Government buildings in New Delhi amongst so many illustrious landmark buildings. The family still live there today with a small staff and provide basic accommodation for those wishing solitude and to commune with the rich ecology of the island, which also hosts a colony of wallabies. The beautiful island retreat, a Natura-2000 site, has both Special Protection Area (SPA) and Special Area of Conservation (SAC) designations.

This off-grid island is a 30-minute boat trip from Malahide Marina, a fashionable part of north Dublin and I sourced Eamon McGrattan who owns a charter boat *'Fish & Trips'* who as the name of his vessel suggests takes fishing trips around Dublin Bay. Fishing trips appeared to be a euphemism for young guys drinking a slab or two of lager with fishing a secondary activity. To supplement his income, he was employed by the Baring family to fetch and carry post, Amazon parcels and supplies to their domain. He was also allowed to take nature walks around the island and visit the historic house. Desperate to get a 'full set' of islands I was to pay the princely sum of 220 Euros for John and myself to take a 3-hour tour.

We drove the 65 or so miles from John's home in Abbeyleix on a beautiful June day safe in the knowledge that weather would not scupper our trip. The M50 Dublin ring road was as busy as ever, but we made the rendezvous outside White's laundry in Malahide Marina on time. Not a soul was around, nor could we spot likely companions who may have also booked the trip with Eamon. After 30 minutes I called our host who was surprised I hadn't received his email postponing the trip because of a forecast 1.5 metre swell. So much for our optimism. He could recognise my utter dejection and offered a free trip several days later on one of his essential commercial trips which would go ahead irrespective of the weather.

Annoyed we turned tail to face the busy M50 again and headed across Ireland the 351 kilometres to *The West Cork hotel*, Skibbereen to tackle the remaining three Irish islands. Hope was triumphing over experience as John had yet to have confirmation of our requests to visit these intriguing island stragglers.

We had few accommodation choices, so I plumped for *The West Cork hotel* which was seriously expensive but with great views over the River Ilen. On arrival we were to take stock of our next moves with **Horse Island**, the remaining inhabited island in the Carbery Hundreds, our target the next day. In the 19th Century around 100 miners worked its copper mines operated by the West Cork mining company. Since then, there had been a succession of wealthy owners who had turned this one-time working island into a luxury retreat.

We hadn't heard from John Kearney, our island contact which troubled us. We anxiously waited in the busy Saturday night lounge bar of the hotel after almost 500 kilometres of driving since setting off from Abbeyleix at 10:30 that same morning.

Over breakfast the next day John realised his phone was on silent and urgently telephoned our skipper who was different in tone from his usual laconic style and instructed us in no uncertain terms that we must meet him at Rossbrin boatyard within the hour as the favourable tide would soon be lost to land on the island.

On arriving at our appointed time at a deserted Rossbrin boatyard we waited for what we expected to be a gruff uninterested and possibly tetchy Irishman. When he arrived by an ex-RNLI RIB with his son, we could not have been more wrong. He was accommodating and knowledgeable and a veteran of ocean exploration in submersibles. Our trip was only a few days after the *Oceangate* tragedy when the Titan submersible imploded on the floor of the North Atlantic whilst visiting the Titanic wreck. His stories were fascinating and he and his son, also called John were ideal guides for our short trip and wanted no fee.

After an exhilarating five minutes we stood ashore and were greeted by a young woman who was from the current family taking custody of the island. We chatted amiably until the light drizzle became a tad more intense when we took shelter in the lee of a cliff overhang. The drizzle abated and we headed back to the mainland to beat the tide with the two Johns (four including John and me!). We had a long drive to our home for the night in the tourist village of Sneem popular with those travelling the Ring of Kerry. John had developed a good rapport with Seamus Galvin, the head gardener of **Garinish Island** who had arranged to meet us at Oysterbed pier the next morning for the short journey to the island.

During initial research the idea we could get access to these exclusive private retreats was ludicrous. After all, why should wealthy, very wealthy, business people break their elected solitude by inviting strangers to their sanctuaries. Our persistent contacts with all four remaining Irish islands proved quite the reverse with representatives of the owners more than willing to give us at least accompanied access or at best guided tours. Seamus was a dedicated landscape gardener of many years' experience and after docking on this verdant sub-tropical paradise was eager to share his floral knowledge with us. We walked slowly up the graded path with tree ferns, Cordyline Australis (cabbage palms) lining our route with Knockanamadane mountain in the distance. A perfect day was cut short only by our need to visit **Foynes Island** 132 kilometres north in Limerick on the Shannon estuary across the Cork and Kerry Mountains and the Killarney National Park. The weather and therefore views were a vast improvement from our earlier trip, which was somewhat spoilt by torrential rain for most of the day

Foynes Island was still an enigma. John had researched a contact in *The Dunraven Hotel*, Adare near Limerick and we were minded to go there and investigate ways of visiting the island. Procrastination is the thief of time and instead of heading there direct we whiled away time in one of Foynes hostelries where helpful bar staff gave us a number for a member of Foynes yacht club, thus widening our contact list. John phoned the contact who said he would contact Alison O'Brien, married into the O'Brien family who owned much of the island.

We decided to overnight in Glin a village overlooking the Shannon estuary a dozen miles from Foynes. Our chosen hostelry was *Geoghegans Bar* with convivial hosts who had run the pub for generations telling tales of the infamous Black and Tans, pillaging the hotel for food and Guinness during their terror grip on Ireland after the Easter uprising.

Rested we went to the **Foynes Island** quay optimistically waiting for a promised call to gain access. The island was no more than 200 metres away, enticing but inaccessible. We were about to leave when John's phone trilled. It was Alison ringing from Dublin and most enthusiastic at our interest in the island and our wish to visit. Sadly, no-one was available to take us, but we exchanged numbers with Alison who was sure we could coordinate a visit when it suited all parties. She even offered to pick us up from Shannon Airport. Twinged with a little sadness that this island 'could be the one that got away' we headed back to Abbeyleix to meet Eamon at Malahide Marina the next day.

We left plenty of time to get through the Wednesday morning rush hour traffic on the M50 and made it to Malahide to meet Eamon again and a number of women on a retreat to Lamby. Their Dutch-born leader had been many times to luxuriate in a week of walks, Pilates, meditation and a little wine, but mostly solitude. The journey was business-like and on arrival John and I had a brief walk to the boathouse and beach whilst supplies were being loaded and unloaded. Regular visitors chit chatted away to old friends in the lee of the harbour.

Time to go was called and my companion in the boat's cabin was a gourmet chef who travels the world providing fine dining for rich clients. She had just finished a spell for the Baring family and was off to the Scottish Highlands to serve the lords and ladies of the large estates during the summer and of course the grouse season.

The trip, whose coordination had taken so much planning, was now over and leaving John Lawlor at Malahide DART station I had enough time to catch the 15:00 ferry back to Holyhead with happy memories, satisfied I had done all I could to complete Ireland's inhabited islands. **Brecqhou** remained!

38. Epilogue

I wasn't expecting to get permission to land on **Brecqhou**, that elusive private island a tantalising several metres across Le Gouliot passage from **Sark** but I emailed the island factotum expecting rejection. I got a reply by return authorising a brief visit but in hostile prose indicating that photographs were severely restricted, with accompaniment at all times and no hospitality during a precisely timed 10 minutes stay on the island.

This was to be an expensive trip with flights and hotels just for a ten-minute stay. Would it be worth it? Steve, over again from California to complete the Channel Islands with me, believed the experience out manoeuvred the cost. We lodged again at the delightful *Fleur du Jardin* on **Guernsey** and made the stringently appointed time for embarkation on the immaculately kept *Brecqhou Chief*. We were somberly greeted by its three-man crew and a workman, the boat filled with supplies for the incumbent staff and Lady Barclay who was due on the island within days of our visit.

A twenty-five-minute trip in calm waters brought us to the island jetty and a meeting with Aidan. His manner and demeanour couldn't have been different from his frosty, terse email. He was a charming Liverpudlian who had served Sir David for thirty or more years and had supervised between 1993 and 1995 the building of the 95-room castle and the landscaping of the island. It was clear that Sir David's death from Covid-19 had hit him hard as he was both a friend and confidant. He was now economising the estate which once boasted three helicopters and 5 full time pilots. **Brecqhou** even had a 'spare' helipad to maximise flying time when weather directions changed.

We climbed aboard a golf buggy and set off exploring the island along hundreds of metres of carefully choreographed granite block roadways.

We were allowed to photograph sparingly but not the main house even though images on the internet are easy to obtain. The trip took in the artificial lake and its waterfall, the islands highest point overlooking **Sark** and the Catholic chapel constructed especially for Lady Barclay.

It transpired that in recent years we were the only visitors other than family and friends given the privilege of setting foot on the island though Prime Ministers especially Thatcher and Cameron along with the Catholic Archbishop of Westminster had been the Barclay brothers special guests. Sir David had been buried on the island and we were taken to the grave as the highlight of the tour.

It is doubtful that the island's exclusivity can be maintained, and Aidan and Sir David's heirs were already thinking of ways to secure its legacy into the future. I liked Aidan immensely with his Liverpool/Irish charm and wished him well in his endeavours to balance the books and preserve the island's exclusivity. I am ambivalent about extolling the virtues of billionaires and their show piece estates but as a pure spectacle of wealth and privilege **Brecqhou** has no equals in the British Isles

Aidan returned us to the jetty after about an hour and the crew whisked us back to the Inter Islands Quay in St Peter Port, convinced, we were sure, that we were important emissaries. It was 10:30 and their day had ended until summoned by Aidan for further trips.

Ending a project of over six years was bitter-sweet but I was going to end on the highest of highs. Steve, ever the adventurer and 'dark' tourist had encouraged me not to forgo **Foynes island** in the Shannon estuary. This is an innocuous looking small, round, wooded island nestling incongruously a few hundred metres from Foynes port, Ireland's second largest port operator. The port processes ten million tonnes of goods annually. The turnover value of current trade handled by the Port is €8.5 billion per annum, with associated economic impacts of a further €1.9 billion supporting over 3,900 jobs. The tranquillity of the island could not have been different from this busy commercial hub

Epilogue

John Lawlor and I had contacted the part owners of the island earlier in the summer and I had politely accepted their generous offer to accompany us to the island at a favourable time for both parties. I wasn't enthusiastic until Steve cajoled me into organising a trip after his adventures in Turkmenistan. Fares from Manchester to Shannon were on the face of it cheap at around £30 return though Ryanair squeeze the lifeblood out of you with 'essential' extras.

I sent a WhatsApp to Alison O'Brien who was only too pleased to meet Steve and me. The last island was on! We met on a drizzly day, Alison having driven all the way from Dún Laoghaire, a suburb of Dublin, with her husband Stephen, the great nephew of the fabled explorer and adventurer personified, Connor O'Reilly. He would have wholly approved of Steve's obsessive wanderlust to obscure countries around the world. My aching bones had become tired of getting in and out of all manner of craft and I was glad this would be the last, taking great care with patient help from Alison to avoid a fall in the gloomy, deep waters of the Shannon.

The metal jetty built to cope with over a 5-metre tidal range was tilted at a steep angle as the tide was low and my footsteps were tentative as I hung onto the cold metal rail and finally onto the grass pathway leading to the grand house, *Monare*. Stephen was waiting. He was a man of my own age and his warmth shone out with our first handshake. We exchanged pleasantries in the porch escaping the early autumn mizzle, before being ushered into their home resplendent with roaring log fire.

We talked animatedly with much in common, our hosts genuinely interested in my random stories, before being offered Bushmills whiskey as an aperitif to a fine lunch. The end to my 223 island visits could not have been orchestrated better. It was as if the O'Reilly's had been sent to me to make amends for all my angst and uncertainties gaining access to remote islands.

We returned to the mainland on a higher tide and even the metal jetties were now almost horizontal as if they too were helping a tired man at the end of a long journey. We paid an emotional farewell to our hosts and drove away contemplating who knows what further adventures.

I needed a suitable time for reflection after completing my island visits which began in April 2016 and ended in early autumn 2023 filling my life with innumerable serendipity moments all the time to the finishing line; through illness and self-doubt and many logistical nightmares. I am still uncomfortable intruding on the isolation of private owners who have chosen their secret lives to escape intruders like me. They or their representatives bar none could not have been kinder in associating themselves with my eccentric pursuits. No charges for transport were ever discussed and in some cases, like **Vaila** in the Shetland islands or **Foynes** in the Shannon estuary, hospitality was beyond any of my expectations with food and alcoholic beverages on generous supply.

I had travelled by road, foot, air and sea to 223 islands and felt my eventual definition of what is a 'permanently' inhabited island held true: an island which is occupied either as a main or second home by persons or families or an organisation and not a holiday let. In the Irish Republic this was difficult as the latest census suggested about a dozen islands with meagre permanent populations, which in reality were holiday lets. This was a ruse for owners to apply for grants from the Gaeltacht to enable essential infrastructure, mostly jetties, to be maintained by the public purse. Sound, functional jetties are expensive to maintain but are the lifeblood of all islands.

I had been on four islands which were 'ruled' by self-appointed kings; an island where apparent nefarious activities had led to a very hostile reception; islands where the only means of transport involved parting with large sums of money for private boat hire; and possibly the most memorable and most dangerous access to **Foulness** in the Thames estuary where inappropriate actions would have led to certain death.

Did I have a favourite? That is an impossible question as most had a unique combination of exciting landscapes and seascapes, beguiling historic legacies and contemporary charm. Even islands whose access was

Epilogue

benign and back stories mundane had a uniqueness simply because they are islands indefatigable in their existence offshore of their neighbouring Irish, British and French Mainland.

There were islands with genuinely sole occupants like **Boreray** in the Outer Hebrides or **Illaunmore** off the coast of Galway whose lifestyles over decades had been defined by solitude. These contrast with the busy metropolis of **Portsea** which contains the city of Portsmouth and often to many defies its description as an island. There are also remote islands like **Foula** some two dozen miles from **Mainland Shetland** in the North Atlantic which still clings onto its school and whose inhabitants speak Norn or a Norwegian dialect and retain the Julian calendar.

The 90 second trip between **Papa Westray** and **Westray** by Loganair on its daily scheduled commercial flight was a special highlight taking off from a remote airstrip only a mile or so from the remains of what is reputed to be one of the oldest houses in northern Europe. A modern sustainable life in the Celtic fringes has been forged by communities proud of their heritage and hopeful about their future survival. This is seen no more so than in the Orkney Islands where ancient cultures were as old or older than archaic Egypt. Skara Brae, the Ring of Brodgar, and the Standing Stones of Stenness, older than the Pyramids or Stonehenge stand cheek by jowl with innovations in creating wave and wind power energy to combat climate change. These sites stand as visible symbols of the achievements of remote societies away from the traditional centres of both ancient and modern civilisation.

This has been a journey through an extraordinary tapestry of islands, an exploration of their diversity of nature, history and culture from **Yell** and **Unst**, the most northerly Shetland Islands steeped in Viking legacies to the Scilly Isles bathed by the North Atlantic Gulf stream, kissing its shores. The journey uncovered the landscapes and cultures through a palimpsest across the centuries where legends and myths have woven themselves into the very fabric of the islands shaping their uniqueness. The resilient and resourceful inhabitants have created a distinctive way of life forged by their remote surroundings. These are my "Treasured islands"

Acknowledgements

I would like especially to thank John Lawlor who not only visited all but one of my Irish islands but edited the manuscript and gave me many ideas in the shaping of this book.

Many others accompanied me on this odyssey:

Sue Ruben and Bob Farquhar who joined me for many of the Welsh islands with Sue joining me for the islands surrounding **Skye**

My university friends Stuart McCulloch, Paul Nicholas and Steve White who joined me on several occasions including many of the Hebridean islands. Steve encouraged me to complete the elusive **Brecqhou** in the Channel Islands and **Foynes** in the Shannon estuary after enjoying a number of other trips with me. His characteristic calmness contrasting with my own impetuosity made possible my walk at low tide to the elusive **Osea island** in the Blackwater estuary, Essex.

Trevor Masterson my friend of over 50 years who accompanied me to the Orkney Islands.

Ian Vesey who accompanied me to the Shetland Islands.

Adrian Wakelin who arranged two attempted visits (one successful) to **St Tudwal's West**, Bear Gryll's island off Abersoch, and **Gored Goch** in the Menai Straits

Commander Ian Pratt of the Royal Navy who kindly gave me exclusive access to **Whale island** in Portsmouth harbour, the Headquarters of the Royal Navy and home to the Royal Marines.

ACKNOWLEDGEMENTS

I could not have completed my full complement of 223 islands without the co-operation of the owners and their representatives of the very many private islands, usually off limits to the general public and thank them for allowing me to invade their privacy.

I owe a debt of gratitude to all these and more who encouraged my trips in spite of the trials and limitations of my poor health and particularly the Covid 19 pandemic right in the middle years of my adventures.

Finally I would like to thank all my friends who helped me assemble photographs of the journey after many of my own photographs had disappeared with my stolen camera. Photos without credit are the author's.

I am indebted to Owen de Visser for editing the chosen photographs and to my great friend Tijana Sekuloska for painstakingly preparing the many maps.

Appendix
Island Statistics

Order of visit	Map no.	Island	Native name	Etymology	Short Meaning	Island Group	Country	Local Authority	Population	Date Visited	Access	Visited	Details of Access
1		Great Britain				British Isles	England, Scotland and Wales	Various	61,370,912	4/6/16	Car	Yes	
2	2	St Mary's	Ennor	Cornish	The Mainland	Atlantic Ocean	England	Isles of Scilly	1,723	4/7/16	Passenger ferry	Yes	Penzance
3	2	Tresco	Enys Skaw	Cornish	Elder Trees	Atlantic Ocean	England	Isles of Scilly	175	4/8/16	Passenger ferry	Yes	St Mary's
4	2	Bryher	Breyer	Cornish	Place of Hills	Atlantic Ocean	England	Isles of Scilly	84	4/8/16	Low tide access	Yes	Tresco
5	2	St Martins	Brechiek	Cornish	Dappled isle	Atlantic Ocean	England	Isles of Scilly	136	4/8/16	Private boat taxi	Yes	Tresco
6	2	St Agnes	Agenys	Cornish	Agnes	Atlantic Ocean	England	Isles of Scilly	82	4/9/16	Passenger ferry	Yes	St Mary's
7	2	Gugh	Keow	Cornish	Hedge banks	Atlantic Ocean	England	Isles of Scilly	3	4/9/16	Low tide access	Yes	St Agnes
8	3	St Michaels Mount	Karrek Loos yn Koos	Cornish	Hoar Rock in the woodland	English Channel	England	Cornwall	35	4/10/16	Causeway	Yes	Marazion
9	3	Burgh	Borough	English	Borough	English Channel	England	Devon	12	4/10/16	Low tide access	Yes	Bigbury on Sea Bay
10	4	Bute	Eilean Bhòid	Gaelic	Fire	Firth of Clyde	Scotland	Argyll and Bute	6,498	5/5/16	Car ferry	Yes	Wemyss bay to Rothesay
11	4	Arran	Eilean Arainn	Gaelic	High Place	Firth of Clyde	Scotland	North Ayrshire	4,629	5/6/16	Car ferry	Yes	Ardrossan to Brodick
12	4	Holy	Eilean MoLaise	Gaelic	High island	Firth of Clyde	Scotland	North Ayrshire	31	5/6/16	Passenger ferry	Yes	Lamlash, Arran
13	4	Gigha	Giogha	Gaelic	God's Island	Islay	Scotland	Argyll and Bute	163	5/7/16	Car ferry	Yes	Tayinloan, Kyntyre to Achamhinish
14	4	Great Cumbrae	Cumaradh Mòr	Gaelic	Large Island	Firth of Clyde	Scotland	North Ayrshire	1,376	5/7/16	Car ferry	Yes	Largs to Cumbrae Slip
15	5	Barrow	Barrae	Old Norse	Bare Island	Furness Islands	England	Cumbria	2,616	5/8/16	Road access	Yes	Barrow in Furness

Island statistics

			Haugr	Old Norse	Hill or Mound								
16	5	Walney				Furness Islands	England	Cumbria	10,651	5/8/16	Road bridge	Yes	Jubilee Bridge, Barrow
17	5	Roa				Furness Islands	England	Cumbria	100	5/8/16	Road causeway	Yes	Rampside
18	6	Islay		Ìle	Gaelic			Scotland	Argyll and Bute	3,228	24/5/16	Car ferry	Yes	Kennacraig, Kyntyre to Port Ellen
19	6	Jura		Diùra	Gaelic	Deer island		Scotland	Argyll and Bute	196	24/5/16	Car ferry	Yes	Port Askaig, Islay to Feolin
20	6	Colonsay		Colbhasa	Gaelic	Columba's Isle		Scotland	Argyll and Bute	124	25/5/16	Car ferry	Yes	Port Askaig, Islay to Scalasaig
21	6	Oronsay		Orasaigh	Gaelic	Tidal island/ Oran's Isle		Scotland	Argyll and Bute	8	25/5/16	Low tide access	Yes	Colonsay Strand
22	6	Luing		Luinn	Gaelic		Slate islands	Scotland	Argyll and Bute	195	26/5/16	Car ferry	Yes	Seil across Cuan Sound
23	6	Torsa		Torsey	Gaelic	Thorir's island	Slate islands	Scotland	Argyll and Bute	1	26/5/16	Low tide access	Yes	Luing via sound near Torsa Beag
24	6	Seil		Saoil	Gaelic		Slate islands	Scotland	Argyll and Bute	551	26/6/16	Road bridge	Yes	B844 over Clachan Bridge
25	6	Easdale		Eilean Èisdeal	Gaelic		Slate islands	Scotland	Argyll and Bute	59	26/5/16	Passenger ferry	Yes	Easdale Sound
26	6	Kerrera		Cearara	Gaelic	Kjarbar's island	Slate islands	Scotland	Argyll and Bute	34	26/5/16	Car Ferry	Yes	Gallanach, 3km south of Oban
27	6	Shuna		Siuna	Gaelic		Slate islands	Scotland	Argyll and Bute	3	27/5/16	Private boat	Yes	Craobh Haven to Shuna House
28		Ireland		Eire	Irish	Abundant Land		Atlantic Ocean	Ireland and Northern Ireland	Various	6,568,839	8/10/16	Air	Yes	Birmingham to Belfast City
29	7	Rathlin		Reachlainn	Irish			Atlantic Ocean	Northern Ireland	Antrim	75	8/11/16	Passenger ferry	Yes	Ballycastle
30	9	Sheppey		Sceapig	Old English	Sheep island	North Sea	England	Kent	40,300	19/10/16	Road bridge	Yes	Sheppey Crossing
31	10	Lismore		Lios Mòr	Gaelic	Great enclosure		Mull	Scotland	Argyll and Bute	192	31/10/16	Passenger ferry	Yes	Port Appin to Port Ramsay

32	10	Mull	An t-Eilean Muileach	Gaelic	Promontory	Mull	Scotland	Argyll and Bute	2,800	31/10/16	Car ferry	Yes	Oban to Craignure
33	10	Ulva	Ulbha	Gaelic	Wolf island	Mull	Scotland	Argyll and Bute	11	1/11/16	Passenger ferry	Yes	Ulva Ferry, Lagganulva, Mull
34	10	Gometra	Gòmastra	Gaelic	Good Man's island	Mull	Scotland	Argyll and Bute	2	1/11/16	Foot bridge	Yes	Ulva
35	10	Erraid	Eilean Earraid	Gaelic	Tidal island	Mull	Scotland	Argyll and Bute	6	2/11/16	Low tide access	Yes	Knockvologan, Mull
36	10	Iona	Ì Chaluim Chille	Gaelic	Island of Columba	Mull	Scotland	Argyll and Bute	177	2/11/16	Passenger ferry	Yes	Fionnphort, Mull
37	11	Northey				Blackwater estuary	England	Essex	1	23/11/16	Causeway	Yes	Greens Farm Lane
38	11	Mersea	Meresig	Old English	Island of the Pool	North Sea	England	Essex	6,925	23/11/16	Causeway	Yes	The Strood
39	12	Sherkin	Inis Arcáin	Irish	Piglet island	Carbery Hundreds	Ireland	Cork	111	14/3/17	Passenger ferry	Yes	Baltimore
40	12	Ringarogy	Rinn Ghearróige	Irish		Carbery Hundreds	Ireland	Cork	84	14/3/17	Road bridge	Yes	R595
41	12	Inishbeg	Inis Beag	Irish	Small island	Carbery Hundreds	Ireland	Cork	34	14/3/17	Road bridge	Yes	R595
42	12	Dursey	Oileán Baoi	Old Norse	Bull island	Atlantic Ocean	Ireland	Cork	4	15/3/17	Aerial tramway	Yes	R572
43	12	Bere	An tOileán Mór	Irish	Big island	Bantry Bay	Ireland	Cork	167	15/3/17	Car ferry	Yes	Castletownbere
44	12	Whiddy	Oileán Faoide	Irish		Bantry Bay	Ireland	Cork	18	15/3/17	Passenger ferry	Yes	Bantry
45	13	Skye	An t-Eilean Sgitheanach	Gaelic		Skye	Scotland	Highland	10,008	10/4/17	Road bridge	Yes	A 87 Skye Bridge, Kyle of Lochalsh
46	13	Raasay	Ratharsai	Gaelic	Roe Deer	Skye	Scotland	Highland	161	10/4/17	Car ferry	Yes	Sconser, Skye to Churchton Bay
47	13	Rona	Rònaigh	Gaelic	Rough island	Skye	Scotland	Highland	3	11/4/17	Private boat	Yes	Portree, Skye
48	13	Scalpay	Sgalpaigh	Gaelic	Ship island	Skye	Scotland	Highland	4	12/4/17	Private boat	Yes	Kyleakin
49	14	Isle of Man	Ellan Vannin	Manx	Isle of Man	Irish Sea	Isle of Man	Isle of Man	84,495	15/5/17	Air	Yes	Birmingham to Ronaldsway
50	14	Calf of Man	Yn Cholloo	Manx	Small island	Irish Sea	Isle of Man	Isle of Man	2	17/5/17	Private boat	Yes	Port St Mary

Island statistics

51	15	South Ronaldsay	Rognvald		Old Norse	Orkney Islands	Scotland	Orkney	909	17/6/17	Car ferry	Yes	"Gills Bay, Caithness to St Margarets Hope
52	15	Burray	Borgarey		Old Norse	Orkney Islands	Scotland	Orkney	409	17/6/17	Road bridge	Yes	Churchill Barriers from South Ronaldsway
53	15	Lamb Holm				Orkney Islands	Scotland	Orkney		17/6/17	Road bridge	Yes	A961 Causeway from Burray
54	15	Orkney Mainland	Megenland	Mainland	Norse	Orkney Islands	Scotland	Orkney	17,164	17/6/17	Road bridge	Yes	A961 Causeway from Lamb Holm
55	15	Rousay	Hrólfsey	Rolf's island	Old Norse	Orkney Islands	Scotland	Orkney	216	17/6/17	Car ferry	Yes	Tingwall to Rousay
56	15	Hoy	Háey	High island	Old Norse	Orkney Islands	Scotland	Orkney	419	18/6/17	Car ferry	Yes	Houton
57	15	South Walls	Vágaland	The southern inlets	Old Norse	Orkney Islands	Scotland	Orkney	See Hoy	18/6/17	Causeway	Yes	B9047 from Hoy
58	16	Shetland Mainland	Megenland	Mainland	Old Norse	Shetland Islands	Scotland	Shetland	18,765	19/6/17	Car ferry	Yes	Kirkwall to Lerwick
59	16	Trondra				Shetland Islands	Scotland	Shetland	135	19/6/17	Road bridge	Yes	B9074 from Shetland Mainland
60	16	West Burra	Barrey	West Broch island	Old Norse	Shetland Islands	Scotland	Shetland	776	19/6/17	Road bridge	Yes	B9074 from Trondra
61	16	East Burra	Barrey	East Broch island	Old Norse	Shetland Islands	Scotland	Shetland	76	19/6/17	Road bridge	Yes	B9074 from West Burra
62	16	Bressay	Brusey	Brusi's island	Old Norse	Shetland Islands	Scotland	Shetland	368	19/6/17	Passenger ferry	Yes	Lerwick
63	16	Muckle Roe	Rau_oy Mikla	Big Red island	Old Norse	Shetland Islands	Scotland	Shetland	130	20/6/17	Road bridge	Yes	Mainland Shetland
64	16	Yell	Jala	Barren	Old Norse	Shetland Islands	Scotland	Shetland	966	21/6/17	Car ferry	Yes	Toft, Mainland Shetland to Ulsta
65	16	Fetlar	Fætilar	Fat Land	Old Norse	Shetland Islands	Scotland	Shetland	61	21/6/17	Car ferry	Yes	Bluemull Sound to Hamars Ness

TREASURED ISLANDS

			_mstr										
66	16	Unst		Old Norse	Pre Celtic	Shetland Islands	Scotland	Shetland	632	21/6/17	Car ferry	Yes	Gutcher, Yell
67	16	Vaila	Valey	Old Norse		Shetland Islands	Scotland	Shetland	2	22/6/17	Private boat	Yes	Burrastow House Hotel, Mainland Shetland
68	16	Whalsay	Hvalsoy	Old Norse	Whale island	Shetland Islands	Scotland	Shetland	1061	23/6/17	Car ferry	Yes	Laxo, Mainland Shetland to Symbister
69	16	Papa Stour	Papey Stóra	Old Norse	Big island of the Priests	Shetland Islands	Scotland	Shetland	15	24/6/17	Car ferry	Yes	West Burrafirth, Mainland Shetland
70	16	Housay	Húsey	Old Norse	House island	Shetland Islands	Scotland	Shetland	50	25/6/17	Car ferry	Yes	Vidlin, Mainland Shetland
71	16	Bruray	Bruray	Old Norse		Shetland Islands	Scotland	Shetland	24	25/6/17	Road bridge	Yes	Skerries Bridge, Housebay
72	16	Fairisle	Fri_arey	Old Norse	Fair island	Shetland Islands	Scotland	Shetland	68	26/6/17	Air	Yes	Tingwall, Shetland Mainland
73	16	Foula	Fugløy	Old Norse	Bird island	Shetland Islands	Scotland	Shetland	38	28/6/17	Air	Yes	Tingwall, Shetland Mainland
74	17	Inner Holm		Old Norse	Inner rounded islet	Orkney Islands	Scotland	Orkney	1	29/6/17	Low tide access	Yes	Stromness Harbour, Mainland Orkney
75	17	Holm of Grimbister			Isle of Grimm's Farm	Orkney Islands	Scotland	Orkney	3	29/6/17	Causeway/ foot	Yes	Holme Point, Mainland Orkney
76	18	Tanera Mòr	Tannara Mór	Gaelic	Harbour island	Summer Isles	Scotland	Highland	4	30/6/17	Passenger boat	Yes	Achiltibuie
77	18	Tioram	Eilean Tioram	Gaelic	Dry island	Loch Moidart	Scotland	Highland	6	1/7/17	Low tide access	Yes	Shiel Bridge
78	18	Shona	Eilean Seòna	Gaelic	Sea island	Loch Moidart	Scotland	Highland	2	1/7/17	Low tide access	Yes	Kylesbeg to Shona Beag

ISLAND STATISTICS

			Eilean nam Muc	Sea pig	Gaelic		Small Isles	Scotland	Highland	27	27/7/17	Passenger boat	Yes	Sheerwater cruise, Arisaig
79	18	Muck	Eilean nam Muc	Sea pig	Gaelic		Small Isles	Scotland	Highland	27	27/7/17	Passenger boat	Yes	Sheerwater cruise, Arisaig
80	18	Eigg	Eige	Notched island	Gaelic		Small Isles	Scotland	Highland	83	27/7/17	Passenger boat	Yes	Sheerwater cruise, Arisaig
81	18	Danna	Danna	Dane's island	Gaelic		Islay	Scotland	Argyll and Bute	1	3/7/17	Road bridge	Yes	Southern end of Taywallich peninsular
82	19	Canvey	Caningaege	Island of Cana's people	Anglo Saxon		Thames Estuary	England	Essex	38,170	27/7/17	Road bridge	Yes	A130 Canvey Way, Essex
83	20	Portsea	Portus/ea	Harbour island	Latin/Saxon		Solent	England	Hampshire	207,100	24/9/17	Road bridge	Yes	M275 from M27
84	20	Hayling					Solent	England	Hampshire	17,379	24/9/17	Passenger ferry	Yes	Eastney, Portsea
85	20	Thorney					Chichester Harbour	England	West Sussex	1,079	24/9/17	Foot bridge	Yes	Across Great Deep, south of Southbourne
86	20	Isle of Wight	Wihtwara	Men of Wiht	Jutish		Solent	England	Isle of Wight	139,800	25/9/17	Hovercraft	Yes	Southsea to Ryde
87	21	Tiree	Tiriodh	Land of corn	Gaelic		Mull	Scotland	Argyll and Bute	653	29/10/17	Car ferry	Yes	Oban
88	21	Coll	Cola		Gaelic		Mull	Scotland	Argyll and Bute	195	29/10/17	Car ferry	Yes	Oban via Tiree
89	22	Annaghvaan	Eanach Mheáin	Marsh	Irish		Gorumna	Ireland	Galway	104	18/4/18	Road bridge	Yes	R374
90	22	Lettermore	Leitir Móir	great rough hillside	Irish		Gorumna	Ireland	Galway	513	18/4/18	Road bridge	Yes	Annaghvaan
91	22	Gorumna	Garmna		Irish		Gorumna	Ireland	Galway	1,019	18/4/18	Road bridge	Yes	Lettermore
92	22	Lettermullen	Leitir Meallâin	rough hillside	Irish		Gorumna	Ireland	Galway	204	18/4/18	Road bridge	Yes	Gorumna
93	22	Furnace	Foirnis	Fort	Irish		Gorumna	Ireland	Galway	60	18/4/18	Road bridge	Yes	Lettermullen
94	22	Crappagh	An Chnapach	The Lump	Irish		Gorumna	Ireland	Galway	1	18/4/18	Road bridge	Yes	Lettermullen
95	23	Barra	Barraigh	St Finbar of Cork	Gaelic		Barra and Vatersay	Scotland	Eilean Siar	1,174	6/5/18	Car ferry	Yes	Oban to Castle Bay
96	23	Vatersay	Bhatarsaigh	Water Island	Gaelic		Barra and Vatersay	Scotland	Eilean Siar	90	6/5/18	Road bridge	Yes	South of Castle bay

97	23	Eriskay	Èirisgeigh)	Gaelic	Eric's isle	Uist and Barra	Scotland	Eilean Siar	143	6/6/18	Car ferry	Yes	Barra
98	23	South Uist	Uibhist a Deas	Gaelic	South Crossing island	Uist and Barra	Scotland	Eilean Siar	1,754	6/6/18	Causeway	Yes	Eriskay
99	23	Benbecula	Beinn nam Fadhla	Gaelic	Pennyland of the Fords	Uist and Barra	Scotland	Eilean Siar	1,330	6/6/18	Causeway	Yes	South Uist
100	23	Eilean na h-Airigh	Eilean na h-Airigh	Gaelic		Uist and Barra	Scotland	Eilean Siar	1	6/7/18	Causeway	Yes	A865 between Benbecula and Grimsay
101	23	Eilean a' Ghiorr	Eilean a' Ghiorr	Gaelic			Scotland	Eilean Siar	1	6/7/18	Causeway	Yes	A865 between Grimsay and North Uist
102	23	Grimsay North	Griomasaigh	Gaelic	Grim's island	Uist and Barra	Scotland	Eilean Siar	169	6/7/18	Road bridge	Yes	Between North Uist and Benbecula
103	23	North Uist	Uibhist a Tuath	Gaelic	North Crossings island	Uist and Barra	Scotland	Eilean Siar	1,254	6/7/18	Causeway	Yes	Benbecula
104	23	Baleshare	Baile Sear	Gaelic	East town	Uist and Barra	Scotland	Eilean Siar	58	6/7/18	Road bridge	Yes	North Uist
105	23	Lewis/ Harris	Leòdhas/ Na Hearadh	Gaelic	Marshy/ Higher	Outer Hebrides	Scotland	Eilean Siar	21,031	6/7/18	Car ferry	Yes	Leverburgh, Harris
106	23	Berneray	Beàrnaraigh na Hearadh	Gaelic	Bjorn's island	Uist and Barra	Scotland	Eilean Siar	138	6/7/18	Road bridge	Yes	North Uist
107	23	Boreray	Boraraigh	Gaelic	Fort island	Uist and Barra	Scotland	Eilean Siar	1	6/8/18	Private boat	Yes	Leverburgh, Harris
108	23	Scalpay	Sgalpaigh	Gaelic	Scallop island	Outer Hebrides	Scotland	Eilean Siar	291	6/8/18	Road bridge	Yes	Harris
109	23	Great Bernera	Beàrnaraigh Mòr	Gaeilc	Bjorn's island	Outer Hebrides	Scotland	Eilean Siar	252	6/8/18	Road bridge	Yes	Lewis
110	24	Anglesey	Ynys Môn	Welsh	Isle of Mon	Irish Sea	Wales	Ynys Mons	69,700	6/9/18	Road bridge	Yes	A5 Menai bridge
111	24	Holy	Ynys Gybi	Welsh	Isle of Saint Cybi	Irish sea	Wales	Ynys Mons	13,660	6/9/18	Causeway	Yes	Anglesey

Island statistics

112	25	Rum	i-dhruim	Gaelic	Isle of the ridge	Small Isles	Scotland	Highland	22	30/10/18	Car ferry	Yes	Mallaig
113	25	Canna	Canaigh	Gaelic	Porpoise island	Small Isles	Scotland	Highland	12	30/10/18	Car ferry	Yes	Mallaig, via Rum
114	25	Sanday	Sandaigh	Gaelic		Small Isles	Scotland	Highland	6	30/10/18	Road bridge	Yes	Canna
115	26	Stronsay	Strjónsey	Old Norse	Good fishing and farming	Orkney Islands	Scotland	Orkney	349	14/6/19	Car ferry	Yes	Kirkwall
116	26	Eday	Eiðoy	Old Norse	Isthmus	Orkney Islands	Scotland	Orkney	160	14/6/19	Car ferry	Yes	Kirkwall and Stronsay
117	26	Shapinsay	Hjálpandisey	Old Norse	Helpful island	Orkney Islands	Scotland	Orkney	307	15/6/19	Car ferry	Yes	Kirkwall
118	26	Graemsay	Grímsey	Old Norse	Grímr's Island	Orkney Islands	Scotland	Orkney	28	16/6/19	Passenger ferry	Yes	Stromness harbour
119	26	Flotta	Flottey	Old Norse	Flat island	Orkney Islands	Scotland	Orkney	80	16/6/19	Car ferry	Yes	Houton on Mainland Orkney
120	26	North Ronaldsay	Rínansey	Old Norse	Ringa's isle	Orkney Islands	Scotland	Orkney	72	17/6/19	Car ferry	Yes	Kirkwall
121	26	Westray	Vestrey	Old Norse	West island	Orkney Islands	Scotland	Orkney	588	18/6/19	Car ferry	Yes	Kirkwall
122	26	Papa Westray	Papey (hin) Meiri	Old Norse	Big island of thr Papa	Orkney Islands	Scotland	Orkney	90	18/6/19	Passenger ferry	Yes	Westray
123	26	Auskerry	Austrsker	Old Norse	East Skerry	Orkney Islands	Scotland	Orkney	4	19/6/19	Private boat	Yes	Mainland Orkney
124	26	Gairsay	Gáreksey	Old Norse	Gárekr's isle	Orkney Islands	Scotland	Orkney	3	19/6/19	Private boat	Yes	Auskerry
125	26	Wyre	Vigr	Old Norse	Spear head	Orkney Islands	Scotland	Orkney	29	19/6/19	Private boat	Yes	Gairsay
126	26	Egilsay	Eaglais	Gaelic	Church	Orkney Islands	Scotland	Orkney	26	19/6/19	Private boat	Yes	Wyre
127	26	Sanday	Sandey	Old Norse	Sandy island	Orkney Islands	Scotland	Orkney	494	20/6/19	Car ferry	Yes	Kirkwall
128	27	Rusheennacholla	Roisín an Chalaidh	Irish	Caeledonian Rose	Mainis Bay	Ireland	Galway	10	21/7/19	Road bridge	Yes	Carna

TREASURED ISLANDS

		Name	Local name	Meaning	Language	Water	Country	County	No.	Date	Access	Visited	Location
129	27	Mweenish	Maínis	Abbey	Irish	Maínis Bay	Ireland	Galway	137	21/7/19	Road bridge	Yes	Rusheennachola
130	27	Inishnee	Inis Ní		Irish	Bertaghroy Bay	Ireland	Galway	43	13/7/19	Road bridge	Yes	Roundstone
131	27	Inishbofin	Inis Bó Finne	Island of the white cow	Irish	Atlantic Ocean	Ireland	Galway	175	13/7/19	Passenger ferry	Yes	Cleggan
132	27	Omey	Iomaidh		Irish	Atlantic Ocean	Ireland	Galway	2	13/7/19	Low tide access	Yes	Claddaghduff
133	27	Inishcottle	Inis Coitil		Irish	Newport bay	Ireland	Mayo	1	14/7/19	Causeway	Yes	Inishnakillew
134	27	Clare	Oileán Chliara	Clara Island	Irish	Clew bay	Ireland	Mayo	159	14/7/19	Passenger ferry	Yes	Roonah Quay
135	27	Inishnakillew	Inis na Coilleadh	Island of woods	Irish	Newport bay	Ireland	Mayo	6	14/7/19	Causeway	Yes	Claggan
136	27	Rosmore	An Ros Mó		Irish	Newport bay	Ireland	Mayo	1	14/7/19	Road bridge	Yes	Newport
137	27	Rossroe	An Ros Rua		Irish	Greatman's Bay	Ireland	Galway	22	14/7/19	Road bridge	Yes	Casla
138	25	Holy	Lindisfarne	Kingdom of pool/stream	Irish/Brittonic	North Sea	England	Northumberland	180	15/7/20	Causeway	Yes	Beal, off A1
139	28	Piel	Fowdrey	Fodder	Old Norse	Furness Islands	England	Cumbria	2	16/7/20	Low tide access	Yes	Snab point, Walney island
140	29	Horsey				Walton Channel	England	Essex	2	1/8/20	Causeway	Yes	Kirby le Soken
141	29	Wallasea	Wala	Old English Foreigner		Rivers Roach/Crouch	England	Essex	?	1/8/20	Road bridge	Yes	Minor road east of Canewdon
142	29	Foulness	Fugla Næsse	Old English Bird Headland		Thames Estuary	England	Essex	131	2/8/20	Low tide access	Yes	via Broomway, Wakering Stairs
143	24	Ynys Gaint	Yny Gaint	Kent island	Welsh	Menai Straits	Wales	Ynys Mons	2	10/8/20	Causeway/foot	Yes	A 545 near Menai village
144	24	Ynys y Big	Ynys y Big	Big island	Welsh	Menai Straits	Wales	Ynys Mons	1	10/8/20	Foot bridge	Yes	A 545 near Menai village
145	24	Ynys Castel	Ynys Castel	Castle Island	Welsh	Menai Straits	Wales	Ynys Mons	1	10/8/20	Causeway/foot	Yes	A 545 near Menai village

Island statistics

146	24	Ynys Faelog	Ynys Faelog	Welsh		Menai Straits	Wales	Ynys Mons	2	10/8/20	Causeway/foot	Yes	A 545 near Menai village
147	30	Lundy	Lundey	Old Norse	Puffin Island	Bristol Channel	England	Devon	28	27/8/20	Passenger ferry	Yes	Ilfracombe
148	31	Ewe	Eubh	Gaelic		Loch Ewe	Scotland	Highland	3	8/9/20	Private boat	Yes	Aultbea jetty
149	31	Dry	Eilean Tioram	Gaelic	Echo	Loch Gairloch	Scotland	Highland	4	9/9/20	Floating bridge	Yes	Aird west of Badachro
150	31	Soay	Sòdhaigh	Gaelic	Sheep island	Skye	Scotland	Highland	3	10/9/20	Private boat	Yes	Elgol, Skye
151	31	Eilean Da Mheinn	Eilean Da Mheinn	Gaelic	Island of two mines	Crinan harbour	Scotland	Argyll and Bute	2	10/9/20	Dinghy with outboard	Yes	Crinan Harbour Jetty
152	30	Flat Holm				Bristol Channel	Wales	City/County of Cardiff	1	15/6/21	Private boat	Yes	Mermaid Quay Cardiff
153	32	Bardsey	Enlli	Welsh	Island of the currents	Irish Sea	Wales	Gwynedd	11	19/6/21	Passenger ferry	Yes	Aberdaron
154	32	Skokholm	Skogwm	Welsh		St Bride's Bay	Wales	Pembrokeshire	2	2/8/21	Passenger boat	Yes	Martin's Haven
155	32	Caldey	Ynys Bŷr	Welsh	short	Bristol Channel	Wales	Pembrokeshire	20	8/2/21	Passenger boat	Yes	Tenby
156	32	Skomer	Sgomer	Welsh		St Bride's Bay	Wales	Pembrokeshire	1	3/8/21	Passenger boat	Yes	Martin's Haven
157	32	Ramsey	Ynys Dewi	Welsh	David's island	St George's channel	Wales	Pembrokeshire	2	4/8/21	Passenger ferry	Yes	St David's
158	24	Ynys Gored Goch	Ynys Gored Goch	Welsh	Red Weir island	Menai Straits	Wales	Ynys Mons	1	11/8/21	Private boat	Yes	Jetty near Pont Britannia
159	33	Coney	Inishmulclohy	Irish		Sligo Harbour	Ireland	Sligo	3	25/8/21	Low tide access	Yes	Cummeen Strand
160	33	Rosbarnagh	Rosbarnagh	Irish		Clew Bay	Ireland	Mayo	1	25/8/21	Road bridge	Yes	Rosentubble
161	33	Achill	Achaill	Irish		Atlantic Ocean	Ireland	Mayo	2440	26/8/21	Road bridge	Yes	Michael Davit Bridge
162	33	Achillbeg	Achaill Beag	Irish		Atlantic Ocean	Ireland	Mayo	1	26/8/21	Private boat	Yes	Southern tip of Achill Island
163	33	Inishbiggle	Inis Bigil	Irish	Vigil	Blacksod bay	Ireland	Mayo	18	27/8/21	Passenger ferry	Yes	Ballycroy, Achill Island
164	33	Collan Beg	Collan Beg	Irish		Clew bay	Ireland	Mayo	2	28/8/21	Private boat	Yes	Rosmoney Pier

		English name	Irish/Other name	Language	Meaning	Body of water	Country	County	#	Date	Transport	Visited	Location
165	33	Clynish	Claidhnis	Irish		Clew Bay	Ireland	Mayo	4	28/8/21	Private boat	Yes	Collan Beg
166	33	Inisturk Beg	Inis Toirc Beag	Irish	Small island of the wild boar	Clew bay	Ireland	Mayo	2	28/8/21	Private boat	Yes	Clynish
167	33	Inishlyre	Inis Laidhre	Irish	Fork	Dorinish Harbour	Ireland	Mayo	4	28/8/21	Private boat	Yes	Inishturk Beg
168	33	Collanmore	Collainn Mohr	Irish		Clew Bay	Ireland	Mayo	7	28/8/21	Private boat	Yes	Inishlyre
169	33	Inishturk	Inis Toirc	Irish	Wild Boar	Atlantic Ocean	Ireland	Mayo	51	29/8/21	Passenger ferry	Yes	Roonah Quay, Louisburgh
170	33	Inishkea South	Inis ge Theas	Irish	Goose island south	Inishkea Islands	Ireland	Mayo	1	31/8/21	Private boat	Yes	Blacksod Pier
171	33	Inishkea North	Inis ge Thuaidh	Irish	Goose island north	Inishkea Islands	Ireland	Mayo	1	31/8/21	Private boat	Yes	Inishkea South
172	33	Arranmore	Árainn Mór	Irish		Atlantic Ocean	Ireland	Donegal	469	1/9/21	Car ferry	Yes	Burtonport Harbour
173	33	Cruit	An Chruit	Irish		Rosses Bay	Ireland	Donegal	60	1/9/21	road bridge	Yes	South of Kincaslough
174	33	Gola	Gabhla	Irish		Gweedore Bay	Ireland	Donegal	5	2/9/21	passenger ferry	Yes	Derrybeg
175	33	Rutland	Inis Mhic an Doirn	Irish		Atlantic Ocean	Ireland	Donegal	6	2/9/21	Private boat	Yes	Burtonport Harbour
176	33	Inishbofin	Inis Bó Finne	Irish	White Cow	Tory Sound	Ireland	Donegal	2	3/9/21	Passenger ferry	Yes	Meenlaragh
177	33	Tory	Toraigh	Irish	Bandit	Atlantic Ocean	Ireland	Donegal	119	3/9/21	Passenger ferry	Yes	Meenlaragh
178	33	Roy	Oileán an Bhráighe	Irish	Island of the captive	Mulroy Bay	Ireland	Donegal	12	4/9/21	Road causeway	Yes	R248 Carrickart
179	33	Aughnish	Eachinis	Irish		Lough Swilly	Ireland	Donegal	2	4/9/21	Road causeway	Yes	Ramelton
180	33	Inch	Inse	Irish	Island	Lough Swilly	ireland	Donegal	438	4/9/21	Road causeway	Yes	Near Burnfoot, close to NI border
181	34	Guernsey	Guernési	Norman		English Channel	Channel Islands	Balliwick of Guernsey	63,026	13/4/22	Air	Yes	East Midlands Airport

ISLAND STATISTICS

182	34	Herm	Eremite		Old French	Hermit	English Channel	Channel Islands	Balliwick of Guernsey	60	14/4/22	Passenger ferry	Yes	St Peterport
183	34	Jethou			Norman	Small Hill	English Channel	Channel Islands	Balliwick of Guernsey	3	14/4/22	Private boat	Yes	Herm
184	34	Alderney	Aurigny		French		English Channel	Channel Islands	Balliwick of Guernsey	2,000	15/4/22	Passenger ferry	Yes	St Peter Port
185	34	Sark	Sercq		French		English Channel	Channel Islands	Balliwick of Guernsey	600	16/4/22	Passenger ferry	Yes	St Peter Port
186	34	Lihou	Iydd		Breton	in or near water	English Channel	Channel Islands	Balliwick of Guernsey	1	17/4/22	Low tide access	Yes	Guernsey
187	34	Jersey	Jèrriais		French		English Channel	Channel Islands	Balliwick of Jersey	100,080	19/4/22	Car ferry	Yes	Guernsey
188	35	Great	An tOileán Mór		Irish		Cork Harbour	Ireland	Cork	12,000	23/6/22	Road bridge	Yes	Flota (suburb of Cork)
189	35	Haulbowline	Inis Sionnach		Irish	Island of Foxes	Cork harbour	Ireland	Cork	216	23/6/22	Road bridge	Yes	Via rocky island and ringaskiddy
190	35	Hop					Loch Mahon	Ireland	Cork	18	23/6/22	Road bridge	Yes	Rochestown
191	35	Inchydoney	Inse Duine		Irish		Clonakilty harbour	Ireland	Cork	183	23/6/22	Road causeway	Yes	Clonakilty
192	35	Clear	Cleire		Irish		Carbery Hundreds	Ireland	Cork	147	24/6/22	Passenger ferry	Yes	Baltimore
193	35	Heir	Inis Uí Driscoil	O'Driscol's island	Irish		Carberry Hundreds	Ireland	Cork	28	24/6/22	Passenger ferry	Yes	Baltimore
194	35	Mannin Beg	Mannainn Bheag		Irish		Carberry Hundreds	Ireland	Cork	1	24/6/22	Road bridge	Yes	Kilcoe
195	35	Long	Inishfada	Long	Irish		Carbery Hundreds	Ireland	Cork	20	25/6/22	Passenger ferry	Yes	Colla Pier south of Schull
196	35	Rossmore					Kenmare river	Ireland	Kerry	8	25/6/22	Road bridge	Yes	N70 east of Tahilla
197	35	Valentia	Dairbhre	The Oak wood	Irish		Atlantic Ocean	Ireland	Kerry	657	25/6/22	Road bridge	Yes	Portmagee
198	35	Samphire					Tralee Bay	Ireland	Kerry	31	26/6/22	Causeway	Yes	Fenit
199	35	Tarbet	Tairbeart	Draw boat	Irish		Shannon estuary	Ireland	Kerry	5	26/6/22	Road bridge	Yes	Near Tarbet ferry

		Name	Irish/Gaelic Name	Language	Alt Name 1	Alt Name 2	Body of Water	Country	County	Pop.	Bridged	Date	Access	Location
200	35	Carrig	Oileán na Carraige	Irish		Carrig island	Shannon estuary	Ireland	Kerry	7	Yes	26/6/22	Road bridge	Aghavallen near Carrigafoyle castle
201	35	Aughinish					Shannon estuary	Ireland	Limerick		Yes	26/6/22	Road bridge	Road to aluminium factory
202	35	Aughinish	Eachinis	Irish			Galway Bay	Ireland	Clare	34	Yes	26/6/22	Road causeway	NW of Kinvarra, Galway
203	35	Inisheer	Inis Oírr	Irish			Aran Islands	Ireland	Galway	281	Yes	27/6/22	Passenger ferry	Doolin
204	35	Tawin Island East	Tamhain	Irish			Galway Bay	Ireland	Galway	12	Yes	28/6/22	Road bridge	Clarinbridge
205	35	Tawin	Tamhain	Irish			Galway Bay	Ireland	Galway	31	Yes	28/6/22	Road bridge	Tawin Island east
206	35	Inishmore	Inis Mór	Irish			Aran islands	Ireland	Galway	762	Yes	29/6/22	Air	Inverin
207	35	Illaunmore	An tOileán Mór	Irish			Killkieran Bay	Ireland	Galway	1	Yes	30/6/22	Low tide access	Kilbrackan
208	35	Inchaghaun	Inis an Ghainimh	Irish			Gorumna	Ireland	Galway	2	Yes	30/6/22	Low tide access	Lettermore
209	35	Inishmaan	Inis Meain	Irish			Aran islands	Ireland	Galway	183	Yes	30/6/22	Passenger ferry	Rossaveel
210	37	Bull or North Bull	Oileán an Tairbh Thuaidh	Irish			Dublin Bay	Ireland	Dublin	12	Yes	27/22	Causeway	Raheny
211	32	St Tudwals West					Ceredigian Bay	Wales	Gwynedd	2	Yes	7/7/22	Private boat	Porthmadog
212	36	Whale					Portsmouth harbour	England	Hampshire	500	Yes	14/7/22	Road bridge	Portsmouth
213	11	Osea	[]sg[]pes []eg	Old English	Osyth's Island		Blackwater estuary	England	Essex	?	Yes	8/8/22	Causeway	near Goldhanger
214	17	Eilean Donan		Gaelic	Island of Donnán		Loch Duich	Scotland	Highland	2	Yes	9/5/22	Road bridge	A82 Dornie
215	22	Flodda	Flodaigh	Old Norse	Float island		Uist and Barra	Scotland	Eilean Siar	7	Yes	9/6/22	Road bridge	Off A865 north Benbecula

ISLAND STATISTICS

216	22	Grimsay South	Griomasagh	Gaelic	Grimm's island	Uist and Barra	Scotland	Eilean Siar	20	9/6/22	Road Bridge	Yes	Benbecula/B891
217	22	Eilean na Cille		Gaelic		Uist and Barra	Scotland	Eilean Siar		9/6/22	Causeway	Yes	B891 South Grimsay
218	38	Holme island				Morecambe Bay	England	Cumbria	2	20/6/23	Low tide access	Yes	Grange-over-Sands
219	35	Horse	Oileán na gCapall	Irish	Horse island	Carberry islands	Ireland	Cork	1	25/6/23	Private boat	Yes	Rossbrin boatyard
220	35	Garinish				Kenmare river	Ireland	Kerry	2	26/6/23	Private boat	Yes	Oysterbed Quay, near Smeen
221	37	Lambay				Irish Sea	Ireland	Dublin	9	28/6/23	Private boat	Yes	Malahide Marina
222	34	Brecqhou		French		English Channel	Channel Islands	Balliwick of Guernsey	22	30/8/23	Private boat	Yes	Guernsey
223	35	Faughnish	Oilean Fainghe	Irish	circular island	Shannon estuary	Ireland	Limerick	2	13/9/23	Private boat	Yes	Foynes

Index

Achill Mayo 354 355 356 357 365 453
Achillbeg Mayo 354 355 356 453
Alderney Balliwick of Guernsey 377 378 382 383 384 385 455
Anglesey Ynys Mons 2 6 43 184 220 222 223 224 226 227 308 325 415 450
Annaghvaan Galway 196 415 449
Arran North Ayrshire 6 31 35 37 39 142 226 444
Arranmore Donegal 284 365 367 368 454
Aughinish Clare 409 412 456
Aughinish Limerick 406 407 408 456
Aughnish Donegal 374 375 454
Auskerry Orkney 239 250 260 261 262 451
Baleshare Eilean Siar 208 209 450
Bardsey Gwynedd 223 229 325 326 329 330 331 335 372 452
Barra Eilean Siar 5 189 200 201 202 203 380 449
Barrow Cumbria 43 44 444
Benbecula Eilean Siar 107 203 204 206 207 208 423 424 425 450
Bere Cork 102 103 285 361 446
Berneray Eilean Siar 208 210 214 450
Boreray Eilean Siar 206 207 208 210 213 214 439 450
Brecqhou Balliwick of Guernsey 377 386 388 427 434 435 436 440 457
Bressay Shetland 135 136 447

Bruray Shetland 152 153 448
Bryher Isles of Scilly 12 19 21 22 444
Bull or North Bull Dublin 96 418 428 446
Burgh Devon 27 28 29 244 444
Burray Orkney 128 131 447
Bute Argyll and Bute 20 31 33 444
Caldey Pembrokeshire 223 308 323 325 332 334 335 453
Calf of Man Isle of Man 118 119 123 446
Canna Highland 109 203 232 233 234 235 237 291 451
Canvey Essex 6 175 176 177 178 182 449
Carrig Kerry 406 456
Clare Mayo 280 281 284 363 452
Clear Cork 98 398 455
Clynish Mayo 284 285 354 359 454
Coll Argyll and Bute 187 188 189 190 191 193 204 449
Collan Beg Mayo 354 359 453
Collanmore Mayo 354 359 362 454
Colonsay Argyll and Bute 49 50 54 55 56 445
Coney Sligo 284 347 349 350 351 453
Crappagh Galway 196 197 449
Cruit Donegal 368 454
Danna Argyll and Bute 165 166 173 174 449
Dry Highland 313 315 317 448
Dursey Cork 100 101 285 446

Index

Easdale Argyll and Bute 57 58 59 445
East Burra Shetland 133 135 447
Eday Orkney 243 245 246 260 263 451
Egilsay Orkney 130 262 263 451
Eigg Highland 164 166 172 173 232 369 449
Eilean a' Ghiorr Eilean Siar 450
Eilean Da Mheinn Argyll and Bute 313 322 453
Eilean Donan Highland 321 424 456
Eilean na Cille Eilean Siar 423 426 457
Eilean na h-Airigh Eilean Siar 450
Eriskay Eilean Siar 201 202 203 450
Erraid Argyll and Bute 80 84 85 446
Ewe Highland 165 170 270 306 313 315 316 453
Fair Isle Shetland 31 60 134 139 149 154 156 448
Fetlar Shetland 141 142 143 144 447
Flat Holm City/County of Cardiff 223 308 325 326 327 328 329 453
Flodda Eilean Siar 206 208 419 423 425 456
Flotta Orkney 130 250 252 253 254 451
Foula Shetland 15 139 147 148 159 160 439 448
Foulness Essex 9 91 92 298 300 303 304 305 438 452
Foynes Limerick 406 407 427 433 436 438 440 457
Furnace Galway 196 449
Gairsay Orkney 239 263 264 451
Garinish Kerry 403 404 427 433 457
Gigha Argyll and Bute 39 444
Gola Donegal 368 369 370 454
Gometra Argyll and Bute 80 81 82 83 84 446
Gorumna Galway 194 196 197 273 449

Graemsay Orkney 250 251 451
Great Cork 393 395 455
Great Bernera Eilean Siar 215 216 450
Great Cumbrae North Ayrshire 31 39 40 444
Grimsay North Eilean Siar 208 209 450
Grimsay South Eilean Siar 206 208 209 419 423 425 426 457
Guernsey Balliwick of Guernsey 3 8 377 379 380 381 382 384 386 387 388 389 390 435 454
Gugh Isles of Scilly 12 19 23 24 444
Haulbowline Cork 393 395 396 455
Hayling Hampshire 6 179 181 182 183 419 449
Heir Cork 285 399 455
Herm Balliwick of Guernsey 377 379 380 455
Holm of Grimbister Orkney 132 161 163 448
Holme Cumbria 427 428 429 457
Holy North Ayrshire 31 36 226 444
Holy Ynys Mons 220 222 223 224 226 325 415 450
Holy Northumberland 226 289 290 291 335 452
Hop Cork 393 396 455
Horse Cork 402 403 427 431 457
Horsey Essex 298 301 302 304 452
Housay Shetland 152 153 448
Hoy Orkney 130 131 250 251 252 253 384 447
Illaunmore Galway ix 197 414 415 439 456
Inch Donegal 375 454
Inchaghaun Galway ix 197 414 415 456
Inchydoney Cork 393 397 398 455

Inishbeg Cork 99 446
Inishbiggle Mayo 354 357 453
Inishbofin Galway 10 276 277 284 347 364 452
Inishbofin Donegal 10 372 454
Inishcottle Mayo 283 284 285 452
Inisheer Galway 71 410 412 456
Inishkea North Mayo 364 365 366 454
Inishkea South Mayo 364 365 366 454
Inishlyre Mayo 284 354 361 454
Inishmaan Galway 71 410 416 417 456
Inishmore Galway 71 410 412 413 456
Inishnakillew Mayo 271 283 285 452
Inishnee Galway 276 452
Inishturk Mayo 280 281 362 363 454
Inisturk Beg Mayo 354 359 360 361 362 454
Inner Holm Orkney 132 161 162 448
Iona Argyll and Bute 59 80 83 84 85 86 209 213 291 335 446
Islay Argyll and Bute 6 47 49 53 54 56 69 80 266 373 375 444
Isle of Man Isle of Man 2 3 4 5 6 8 119 120 122 185 212 317 381 382 446
Isle of Wight Isle of Wight 2 6 7 9 35 50 179 181 183 184 222 337 398 449
Jersey Balliwick of Jersey 3 8 377 382 388 389 390 455
Jethou Balliwick of Guernsey 377 379 380 384 388 404 455
Jura Argyll and Bute 5 6 49 50 51 52 55 56 69 173 174 445
Kerrera Argyll and Bute 61 62 77 80 445
Lamb Holm Orkney 447
Lambay Dublin 427 428 430 457
Lettermore Galway 196 197 415 416 449
Lettermullen Galway 196 449

Lewis/ Harris Eilean Siar 2 5 6 107 108 154 157 179 205 207 208 210 211 212 215 216 217 218 219 222 269 450
Lihou Balliwick of Guernsey 377 387 388 455
Lismore Argyll and Bute 77 79 80 445
Long Cork 285 401 455
Luing Argyll and Bute 57 58 59 445
Lundy Devon 308 310 311 312 326 328 453
Mannin Beg Cork 400 455
Mersea Essex 91 93 301 446
Muck Highland 164 166 232 449
Muckle Roe Shetland 140 447
Mull Argyll and Bute 6 10 68 77 78 79 80 81 82 83 84 85 209 222 291 320 445
Mweenish Galway 274 275 276 452
North Ronaldsay Orkney 243 254 255 261 451
North Uist Eilean Siar 5 15 31 204 206 207 208 209 211 423 425 426 450
Northey Essex 73 91 92 446
Omey Galway 278 279 285 452
Orkney Mainland Orkney 163 239 245 247 252 253 262 263 264 266 269 384 447
Oronsay Argyll and Bute 54 55 289 445
Osea Essex 73 91 92 93 286 298 306 419 422 440 456
Papa Stour Shetland 139 150 151 448
Papa Westray Orkney 246 257 258 259 414 439 451
Piel Cumbria 43 45 292 293 294 296 297 300 372 452
Portsea Hampshire 4 6 179 181 183 439 449

Index

Raasay Highland 107 110 111 113 446
Ramsey Pembrokeshire 325 332 335 338 339 453
Rathlin Antrim 64 67 68 70 236 278 328 445
Ringarogy Cork 99 446
Roa Cumbria 43 45 294 297 445
Rona Highland 8 107 112 113 114 157 446
Rosbarnagh Mayo 353 453
Rosmore Mayo 283 285 286 452
Rossmore Kerry 402 403 435
Rossroe Galway 287 291 452
Rousay Orkney 129 130 262 263 447
Roy Donegal 374 375 454
Rum Highland 109 172 232 233 235 236 451
Rusheennacholla Galway 271 273 274 451
Rutland Donegal 367 368 370 454
Samphire Kerry 405 406 455
Sanday Highland 232 233 235 237 451
Sanday Orkney 243 244 245 265 266 451
Sark Balliwick of Guernsey 377 380 381 385 387 435 436 455
Scalpay Highland 9 107 109 114 115 116 446
Scalpay Eilean Siar 212 213 450
Seil Argyll and Bute 57 58 216 445
Shapinsay Orkney 248 249 260 263 451
Sheppey Kent 6 73 74 75 445
Sherkin Cork 97 98 103 285 446
Shetland Mainland Shetland 6 9 15 128 129 133 135 136 139 141 151 152 156 222 439 447
Shona Highland 57 164 165 166 170 171 172 448
Shuna Argyll and Bute 60 61 445
Skokholm Pembrokeshire 224 325 332 333 334 335 453
Skomer Pembrokeshire 224 325 332 333 334 335 336 337 339 453
Skye Highland i 6 8 9 80 82 106 107 108 109 110 111 112 113 115 170 203 211 215 219 222 270 286 306 313 315 319 320 321 423 424 440 446
Soay Highland 9 107 109 116 170 172 215 219 237 270 286 306 313 315 319 320 321 453
South Ronaldsay Orkney 128 129 131 242 447
South Uist Eilean Siar 202 203 204 205 206 208 209 215 425 450
South Walls Orkney 131 447
St Agnes Isles of Scilly 12 18 19 23 24 444
St Martin's Isles of Scilly 12 18 19 21 22 23 444
St Mary's Isles of Scilly 12 13 16 17 18 19 20 21 23 26 264 444
St Michael's Mount Cornwall 27 28 29 444
St Tudwal's West Gwynedd 323 325 339 341 344 379 424 440 456
Stronsay Orkney 243 245 263 451
Tanera Mor Highland 165 166 167 448
Tarbet Kerry 406 455
Tawin Galway 412 413 456
Tawin East Galway 412 413 456
Thorney West Sussex 9 179 182 449
Tioram Highland 164 165 170 171 448
Tiree Argyll and Bute 187 188 189 449
Torsa Argyll and Bute 57 58 59 445
Tory Donegal 15 21 365 370 372 454

Tresco Isles of Scilly 12 18 19 21 22 444
Trondra Shetland 133 135 136 447
Ulva Argyll and Bute 80 81 82 83 84 446
Unst Shetland 135 141 144 145 389 439 448
Vaila Shetland 9 139 140 141 145 147 151 438 448
Valentia Kerry 404 405 455
Vatersay Eilean Siar 200 201 202 449
Wallasea Essex 298 301 302 303 304 452
Walney Cumbria 6 43 44 293 445
West Burra Shetland 131 133 135 449
Westray Orkney 243 246 257 258 239 263 414 439 451
Whale Hampshire 298 419 420 421 440 456
Whalsay Shetland 148 149 448
Whiddy Cork 102 103 104 285 446
Wyre Orkney 130 262 263 264 431
Yell Shetland 141 142 143 439 447
Ynys Castell Ynys Mons 229 230 325 452
Ynys Faelog Ynys Mons 224 229 231 325 453
Ynys Gaint Ynys Mons 224 229 230 325 452
Ynys Gored Goch Ynys Mons 224 229 325 339 340 440 453
Ynys y Big Ynys Mons 224 329 330 325 452